W9-BMN-898

EDWARD
TELLER ✳

Also by Stanley A. Blumberg

Energy and Conflict: The Life and Times of Edward Teller
  (with Gwinn Owens)

The Survival Factor: Israeli Intelligence from World War II
  (with Gwinn Owens)

EDWARD TELLER ⚛

Giant of the Golden Age of Physics

A BIOGRAPHY BY

Stanley A. Blumberg
and Louis G. Panos

Charles Scribner's Sons
New York

Copyright © 1990 by Stanley A. Blumberg and Louis G. Panos

All rights reserved. No part of this book may be reproduced or
transmitted in any form or by any means, electronic or mechanical,
including photocopying, recording, or by any information storage
and retrieval system, without permission in writing from the Publisher.

Charles Scribner's Sons
Macmillan Publishing Company
866 Third Avenue, New York, NY 10022
Collier Macmillan Canada, Inc.

Library of Congress Cataloging-in-Publication Data
Blumberg, Stanley A.
  Edward Teller : giant of the golden age of physics : a biography /
by Stanley A. Blumberg and Louis G. Panos.
      p.   cm.
  Bibliography: p.
  Includes index.
  ISBN 0-684-19042-7
  1. Teller, Edward, 1908–   .   2. Science and state—United States—
History.   3. Physicists—United States—Biography.   I. Panos, Louis G.
II. Title.
QC16.T37B57   1990
530′.092—dc20   89-6262
[B]   CIP

Macmillan books are available at special discounts for bulk purchases
for sales promotions, premiums, fund-raising, or educational use.
For details, contact:

                    Special Sales Director
                    Macmillan Publishing Company
                    866 Third Avenue
                    New York, NY 10022

10   9   8   7   6   5   4   3   2   1

Printed in the United States of America

To Berty Blumberg and Aphrodite Panos

CONTENTS

ILLUSTRATIONS

PREFACE

Most of us live out our span without once influencing the course of history. A great man or a great woman may do so once in a lifetime. Edward Teller has done it not once but three times over the course of half a century. He helped create the atomic bomb. He designed the hydrogen bomb. He was the dominant figure in the development of the strategic defense initiative (SDI), or "Star Wars." Throughout that time, he has been a complex, enigmatic, and colorful character, revered or reviled but never ignored.

When SDI emerged in 1983 as a revolutionary concept in national defense, Teller was well into his seventies. Most of the giants of science with whom he had crossed paths—Albert Einstein, Werner Heisenberg, Enrico Fermi, Niels Bohr, Leo Szilard, J. Robert Oppenheimer, and others— were dead. But even at his forbidding age, Teller not only vigorously promoted SDI but also took on still another, related pursuit. He became a significant contributor to the defense of Israel, the land of his forebears but, paradoxically, a land about which he had expressed little concern or understanding until his declining years.

Our interest in the unorthodox manner and the rare vigor of Teller in such late endeavors and, more importantly, in the results of his efforts led to the writing of this book. History has produced greater scientists and greater politicians, but it would be difficult to find one who has straddled both fields with such great effect on how humans live and, perhaps, on human survival.

This work was begun in the summer of 1985 with an assurance and an admonition from Teller. The assurance was that he would try to make himself available for interviews and his papers available for inspection. He did. The admonition was that we try to avoid painting a wholly complimentary portrait of him. We did. Among those who have known and worked with Edward Teller, we found no neutral ground but a vast acreage of conflicting argument from which we tried to sift the most persuasive elements. Our objective was not to support or to undermine Teller's position on any of the many vital controversies engulfing him but to try to understand that position and, if possible, to understand and describe the personal forces driving him to it.

We do not know whether our quest has been successful. We do know that it has been fascinating, and we are grateful to those who have helped make it so.

Foremost among them is Teller, who shared more of himself with us than we believe even he intended. Despite his advanced age, uncertain health, and difficult schedule, he took time to answer our questions on dozens of occasions, each lasting from a few minutes to many hours. These interviews were conducted over meals, on automobile trips to airports, and in meeting rooms on both American coasts—at his favored Cosmos Club in Washington, D.C., in Baltimore, Maryland, and at his home in Palo Alto, California.

Also due more gratitude than can be expressed here are those others—his colleagues, relatives, friends, and opponents—who contributed their time and their recollections to help make this account possible. When practical, these have been identified in the text, but special mention should be made of James Abrahamson, Hans Bethe, Norris Keeler, George A. Keyworth, Yuval Ne'eman, James Watkins, John Archibald Wheeler, and Lowell Wood. We relied heavily, too, on official histories of projects and events embracing Teller's work, such as those recording the operation of the Atomic Energy Commission (AEC) and the Los Alamos National Laboratory. Greatly easing our burden throughout this work have been the help and counsel of Gwinn Owens, an old friend, and Edward T. Chase, our editor and new friend.

A book of this kind is hobbled by legal and moral restrictions involving the security of the United States. Our efforts to observe both have convinced us that the moral restrictions are often more sensible than the legal ones. Our prayer is for a day when neither will be necessary.

ACKNOWLEDGMENTS

In addition to those named in the preface, many persons made significant contributions to the completion of this book. Identifying all would not be practical. There are too many, and some, such as the diligent and ever-courteous staff members of the Baltimore City and Baltimore County Library System, contributed in anonymous but nonetheless valuable performance of routine duty. Our heartfelt thanks to them and, among many others, to these:

Mici Teller, Wendy Teller, Emmi Kirz, and Janos Kirz, for helping assemble the composite portrait of Edward Teller as husband, father, brother and uncle;

Hans Mark, chancellor of the University of Texas at Austin, for sharing his views on Teller as a person and fellow physicist;

Aron Moss, director of Israeli liaison with the Strategic Defense Initiative Organization (SDIO), for his account of Teller's influence on Israeli defense;

Victor Weisskopf and William O. Baker, for their complementary accounts of White House events on the evening of Ronald Reagan's SDI speech;

Gen. Daniel O. Graham (USAF, ret.), for sharing his different perspective on SDI from High Frontier, and Karl Bendetsen, for his account of early support for SDI;

Lt. Col. Donald R. Baucom, historian of the Strategic Defensive Initiative Organization, and Major Alan Freitag, its external affairs officer, who showered us with more information about the nuts, bolts, and dreams of SDI than we could use, absorb, or need;

U.S. Senator Rudy Boschwitz, of Minnesota, and Tom Schroeder, an intern on his staff, for helping illuminate Teller's work on Capitol Hill as an SDI advocate;

John Archibald Wheeler, for many details of his half-century association with Teller as friend and colleague;

Abel Wolman and John Toll, for recalling Teller's roles in nuclear safety and nuclear research projects on which they worked with him;

Dr. Elena Bonner, for permission to quote from her letter to Edward Teller about the strikingly similar paths followed by him and by her husband, Dr. Andrei Sakharov;

James Houtrides and Mike Lewin, for their descriptions of Teller as a network television subject and fellow investment counselor, respectively;

William F. Buckley, Mike Wallace, and Ira Rosen, for contributing to the accounts of Teller's appearance on the *Firing Line* and *60 Minutes* television programs;

Robert R. Budwine, for shepherding us about the Lawrence Livermore National Laboratory, and his fellow physicists there—John Nuckolls, John Anderson, Rod Hyde, George Chapline, Morton S. Weiss, Joseph B. Knox, and Richard Briggs—for their accounts of Teller as a colleague;

Andrew Burgess, M.D., chief of the orthopedic surgery team at the Maryland Shock Trauma Center, and James Maxfield, M.D., Teller's personal physician, for their help with passages involving his health;

Judith Schoolery, Genevieve Phillips, and Gloria Purpura, for easing our climb up the mountain of papers and records reflecting the work and life of our subject; and

Robbie Robinson, Alan Doelp, Angela Parks, James Brown, and Ann Zylstra, for help ranging from technical advice to preparation of photos and manuscript.

Their support is largely responsible for whatever is worthy in the pages that follow. We alone are responsible for what is not.

STANLEY A. BLUMBERG
LOUIS G. PANOS

Baltimore, Maryland

Chapter 1

THE SPEECH

Like so many other White House guests that evening of March 23, 1983, Edward Teller did not know why he had been invited. The only hint had come from George A. Keyworth, the president's science adviser.

"How important is it that I be there?" he had asked Keyworth on the telephone.

"It's important, Edward."

"But the board of regents is visiting the laboratory, and I really should be here unless it is urgent."

He was at the Lawrence Livermore National Laboratory, the weapons facility he had helped found near San Francisco more than thirty years earlier. The University of California operated it under contract with the Department of Energy (DOE). As the governing body of the university, the regents made periodic oversight visits to Livermore.

Keyworth could not be more specific without violating security. But he tried to save Teller from what he knew would be lasting disappointment if this invitation from the president went unaccepted.

"Edward," he said, "I can tell you this. It's what you always wanted."[1]

So Teller booked a flight east, as he had done so many times in the last four decades. But this flight was different. In the past, his reason for traveling to Washington was clear. As one of the world's foremost physicists and an expert on nuclear defense, he had frequently testified before congressional committees and had met with Pentagon and security officials and with fellow members of the White House Science Council. Invariably, he had wound up in the middle of controversy.

On one series of visits in the late 1940s and early 1950s, he had helped persuade government officials of the need for thermonuclear weapons, a success that brought him the tag he hated, "father of the H-bomb."

On another trip he testified in 1954 as a key witness in the AEC hearings

1

on whether J. Robert Oppenheimer, the great scientist who had directed the World War II development of the atomic bomb, should be stripped of his security clearance because of Communist connections. It was a turning point in the lives of both Teller and Oppenheimer.

In 1970, when he was urging Congress to strengthen national defense in the face of a Soviet nuclear arms buildup, students on the University of California campus at Berkeley rose up against him. Accusing him of being a war criminal, they held a mock trial, found him guilty, then marched on his nearby home. When police intercepted them at an intersection a block away, they burned Teller in effigy.

But Teller had also collected many honors through the years both as a scientist recognized for his contributions to theoretical and applied physics and as a citizen promoting defense to prevent war.

An indication of the contrasting opinions he was capable of generating, even among normally objective observers, came from two distinguished colleagues, both longtime acquaintances, both Nobel Prize–winning physicists. Eugene P. Wigner, one of them, said, "He is the most imaginative person I have ever met, and this means a great deal when you consider that I knew Einstein." The other, I. I. Rabi, saw Teller differently. "He is a danger to all that is important," he told us. "I do really feel it would have been a better world without Teller . . . I think he is an enemy of humanity."*

Against that background, what could transpire during this White House visit to justify Keyworth's assurance "It's what you always wanted"?

The answer came shortly after the White House limousine dropped Teller off at the southwest gate. It was 6:10 P.M., and the mid-forty-degree mildness of the afternoon had given way to a slight chill. Teller, limping slightly on the prosthesis replacing the right foot he had lost in an accident fifty-five years earlier, followed an escort up the grand staircase to the Blue Room. About three-dozen seats had been set up, and many of them were already filled or about to be filled with those still being greeted by Keyworth and John Poindexter, President Reagan's deputy national security adviser.

Teller spotted Defense Secretary Caspar W. Weinberger, Secretary of State George Shultz, and a host of prominent scientists. Among them were physicists Harold Agnew, former director of the Los Alamos laboratory where the first atomic bomb was built; John Foster, former director of the Livermore laboratory; and Victor Weisskopf, another member of the nuclear weapons pioneering team at Los Alamos, who had once joined

---

* Both assessments were offered to us in 1975 interviews; Rabi repeated his when we asked him again in 1981.

Teller and the great Italian physicist Enrico Fermi in writing a paper on atomic particles called mesotrons.

But curiously enough, Teller either did not notice or subconsciously blocked out recognition of Hans Bethe. Bethe was not only one of the most widely recognized and highly acclaimed scientists in the room but was also Teller's oldest personal friend and strongest public opponent of the issue that had brought them to the White House that evening.

That issue, as Poindexter and Keyworth explained to the guests when they had settled down, was a historic change in national defense policy to be announced by the president in a televised address at 8:00 P.M. The change would replace the policy of pinning hopes for peace mainly on a buildup of nuclear arms in the belief that only fear of catastrophic retaliation would discourage the United States and the Soviet Union from attacking each other—the policy of mutual assured destruction, or MAD.

In its place, the White House guests were told, the president would propose a policy emphasizing a defense built on modern technology, one capable of intercepting and destroying long-range nuclear missiles before they reached their targets. Teller's heavy black eyebrows arched in surprise, and his rugged features broke into a grin.* His role as a scientist trying to influence U.S. policy seemed to have come full cycle.[2]

Forty-three years earlier, on May 10, 1940, he had heard a call for help from another president, Franklin Delano Roosevelt. Teller had not even planned to attend the meeting being addressed by Roosevelt, the Eighth Pan American Scientific Conference in Washington. As a young theoretical scientist, he felt committed to pure investigation of the world and its makeup. Even though he had come to the United States to escape the shadow of anti-Semitism cast over his native Hungary by Adolf Hitler, he hoped he could pursue a career free of distortion or taint by political considerations.

Earlier that day, just after dawn came to western Europe, Hitler's Nazi troops had invaded the Lowlands of Europe. It was Hitler's most violent move since his swift invasion of Poland, on September 1, 1939, had triggered a declaration of war on Germany by Great Britain and France. Now, with this westward thrust positioning Hitler for strikes at British and French soil, the war had taken on a new dimension. Roosevelt was expected to discuss this, and possible U.S. reaction, in his speech. Teller decided to attend.

Roosevelt began the address by deploring the invasion of Holland,

---

* Keyworth related this to us in a 1986 interview. Bethe described it on a PBS television program originally broadcast on April 22, 1986.

Belgium, and Luxembourg. He pointed out that a free meeting of the type he was addressing could no longer take place in a large part of the world. Until the assault on the Lowlands, he said, because a great ocean separated their country from Europe, too many Americans believed themselves safe from "the impact of attacks on civilization." But this should convince them otherwise, he suggested.

Roosevelt then turned to the role of the scientists in world affairs and made this appeal: "You . . . may have been told that you are partly responsible for the debacle of today because of the processes of invention for the annihilation of time and space, but . . . the great achievements of science . . . are only instruments by which men try to do the things they most want to do. If death is desired, science can do that. If a full, rich, and useful life is sought, science can do that also. . . . I am a pacifist. You, my fellow citizens of twenty-one American republics, are pacifists, too. But I believe that by overwhelming majorities in all the Americas you and I, in the long run if it be necessary, will act together to protect and defend, by every means at our command, our science, our culture, our American freedom and our civilization."

Teller, then thirty-two, was profoundly stirred by Roosevelt's message. As he interpreted it, the president was not merely suggesting something that scientists might do. "He was talking about something that was our duty and that we must do—to work out the military problems, because without the work of the scientists the war and the world would be lost," Teller told us in recalling that moment in an interview nearly half a century later.

"I had the strange impression that he was talking to me. My mind was made up, and it has not changed since."[3]

That speech changed Teller's life. It moved him from the world of pure, politically uninvolved physics into an arena in which science responds directly to the immediate problems of society and government. It was an arena in which he was to know painful, lonely defeat. There he was also to feel the satisfaction of knowing that he had helped shape the course of history at three critical points: One involved production, during World War II, of the atomic bomb, which he helped develop but which he did not want used against the Japanese without prior demonstration in an unpopulated area. Another came in 1952, when his design of a hydrogen bomb was successfully tested. The third was the policy being announced by President Reagan on this March evening of 1983.

Teller was anxious to hear the details of Reagan's plan and to see how it would be received. Teller, who had zigzagged in and out of defense developments since the day of that Roosevelt speech in 1940, had worked on the concept of SDI for many years. He believed in its technical feasibility but until a few months earlier was discouraged about the prospect that it would ever gain political acceptance.

As early as August 20, 1963, he had publicly declared his conviction that effective defensive measures against ballistic missiles could be developed. At the time, he appeared before the Senate Foreign Relations Committee on the proposed ratification of a treaty banning nuclear tests in the atmosphere. Teller opposed ratification.

Proponents argued that the prohibition of atmospheric testing would slow the nuclear arms race and eliminate or greatly reduce radioactive fallout, thereby improving the international political climate and the quality of the environment at the same time.

But Teller was suspicious. He had not trusted Communist leaders since his boyhood days in Hungary, when Soviet-backed revolutionaries had seized control of the country and made a shambles of its economy and social order. Now he was convinced that the Soviet Union would welcome a test ban because it had recently conducted a successful test series and had forged ahead of the United States in the arms race. That, he said, explained why Soviet First Secretary Nikita Khrushchev had changed his mind about entering into the treaty.

"In 1960, he wasn't willing to sign, but now he had these magnificent test series in 1961 and 1962," Teller suggested to the committee. "He now knows how to defend himself. . . . He has the knowledge, and he is now willing to stop and prevent us from obtaining similar knowledge."

Teller then referred to reports that the Soviets had run at least fifty atmospheric nuclear tests beginning on September 1, 1961. He said a panel of experts appointed by President John F. Kennedy had analyzed debris from the tests. There was evidence that the Soviet Union was developing an antimissile missile.

"A few years ago I believed that missile defense was hopeless," Teller testified. "I am now convinced that I was wrong. . . . I am now convinced that we can put up a missile defense that can stop the attack of any weaker power, such as China, for at least the next two decades. In a time when we rightly worry about proliferation, we must not neglect our defenses against an attack from a quarter other than Russia. In addition, I also believe that our defense can be partially effective against the Russians. . . . Missile defense, by deterring the Russians, may make the difference between peace and war."[4]

Defense Secretary Robert S. McNamara, testifying the previous day for ratification, told the committee that the United States was stronger than the Soviets, had more missiles than they, and, if challenged by them in a stepped-up arms race, could outbuild them. Ratification of a test-ban treaty would not prevent the United States from proceeding with its only antiballistic missile defense, he said.

On this point, Teller said the United States could *proceed* with such a defense but could not *complete* it under a test-ban treaty because tests were necessary for development of an antimissile defense. In the end, approval was given to the Limited Test Ban Treaty of 1963, which prohibited testing in the atmosphere but not underground.

From that point to this, Teller had witnessed the groping by one set of negotiators after another for an answer to the arms-race dilemma. In 1967, President Lyndon B. Johnson met with Soviet Premier Aleksei Kosygin at Glassboro, New Jersey, in the hope of getting an arms agreement. This effort failed, but negotiations continued through the end of Johnson's term in 1969. Finally, an antiballistic missile treaty was negotiated and signed in Moscow on May 26, 1973, by President Richard Nixon and Soviet Chairman Leonid Brezhnev. This limited each side to one site to be defended and to the deployment of 100 antiballistic missiles for that purpose. The Soviets chose to defend Moscow. The United States chose a missile site in North Dakota, did not complete installation of the allowed 100 missiles until 1975, then dismantled the system a year later because the march of offensive technology rendered it obsolete.

Teller had given Ronald Reagan his first taste of the SDI idea in 1966, shortly after Reagan's election as governor of California. Visiting him in Sacramento, Teller invited him to Livermore for a look at some of the work being done there. Reagan went and was impressed. By the time he was elected to Washington fourteen years later, he was looking for an alternative to MAD.

In the intervening years, Teller also searched for a way to realize his dream of an antimissile system to blunt the menace of the nuclear weapons he had helped bring into the world.

He helped assemble a special team of brilliant young scientists at Livermore and kept close watch on their work in X-ray lasers and other potential weapons of modern defensive technology.

He met with several groups sharing Reagan's search for an alternative. One was linked both to the exclusive Bohemian Grove in California and to the Heritage Foundation, a conservative "think tank" based in Washington. Its members included Karl R. Bendetsen, retired chairman of Champion International Corporation, and Joseph Coors, the brewing magnate. Another group was High Frontier, a pro-defense civilian unit headed by retired Gen. Daniel O. Graham, former chief of air force intelligence and Reagan's presidential campaign military adviser. There was much cross-pollination between the Bendetsen and High Frontier groups, with experts like Teller and George Keyworth attending some meetings of both.

Teller left few areas unworked in campaigning—"on the whole, without success," he said—for support of his ideas on defense. He had been gathering evidence that Soviet work on antiballistic missiles dated back to 1956, and on innovative defense technologies, such as those he was urging the United States to pursue, to 1966. His cause moved a big step forward on June 15, 1982, when he was invited to appear on *Firing Line*, the Washington-based interview program hosted by journalist William F. Buckley.

After hearing Teller's version of SDI, Buckley shrugged and offhandedly suggested, "Well, all right, why don't you go to President Reagan and ask him for thirty billion dollars to do it?"

"I said, 'I'd love to,' " Teller recalled in discussing it with us later. " 'In fact, I don't need thirty billion. Right now I would be satisfied with one percent of this amount—three hundred million. But unfortunately, I have not once seen the president since he has been president.' "

Ronald Reagan was disappointed in this remark, Teller said. "In some mysterious way, this got back to the president," he said. He did not know how, but he assumed that someone on Reagan's staff had seen the program and told him about it. Buckley thought he knew better. In a letter to the authors, he said he had written Reagan, calling his attention to Teller's proposal.

But George Keyworth learned that both Teller and Buckley were wrong about how Reagan became informed. "He never misses Buckley," Keyworth told us. "If he can't see him live, he has the program taped so he can watch it later. And he certainly saw this one." Keyworth said he became aware of this some weeks later, probably in July, as a White House meeting of the National Security Council (NSC) was breaking up and Reagan asked him to stay for a moment longer.

Describing Teller's complaint, Reagan expressed puzzlement. "You know I've never been unfriendly to Edward Teller," he said.[5] Keyworth, a former physicist at Los Alamos, had been recommended by Teller for his job as science adviser to the president. Reagan wanted to believe there was something to the new-defense idea of Teller and his fellow advocates. But he also knew it would be difficult to budge the Defense and State departments from MAD, the policy of deterrence now widely likened to two men holding cocked pistols at each other's head. That policy had prevailed over a period of more than thirty years of peaceful, however jittery, coexistence. But Reagan did not want to offend Teller. He directed Keyworth to assure Teller that he and his views were always welcome in the White House. A short time later, Teller received a call from Keyworth, notifying him that he had been scheduled for a meeting with Reagan on October 1, 1982.

The meeting lasted thirty minutes. Joining Reagan and Teller were Keyworth and William Clark, the president's adviser on national security. Teller referred to the development of a third generation of weapons as a logical succession to the generations of atomic and hydrogen bombs. He spoke of work at Livermore and elsewhere on lasers and supercomputer systems capable of directing such third-generation weapons to seek out and destroy enemy missiles. Clark, indicating doubt, questioned Teller closely. Teller considered it a positive meeting. He thought the president was receptive. "When we were through," he told us, "the president said, 'When the submarine was first proposed, nobody believed it.' To my ears it almost sounded as a not quite small amount of interest."

Another key meeting attended by Teller and leading to the president's policy-change announcement was held on January 20, 1983, in the Pentagon office of Adm. James Watkins, chief of naval operations. Watkins, anxious to learn more about Teller's proposal, invited him to lunch.

Unknown to Teller at the time, Watkins was desperately seeking a way out of the hopeless trap he believed MAD to be. Over a period of many months, the Joint Chiefs had thrashed through forty-two meetings in search of an effective way to protect MX missiles, the nation's prime retaliatory weapon, from a Soviet first strike. Watkins was convinced that neither Congress nor the public would accept the method inherited as a recommendation from the Carter administration. This called for the installation of missiles in closely based silos so that if a Soviet nuclear missile exploded on or near one of them, radioactive debris from the explosion would destroy or divert missiles aimed at the other silos, leaving the missiles in those silos available for a retaliatory strike.

Also unknown to Teller was the fact that Robert McFarlane, Clark's deputy, was more concerned than Clark about the need for drastic revision of defense strategy and was moving to shape some change. Pressure for a nuclear freeze was growing in Congress, and disarmament talks in Geneva were foundering. McFarlane mentioned this to Reagan, who had already indicated a desire for a new approach, and then to Clark. But the selling of any massive change would require endorsement by political leaders and experts outside the White House, preferably among the military. With such backing, a missile defense program emphasizing research on new technology could be put forward as a nonpartisan proposal worthy of public support. Down the line, it might also bring some movement in Geneva. Knowing of the dilemma confronting the Joint Chiefs over how to protect the nation's retaliatory-weapons arsenal, McFarlane decided to talk it over with Watkins.

When Teller arrived at the Pentagon for his January 20 meeting with Watkins, the admiral had already consulted with McFarlane. Watkins had been urged by Capt. Jake Stewart, a long-range planning adviser, to hear what Teller had to say. Watkins told us about it on September 26, 1986, at a meeting in his office. As Watkins, Teller, and two of the admiral's aides had done at their meeting, we sat on leather sofas flanking a rectangular cocktail table. Looking down on us from a high wall was the portrait of a stern-looking Adm. Arleigh Burke, the World War II hero who was a Watkins favorite.

Watkins said he had turned to Teller for help while searching for an alternative to MAD.

"Mutual assured destruction was losing its grasp . . . on the strategic thought process," he said. "I continued to find it morally repugnant as a concept for this nation. . . . We were walking into a strategic cul-de-sac from which we couldn't extract ourselves." So in response to Stewart's suggestion, "I said I'd like to hear from Dr. Teller. . . . I'm at a point now where I am inadequate in my understanding of where we are technologically. . . . I've got to talk to a visionary."[6]

Teller's presentation of his basic idea of an antimissile defense lasted nearly an hour, with only an occasional pause for a question from Watkins. They then adjourned to the flag mess across the hall and continued their discussion over a luncheon of shrimp-stuffed filet of sole Provençale.

At the end, Watkins said, "Dr. Teller, I am fascinated by what you tell me, and what you are saying is giving me new hope that the technology may well be in hand at the turn of the century to shift to this concept of defense. . . . Is the technology within our grasp?"

"It is," Teller replied, then began a detailed explanation of what he understood the Soviets to be doing in defense. Watkins was impressed. Their intelligence sources obviously differed, but their conclusion was the same: The Soviets were ahead of the United States by at least ten years in some areas of antimissile defense. Teller's sense of urgency was contagious.

Two weeks after his meeting with Teller, Watkins and the rest of the Joint Chiefs were to meet on February 5, 1983. William Clark had sent word that the president wanted their recommendation. Watkins, preparing a presentation urging a shift from MAD to strategic defense, conferred several times with Keyworth. On the day of the meeting, he was not certain that the impasse prevailing over the previous forty-two meetings would be broken. "I decided to give it my best shot," he said. When he finished his presentation, they voted. It was unanimous. Reagan now had the support critical to his announcement.[7]

*   *   *

Preparing the assembled White House guests for the president's speech, Poindexter explained that Reagan was about to propose a significant change in U.S. defense policy. He then introduced Keyworth, who said the change was based on scientific developments that could produce a "shield" of antimissile weapons to intercept and destroy nuclear missiles fired at the United States and her allies by any enemy.

Teller's happy reaction to the briefing by Poindexter and Keyworth was not shared by many of the other scientists in the room. Hans Bethe and Victor Weisskopf, longtime colleagues of Teller who had disapproved of his stand on a number of defense issues, made no attempt to hide their disappointment.

Bethe expressed doubt that such a shield was feasible.

"It won't work," he said to Keyworth as the briefing ended and the group was led from the Blue Room to the Red Room for cocktails. Bethe and Weisskopf had opposed Teller's efforts thirty years earlier to speed up work on the H-bomb. Bethe had also differed with Teller on the test-ban treaty twenty years earlier and more recently had cautioned against goading the Soviets into stepping up the pace of the arms race. The only sane course, they had insisted throughout, was disarmament.

Shultz, walking along with Teller, looked worried. "Are you sure this will be one hundred percent effective?" he asked.

"No," said Teller. Then he repeated what was to become his controversial theme throughout the continuing SDI debate. "No defense is one hundred percent effective, but a partial defense is better than no defense if it discourages an aggressor from attacking."

Defense Secretary Weinberger was among the believers. He had been convinced since September 1982, when he saw an antimissile missile in a test off the coast of Florida hit its target on the nose.

Teller's good feeling over what was unfolding that evening was nearly matched by Keyworth's sense of satisfaction. Keyworth had played a major role in drafting the president's speech. A native of Boston, he was a 1963 Yale graduate and received his doctorate in nuclear physics from Duke University in 1968. He spent the next thirteen years at Los Alamos, the last three as director of its experimental physics division, which included several hundred scientists and technicians involved in their basic research emphasizing nuclear work. His appointment as director of the White House Office of Science and Technology Policy, or science adviser to the president, was confirmed by the Senate on July 24, 1981, two months and five days after it was announced.

Teller's recommendation of Keyworth for the job was built on an association dating back to Keyworth's middle years at Los Alamos, where Harold Agnew, then director, introduced them. They discovered they had a mutual interest in the action of the nuclei of fissionable materials at ultra-low temperatures.

One of Keyworth's notable acts after joining the president's staff was his setting up the White House Science Council in early 1982 to fill the vacuum left when the president's Science Advisory Committee was terminated by Richard Nixon during his presidency in the 1970s. Teller was among those appointed to the new council. One of its early assignments was the creation of a subgroup to look at emerging technologies and report on how they could influence the president's defense policy. A key feature of that report—only one copy is said to have existed long after it was issued in the fall of 1982—was its conclusion that one option lay in strategic defense but that strategic defensive weapons in space would be vulnerable to enemy attack.

We asked Keyworth about this in the Georgetown office he had set up as a consultant after leaving the White House in 1986. Without referring to the report itself, he said scientists had come up with a way to circumvent the vulnerability problem of weapons in space: Base them on the ground. He said this was made feasible by the advent of a new class of ground-based lasers and the possible use of space-hung mirrors off which the laser beams could be bounced.

"There was a promise that advanced optics could be developed to correct for the effects of the earth's atmosphere on the laser beam," he said. "They noted that some astronomers had been successful in taking the twinkle out of the stars. The same techniques could be used in reverse to compensate for the distorting effects of the atmosphere on a laser beam." Keyworth said it was difficult to overemphasize the importance of this. "It allows one, for the first time, to think seriously about putting the expensive component of a strategic defense system on the ground."

Keyworth said Reagan had expressed concern to him very early about whether the nation's defense had kept pace with available technology. "Not long after my arrival in Washington, I had sat down in the Oval Office with the president and discussed the fact that the strategic modernization decision, modernizing our strategic forces—that means airplanes, missiles, submarines, command and control—was a primary objective in his administration. And he asked me if I would help to clarify the issues before him on that."

Keyworth said Teller, at the meeting set up with Reagan in 1982 as a result of the Buckley program, referred to the nuclear freeze movement. He then expressed his deep concern over the possibility that the Russians could be developing a bomb-pumped X-ray laser. Using energy from a nuclear bomb, this device would concentrate it into a narrow beam flashing across thousands of miles of space with enough power to destroy an intercontinental ballistic missile. "Edward was very technical and specific in that brief discussion with the President about the promise and the threat of the X-ray laser," Keyworth recalled. "It could be the means, he argued, of creating a better balance in the nuclear area."

After that and many other meetings, Reagan called Keyworth in and asked the critical question "Is it now feasible to initiate a major research effort to develop these defenses?"

"And the answer I could give him," Keyworth said, "based upon what Edward and many other people had done and the state of the technology in general, was categorically yes."

The half-hour cocktail reception over, the White House guests on that evening of March 23, 1983, were escorted from the Red Room into the cross hall leading to the state dining room. There a half-dozen tables, each seating six, were set up for a buffet dinner of roast beef and green beans amandine. Spotted around the room were television sets offering a clear view from almost any seat.

The group had barely finished their dessert of chocolate mousse when the president, seated at his desk in the Oval Office and reading from teleprompters, began his speech.

"The subject I want to discuss with you, peace and national security, is both timely and important," he said. What followed would be referred to formally thereafter as the president's SDI speech. In the media it became known, after the movie featuring ray-gun battles in space, as the "Star Wars" speech.

To a weary Keyworth, who listened to the speech with an especially sensitive ear, it was Speech Draft No. 17, revised. After spending all weekend closeted in his office and going over one version after another, he and McFarlane had finished the seventeenth and final draft in time for presentation to the president on Tuesday, the day before delivery. It was identified by number and by the date and time of its delivery to the Oval Office: "03/22/83 . . . 0930."

Keyworth had dropped it off, then returned near the end of the lunch hour to pick it up, with any last amendments penned in by Reagan. Accepting it from the president, he glanced through the first few pages and froze, a look of surprise on his face. Page after page bore a number of largely stylistic changes made in Reagan's strong, clear handwriting.

"Why do you look startled?" Reagan asked.

"Well, Mr. President, I thought it was a pretty good speech."

Reagan smiled. "Just a few small changes," he assured Keyworth.

In delivery, Reagan stuck to the final, revised draft, whose changes for the most part were, as he assured Keyworth, minor.

For example, after asking whether it would not be better "to save lives than to avenge them" (as in MAD), he was to have said this:

After careful consultation with my advisers, including the Joint Chiefs of Staff, I believe there is a way, and I would like to share with you what I believe is a vision of the future which offers hope.

On delivery it came out like this:

After careful consultation with my advisers, including the Joint Chiefs of Staff, I believe there is a way. Let me share with you a vision of the future which offers hope.

Then he was to have described the hope like this:

We can and must embark upon a program dedicated to countering the awesome Soviet menace with measures that are defensive.

Instead, he said it like this:

It is that we embark on a program to counter the awesome Soviet threat with measures that are defensive.

The president then picked up the Draft No. 17 version:

What if free people could live secure in the knowledge that their security did not rest upon the threat of instant U.S. retaliation to deter a Soviet attack, that we could intercept and destroy strategic ballistic missiles before they reached our own soil or that of our allies? . . . This is a formidable task, one that may not be accomplished before the end of this century. Yet current technology has attained a level of sophistication where it is reasonable for us to begin this effort on many fronts. . . .

Here Reagan inserted this additional thought:

. . . and as we proceed we must remain constant in preserving the balance and maintaining a solid capability for flexible response.

Then came another change. Draft No. 17 called for this:

In the meantime, we must aggressively pursue reductions in nuclear arms.

It was delivered like this:

In the meantime, we will continue to pursue real reductions in nuclear arms.

Near the end of his address, the president had amended the last draft in a way that struck home with Teller. It originally read like this:

I call upon the nation, our men and women in uniform, our scientists and engineers, our entrepreneurs and industrial leaders, all our citizens . . . (to support this proposal).

It came out like this:

I call upon the scientific community, which gave us nuclear weapons, to turn their great talents to the cause of mankind and world peace.

It was almost, Teller later told us, as if he had been transported back more than forty years in time to that day when Franklin Roosevelt had issued an almost identical challenge.

When the speech ended and coffee and liqueurs were being served in the Blue Room, Reagan, obviously elated, entered and began accepting congratulations from his staff and other supporters of the new defense initiative.

Teller was among the most enthusiastic greeters. But there would be many times in the years ahead when he might well wonder whether his enthusiasm was justified.

Chapter 2

CULTURE AND CHAOS

For the first three years of his life, Edward Teller showed few recognized signs of exceptional intelligence. On the contrary, he had not even begun to speak, prompting his maternal grandfather to suggest that he lacked even normal intelligence. The grandfather thus became the first of many critics disproved by Edward in a long life of frequent criticism.

Edward was born on January 15, 1908, to Max and Ilona Teller, an upper-middle-class couple residing in the Pest section of the twin-city Hungarian capital composed of Buda and Pest. A daughter, Emmi, had been born twenty months earlier. Edward's father was a lawyer. His mother was the daughter of a cotton-mill owner and banker from Lugoj, in eastern Austria-Hungary. Both parents were of Jewish heritage. But like many of the 1 million Jews comprising about 5 percent of the Hungarian population, both families had generally assimilated into the predominantly Christian community and confined the expression of their religious beliefs primarily to ceremonial occasions and high holidays.

Many details of Edward's early life were passed on to us by his sister, Emmi, by other relatives, and by Magda Hess Schutz, who was the governess of the Teller children from the time Edward was nine until he reached fourteen. We met and interviewed them in their homes and by telephone after they immigrated to the United States.

One reason for Grandfather Ignac Deutsch's concern over Edward's early silence might have been a special fondness for him because of his close resemblance to Ignac: stocky frame, dark hair, thick eyebrows, broad forehead. In any event, the grandfather is said to have tried unsuccessfully to coax some coherent speech from Edward and then to have glumly suggested to Ilona, "I think you should prepare yourself for the possibility that you have a retarded child."[1]

But when Edward did begin to speak as he turned four, Emmi told us,

15

it was almost as if a dam had collapsed. The words gushed forth in polysyllables, understandable phrases, complete sentences. Soon he also began demonstrating exceptional aptitude in mathematics and music. Even before he was six, he would lie in bed at night and induce sleep by working multiplication problems: How many seconds in a minute, hour, day, week, year? Also, before long, he was playing the piano so well that his mother began nurturing the dream that he might achieve fame as a concert pianist.

Teller's father was born in Ersekújvár, a small town in the Hungarian province of Moravia. After graduation from secondary school in nearby Pozsony (Bratislava), he enrolled at the University of Budapest and received a law degree there in 1895. At thirty, having fulfilled the traditional European responsibility of seeing his three sisters married before thinking of taking a wife for himself, he met Ilona Deutsch, a petite blue-eyed blonde eleven years his junior who was visiting a friend in Budapest. Sixteen days later Max and Ilona were engaged, and in two more years, on May 29, 1904, they married.

Edward Teller's mother was talented at the piano and, besides her native Hungarian, spoke English, German, French, and Italian. Relatives remember her as intense and extremely protective of her children. Magda Hess, the governess, told us of one swim outing during which Ilona tied strings around the waists of young Emmi and Edward, enabling her to give a precautionary tug if they ventured too far.

The Hungary of pre–World War I days was stirred by political crosscurrents of nationalism whipped up by the Slovenes, Croatians, Romanians, and Slovaks, who made up 50 percent of the population, but they held less than 1 percent of the voting strength in a national parliament dominated by a Hungarian upper class. Hints of revolt by one or another of the underrepresented national groups were common. Also contributing to the unsettled political climate within Hungary was the outbreak of three wars between 1911 and 1914 in neighboring Balkan countries. Still another ominous factor was the combination of widespread economic problems and social discontent propelling much of the world toward World War I.

Against this uncertain background, the newly married Tellers settled into a spacious apartment overlooking the main square of Budapest, on the Pest side of the historic Danube. Max made a law office of one room in the apartment, which was conveniently located near the courts and government offices. Emmi and Edward were both born at home.

At the age of six, Edward was enrolled in the Mellinger School, a small private school occupying the third floor of a building near the Teller home. From 9:00 A.M. to 1:00 P.M. pupils were exposed to arithmetic, spelling, reading, German music, and the fairy tales of Grimm and Andersen. He excelled in class and in footracing, soccer, and other games played in an area laid out on the roof over the school. He also displayed an incisive curiosity that sometimes led to awkward moments. On one occasion, when a religion instructor stated that God created earth, Edward asked, "Who created God?" When the instructor continued with an account of how the biblical serpent was punished by being made to slither about on its belly, Edward asked how it got around before the punishment was imposed.[2]

At home, Edward sometimes demonstrated a combination of childish egocentricity and adult profundity. He retreated frequently into periods of silent concentration, sometimes extending these even through mealtime. "Please don't talk to me," he would say. "I have a problem."

"It was more of a plea than rudeness," Emmi told us when we asked about this more than seventy years after the fact. "He would say it very politely, and he would apologize. We knew he was thinking about something he considered very important at the time, and we understood."[3]

But Edward's precocity was less appreciated in school. Older pupils zeroed in on him as a target for taunts and pranks. During one stretch his trip home from school became a gauntlet flanked by bigger boys taking much sport in pushing and harassing him. In the young world of Edward Teller, the situation reached crisis proportion.

Sharing the crisis was Magda Hess, whose efforts to help included an aborted plan to accompany him on the after-school walk home. "I'm working on something," he assured her. "Don't worry."

"The next day he wanted a longer book strap," Magda recalled. En route home that afternoon, as the school bullies approached, Edward responded by swinging the strapped books in a powerful arc that sent the foremost of the tormentors sprawling and discouraged the rest. "They never bothered him again," said Magda.[4]

During the buildup to World War I and for a brief period after its outbreak, there was little change in the life-style of the Tellers and most of their neighbors near the downtown square in Budapest. But by the winter of 1915, less than a year after the conflict was triggered by a Serbian terrorist's assassination of the Austrian archduke, Budapest began to feel the pinch of food and coal shortages. Lines formed at butcher shops. Among institutions forced to close at least temporarily for lack of heat was the Mellinger School, but Edward maintained his studies and completed the four-year course with honors in the spring of 1918.

In the meantime, military and political developments set the stage for a Communist takeover of Hungary. The Bolshevik Revolution had forced first Czar Nicholas, then his brother, Michael, from power in 1917. With the entry of the United States into the war on the side of the Allies, the capitulation of the Central Powers—Germany, Turkey, and Austria-

Hungary—became inevitable. Barely four months after the armistice of November 11, 1918, the Socialist party of Hungary set itself up in Budapest on March 21, 1919, as the power controlling the "workers' and peasants' state" under the leadership of Béla Kun, a Hungarian lawyer and journalist indoctrinated in Russia.

For the Tellers, a major decision during the period was the selection of a middle school for Edward. They ruled out one of three schools because, despite its excellence, the Piarist Catholic priests running it required that enrollees become Christians. Another, operated by the Lutheran church, was rated scholastically inferior to the others. As a result, in the fall of 1918, Edward entered the remaining possibility, the Minta, or "model," a school established by Moritz von Karmann. His son, Theodor von Karmann, was to become one of America's most highly acclaimed aeronautical engineers.

Edward plunged into the limitless world of books and was especially drawn to the science fiction of Jules Verne. But his adjustment to the Minta and his new schoolmates was not easy.

He found Latin unworthy of serious study and grudgingly conceded it just enough effort to get by. But his difficulty with mathematics presented a different kind of dilemma. Here the problem was not indifference to the subject but boredom. His keen interest in mathematics had propelled him into the realm of basic algebra, and he was so far ahead of the class that he seemed apathetic.

An incident illustrating the problem involved Dr. Karl Oberle, who served as both principal and mathematics instructor at the Minta. In one version of the incident, Oberle demonstrated the solution to an algebra problem on the blackboard. On turning around to face the class, he saw Teller signaling with upraised hand. When he called on Teller, Edward is then said to have suggested a better method of solving the problem. Invited to demonstrate, he walked to the board and did so.

"So, you are a genius," the embarrassed instructor said. "Well, I don't like geniuses."

This version comes from Teller's sister, Emmi, who recalled hearing it from Edward himself shortly after the incident. Another source of the same version was Miklos Wenczel, one of Edward's classmates at the time. Wenczel described the incident to us more than half a century later at his home in Silver Spring, Maryland.[5]

But in reviewing this account with us in late 1987, Teller questioned its accuracy and gave this version:

"The method was that there would be questions, and whoever knew the answers would raise his hand. And I think that the correct version is that I answered the question—I remember it—and I shouldn't have known the answer, but I did. The teacher did not say anything at all. That was in advance of what we should have known. I put up my hand. I don't know whether I was the only one or not. But he asked me and I answered. And then he asked me, 'What are you, a repeater [one who had taken the course before]?' I said no. And from then on, for at least a couple of months, he would never ask [call on] me. He ignored me completely. I was afraid I would get a bad mark. But that did not happen. On three or four occasions, out of a hundred or more, he did ask me. My answers were right. And I got the best grade. That was all there was to it. Nothing dramatic of that kind."[6]

In light of the military and political unrest throughout his years at the Minta, and its potential for unsettling adolescent students, Edward's scholastic achievements seem extraordinary. Much has been written about the group of Hungarians who emerged from that period and, after emigrating to the United States and working on nuclear-weapons projects, gained international recognition. Besides Teller, the group included such renowned physicists as Eugene Wigner, the 1963 Nobel laureate, and Leo Szilard, who, with Italy's Enrico Fermi, in 1942 produced the world's first controlled nuclear reaction. Others in the group were Theodor von Karmann, mentioned earlier as the distinguished aeronautical engineer, and John von Neumann, regarded by many as the finest mathematician of his day.

Such group excellence defies explanation. There is no obvious common thread. These exceptional minds did not all come under the influence of the same gifted teachers. No government or local education system laid out a stimulating and demanding study plan. Wigner and von Neumann both attended the Lutheran school considered inferior by Teller's parents. Teller and Szilard had no teachers in common with the others.

Eugene Wigner thought part of the answer lay in the stimulating intellectual climate pervading Hungary at that time. "You heard a great deal more erudite conversation than you hear in the United States," he told us. "People talked more about culture, about art, about literature."[7]

But part of the answer may simply lie in the pure coincidence that each, like Edward, came from a closely knit family that placed high value on education. In later life, such as during their war work in the United States, the unusual intelligence of the group amazed American colleagues, who joked that they must have descended from another planet and therefore referred to them as "the Martians." The joke stuck, and Edward himself, asked by us to explain the Hungarian phenomenon, merely smiled, shrugged, and said, "Martians."

Making their educational progress even more remarkable was that it continued through the years of political unrest and economic uncertainty. Béla Kun's tenure lasted only four months, but its damage lasted far beyond. His decree nationalizing all commerce, industry, and real estate resulted in collapse of the nation's economy, followed by a suspension of domestic law. For all citizens, this meant a curtailment of basic rights. For Max Teller, it also meant some curtailment of his livelihood.

It was apparent that the Communists were unable to build widespread popular support. Signs of resistance developed, which generated repressive measures. Revolutionary forces and resistance units, including remnants of the Hungarian army defeated in World War I, clashed in the streets. Among those killed in such outbreaks were unaligned civilians, including the son of a janitor in the Teller building. The arrest and shooting of "traitors" was an almost daily occurrence. Reminders of the fate awaiting dissidents appeared in the form of corpses hanging from lampposts.

Amid all this, there was little change in the life-style of the Teller family. Although his practice was reduced by the suspension of domestic law, Max continued to serve clients in need of wills to be written, changed, or administered. With income from such work and with reserves built up in better times, Max managed to support his family without serious hardship. Emmi and Edward, now twelve and ten, continued their attendance at school but were closely protected by their parents from the sporadic street violence.[8]

The most direct impact of the political situation on the Tellers was the billeting of two Communist soldiers in their apartment. They were generally restrained and courteous, but their mere presence introduced tension into the daily life of the family.

An uglier aspect of the brief revolutionary period was its fanning of latent anti-Semitism among the general Hungarian population. Béla Kun was a Jew. So were eight of his eleven commissars. As intellectuals and activists who had been weaned on Karl Marx, they shared little in goal or purpose with the middle-class Jews who had achieved success in the professional and cultural mainstream of Hungarian society. This successful element of Hungarian Jewry was not politically active but, as part of the nation's professional and business leadership, had enjoyed a mutually respectful relationship with moderate government officials and with its fellow citizens. Now, in the early 1920s, Jews not involved in politics began to sense the rising resentment and hostility engendered among the aristocracy and non-Jewish middle class by the Kun organization. Magda Hess recalled that Ilona Teller expressed her concern to her, saying, "I shiver at what my people are doing. When this is over, there will be terrible revenge."

To protect the children during this turbulent time, the Tellers gained permission to send Edward and Emmi to stay with Ilona's parents in Lugoj in the fall of 1919. Ignac Deutsch had maintained his substantial position in this eastern Hungarian community, and it was felt that a healthier, more stable environment could be provided there for the children.

By midsummer of 1919, a counterrevolutionary coalition had emerged in the southern Hungarian city of Szeged under the leadership of Adm. Miklós Horthy, a wealthy landowner and Hungarian war hero of World War I. Béla Kun stepped down on August 1. After a brief occupation of Budapest by Romanian troops, Horthy led his new Hungarian national army into the city on November 16 and took over.[9]

Emmi and Edward remained in Lugoj with Ilona's parents until the spring of 1920, when they returned to Budapest and resumed their education. Emmi, now fourteen, reentered a *Gymnasium*, or middle school, named Marie Tereze. Edward, twelve, resumed his courses at the Minta. Magda Hess said Edward during this period made excellent progress in developing self-confidence, intellectual growth, and athletic ability. The crisis of the Minta bullies but a dim memory, he built a new circle of friends and sharpened his zest for mathematics, chess, and the piano, often becoming engrossed for hours at a time in the sonatas and fugues of Bach, Beethoven, and Mozart.

With the rule of law established again, Max resumed full practice. He also reestablished regular contact with his closely knit group of friends, most of them middle-class Jewish professionals and intellectuals. Their tendency to assimilate, hardly rare in the old days, was intensified under the pressure of anti-Semitic incidents. Ilona's fears of a post-Kun backlash against the small Jewish segment of the population were shared by her husband. They also proved to be well-founded. In his drive to oust the Communists, Horthy had appealed to the kind of superpatriotism that has historically produced polarization and suppression of minorities.

On his arrival in Budapest, Horthy had declared, "This city disowned her millennial tradition [and] dragged the Holy Crown and national colors in the dust. . . . We shall forgive this misguided city if it turns from the false gods to the love of our fatherland . . . if it reveres the Holy Crown once more."

Almost, as if in response, patriotic societies sprang up throughout Budapest. Some were secret. Some were open. Most were plainly anti-Semitic, and they flourished under an obvious policy of encouragement by the Horthy government. Jews were not prohibited from entering government work or educational institutions, but discriminatory quotas were established.

With this increase in outright hostility, the number of Jews professing conversion to Christianity increased. "The type of society to which our family belonged was really trying to assimilate," Edward Teller said. He recalled his father's bringing the subject to his attention. "I think it was the first time I was deeply impressed by my father," Edward said. "He said anti-Semitism was coming. To me, the idea of anti-Semitism was new, and the fact that my father was so serious about it really impressed me."

The Tellers did not experience the physical violence felt by some Jews, such as Eugene Wigner, for example, who was beaten by a mob. But Edward did not escape the psychological violence that also accompanies prejudice. One teacher in the Minta sarcastically addressed his class as "Gentlemen, Jews, and Polacks." He did not know whether certain pupils of Polish ancestry were also Jewish.

Although behind Emmi in grade, Edward was far enough advanced in mathematics to help her with her algebra homework. This impressed their parents, but it also generated fear in Max Teller that his son's devotion to mathematics might lead him into a career as an underpaid teacher. For help, the father turned to Leopold Klug, a friend and professor of mathematics at the University of Budapest. Klug was invited to meet Edward in the Teller home for an appraisal of the boy's aptitude in mathematics. At Klug's suggestion, he also bought Edward a copy of Euler's geometry.

Klug discussed the contents of the book with Edward and challenged him with geometry theorems. After a half-dozen visits over the next few weeks, he told Max, "Your son is exceptional."

For Edward the meetings were inspirational. Klug seemed to possess a zest for life and for his work, a rarity among the adults Edward knew. "More and more," Edward told us, "I was convinced that I didn't want to grow up and become bored like the rest of them." Klug was the kind of man he would like to emulate.

At fourteen, after devouring Euler's text, Edward pitched into a book on Einstein's special and general theories of relativity. He was now in only the fourth year of the eight-year Minta curriculum but was already poring over the works of a great living mathematician with whom he would one day share a critical role in the development of the U.S. nuclear weapons program.

Despite Klug's assurance and Edward's proficiency in mathematics, Max Teller could not shake his uneasiness. He felt that Edward, as a Jew facing a government and an educational system with built-in anti-Semitic quotas, should prepare for a professional career offering greater security. But Edward persisted. He had gained confidence from his remarkable scholastic progress and from his development as a robust adolescent. He had also developed a close circle of friends. Magda described how members of the group, all in their early teens, would spend hours on summer evenings walking about the Budapest square and the surrounding neighborhood, discussing science, philosophy, the universe, and its meaning.

The member of the group closest to Edward was Edward Harkanyi. Affectionately known as Suki, young Harkanyi had a brilliant mind, an articulate delivery, and a bright sister, Augusta Maria. Nicknamed Mici, she was also an unusually attractive and lively young lady. Edward noticed. By 1925, when he was seventeen and she was sixteen, their devotion to each other was obvious. It was to last a lifetime.

Mici's parents were among the many Hungarian Jews who had converted to Christianity. There was never a suggestion that this adopted religious difference might hinder the relationship of the young couple.

For Edward it was a time of major decisions, scholastically as well as romantically. As his graduation from the Minta approached, he entered sometimes unpleasant discussions with his parents about the next step in his education. At Ilona's insistence, he enrolled at the University of Budapest and continued to live at home. Max had also prevailed on him to forgo mathematics as his main subject and pursue a more promising career in engineering even though Edward had finished at the top of his class in both mathematics and physics on the university's qualifying examinations.

But after a brief trial at the hometown university, neither Edward nor his father was satisfied with the decision, and they shaped a compromise. Edward would withdraw and enroll at the Institute of Technology in Karlsruhe, on the bank of the Rhine River in southwestern Germany, to study chemical engineering. Supported by the I. G. Farben empire, the institute was internationally recognized. Its graduates were prized by industry. Part of the compromise was that Edward would be allowed to study mathematics as a second major subject.

When the train left Budapest for Karlsruhe on New Year's Day, 1926, Edward Teller was on it.

Chapter 3

THE MAKING OF A SCIENTIST

Despite the devastation of World War I and dismaying political turmoil, the Germany that received Edward Teller as a young student in the 1920s was a nation aglow with intellectual and creative genius. The war and its painful aftermath served as a catalyst for pioneering creative work in art, literature, and the sciences.

Emerging during this period were such giants as Walter Gropius, Ludwig Miës van der Rohe, and Marcel Breuer in architecture and Paul Klee, Wassily Kandinsky, and Lyonel Feininger in art.

In *Im Westen nichts Neues*, the world-famous novel popularized by Hollywood as the film *All Quiet on the Western Front*, Erich Maria Remarque gave voice in 1929 to the pacifist sentiment enveloping most of Europe. Thomas Mann's masterpiece, *The Magic Mountain*, and such other notable works as his allegorical tale "Mario and the Magician," were published in the years 1925–30.[1]

It was almost as if four years of contained creative energy had been freed in a cultural explosion.

But perhaps the greatest impact from the released creativity of this period was delivered by those geniuses who passed endless hours in the physics laboratories and classrooms, prodding a reluctant universe to surrender its truths. Bit by bit, they teased out first one of its secrets, then another and another. Now, with the war and its tragic insanity behind them, they could turn once more to pure science with renewed vigor and freedom.

Leading the exploration were Max Planck and Albert Einstein. They had startled the scientific community with a new conception of the world—what it is made of, how it works. Planck had published his landmark work on radiation and energy in 1900, and Einstein revealed his special theory of relativity in 1905. Although they had laid this foundation twenty years earlier, they were still active in the 1920s, when their theories inspired

24

spectacular developments by the cadre of brilliant physicists then flourishing in Europe. It was a momentous period.

Planck theorized that radiation, such as light of a given color, was not emitted or received in indefinitely small amounts or as a mathematically continuous shaft. Instead, it was emitted or received by a series of steps or discrete—that is, separate and distinct—packets, which he called quanta. One example used to promote an understanding of this theory suggests that we try to imagine a faucet surrendering water in amounts of only one cup or two or three, but never half a cup or any other fraction of a cup.

From Einstein's theory of special relativity emerge many ramifications, but among the most basic is that matter and energy are convertible into each other. To express the energy content of matter, he offered the most remarkable equation of the age: $E = mc^2$, with E representing energy; m, mass; and c, the speed of light. In his exposition of relativity, Einstein buttressed Planck's quantum theory by postulating that light is not a continuous wave but a series of packets, like Planck's radiation packets.

Hot on the trail blazed by Planck and Einstein was a band of scientists bent on refining and extending the application of their theories. In 1913, Niels Bohr of Denmark applied his quantum theory to the movement of electrons around an atom, which revolutionized the traditional representation of electrons as blips around the nuclear center of the atom, like planets orbiting the sun. In the Bohr concept, the energy of the electron is quantized or assigned a measurement that changes as it absorbs or emits energy (in this case, light). Absorption of a necessary amount, or quantum, causes the electron to jump to a higher orbit; later emission of the same amount causes it to leap back to its original orbit.

About to peak at the time of Teller's enrollment at the Karlsruhe Institute of Technology in 1926, this golden age of science was to last only another decade in Germany before its demise under the regressive policies of Adolf Hitler.

In the meantime, Teller's exposure to such an environment intoxicated him more than any other intellectual experience he had known. His arrival in Germany also began a half century of friendships and professional relationships with scientists who, like Teller, would become known to virtually every student in their field: J. Robert Oppenheimer, Bohr, Hans Bethe, I. I. Rabi, Eugene Wigner, Leo Szilard, John A. Wheeler. All would be among his colleagues, his collaborators on research, or his co-workers on nuclear weapons projects in the years to come.

The Karlsruhe of that day offered a hospitable climate for a young student of chemical engineering. The city, six miles east of the Rhine River, included an older section of pleasant architecture surrounding a palace historically serving as the headquarters of the duke of Baden. There was also a less attractive sprawl of factories, reflecting the importance of the city as a railroad hub. But the dominant feature in the city's character was the I. G. Farben chemical works, which was both the major employer in Karlsruhe and the underwriter of the institute.

After renting a room near the institute, the eighteen-year-old Teller settled down to the serious business of learning and working toward a doctor of philosophy degree. "I studied virtually all the time," he later recalled. He complained about the unexpectedly heavy demand on his time required by the laboratory work in his chemistry course. "I broke a lot of test tubes, cut my fingers, and nearly put my eye out on one occasion," he told us.

Despite the heavy workload, Edward was able to take occasional breaks for table tennis, skiing, or hikes through the countryside. Among his happier memories were those of the enduring friendships he built at Karlsruhe, the brightest of which were relationships established with Herman Mark and Peter Ewald, both professors. Teller found Mark especially likable. He was an outstanding lecturer, and his contagious enthusiasm for his subject influenced Teller to switch from chemistry to mathematics. Some years later, Ewald's daughter, Rose, was chaperoned by Edward and Mici Teller on a trip across the United States with the man she would later marry. He was Hans Bethe, the physicist with whom Teller had shared a long and fast friendship—only to have it founder in a sea of philosophical and personal differences in their twilight years. It was one of the many ironies marking the long, bumpy road traveled by the enigmatic Edward Teller.

Herman Mark, still in his twenties at the time he taught Teller, later moved to the United States and became board chairman of Brooklyn Polytechnic Institute. In a 1973 interview with us, he described his former student and the great attraction that the Germany of that time held for young scientists. "There was Planck, there was Einstein, there was [Max von] Laue, there was [Lise] Meitner," he said, rattling off the names of some of the most distinguished scientists of that time.[2] Otto Hahn and his associate, Fritz Strassmann, first split the nucleus of the atom. Meitner and her nephew, Otto Frisch, performed the earliest experiments recording the tremendous release of energy in nuclear fission.

Unlike Oberle, the teacher who was said to have openly expressed resentment of Teller's classroom critiques many years earlier, Mark spoke appreciatively of similar interruptions by Teller in class at Karlsruhe. "Teller really wasn't a good-looking man," he said. "He was stubby and fat and always a little pale. But if he wasn't handsome, he was always kind. Teller was popular, too. The other students respected him. Very frequently during a lecture he would say, 'Well, I think that was very interesting but if you don't mind, I presume what you really wanted to tells us was this.'

And he'd explain his idea in a Hungarian accent, and he was always right."

Mark was among the intellectuals leaving Germany because of rising Nazi anti-Semitism. But unlike many who were forced to abandon most of their life savings before fleeing, he was said to have salvaged a substantial portion of his own by converting his assets into platinum wire. The wire was fashioned into clothes hangers, which, coated with black enamel and hung with light garments packed for the trip, escaped detection during Mark's passage out of the country.[3]

During holiday and summer vacation periods, Edward returned to Budapest. One result of these sojourns was the growth of his friendship with Mici into a full-blown romance. Another was his finally gaining his father's permission to study physics, provided he also continued his studies in mathematics. As a result, in 1928 young Teller entered the University of Munich, where he could enroll in a class under Arnold Sommerfeld, a physics teacher of international reputation. But Edward was not impressed. "He was not terribly inspiring," Teller recalled, "but the subject *was* inspiring."

In Munich, Teller met Hans Bethe, then also a student. But their friendship would not ripen—or overripen—until years later, when both had moved to the United States and each had carved out a lofty niche for himself in the world of science.

It was also in Munich that Teller met tragedy. It struck near the end of his first semester during what was planned as a day of relaxation and enjoyment—on an excursion into the countryside. The date was July 14, 1928. Edward boarded a streetcar for the ride to the railroad station, where he was to join friends for the outing. Absorbed in thought, he looked up after a while and noticed that the three-section streetcar had pulled into his stop. Getting to his feet as the vehicle started up again, he made his way to the exit and leaped from the moving car. But the force of his landing and the awkward weight of his rucksack and other hiking gear spun him off balance and sent him sprawling.

His recollection of the accident a half century later was still vivid but unemotional: the sound of the streetcar rumbling on, an apparent feeling of relief in the mistaken belief that he had escaped its wheels, then the curious realization that he had not.

"I saw the streetcar going by. I remember a sense of relief. And for a reason I did not know—and do not know—I did not try to get up but looked back. And then I saw my boot lying there, and I wondered, How will I go hiking? And only after that I looked at my foot that was gone, and I wondered why I don't feel anything. And then I started to feel it."

Teller had no accurate sense of how long it took for help to arrive, but he recalled no feeling of impatience while waiting for the ambulance. He did not remember receiving any sedative or anesthetic en route to the hospital. "I may have been on the operating table half an hour after jumping off the car—maybe more, but not much more. There was this man, Dr. Von Lossow, who asked me what he should do, what kind of operation I wanted. And I wished only that he would tell me, but he wanted to know what I wanted. He was very nice about it."

One choice was what Teller described as the "standard" operation, in which the remainder of his foot, the part not severed or crushed by the wheels of the streetcar, would be removed by amputation above the ankle. "And then I would get a very nice, appropriate prosthesis." An alternative was a procedure that he recalls being attributed by Von Lossow to a Russian surgeon. He apparently referred to Nikolai Ivanovich Pirogov (1810–81), whose works are still a beacon in modern limb surgery. In this procedure, part of the heel bone and the heel pad are saved and are pulled forward and upward for fusion with the tibia, or major bone of the lower leg. This, Teller was told, would produce a padded stump on which he could walk without a prosthesis. "That was the one I chose," he said. [4]

Near the end of Teller's two-month hospital stay, a mystery unfolded. "One day, without notice, Von Lossow disappeared," he said. "I later found out he went to South America. He was very nice, and I liked him. But I was upset that he did not say good-bye." Teller learned that the surgeon was a brother of Gen. Otto von Lossow, the Bavarian army commander who had testified against Hitler at the Nazi leader's trial for treason after the unsuccessful Munich Beer Hall Putsch in which the Nazis unsuccessfully tried to overthrow the government in November 1923. [5] With Hitler's release nine months later and his star again on the rise by 1928, former enemies such as General von Lossow—and their relatives— sought healthier climates. Accordingly, Dr. Von Lossow was thought to have taken up practice elsewhere. Rumors mentioned South America most frequently. Whatever the reason for his sudden departure, Teller never heard from him again.

Perhaps because of the support and concern shown him by Von Lossow at the outset, perhaps because of his own constitutional toughness, Teller refused to let the accident crush his spirit. Asked if there was some other factor—religion, family, or both—that helped sustain him during his convalescence in Munich and during a later, equally long one in Budapest, Teller shook his head. "My whole family came out, and my mother stayed until I was well enough to come back to Budapest," he said. "She did not want to go. I wish she had. At that time I was not in need of being sustained." [6]

Because he had philosophically accepted his misfortune? "I don't know. I know that I was not in need." Besides his work, he still had a keen appreciation of the piano and chess, two of his favorite forms of relaxation, and the ability to play them well. He also recovered from surgery and adapted to his artificial foot well enough to regain a great degree of mobility remarkably soon.

Toward the end of autumn, Teller felt well enough to resume his studies. Sommerfeld, who had been a major attraction for Teller at Munich, was now on leave of absence. But there was an even greater attraction at the University of Leipzig in the person of Werner Heisenberg. Later to be recognized as one of the world's great physicists, Heisenberg was at this point still a young teacher. But he had already excited the scientific community with his uncertainty principle, a major contribution to a wider understanding of the theory of quantum mechanics. Basically, Heisenberg's principle held that the behavior of subatomic particles was governed not by causality but by statistical laws—not on the basis of constant certainty but only on the basis of probability. One cannot state that a particle will behave in a certain manner, Heisenberg said, but only that it *probably* will behave in that manner. It was a controversial idea, and among those who disagreed was Einstein. "Highly disagreeable," he said. "God does not play dice with the universe."

Einstein nothwithstanding, the opportunity to study with Heisenberg was irresistible to Teller. He later described Heisenberg as "the one who gave me a start." The admiration was mutual. Heisenberg recalled Teller's arrival at Leipzig and his presentation of his transcripts. "They were excellent, excellent, excellent," Heisenberg said. "From that time on, he was one of the most interested, as well as the most interesting, members of my seminary."

Leipzig in the 1920s was an intellectually stimulating city. With its scholars, its many structures dating back to the sixteenth and seventeenth centuries, and its history enriched by the contributions of sons such as Martin Luther, Johann Sebastian Bach, Goethe, Schumann, and Mendelssohn, it offered an ideal environment for a young student. "An extremely happy life," Heisenberg recalled. "We worked hard, but we went on excursions or we met at the swimming pool. It was not only a gay life but a time of great scientific progress, accomplished by very young people, most of them under thirty. They did important work on the theory of metals, the electric conduction of metals, the theory of magnetic behavior, the theory of molecules, and even astrophysical problems. It was an extremely interesting time." For Edward it was one of the happiest periods of his life.

One reason for Teller's happy recall of his days at Leipzig was the rapport he established with Heisenberg. This also seemed to be true of Heisenberg and many of his other exceptional students, but the relationship with Teller might have been strengthened by many similarities in their backgrounds.

Heisenberg was born in 1901 in Würzburg, Bavaria. His father, like Teller's, was a professional. He was a teacher in the *Gymnasium*, or the fifth-through-twelfth-grade middle school common to educational systems in many European countries at the time. And as Edward was to do later, young Heisenberg demonstrated early an exceptional aptitude in mathematics. When Werner was eight, his family moved to Munich, where the university had offered his father a professorship in medieval Greek literature and history. By the time he was twelve or thirteen, Werner had surged beyond the mathematics texts used in his own school and was immersed in differential equations and calculus.

After the war, as Edward was to do, Heisenberg redirected his main interest from mathematics to physics and studied at the University of Munich under the same professor Sommerfeld who was later to teach Teller. The theory of relativity was popular at the time, and Werner had read all the books he had found on the subject before he was twenty and ready to enter the University of Munich. From Sommerfeld he learned about Niels Bohr's theory of the atom. Two years later, in 1922, Sommerfeld invited Heisenberg to attend a series of lectures by Bohr at the University of Göttingen. There Heisenberg met the great Danish physicist himself.

In 1928, Heisenberg was called to Leipzig, where he set up the seminary that attracted aspiring physicists like young Teller.

Teller was among the group of students who regularly socialized with their teacher when the formal workday was done. Most students, like Teller, were of modest means and rented rooms in the homes of families needing extra income. They ate most of their meals in nearby inexpensive restaurants. Heisenberg occupied bachelor's quarters on the second floor of the building in which he also taught class, and he would join students on Tuesdays for evening tea in the downstairs room where he conducted daytime seminars. These extracurricular sessions frequently turned out to be extensions of classroom physics discussions, but they were also enlivened by table-tennis competition waged throughout much of the evening only a few feet away in the same room. By now Teller had adjusted to his artificial foot well enough to resume playing with much of his former skill.

Between sips of tea, members of the seminar and Heisenberg would chat and exchange talk liberally laced with physics. Many would disengage themselves in turn to drift off and challenge the reigning player of the evening. That was often Teller, and it was his competitive spirit and talent in the sport as well as in class that so deeply impressed Heisenberg.

He admired the manner in which Teller had overcome his handicap. "I could see in the beginning that he really suffered from it, not just bodily, but also mentally," Heisenberg said. "But I think he overcame it rather soon. I think in a year or so he was quite stabilized in his mind." Heisenberg noted that even after Teller made such progress he could not compete in most sports against young men. But table tennis was an exception. "He became an excellent player just because he wanted to become one," Heisenberg said. "There I could see the force in the man. When he was hampered by some outer fact which he couldn't change, he really would try with all his strength to make up for it—and he did make up for it."[7]

These evening sessions often ran until two or three o'clock in the morning, which required little adjustment for Teller. He had already developed a late-to-bed, late-to-rise schedule for work and play. His nocturnal work habits led to a joke about his predawn use of a mechanical calculating device to work on the problems assigned to him by Heisenberg. Unlike the quiet electronic models of later years, Teller's primitive calculating machine clanked, rumbled, and banged, sending its powerful vibrations throughout the barnlike classroom building, including the second-floor bedroom of his professor. In one of his occasional efforts at subtle self-deprecation, Teller would suggest that Heisenberg's awarding him his doctorate was an act of self-preservation born of a desperate need for a good night's sleep.

Among Teller's closest friends at the University of Leipzig in 1929 was Carl F. von Weizsaecker, a student whose father was a German admiral who would one day become under secretary of state in the Nazi regime. Young Weizsaecker and Teller frequently engaged in philosophical arguments that tested but did not break their friendship.

A product of Prussian aristocracy, Weizsaecker tended to rationalize early Nazi excesses. He saw Hitler as a protector against the threat of communism. Teller, having personally experienced the excesses of communism during the Hungarian uprising, shared his friend's distaste for it. But he was troubled by the anti-Semitic note in the Nazi theme.

In still another of the many ironies dogging Teller, his teacher, Heisenberg, and his good friend, Weizsaecker, later became part of the German scientific team furthering the Nazi war effort, while Teller joined the growing group of Europeans who emigrated to the United States because of the Nazis and joined the war effort that brought victory to the Allies.

Weiszaecker and Teller reestablished their friendship after the war, and Weizsaecker visited his old classmate at Livermore in 1976.

Coincidentally visiting the United States at the time of Weizsaecker's 1976 trip was Heisenberg. In the same interview during which he offered us many of the preceding recollections, he said his decision to remain in Germany during the war was a painful one. He arrived at the decision, he said, after consulting Max Planck for advice. The great developer of the quantum theory told Heisenberg that war would come and that the Allies would win. Then, Heisenberg recalled, Planck told him that Germany would desperately need scientists to help in its postwar reconstruction. So Heisenberg stayed.[8]

Accepted at face value, Heisenberg's account might stand as an example of the blindness frequently shown by brilliant scientists to sociopolitical reality. Only in this light could one accept the explanation that one of Heisenberg's stature would rationalize his enlistment in Hitler's cause. Heisenberg later masterminded Germany's own nuclear weapons project and, as will be seen later, was distressed by his failure to beat the Allies to the finish line in the atomic bomb race.

Teller won his doctorate at Leipzig in 1930. In his final semester, he joined a group of a dozen students accompanying Heisenberg on several visits to Berlin. On one such trip he heard Albert Einstein at a seminar at the Kaiser Wilhelm Institute. He also met Eugene Wigner, one of the brilliant Hungarian physicists, with whom he established a long, warm friendship. Einstein discussed his unified field theory, but it was over Teller's head. "I listened; I didn't understand a syllable," he said.

Later, on a similar trip with Heisenberg and classmates, Teller visited Copenhagen for two weeks to hear several lectures by Niels Bohr. As was customary, Bohr received the foreign students at tea. At one of these sessions, Teller engaged him in a profound discussion of Bohr's theory of the atom. Is an electron, he asked, a particle or a wave? Then the newly made Ph.D. charged ahead with his own, somewhat presumptuous impression of basic concepts in physics.

In mid-pronouncement he observed that the great scientist's eyelids had dropped to half-mast. Teller stopped talking and uncomfortably wondered whether he had bored his illustrious listener to sleep. Seconds passed. Then Bohr opened his eyes and said, "You might just as well say we are not sitting here drinking tea, but are only dreaming all this."[9]

On the entire return trip to Leipzig, Teller pondered the puzzling remark. Had Bohr said it merely as a philosophical extension of a physics theory? Or was he suggesting, as Teller feared, that Teller had talked too much?

Teller thought about returning to Copenhagen for a longer stay but instead remained in Germany to accept the offer of an assistantship at the University of Göttingen. He arrived in Göttingen in the fall of 1930. The record of his stay suggests no notable developments in his professional or personal life until he took a brief leave in the spring of 1932 to visit Italy for a series of seminars with Enrico Fermi at the University of Rome. Fermi, who was then gaining recognition as an important experimental physicist, was also greatly admired as a generous and kind human being. Among those Teller was able to meet and work with at the Fermi series were Hans Bethe, Rudolph Peierls, and two Fermi associates, Emilio Segrè and Franco Rassetti.

It was Teller's second meeting with Bethe, and it brought them into closer contact than the earlier one, in Munich. Bethe later remembered especially the taunting of Teller by George Placzek, who was attending the Fermi seminar and with whom Teller had been working on a paper in Göttingen. A Czech who had grown up in Vienna, Placzek tended to dominate the group of young physicists from Germany.

"He was a man of the world, much more sophisticated than Teller or I," Bethe said. "He had dated girls in large numbers, and he spoke eight or ten languages, all very well, and was well versed in literature and all sorts of things."

Bethe recalled that Placzek made sport of Teller with comments like "Well, this isn't much, Teller." Teller's wearing of a hooded raincoat also earned him the nickname *Il Pellegrino*, "the Pilgrim." Teller was uncharacteristically humble toward Placzek during these teasing sessions, Bethe said.

In the few years before Teller's arrival in Germany, despite its rapid development in the arts and sciences, the nation struggled to regain the economic health sapped by World War I and its aftermath. Even though a relatively small portion of the conflict was waged on her soil, Germany staggered under the burden placed on her by the Treaty of Versailles, which she was compelled to accept on June 28, 1919. The territorial provisions of the treaty had stripped her of 14.6 percent of her arable land, 74.5 percent of her iron ore, 68.1 percent of her zinc, and 26 percent of her coal. Inflation drove the German mark from its normal rate of 4 to the dollar up to 191.8 by January 1922. One year later it hit 17,920, and by November 1922 it had soared to 4.2 million marks to the dollar.[10]

Against this background, the German Republic reeled from crisis to crisis. As in Hungary, superpatriots in search of scapegoats resorted to anti-Semitism. By 1929, exploiting the sagging economy and resultant political unrest, the Nazis had elected 107 delegates to the Reichstag. Teller's prospects for a long stay in Göttingen darkened. On January 30, 1933, President Paul von Hindenburg called on Hitler to form a government. Within a month came the destruction of the Reichstag building by a mysterious fire, then Hitler's demand for emergency powers to maintain order. Once obtained, they enabled him to stifle not only opposition from the left but the already weak voices of moderation. Next came a stepped-up campaign against Jews, with intellectuals and scientists especially targeted. Einstein himself was selected as a primary victim, with even a German

Nobel laureate, Philipp von Lenard, publicly branding him as "the most important example of the dangerous influence of Jewish circles on the study of nature."[11]

Inevitably, this intensified wave of anti-Semitism cost Germany an unbearable price in brainpower as Jewish artists, scientists, and teachers left the country for havens abroad. Many wound up in the United States and England, where they were able to contribute enormously to the military effort that spelled defeat for their Nazi oppressors. Among them was Edward Teller. Returning to Göttingen after a vacation with his family in Budapest, Teller found that the exodus had begun. Teller himself had already started preparations for his departure by applying for a Rockefeller Foundation fellowship grant to study at the Copenhagen Institute for Theoretical Physics, which Bohr had founded in 1919. "The hope of making an academic career in Germany for a Jew existed before Hitler came—and vanished the day he arrived," Teller said. He then acknowledged a political naïveté born of apathy. "In the day-to-day politics I still was hardly interested, except that I wanted to continue my work. It was obvious that I had to leave Germany."

But leaving Germany turned out to be only part of the problem. The other, more difficult part involved winning the fellowship at Copenhagen without demolishing his plans for matrimony.

Chapter 4

CROSSROADS

Teller's desire to enlist in the growing band of Niels Bohr's followers at the Copenhagen Institute for Theoretical Physics took root during his brief earlier visit there in 1930 with Werner Heisenberg and his fellow students. He had considered applying for a Rockefeller Foundation fellowship at the institute while he was teaching at Göttingen, but he did not actually apply until after the Nazis had seized control of Germany in 1933. Then, before gaining approval of the application, he had to clear several hurdles.

One of them was his lack of a stable address and a regular source of income. Another was his plan to marry Mici in December 1933, less than a month before the start of the fellowship.

He eased over the first barrier with the help of George Donnan, a British biochemist noted for his work involving the balance of fluids on opposite sides of a membrane. Donnan had helped many scholars and scientists regain professional stride after being driven from Germany by the political climate, and he offered Teller an assistantship in physics at the University College in London. This enabled Teller to fulfill the residence-income requirements for the Rockefeller fellowship.

The London job also resulted in a renewal and strengthening of Teller's acquaintance with Hans Bethe. Among those who slipped out of Germany because of the Nazi rise, Bethe had wound up in England, working on a project at the University of Manchester with Walter Heitler, still another scientist self-exiled from Germany. Bethe, working on his part of the project, which dealt with electronics and gamma radiation, arrived at a calculation that Heitler had great difficulty accepting. To help settle the issue, the two collaborators agreed to travel to London and lay the question before Teller, their old colleague from Göttingen. Bethe was pleased by the result.

"Teller immediately grasped the idea of my calculation and very effectively persuaded Heitler that I was right," he said. "This was, I think, the first time that Teller had participated directly in something I had done. I was very much impressed by his quick understanding and in the way he then explained it. From this time on I had great respect for him."[1]

Clearing the other barrier, resolution of his marital status, proved to be a more complex and vexing problem for Teller. During his visit home on summer vacation from Göttingen in 1933, he and Mici had agreed to be married during the Christmas vacation and, if he won the fellowship, to start life together in Copenhagen in January. Their decision had followed a two-year separation during which Mici had left Budapest for graduate study in the United States at the University of Pittsburgh. Edward had not been made fully aware of her plan to do so, and they had quarreled. Reunited now in 1933, they were determined to avoid another long separation.

It was therefore with some perplexity that Teller considered his answer to that part of the foundation questionnaire asking, "Married or Single?" For advice he turned to Donnan, who suggested that he answer with an asterisk and a full explanation on a separate sheet of paper. He did so, and in response he received a telegram from the Paris headquarters of the foundation. It said a meeting to award fellowships was being held the next day. Then it added:

NEED INFORMATION IMMEDIATELY ON WHETHER YOU INTEND TO GET MARRIED.

At Donnan's suggestion, Teller took the next train to Paris to present his case in person to the Rockefeller representative there. But instead of agreeing that love must find a way, the official cited an earlier incident involving a Hungarian recipient of a fellowship who had married and run off on an extended wedding trip. "We do not," the interviewer said, "award Rockefeller fellowships to send Hungarians off on honeymoons."

Edward broke the news to Mici by telephone. Though unable to disguise her disappointment, she agreed to an indefinite shelving of their December wedding plans. Disconsolate, Edward also shared the word with James Franck, one of his former colleagues at Göttingen and now among the emigrants reestablished in the United States. Teller had written him earlier about his engagement to Mici and merely wished to bring him up-to-date. But before long, back came a letter from Franck declaring that he had been unable to contain his outrage over this assault upon the institution of marriage and its potential for slowing the march of science. He had personally lodged a protest with the Rockefeller Foundation at its New York headquarters. He made the case so vigorously and logically, he reported, that he had persuaded the foundation to modify its position. But, he added,

Teller should write a letter to the foundation. To ease the discomfort and avoid possible embarrassment to officials there, the letter should say that Edward could not bear single status much longer and that his work would suffer unless he carried out his marriage plans.

A few days after mailing the letter, Teller received a cryptically worded response whose ambiguity pained him until he reached the final sentence: "Will you kindly inform us of the date of your wedding?"

Edward and Mici were united in a civil ceremony attended by immediate family members and a few friends. The notary public who performed it in his office, across the street from the apartment of the wedding couple, expressed respect for their homeland by decorating his generous waist with a sash in the red, white, and green colors of Hungary. At the insistence of his mother-in-law, Edward established a precedent by wearing a hat. It was February 26, 1934. [2]

Teller's eight-month fellowship at Copenhagen was memorable in many ways. In a letter to Bohr more than twenty years later, he called it "among the most important and wonderful periods of my life." Besides being married, he made great strides professionally, producing creditable, original work and benefiting from exposure to many of the finest scientific minds of that era. At the center of it all was Bohr himself.

Tall and sad eyed, Bohr made an imposing figure as he glided about the streets of Copenhagen on a bicycle that resembled a toy under his huge frame. Bohr had won the Nobel Prize in physics for his work on atomic structure in 1922, twelve years before Edward's arrival at the institute. He was the latest in a long line of distinguished, frequently colorful Danish scientists.

Among the earliest and most colorful was Tycho Brahe, who, in the sixteenth century, alternated between fame and notoriety as an astronomer. Known for his brilliance and arrogance, he dueled with a fellow student at the University of Rostock to settle a dispute over which was the better mathematician. Brahe's nose was sliced off, and he personally fashioned a metal replacement that he wore the rest of his life. [3]

Bohr was to earn the admiration and acclaim of his countrymen for his courage as well as for his scientific achievements. After graduating from the University of Copenhagen, he had gone to England for research under Sir Joseph J. Thomson and Lord Ernest Rutherford. In 1913, at the age of twenty-eight, he published three papers regarded as the theoretical basis for much of modern thought on the structure of the atom. (Thirty-six years later, in collaboration with John A. Wheeler at Princeton, he announced the identity of uranium-235.)

At the outset of World War II, Bohr was in the prime of his career.

When the Nazis invaded Denmark, in protest he suspended his atomic research. In 1943, he secretly slipped out of the country on a fishing vessel bound for Sweden. From there, hidden in the bomb bay of a Royal Air Force plane with his priceless research documents beside him, he was flown to England and later to the United States for completion of work on the atomic bomb.

Assessing Bohr and his work from the perspective of half a century after their first meeting, Teller assigned him unique status. Teller suggested that unlike many other developments in science the theory of complementarity would not have come about without Bohr.

"The constituents of the atom cannot be described in a complete manner as particles," he explained. "They sometimes appear as particles, and they sometimes appear as waves, depending on what kind of experiments are performed on them."

What are electrons?

"The answer that has been given by many tentatively, and by Bohr in a very concrete and definite way, is, the electrons really are neither waves nor particles. To describe them completely, it is necessary to use sometimes the wave picture and at other times the particle picture. . . ."

Bohr invented the word *complementarity*, and he developed a remarkable philosophy around this word. "The idea of complementarity is that in order to describe a situation you have to use (at least on certain occasions) two mutually exclusive approaches. If you omit either, the description is incomplete. Both must be used. Because they are mutually exclusive, it is necessary to adjust the two approaches in a manner that is by no means obvious."

By way of illustration, Teller asked, "What are you?"

Looking into a mirror, the respondent might say, "A piece of matter."

"But if, instead of looking into the mirror, you look at yourself with your eyes closed, you just know that you are there. If you look at yourself from the inside by indulging in the strange sport of introspection, you don't appear to yourself to be matter. It's not quite clear what you are. Shall we say, spirit? I don't know what. . . .

"Bohr's very natural statement would be that the description of a person will be incomplete—ridiculously incomplete—unless he is described as both the thing he appears to be from the outside, which is subject to laws of physics, and as the entity he appears to be from the inside, which might conceivably be subject to laws of psychology, if any."

The idea of complementarity was commonplace, Teller said, but its incorporation into a rigorous theory of physics, he added, was new and exciting. This led to his appraisal of Bohr as unique.

Teller had earlier indicated a belief that much of scientific development was probably inevitable because "if a sufficient number of semi-intelligent people (like ourselves) look at the world, they are bound to arrive at some conclusions." If Scientist X had not come along with a particular discovery or development, Scientist Y or Z would probably have come along with it, anyway. But Teller expressed doubt whether, in certain exceptional cases, a particular development would ever have unfolded unless a certain individual had come along when he did. "Bohr's idea of complementarity," he said, "is an example."[4]

Both the resumption of friendships formed in his student days and fresh opportunities to rub elbows with physicists who had already achieved or were bound for greatness contributed to Teller's pleasure during his fellowship year at Copenhagen. But the newly nurtured relationship proving especially influential in Teller's life from that point on was his friendship with George Gamow, a Russian refugee and internationally known physicist. A big man with an easy, brusque manner, he was four years older than Teller and shared the latter's abhorrence of Communists. During Easter vacation Gamow and Teller spent the holiday riding across Denmark and back on Gamow's motorbike. Their discussions on physics in general and quantum mechanics in particular during the trip strengthened Gamow's professional respect for Teller. It also helped shape Teller's career, for when Gamow was established in the United States one year later, he offered Teller his first job outside Europe.

While in Copenhagen, Teller produced what was generally considered his most important work up to that point in his career, a paper dealing with molecular behavior. Coauthored with one F. Kalchar, a young Dane, it was titled "Theory of the Catalysis of the Ortho-Para Transformation by Paramagnetic Gases."

In the fall of 1934, shortly after Teller returned to the University of London as a lecturer in chemistry, he found two letters offering positions in America. One was for a lectureship at Princeton. The other was from Gamow, now head of the physics department at George Washington University. It offered a full professorship. For a twenty-six-year-old scientist, it seemed irresistible.

A fretful period followed during which Teller unsuccessfully applied for a visa as a nonquota immigrant. After this rebuff, he once again sought help from an influential friend, this time Thomas Balogh, a Hungarian who had emigrated to London as a young man and had gained a reputation as an economist. Balogh learned that the basis for the rejection of Teller's request for a nonquota visa was his lack of two years of university teaching experience in the subject he was hired to teach in the United States. His Copenhagen experience did not count toward the requirement because of his status there as a fellow, not a teacher.

But in bureaucracy as in science, simple answers sometimes lie awaiting discovery while searchers fruitlessly explore complicated avenues. In the end, it was realized that under a U.S. law that admitted immigrants from foreign countries according to the numbers of their nationality already in this country, the Tellers were eligible for visas within the Hungarian quota.[5] They set sail in August 1935.

Chapter 5

STATESIDE

The hiring of Teller at George Washington University in 1935 was plotted by George Gamow one year earlier, when Gamow himself had been offered the chairmanship of the physics department. Cloyd H. Marvin, president of the university, had approached Gamow at the suggestion of Merle Tuve, whose advice he sought on how to strengthen his basic science program.

Tuve, then director of the Department of Terrestrial Magnetism at the Carnegie Institution in Washington, later recalled that he dissuaded Marvin from his initial inclination to concentrate on the hiring of experimental physicists. Because of laboratory and equipment costs, he noted, the $100,000 earmarked for buttressing the program would not go far in this direction. But theoretical physicists, he added, need only pencil, paper, meetings with colleagues, and travel expenses to and from the meetings. He recommended Gamow as a physicist whose penetration theory was a significant contribution to quantum mechanics and whose reputation in the field would grow brightly for many years.* At Marvin's request, he agreed to see if the young Russian might be interested in the post.

Gamow set two conditions for his acceptance. One was that he be given free rein to hold an annual conference of the world's top physicists, much like the meetings held by Niels Bohr in Copenhagen. The other condition, stipulated with Teller firmly in mind, was that he be allowed to add a second theoretical physicist to the George Washington faculty.

Gamow was six feet three, blond, shaggy, and fun loving. He had a big appetite, and a thirst to match, but paid little attention to details like money. Friends were often touched, especially near the end of the pay

---

* Gamow presented calculations supporting his theory that there is a mathematical probability that a small percentage of subatomic particles can penetrate the electrical barrier around a nucleus if the barrier has a higher charge than the particle.

period. Hans Bethe was innocently drawn into one of his jokes, a prank involving a paper Gamow had produced with a collaborator, Ralph Alpher. He inserted the name of his colleague from Cornell into the credit line so that it read, "Alpher, Bethe, and Gamow."

Gamow exercised a random brilliance that led him to toss theories about like lawn seed. Teller would frequently be roused by a morning telephone call from the big Russian extrovert eagerly propounding an idea.

"Now, Gamow had a fertile imagination," Teller recalled. "He was an exceedingly nice guy, and furthermore, he was the only one of my friends who really believed I was a mathematician. . . . Now, I'm sorry to say that ninety percent of Gamow's theories were wrong, and it was easy to recognize that they were wrong. But he didn't mind. He was one of those people who had no particular pride in any of his inventions. He would throw out his latest idea and then treat it as a joke. He was a delightful person to work with."

At twenty-seven, Teller, despite his choice of theoretical physics over his father's recommendation of a career in chemistry, had achieved security and professional status. Like Gamow himself, he was a a full professor, with a yearly salary pegged at about $6,000, excellent compensation in a depression-ridden era when police were paid $45 per week and many educators received only a bit more.

Also like Gamow, Teller in those days had a reputation for gregariousness and wit. But he was still given to sieges of moodiness and isolated contemplation that marked his life from boyhood to his late years. Again like Gamow, he developed a widespread reputation as an outstanding lecturer. In addition to classes on his home campus, Gamow lectured at Johns Hopkins University in Baltimore, and students from Johns Hopkins often traveled the forty miles to Washington to hear Gamow and Teller.

Before teaming up with Gamow, Teller had worked primarily on the applications of atomic physics to molecules. But their association influenced him to transfer his emphasis to nuclear physics. As a result, instead of probably spending most of his working life in front of a lecture hall filled with students, he stepped onto a path leading to the development of nuclear energy for purposes of war and peace. It was a fateful shift.

Teller held the Washington assignment for six years, up to that time his longest stay in one place since leaving Budapest to study at Karlsruhe. Again, because of Gamow's insistence on holding annual conferences in the style of those they had both known at Copenhagen under Niels Bohr, Teller found himself at a crossroads for outstanding theoretical physicists.

Shortly after their arrival in the United States, the Tellers had moved into a brown-shingled house on Garfield Street in northwest Washington.

Their home, off Connecticut Avenue and near the Sheraton Park Hotel, then known as the Wardman Park, became a favorite gathering place for both visiting scientists and many from throughout the Washington area. Among them was Alfred Sklar, a Baltimore physicist who regularly made the trip to Washington to attend Teller's course on atomic spectra. Sklar remembered the extracurricular soirees at the Teller home as gatherings where talk centered on new scientific thought.

"It soon got about in the local community that Teller was interested in the whole gamut of chemical and physical problems, that he was happy to talk about your problems, and that you would come away with some new approach or a new avenue through your specific maze. Among those who came and went were James Franck, who talked about fluorescence and photosynthesis; Merle Tuve, Larry Hafstad, and Charles Critchfield on nuclear phenomena; F. O. Rice on mechanism of chemical reactions; Herta Spooner, K. F. Herzfeld, and myself on light absorption and molecular spectra; Stephen Brunauer on absorption; and a host of specialists from the government bureaus." Sklar said such visitors were almost invariably impressed by Teller's ability to recognize the kernel of a problem and then to fulfill his jocular promise "I don't understand it, but I will explain it to you."

Also among visitors to the Teller home was Hans Bethe. "There were always people in their house," Bethe recalled, "graduate students of his own as well as young chemistry professors who wanted his advice on chemical problems. He had always worked on molecular physics, which borders on chemistry, and he had a very close connection to the chemists in the Washington community."

The Teller-Gamow friendship throughout Teller's stay at George Washington University survived many challenges. Teller, while tolerant of Gamow's penchant for play, burned with stronger ambition. A test of their friendship developed during a Christmas vacation shared by Gamow and his wife with the Tellers.

"When we arrived in Miami," Teller recalled, "it started to become obvious that Joe [a nickname, apparently from the abbreviation of his first name, Geo.] was violently unhappy. Well, his wife—it just burst out of her—said Joe was unhappy because there were so many Jews in Miami, because Joe is really an anti-Semite. Joe got very red in the face and admitted that this was true. Well, his best friend in Russia was a Jew. The man he invited to be his colleague and collaborator—myself—was a Jew. Yet he was anti-Semitic."

The problem was "solved" by yielding to Gamow's petulance. "We moved out and over to the west coast of Florida, where we had a very fine time," Teller said. The west coast was less popular with Jews at that time. In recounting the incident to us, Teller described Gamow's anti-Semitism as "not real" and one that "shouldn't be taken seriously."

"I sensed that the real part of it was that Gamow was violently anti-communist and that communism in Russia had been carried out to a great extent by Jews. So the discussion of anti-Semitism within a few minutes became a discussion of what the communists were doing to Russia. . . . This was the first time we had discussed politics, and once he had started, Gamow really let go and told me about all the harassments the physicists had from the communist philosophers, from the dialectical materialists."[1]

Teller's explanation indicates more than mere tolerance for Gamow's bigotry: Even though he himself had been driven from the land of his birth by anti-Semitism, he did not yet fully appreciate the potential, unacceptable danger of religious prejudice in any form, even the latent brand harbored by Gamow.

During Teller's second and third years in Washington, he and Gamow pressed on with theoretical work on thermonuclear energy. In 1937 they published a paper on the subject, and in 1938 they made it the theme of the annual Washington Conference on Theoretical Physics. Among those who found the subject provocative was Hans Bethe, who came away interested enough to join Teller and Critchfield, then a Teller student, in publishing a paper on the theory of energy production in the sun. Bethe later referred to this as the meeting that led to his work on the source of the energy of the stars, for which he won the 1967 Nobel Prize in physics.[2]

The Bethe-Teller friendship was at its warmest during this period. Bethe, who had joined the Cornell University faculty, usually stayed at the Teller home during his visits to Washington from Ithaca, New York, and he and his fiancée, Rose Ewald, joined the Tellers on a motor trip across the country in 1937. A highlight of the trip was a reunion in California with Enrico Fermi, who was visiting Stanford.

The otherwise pleasant early years of the Tellers in the United States were marred by political developments in Europe. After their first year in Washington, the Tellers made the first of what they hoped would be regular semiannual trips to Hungary to visit their families. But Hitler's annexation of Austria and his creeping influence over Hungary chilled their hope of further visits. The 1936 trip marked the last time Teller saw his father. Max died fourteen years later. Still another nine years passed before Edward was reunited, in 1959, with his mother and sister.

In that summer of 1937, when the Tellers drove to the West Coast with Bethe and Rose Ewald and met with Fermi, Teller also visited Berkeley to address a physics colloquium at the University of California. This led to his first meeting with J. Robert Oppenheimer, who invited him to dinner in a Mexican restaurant. Teller said he found the eminent scientist "over-powering." But there was no indication that Teller made any lasting impression on the man destined to be a principal antagonist in the crisis costing one his career and the other a lifetime of respect among many whose esteem he cherished.

But back in those exciting days of the 1930s there was no hint that this or any other cloud would darken the future of Edward Teller as a professor of top rank and as a mentor of bright young physicists. Many of them, like Teller, had fled to the United States in search of sanctuary from Nazi oppression. However, once secure in their new haven, they immersed themselves in their work and seldom looked back. Surprising though it may seem in retrospect, except for periodic expressions of concern about relatives who had stayed behind, the scientific community in America showed little interest in the political affairs of Europe.

The rhythm of this cozy academic world was interrupted for all time in 1939. On January 16 of that year, Niels Bohr arrived from Europe aboard the *Drottningholm* with word that the nucleus of the atom had been split. John A. Wheeler, then a young Princeton physicist, met Bohr at the pier when his ship arrived in New York. Also greeting him were Enrico and Laura Fermi, who had left Italy only three weeks earlier. Appearing tired and tense, Bohr commented apprehensively on the rising Nazi tide in Europe. Then, during the customs check of his luggage, he took Wheeler aside and told him in confidence that two German chemists, Otto Hahn and Fritz Strassmann, had done what scientists had considered impossible. The Greek word *atom* itself means "indivisible."

In an experiment completed only one month earlier and still kept secret beyond Nazi borders, Hahn and Strassmann bombarded uranium with neutrons. Then they analyzed the uranium and found that parts of it had become barium, which is a different, lighter element. What kind of explanation could they offer? The only supportable one was that the nucleus of the uranium had been split and that fractions resulting from this division were lighter—had fewer protons and neutrons—than uranium. Implicit in the discovery was the accompanying fact that with the dynamic change of one element into another enormous quantities of energy were released.

To ease his lingering doubt, Hahn described the experiment in a letter to Lise Meitner, a Jewish former associate who had fled to Sweden to escape the Nazis. Meitner discussed it with Otto Frisch, her nephew, who was also a refugee physicist and was visiting her from his sanctuary in Denmark. On his return to Denmark, Frisch repeated the experiment and measured not only the chemical transformation of the bombarded uranium but the release of energy as well.

Frisch shared the news with Bohr, who was preparing to leave for a stay of several months in the United States. One of Bohr's earliest engagements was the Washington Conference on Theoretical Physics, with Gamow and Teller as hosts. Bohr was due there January 26, ten days after his arrival from Denmark. One version is that Bohr announced the Hahn-Strassmann discovery in a lecture at Princeton on the same day he arrived in the United States.[3] But by the account of Teller and others the first public disclosure did not come until more than one week later. Teller said he received a telephone call from an excited Gamow on late January 25, the eve of the Washington conference. "That Bohr has gone crazy," he quoted Gamow. "He says the uranium nucleus splits." Then, said Teller, Gamow announced at the convening of the conference on the following day that the agenda had been revised to make way for a presentation by Bohr.[4]

The Bohr disclosure touched off a sensational round of discussion and debate over the implications of the experiment. It also raised questions, such as, if energy is really released, how much? Teller asked one of the most provocative questions: What if the nucleus splitting frees more neutrons and thereby starts a chain reaction?

Before the day was out, many conference participants were back in their laboratories, trying to repeat the classic experiment. By afternoon a contingent from Johns Hopkins University had hurried back to Baltimore, pressed their accelerator into action, and split the uranium nucleus before nightfall. The Washington performance was directed by Merle Tuve at the Carnegie Institution for a group that included Teller, Bohr, and Leon Rosenfeld, a Bohr colleague who had accompanied him on the trip from Sweden. Peering at the oscilloscope as the uranium responded to bombardment by the neutrons, they observed the green line dancing across the screen, then shooting up to measure the burst of energy when the nucleus was split. "The state of excitement challenged description," Rosenfeld recalled. But Teller reacted with the aplomb of a theoretical physicist to whom the mind-picture of a new idea is exciting and the laboratory demonstration is anticlimactic. Recalling the moment for us years later, he said, "I just wasn't excited." Physicists had been bombarding various elements with neutrons for years, and this experiment was relatively simple. "It had been lurking under the surface for years, waiting for someone to discover it," Teller said.

Few shared Teller's restraint. Leo Szilard, who had drawn one of the earliest maps of the nuclear wilderness, was among the most excited. He had been too ill in Princeton to attend the Washington conference. But within the next day or so he was on a train headed for Washington and a meeting with his fellow Hungarian, Edward Teller.

Although compatriots, Szilard and Teller had crossed paths infrequently during their early careers. But their mutual interest in nuclear physics was to bind them through later years in a close, frequently turbulent relationship. Szilard was more than simply a pioneer in nuclear research. He was also an eccentric visionary in the field and a political activist, which made him an ideal opponent for the comparatively low keyed Teller when they later staged several memorable post–World War II debates on nuclear arms.

Szilard was credited with being the first to propound the theory that the neutrons of an atom are held together by some binding force. This mystery continued to intrigue physicists for generations after Szilard first came up with it in 1934, only thirty-eight years after Antoine-Henri Becquerel's discovery of radioactivity. In the meantime, science had given a name to the kind of radiation that caused Becquerel's uranium-bearing pitchblende ore to fog photography plates even though they were wrapped in black paper. The radiation penetrating the paper was made up of what are now known as *alpha* particles. They cannot penetrate material much heavier than paper or travel more than a few inches before dissipating. Two other types of particles may also be emitted by radioactive materials. One type is the *beta* particle, which penetrates more deeply than alpha but can be blocked by heavy cardboard or thin sheets of metal or which dissipates within a distance of a few feet. There are also *gamma* rays, which penetrate several inches of metal.

For many years scientists had used radioactive particles to bombard basic elements of matter and to study the effects. A fascinating aspect of the process was that certain elements, when bombarded in this manner, themselves became radioactive.

Szilard's interest in the mysterious force that bound the nucleus particles was not merely academic but zeroed in on the ultimate question. If a nucleus is bombarded by a neutron from another source and this shatters the bond holding the neutrons within the nucleus itself, might not these neutrons then go shooting off to bombard other nuclei, thus repeating the process in an energy release of a devastating chain reaction?

Szilard had suggested such a possibility as early as 1934 to Ernest Rutherford, the physics pioneer at Cambridge. Teller told us that Szilard later summed up the outcome of his visit by saying, "I was thrown out of Rutherford's office." Teller said Szilard was so indignant over his treatment by Rutherford that he took out a patent on his chain-reaction process and after World War II sold it to the U.S. government for something of a bargain—$20,000. Even though Szilard missed Bohr's dramatic announcement of the atomic nucleus splitting, he more than made up for his absence. Beginning with his visit to Teller, he exerted an initiative largely responsible for getting a U.S. nuclear weapons program under way. The purpose of his visit to Teller was to solicit support for work on nuclear fission. Szilard made a similar stop at Princeton to speak with Eugene Wigner, the brilliant Hungarian physicist, for the same reason.

Five weeks later, Teller recalled, he was home, relaxing by playing a Mozart sonata on the piano, when Szilard called. He spoke in Hungarian. On his return to New York from their January meeting, he had resumed his experiments with Walter H. Zinn at Columbia. By exposing beryllium to gamma rays from radium, they irradiated it, causing it to fire off a stream of neutrons. These were directed at uranium oxide but were first passed through a paraffin barrier to slow them down. As a result, the uranium nucleus absorbed, or "captured," the neutrons and split, releasing some of its own neutrons and creating a chain reaction. This was the essence of Szilard's call to Teller.

"All my worries about nuclear energy," said Teller, "the full realization that it was coming, and coming very soon, and that it would be very dangerous, date back to that time in March 1939, when I was interrupted in the middle of a Mozart sonata."[5]

Chapter 6

TO LOS ALAMOS

Leo Szilard's call to Edward Teller on that March evening in 1939, announcing the world's first known nuclear chain reaction, marked a momentous first step toward the making of an atomic bomb. But the test proving that the bomb could be made did not come until six years and four months later. Between those two events lay an agonizing trail of moral soul-searching and bureaucratic delay as well as much groping and stumbling along the dark corridors of science.

Part of the problem resulted from the paradox that Szilard and some of his fellow immigrant scientists were not trusted by U.S. officials to participate fully in the project.

Szilard has been called the father of the atomic bomb. Teller, who himself later deplored being called the father of the even more powerful hydrogen bomb, referred to Szilard as the one "who initiated the atomic age." He also called Szilard "the most stimulating of all the people I have known"[1] and "the only one of all my friends whom I would have liked to imitate."

Szilard actually conceived the idea of a chain reaction as early as 1933, the year before he unsuccessfully visited Ernest Rutherford in his Cambridge office to discuss it. It had taken clear shape in Szilard's mind while he was walking on Southampton Row, London, and waiting at an intersection for a red light to change.[2] One reason for his failure to press ahead with the chain-reaction concept and for the resultant delay in its development was his aversion to detailed laboratory work. He was repelled by the thought of sifting through the ninety-two then-known elements to see which, if any, would produce fission when its nucleus was bombarded by neutrons.

But by far the greatest reason for the slow pace of development was the combination of bureaucratic inertia and the absence of substantial support from the scientific community. Even after obtaining the patent, Szilard failed in an attempt to assign it to the British War Office as a means of keeping it from competitive, and perhaps hostile, hands. The War Office turned it down with an explanation that there was "no reason to keep the specifications secret."[3] Szilard turned next to the Admiralty, which accepted it on behalf of the Royal Navy, then shelved it.

Even after Szilard had moved to the United States, had shared the excitement of Bohr's announcement that the atomic nucleus had been split, and had produced the world's first known chain reaction, he found the going rough and slow.

First, he unsuccessfully sought the help of Enrico Fermi, who was then at Columbia. He felt that Fermi's participation would have drawn strong support for the experiment in the scientific community and for the overall chain-reaction project from government funding sources. But Fermi, known for his gentility and consummate courtesy, did not condone Szilard's flamboyant life-style and blustery mannerisms. He had declared his office and home off limits to the unorthodox Hungarian. Laura Fermi, the Italian physicist's widow, much later explained to us, "They didn't get along well, you know."

Fermi's rejection was followed by a similar response from financier Lewis L. Strauss. Szilard, who had earned only $1,000 in 1938, approached Strauss for funds needed to rent a small quantity of radium necessary for the experiment. He came away empty-handed. Szilard then turned to Benjamin Liebowitz, an inventor and friend, and finally came up with a loan of $2,000.

Next, he requested permission for use of space in the Pupin Laboratory of Columbia University. George P. Pegram, dean of Columbia Graduate Faculties, pronounced the work "too fantastic to be entirely respectable." But he did grant permission—for only temporary use of the space.

With Walter Zinn agreeing to handle the laboratory details that Szilard found so onerous, the project finally got under way. Within weeks, on the afternoon of March 2, 1939, they had their answer: a laboratory screen flashing signals produced by the emission of neutrons from bombarded uranium. The telephone call to Teller—"We have found the neutrons"— came that evening.

In their experiment, Szilard and Zinn made beryllium radioactive by exposing it to the gamma rays of radium. Once radioactive, the beryllium began emitting neutrons, which were directed at uranium oxide. Under normal conditions, such neutrons move at a speed nearly as great as that of light and are called *photoneutrons*. But there was a stronger likelihood that the neutrons could be absorbed, or "captured," by the uranium nucleus if they could be slowed down to the speed of *thermal neutrons*. To accomplish this, Szilard and Zinn passed them through paraffin. This brought about the absorption of the neutron by the uranium nucleus, which then divided and in the process released neutrons. These, in turn, were captured by other nuclei, causing them to split, and so on, continuing the chain reaction.

Kept under control, the chain reaction could serve as a rich source of energy. Unleashed, it could result in an explosion more devastating than anything previously devised by man.

Fermi soon duplicated the experiment and confirmed the findings of Szilard and Zinn. This raised Szilard's hopes for further funding, but his optimism was unjustified. Fermi was granted an audience before a military committee to request support. After making his presentation in his heavy Italian accent, he was politely dismissed.

Later that spring, Szilard sought help from Niels Bohr, whom he saw at a Princeton meeting. Joining them were Teller and Eugene Wigner. Both offered their support, but Bohr insisted it was impractical. "It can never be done," he said, "unless you turn the whole United States into one huge factory."[4]

Summer brought little change in Szilard's prospects. He and Fermi had joined forces in the cause of nuclear physics and in a shared abhorrence of Nazism. They also shared a fondness for Teller and urged him to join them at Columbia to help with their project during the summer. But the deliberate, gentle Fermi and the flamboyant, unpredictable Szilard had little else in common. Obviously, Teller was tapped to play the triple role of scientist, mediator, and catalyst. Accordingly, Teller and Mici closed down their Washington home for the season and took a place in Morningside Heights.

"We had a nice apartment near Columbia," Teller recalled, "where the wind blew in one window and out the other, even though the two windows were in the same wall. I never understood the hydrodynamics, but it is a fact." He was assigned to lecture graduate students and to advise the Fermi-Szilard team working to build a reactor.

But there was little opportunity to advise. Fermi left Columbia for the summer to teach at the University of Michigan in Ann Arbor. Compounding this setback, Dean Pegram notified Szilard that the experiment could not proceed until Fermi returned from his summer assignment in Michigan. Szilard wrote, but Fermi's answers offered no encouragement.

Szilard then turned to the Naval Research Laboratory for support but was rejected. His frustration mounted further with news that the Germans had embargoed uranium shipments. He feared that they might look toward the rich Belgian Congo deposits for a fresh supply of the vital element.

At this point, Szilard hit on the idea of asking for help from Albert

Einstein, who had been his teacher and with whom he had collaborated on the design of a refrigerator pump. He knew Einstein was an old friend of Belgium's Queen Mother Elizabeth. Some years earlier they had played violin together in a string ensemble. Szilard hoped that Einstein might urge the Belgians to refrain from selling the critically needed uranium to the Nazis. Tracking Einstein from his Princeton office to a summer cottage at Peconic, on Long Island, Szilard called on Wigner to drive him there on Sunday, July 30, 1939.

After his visitors stated their mission, Einstein agreed to write not to the dowager queen but to a Belgian cabinet member he knew. But before the letter could be mailed, Szilard decided that a more effective approach would be to prod the U.S. government into supporting nuclear research aimed at production of the atomic bomb. He approached Alexander Sachs, who had served as economic adviser to Franklin Roosevelt in his 1932 presidential campaign and as chief economist of the National Recovery Administration (NRA) in the early days of the Roosevelt administration. Sachs suggested that Szilard persuade Einstein to write a letter to Roosevelt. He offered to deliver it personally. Szilard was delighted.

Three days after he and Wigner had visited Einstein, Szilard popped into Teller's office at Columbia and asked for a lift to Long Island.

"Where in Long Island?" Teller asked.

"Wherever Einstein lives."

Teller recalled to us that "after one minor breakdown" they reached the general vicinity of Peconic, then began looking for help. "Finally, we found a little girl about ten years old with pigtails, but she couldn't help us when we asked for Dr. Einstein. Then Szilard said, 'You know, he's the man with the long flowing white hair.' That was enough. Then she knew where he lived."[5]

"We had the letter already typed, so Szilard just handed it to Einstein, who had greeted us wearing old clothes and slippers," Teller said. "He gave us some tea and drank some himself while he read the letter. Then he signed it. His only remark was that this would be the first time that man exploits nuclear energy directly rather than indirectly through solar radiation, where the origin was nuclear in any case."[6]

Dated August 2, 1939, the historic letter was addressed to "F. D. Roosevelt, president of the United States" and began by referring to "some recent work by E. Fermi and L. Szilard." Einstein said this work led him to expect that uranium could be converted soon into a new and important source of energy.

He suggested that this work and the work of the Joliot-Curies in France might make possible a nuclear chain reaction in a large mass of uranium, by which vast amounts of power and large quantities of new radium-like elements would be generated.

This new phenomenon would also lead to the construction of bombs, and it is conceivable—though much less certain—that extremely powerful bombs of a new type may thus be constructed. A single bomb of this type, carried by boat and exploded in a port, might well destroy the whole port together with some of the surrounding territory.

The next sentence illustrates the uncertainty of the project, even for those who helped get it launched:

"However, such bombs might very well prove to be too heavy for transportation by air," Einstein wrote. Six years and four days later, such a bomb was transported by air from an American air base in the Pacific and dropped on Hiroshima.

Historians differ on the question of who actually composed the letter that was signed by Einstein and that set in motion one of the most fateful decisions in the human story. Teller brushed aside the question.

"Szilard always represented the letter as written by Einstein," he said, "but I am convinced that Szilard was lying. The man who wrote that letter, in my opinion, was none other than Szilard, with some possible assistance from Eugene Wigner. Einstein did not impress me like the man who had written the letter, though he may have done so."

Whatever its authorship, the letter was received by Alexander Sachs from Szilard on August 10. Sachs did not complete the relay to the president until early in October. In the meantime, Hitler invaded Poland on September 1. Two days later, the British and French declared war on Germany, and Roosevelt quickly followed this by declaring a national emergency and asking Congress to lift the embargo on overseas arms shipments.

After discussing Einstein's letter with Sachs at an October 11 meeting and over breakfast the next day, Roosevelt called in his secretary, Brig. Gen. Edwin M. ("Pa") Watson. Handing him the proposal, he said, "Pa, this requires action."

When Szilard heard Sachs's report, he was ecstatic. But the ecstasy turned to frustration as time after time over the next three years, despite Roosevelt's call for action, Szilard ran into one roadblock after another. The first materialized nine days later at an October 21 meeting of the newly created Uranium Committee.[7] Sachs suggested that Szilard be invited to the meeting, and Szilard suggested that Fermi, Wigner, and Teller also be included. But Fermi declined the invitation even after Teller made a special trip from Washington to Columbia to persuade him at Szilard's request. Instead, Fermi insisted that Teller go and speak for him. "Having started my career in atomic energy as a chauffeur," Teller told us with a slight smile, "I was now going to continue it as a messenger boy."

Chaired by Lyman J. Briggs, a sixty-five-year-old veteran who had spent forty-three years inching up the bureaucratic ladder from Department of Agriculture soil physicist to the directorship of the Bureau of Standards, the committee included a navy ordnance officer and an army colonel. Szilard, Teller, and Wigner went before them to press their case for money to buy the graphite needed in a system to produce a chain reaction. Briggs and the navy man, Comdr. Gilbert C. Hoover, sat expressionless. The colonel, Keith F. Adamson, was even less encouraging. He expressed disbelief in the need for complex devices and quoted a military maxim that a new weapon remains unproven until successfully used in two wars. He declared that troop morale outweighed weapons on the scales of victory.

Teller interrupted the colonel's dissertation to suggest that money was needed for the project approved by the president. How much money? the colonel asked. Tuve had specified to Teller a need for pure graphite and had estimated that the atomic-pile project could be brought in for about $15,000. Sensing the temper of the committee, Teller suggested an allotment of $2,000 for graphite and $4,000 for all other items. Szilard agreed. "All right, all right," the colonel shot back. "You'll get your money."

For $6,000 the U.S. government agreed to undertake an atomic bomb project that ultimately would cost the nation $2 billion.

But the amount agreed upon was not delivered until four months later, on February 20, 1940. In the meantime, Briggs submitted a report to Roosevelt downplaying the potential value of the chain-reaction project for bomb production. He acknowledged it only as a possible power source for submarines.

With the project thus bogged down, Teller and Wigner resumed teaching at George Washington and Princeton universities, respectively, and Fermi worked on his cosmic-ray experiments.

Even without the bureaucratic stall and the doubts raised by Briggs, there was no assurance that an atomic-bomb project would be an early success. Many scientific puzzles still remained to be solved on the blackboard and in the laboratory. One indication of how formidable these would be came in the form of a discouraging report by Niels Bohr and John A. Wheeler. In a *Physical Review* article entitled "The Mechanism of Nuclear Fission," they said uranium in its basic state, U-238, was not fissionable. Another uranium isotope, U-235, was fissionable, they said, but it accounted for only 1 part in 140 of ordinary uranium. Therefore, it would be necessary to separate this small part of U-235 from U-238 to produce an explosion.

That seemed too complex, expensive, and time-consuming for practical pursuit. In the end, Bohr's statement about converting the entire United States into one big factory turned out to seem only slightly exaggerated.

Meanwhile, discouraging news arrived from Germany. As Einstein wrote Roosevelt in a second letter, dated March 7, 1940, "Interest in uranium has intensified in Germany." Szilard learned that a major section of the Kaiser Wilhelm Institute had been committed to a uranium project. Einstein's letter drew a reply from the White House, but not from the president. It came from General Watson, who noted that the Briggs committee felt that "the matter should rest in abeyance" until further evaluation. At Szilard's suggestion, Einstein wrote another letter to Roosevelt. Dated April 25, 1940, it recommended the creation of a separate unit to look into "practical applications" of the atom "with greater speed and on a larger scale."

As a result of the pressure generated by Szilard, Briggs agreed to call a meeting of the Uranium Committee but pointedly excluded Szilard and Fermi because they were not U.S. citizens and therefore were considered untrustworthy in security matters. After Sachs protested, Briggs relented to the extent of appointing them and Wigner, a recently naturalized citizen, to a scientific subcommittee. Then, at its first meeting, on June 13, Briggs announced that the subcommittee was being disbanded. The reason, he said, was that the chain-reaction project might fail and thereby trigger a possible congressional investigation into the use of noncitizens for a critical, federally funded project.

Szilard's resulting criticism, capped by a prediction that Germany might win the war, brought him to the attention of security investigators. An army intelligence reported dated October 1, 1940, said:

> Mr. Szilard is said to be very pro-German and to have remarked on many
> occasions that he thinks the Germans will win the war. Reliable contacts
> among the faculty and authorities at Columbia University state they would
> not care to guarantee his discretion, integrity and loyalty to the United
> States.[8]

Throughout most of Szilard's frustrating episode, Teller's role was limited to his driving Szilard to Einstein's summer home and his appearance with Szilard and Wigner at the Briggs committee session producing the $6,000 pledge for research. Teller shared the concern of most immigrant scientists over the Nazi threat, but he was not yet prepared to abandon his work in theoretical physics for an all-out campaign in support of an atomic bomb project.

"To deflect my attention from physics, my full-time job, which I liked, to work on weapons was not an easy matter," he said. "And for quite a time

I did not make up my mind. But this is one of the few instances where I can tell you, within an accuracy of twenty minutes, when I made up my mind."

When and why did he decide to do so?

The date was May 10, 1940, when President Roosevelt addressed the Eighth Pan American Scientific Congress in Washington.

As noted earlier, the speech turned out to be a call upon Western Hemisphere scientists to join in the defense of "our science, our culture, our American freedom and our civilization." Also as noted, Teller's reading of the president's message was clear: "Without the work of the scientists, the war and the world would be lost." And Teller felt that Roosevelt was speaking directly to him.

Within weeks, in June 1940, Roosevelt announced the creation of the National Defense Research Committee to recruit scientific talent for national defense. Vannevar Bush, president of the Carnegie Institution, was named chairman. The Uranium Committee, headed by Briggs, was redrawn as a unit within the National Defense Research Committee. Briggs was retained as chairman, but the new membership consisted of Pegram; Harold Urey; Jesse Beams, a University of Virginia centrifuge expert; Merle Tuve; and Ross Gunn, the technical adviser at the Naval Research Laboratory. All were native-born Americans. Significantly, Fermi and the Hungarian triumvirate—Szilard, Wigner, and Teller—were appointed as consultants and were admitted to committee meetings only after Sachs protested their exclusion.

At this point in 1940, research in this field focused on construction of a reactor capable of sustaining a chain reaction and on finding a practical way of extracting fissionable uranium, U-235, from common uranium atoms, U-238. Only 1 of every 140 atoms was of the fissionable U-235 variety.

For the rest of 1940 and most of 1941 the Columbia team, led by Fermi, carried the brunt of nuclear research in the United States. Its main objective was the development of a sustained slow-neutron reaction. Among those contributing to this effort were Szilard, Pegram, Urey, Anderson, Zinn, and Teller.

Simultaneously, important work was progressing at the University of California at Berkeley and at England's University of Birmingham. At Berkeley, major breakthroughs had been scored by three researchers. One was the invention of the cyclotron by Ernest O. Lawrence. The other was the use of this cyclotron by Edwin M. McMillan and Glenn T. Seaborg to bombard uranium with neutrons in a way producing two new elements, numbers 93 and 94, which they named neptunium and plutonium, respectively. Both elements were found to be fissionable, greatly reducing the need to rely on the use of rare U-235 for a sustained nuclear reaction. In England, James Chadwick came up with a gaseous diffusion process dramatically reducing the complexity and expense of separating U-235 from U-238.

But progress in the laboratory was not matched by progress in the bureaucracy. Much of the blame for this was directed at the Uranium Committee and its chairman, Lyman Briggs. It seldom met, and even when it did, it moved slowly.[9] Complaints about its creeping pace were heard from Ernest Lawrence, Karl Compton, Harold Urey, and other leading scientists.

Such complaints, combined with reports of British progress on an atomic bomb project, helped prod Briggs into a faster pace. He proposed a budget of $167,000 for chain-reaction research, most of it at Columbia, Chicago, and Princeton. He proposed another $120,000 for research on methods of separating U-235 from U-238 and only $8,000 for research on plutonium as a fissionable element.

Through much of this, Edward Teller was absorbed not only in his work at George Washington University and in consulting with the Fermi-Szilard group at Columbia, but also in the process of becoming an American citizen. He and Mici were naturalized in March 1941. They also bought a new home in Country Club Hills, a development in the Virginia suburbs of Washington. But just three months after the move Teller was invited to take leave from George Washington and to spend a year at Columbia University. Hans Bethe was winding up a summer there as a teacher and researcher on leave from his faculty post at Cornell. Columbia and the Fermi-Szilard group needed someone to succeed him, and Bethe recommended Teller.

In the meantime, Roosevelt had stripped away much of the red tape hampering the nuclear effort by setting up a new agency on June 28, 1941. Named the Office of Scientific Research and Development (OSRD), it superseded the National Defense Research Committee and was given authority over all scientific defense work. Vannevar Bush was appointed its director. James B. Conant, chemist and president of Harvard University, was appointed to succeed Bush as head of the National Defense Research Committee.

In July, Bush learned that researchers working in England at the University of Birmingham had arrived at an amazing conclusion. Instead of the huge amounts estimated by the Americans, ranging up to 100 tons, only 5–10 kilograms of pure uranium might be necessary to build the bomb.

But these calculations had taken a year to wend their way through the British bureaucracy before drawing significant notice. Now that they had, the London scientific community was impatient for action. Even with adequate financing and materials the government could not be expected to produce a bomb within two years. Meanwhile, Nazi firebombers continued their assaults on English cities.

Armed with this information, Bush met with President Roosevelt on October 9, 1941, to urge an all-out effort. He emerged from this meeting with authority to go the limit on research and development. Funds would be drawn from the president's own emergency account. A new unit, Section 1, would be created within the OSRD to give top-level directions to the effort. Mere knowledge of its existence would be confined to the president, the vice-president, James Conant, Secretary of War Henry L. Stimson, and Army Chief of Staff George Catlett Marshall. They would refer to the project as S-1.[10]

Two years had passed since Alexander Sachs had handed Roosevelt the letter signed by Einstein during that visit to his Long Island summer cottage by Teller and Szilard. Finally, the idea proposed in that letter was given the green light.

Chapter 7

ASSEMBLY OF A BOMB TEAM

A neatly drawn conclusion would be that the United States, once President Roosevelt gave the go-ahead, blended scientific genius and keen military planning for the smooth and swift completion of its atomic bomb project. It would also be a false conclusion.

The green light given at the White House at that meeting on October 9, 1941, signaled the end of worries about skimpy financing for the project. But still to be solved was the big problem of how to produce enough fissionable uranium or plutonium to make a deliverable bomb. Also still ahead was the challenge of forging a productive team from an unlikely union of disciplined militarists and free-thinking multinational scientists with strong personalities, competing ambitions, and psychological cross-currents.

A major ingredient in that mixture was Edward Teller and he did not mix well. For those running the project, he and his eccentricities were also a distinct part of the challenge, one that was never completely resolved but often aroused their frustration, puzzlement, and, sometimes, anger. His being asked to join the project team was a tribute to his top ranking as a theoretical physicist. His being kept on the team was a tribute to the diplomacy and patience of those in charge. He brooded over what he felt was a broken agreement to let him pursue research on the hydrogen bomb as well as on the atomic bomb. At a critical point, he balked at doing a job his superiors considered vital to the war effort. For good measure, he antagonized neighboring colleagues by disturbing their rest with late-night piano playing.

An irony in all this was that Teller himself had been regarded as something of a diplomat and peacemaker when he was first drawn into the small circle of those working on a nuclear chain reaction. As Enrico Fermi's wife told us, Teller was called from Washington to New York in the fall of 1941 partly as a catalyst to ease the friction between Fermi and Leo Szilard during their collaboration at Columbia University. "I certainly tried to make peace," Teller acknowledged, "but I believe I failed."[1]

It was during this period, while he and Fermi shared a quiet lunch break from their work at Columbia, that Teller was hooked by an idea that was to influence the rest of his life. Discussing strides already made toward nuclear fission, the two agreed that a controlled chain reaction seemed feasible, and with it, production of an atomic bomb. But neither had stopped there. Both looked beyond nuclear fission and ahead to nuclear fusion.

Teller and Fermi were fully aware of the pioneering work already done by George Gamow and Hans Bethe to explain the source of energy in the stars. Gamow and Bethe had found that intense heat caused light nuclei, such as those in hydrogen, to fuse and thereby generate fantastic quantities of energy. Suppose, Fermi suggested, such intense heat could be produced on earth by a nuclear-fission, or atomic, bomb? Would this not result in the fusion of hydrogen nuclei and the release of even more energy than that released in fission? Was such a fusion, or thermonuclear, bomb in the cards?

Teller was entranced. "If my husband expressed an idea, it vibrated in Teller and came back," said Laura Fermi. She added that Fermi considered Teller "scientifically the most congenial of the physicists, and the most stimulating."[2] Fermi spoke of deuterium, or heavy hydrogen. Its nuclei, he suggested, would probably fuse more readily than those of ordinary hydrogen. Although deuterium is found as only 1 part in 5,000 of ordinary hydrogen, science had already learned that its atoms could be corralled with relatively little difficulty and expense.

The idea of nuclear fusion absorbed Teller. "At that time," he told us, "physics had moved closer to the grim realities of war. Many of us had started to work on the fission bombs. It had become clear that these atomic bombs would be powerful but expensive. If deuterium could be ignited, it would give a much less expensive fuel."

With this economic justification reinforcing his instinctive curiosity as a theoretician, Teller plunged into calculations on the likelihood of a thermonuclear bomb. For weeks he dogged the answer. But somewhere along the line the calculations became *mis*calculations. He became convinced that the idea would not work. "I decided that deuterium could not be ignited by atomic bombs," he told us. "I reported my results to Fermi and proceeded to forget about it."

In the meantime, Mici Teller had adjusted to the move from Washington and fit easily into the rhythm of New York. She and Laura Fermi built a good friendship. The Fermis lived in Leonia, New Jersey, and the

Tellers often visited. "At that time," Mici was to tell us years later, "I still enjoyed the fact that Edward was famous."[3]

International tensions preceding the Japanese bombing of Pearl Harbor on December 7, 1941, had been accompanied by stepped-up activity on the atomic bomb project. In November, the National Academy of Sciences review committee produced a report estimating that within three or four years the United States could produce a bomb powerful enough to "devastate Germany's military and industrial objectives."[4]

At the same time, on December 6, James Conant, acting in the absence of Vannevar Bush, called a meeting of Section 1, the hush-hush bomb unit within the OSRD, and announced a plan to fast-track the bomb project. As part of the plan, S-1 would report directly to Bush as chief of the OSRD instead of to the intervening layer of authority of the National Defense Research Council headed by Conant. Bush's representative in the realigned Section 1 would be Conant himself.

Other members of the revamped Section 1 would represent individual projects, including several aimed at solving the big problem: How could the U-235 isotope be separated from U-238 for use as the more readily fissionable ingredient of the atomic bomb? Arthur H. Compton, chairman of physics at the University of Chicago, would head the chain-reaction project then centered at Columbia but also including work being done at Princeton and Chicago.

By January 1942, Compton concluded that the chain-reaction project should be consolidated in one location. He directed that the Columbia and Princeton units be transferred to Chicago. This meant still another move for Teller, who was barely settled in at Columbia and was to work on the consolidated project with a high-powered group that included Fermi, Szilard, Wigner, and John Wheeler. But the transfer took most of the year to complete.

In the meantime, the structure of S-1, originally created as the Uranium Committee, was revised again in May 1942 as the S-1 Executive Committee of the OSRD. Conant was named chairman. The main thrust of the unit, once regarded as an experimental agency in the field of energy production, had clearly shifted to bomb production. To pave the way for the transfer of project control to the military, Bush and Conant presented a reorganization plan on June 13 to the presidential advisory group, including Vice-President Wallace, Secretary of War Henry L. Stimson, and Gen. George C. Marshall, Army Chief of Staff. Within a week, on June 18, Brig. Gen. W. D. Styer, staff chief for Services of Supply, ordered the creation of a top-secret unit under the Army Corps of Engineers to take over supervision of the atomic bomb project. It was to be known officially as the Manhattan District.

On September 17, the project was placed under the command of Leslie L. Groves, an obscure Corps of Engineers colonel. Groves was crushed. He had believed he was in line for an overseas assignment that would lead to a more rapid rise in rank. He did receive a promotion to brigadier general, but his appointment was welcomed neither by him nor the scientists he was to command. Tall and obese, he typified qualities that intellectuals abhor in the military stereotype—arrogance, insensitivity, and distrust of free thought. Many scientists felt that Groves was too short on scientific background for competent direction of such a large and complex project.

By contrast, Groves felt that scientists, especially theoreticians, spent too much time dreaming and talking and too little time working for the common good. He also perceived in them a lack of discipline, a perception somewhat paradoxical. For although Groves was rigid in many areas of self-discipline (he did not drink, smoke, or condone profanity), he yielded shamelessly to temptation by chocolate candy and kept an endless supply of one-pound boxes of it stashed in his office safe. His weight, a secret nearly as tight as the inner workings of the bomb project itself, was variously guessed at between 250 and 300 pounds.[5]

All this considered, the general and his charges adapted to each other surprisingly well. Teller, no great admirer of military martinets, remembered him favorably. "With all of his shortcomings, his lack of technical knowledge, his lack of tact, he was a man of his word," he said. "He was industrious. He kept after the job, and he made sure that everybody else did. And whatever else you might say about General Groves, he was capable of learning."

A less charitable view was held by Szilard, who clashed with Groves repeatedly on issues as lofty as the potential effect of the bomb on postwar international relations and as base as the dollar value of Szilard's nuclear-chain-reaction patent. The Szilard-Groves dispute was the most bitter, but other conflicts marked the stuttering progress of the project. Among them were differences between Szilard and Fermi, Teller and Oppenheimer, and Teller and Bethe.

Arthur Compton had also brought Oppenheimer aboard in January 1942 to help with the theoretical phase of the project. By spring it became apparent that Gregory Breit, the Russian-born physicist who first headed that phase, was ready to resign. He did so on June 1, and Compton named Oppenheimer to succeed him.

One of Oppenheimer's first acts as chief was to call a summer conference at Berkeley for top-flight physicists assigned to the Manhattan District. The lineup included Edward Teller, Hans Bethe, Felix Bloch, Robert Serber, Emil Konopinski, S. P. Frankel, Eldred Nelson, and J. H. Van

Vleck—a group as strong as many of those that had gathered in the old days at Göttingen and Copenhagen or more recently at the conferences held by George Gamow and Teller in Washington.

The inclusion of Teller among those invited by Oppenheimer helped resolve an awkward situation while at the same time setting up one of the ironies that marked Teller's history. The awkwardness had developed after Compton announced that all chain-reaction work was to be centralized at the University of Chicago. Teller was not included among those directed to make the move from Columbia. The official explanation given by Compton was that Teller was not needed in Chicago because "all the theoretical problems connected with nuclear reactors had been solved." The real reason, Teller later learned, was that his parents and other relatives were still in Nazi-occupied Hungary and he therefore could not be given security clearance for secret work. The irony developed from the fact that the lid on Teller's security clearance was lifted at the request of Oppenheimer, whose own clearance was to be withdrawn more than a decade later as a result of a hearing at which Teller was cast as a key witness against him.[6]

Before leaving Chicago for Berkeley, Teller suggested to Konopinski that one of their contributions to the Berkeley conference could be a report on "why deuterium could not be ignited by an atomic bomb." Konopinski agreed, and they hauled out Teller's earlier calculations and began sifting through them for material to include in their report. "We wanted no one else to waste valuable time investigating Fermi's curbside suggestion," Teller recalled.[7]

"But the more we worked on our report, the more obvious it became that the roadblocks I had erected for Fermi's idea were not so high, after all. We hurdled them one by one and concluded that heavy hydrogen actually could be ignited by an atomic bomb."

The stated purpose of Oppenheimer's conference on the Berkeley campus was to investigate how atomic bombs could be made and would behave. But before long, the entire group, assembled in LeConte Hall under maximum security conditions, was absorbed in a discussion of the thermonuclear question raised by Teller. Could a hydrogen bomb be produced by using an atomic bomb to create enough heat to explode deuterium?

"I presented a rough proof of what could be done and how," Teller later wrote. "My theories were strongly criticized by others in the group, but with the new difficulties, new solutions arose. . . . We were all convinced, by summer's end, that we could accomplish a thermonuclear explosion—and that it would not be too difficult."

Teller has written that Oppenheimer "was as interested in the prospect as any of us."[8] But discussion of the H-bomb idea diverted the gathering from its main purpose, an exchange of ideas on the A-bomb. Also diverting, especially for Oppenheimer, was Teller's explanation of his calculations on the amount of heat that might be yielded by the atomic explosion triggering the H-bomb. In the midst of the explanation there flashed through Oppenheimer's mind the question of whether such heat could, in the process, ignite not only the deuterium in the hydrogen bomb but also the deuterium, or heavy hydrogen, found in seawater and even the nitrogen making up 80 percent of the earth's atmosphere. He insisted on weighing this danger of planetary holocaust.

Even though no one at the conference would place the mathematical possibility of such an occurrence at more than 1 in 3 million, such odds were not reassuring enough. Oppenheimer suspended further sessions until he could consult with Arthur Compton, who was on vacation. Oppenheimer tracked him down at a general store near his Otsego, Michigan, vacation spot. They met two days later at the small Otsego railroad station and drove to a little-used beach, where Oppenheimer laid out his concern.

Compton shook his head. The project would have to be jettisoned unless the question of possible cataclysm could be answered satisfactorily. "Better to be a slave under the Nazi heel," he said, "than to draw down the final curtain on humanity."[9]

At that clandestine meeting and others held in the Michigan vacation area the rest of that week, Oppenheimer and Compton also discussed the possibility of moving directly to work on the thermonuclear bomb.[10] (By now the H-bomb was variously referred to as the fusion bomb, the thermonuclear bomb, the superbomb, and among those deeply involved in nuclear weaponry, "the super.") Besides putting the project on hold until someone came up with convincing evidence that an atomic explosion could be controlled, Compton recommended a special meeting to explore the subject of thermonuclear reaction.[11]

On his return to Berkeley, Oppenheimer picked up the discussion. Teller later said it did not produce total agreement among the theoreticians that a thermonuclear reaction would occur but did rule out any considerable probability of an earth-consuming nitrogen holocaust.[12] The conference adjourned on this note, with its participants stimulated by thoughts of incredibly great amounts of energy being released through thermonuclear reaction but, despite Teller's assurance, also nagged by lingering doubts about controlling it.

Even more immediately disquieting to Washington were military developments abroad and lack of scientific developments at home.

U.S. troops had joined in the fighting and were engaged in a North African offensive against the wily German general Erwin Rommel. England had come under daily pounding by Nazi bombers. Hitler's troops had stabbed deeply into Russia. At home, newly promoted Brig. Gen. Leslie Groves had reluctantly accepted command of a nuclear weapons program dependent on the meshing of many parts but still sputtering at the starting line. On the squash court under the west grandstand of Stagg Field at the University of Chicago, many of the world's foremost physicists labored to build their first atomic pile.

At Berkeley, the project for electromagnetic separation of fissionable U-235 from U-238 had been placed on standby. The centrifuge method of separation had been aborted as unfeasible. The S-1 committee had decided as its first choice to go with the gaseous-diffusion method at the rambling plant at Oak Ridge, Tennessee, a process entailing six hundred steps and guaranteeing nothing.

Into this dark setting strode Leslie Groves, the reluctant colonel-turned-general. After a briefing from Lt. Col. Kenneth D. Nichols, a West Pointer with a Berlin doctorate in engineering and now coordinator of the army's participation in the A-bomb project, Groves issued his first order: Find a supply of uranium and have it delivered to the Manhattan District. Within 24 hours Nichols had a sales agreement with a Belgian firm for 1,250 tons of the ore.

On adjournment of the Berkeley conference, Mici Teller had returned to New York to finish packing for the transfer to Chicago. Including the moves to and from Berkeley, this was to be her third while awaiting the birth of her first child. Edward returned from Berkeley later, "just about the time I had everything packed," she said with a hint of humor.[13] In Chicago, the Tellers moved temporarily into the Fermi apartment before finding one of their own on Kimbark Avenue, near the Chicago campus. They and the Fermis occasionally met for an evening of cards. "Good friends, bad bridge players," Laura Fermi recalled.[14]

In need of furniture, the Tellers learned of a dispersal auction at the old Congress Hotel in Chicago. They came away with a heavy oak living-room suite and the piano that was to sustain Edward through many burdensome times. A Steinway, it has been part of the Teller home for more than forty-five years, whether home was Chicago, Los Alamos, Berkeley, or, most recently, Palo Alto. It cost $200.

By November 1942, Groves, having gathered a substantial supply of uranium, bought under the agreement negotiated by Nichols, had also completed a reconnaissance swing around the circuit of A-bomb laboratories. Visiting Chicago on October 5, he had crossed swords with Arthur Compton, whom he privately called "Arthur Hollywood" because of the Metlab (Metallurgical Laboratory) director's theatrical manner.

Groves's next stop was Berkeley, where an ebullient Ernest Lawrence told him about the uranium separation by the Calutron, Lawrence's new 184-inch cyclotron. After fourteen to twenty-four hours, it produced a series of green smears, only micrograms of U-235. Groves made clear his disappointment over the amount and its quality—only 30 percent pure.

But Lawrence introduced Groves to Oppenheimer, his ultimate choice as top scientist on the Manhattan Project (as the Manhattan District soon became familiarly called). It would be difficult to find two more disparate collaborators in the entire nuclear weapons program.

Groves was the straitlaced son of a straitlaced Presbyterian army chaplain. At eleven, he earned spending money as a walnut picker. At the same age, Oppenheimer, the son of a successful Jewish importer from New York, spoke classical Greek.

A nose-to-the-grindstone West Pointer, Groves was all army, an engineer who translated drawn lines into buildings and carried a .32-caliber Colt automatic on a .25 frame.

Oppenheimer was a loner who at eighteen sailed his own twenty-eight-foot sloop. He graduated from Harvard summa cum laude in three years, studied in Germany and England, spoke French and German fluently, and learned Sanskrit for relaxation. As a youth, he was confined to bed for five months by tuberculosis and had looked cadaverous ever thereafter. A popular teacher, he rebuked less gifted students, was assailed by fits of melancholy, and was once diagnosed as a case of dementia praecox, or schizophrenia.

As Lawrence suggested, Groves questioned Oppenheimer about the little green smears of fissionable U-235 grudgingly surrendered by Lawrence's pet cyclotron. Oppenheimer did not pretend to know the answers but responded clearly, honestly, and, for him, modestly. Groves congratulated him on his skillful, forthright answers. "There are no experts," Oppenheimer shrugged. "The field is too new."[15]

Besides selecting Oppenheimer to run the science phase of the atomic-bomb project, Groves accepted Oppenheimer's recommendation of the place where it should be launched. Groves had rejected an earlier recommendation from an army colonel assigned to scout possible locations. The site chosen consisted of a resort hotel and a few neighboring buildings near Jemez Springs, New Mexico, about fifty miles north of Albuquerque. Oppenheimer, who had spent several summers in the area and owned a ranch there, suggested that they settle instead on the nearby Los Alamos Ranch School.

One week later, on December 2, 1942, another milestone on the road to the making of an atomic bomb was reached in Chicago. The moment had arrived for the key step in the chain-reaction test planned for months by the team working under the Stagg Field grandstand—Compton, Fermi, Szilard, Wigner, Teller, and the others.

The object of the test was to produce a chain reaction. The critical question here was known as the k, or *reproduction*, factor. When a nucleus was bombarded by neutrons, would the bombardment cause the release of more neutrons than the number used in the bombardment? If not, the k factor would be less than one, and the reaction, instead of sustaining itself, would fizzle. But if the number of released neutrons exceeded the number used to strike the uranium nucleus and they, in turn, went flying into other nuclei and released still more neutrons—if the k were more than one—the reaction would continue, building up heat, an atomic "fire." If the heat were built up fast enough, the result would be an explosion.

For two hours the experiment proceeded, slowly building up heat until measuring graphs showed that the world's first man-made nuclear chain reaction had been achieved. Satisfied, Fermi ordered that the atomic furnace be banked.

Eugene Wigner opened a bottle of chianti to toast the achievement and its achievers. It was an exciting night for those present, but Edward Teller was not among them. As on that night in Washington nearly four years earlier when he had unexcitedly witnessed the repeat of the nucleus-splitting experiment, he could not get worked up over the actual event. For him the excitement lay in exploration of the universe through the magic transfer of ideas onto the blackboard. Confident that the chain-reaction test would succeed, he had chosen not to be present for what he considered the anticlimax.[16]

It was not long before the focus of the bomb project shifted back to Los Alamos, where it was to stay until bombs fell on Hiroshima and Nagasaki. By the end of 1942, an advance crew of construction workers, the first of an ultimate 3,000, had moved onto the mesa. For the next three years it would be home to Teller and that select band of scientists, not all of whom were pleased by the thought of life in such a remote sanctuary. Oppenheimer later disclosed that even before steering Groves to it he had secretly fixed on Los Alamos as his first choice for the project. His attachment to the area dated back to 1928, when he leased his ranch and named it Perro Caliente. That is Spanish for what he exclaimed when he first saw it, "Hot dog!"[17]

Chapter 8

MAVERICK ON THE MESA

The scientists building the atom bomb at Los Alamos were ill suited by temperament and training for life on the mesa. They were unused to the kind of regimen and regimentation dictated by security requirements and by the remote location of the project. Edward Teller was even less adaptable than most. Before arriving in New Mexico, he believed he had been promised enough latitude to pursue his interest in thermonuclear weaponry while also working on the A-bomb. But once there, he was denied this. His resentment was reflected in increasingly difficult relationships with Oppenheimer and Bethe. His disposition was not improved by the generally frustrating work and living conditions necessarily imposed on scientists and their military counterparts alike.

Steered by Oppenheimer, Groves made what was generally greeted as an excellent choice in selecting the Los Alamos Ranch School as the site for the atomic bomb project. Now established as a major effort, the project had received a $400 million commitment from President Roosevelt.

The site, the Los Alamos ("the Poplars") Mesa of the Pajarito ("Little Bird") Plateau, met every criterion. It was big enough to provide a testing ground. Its climate made outdoor work possible through the winter. It was accessible by road and rail for transportation of personnel and materials. Sources of construction material were near enough to avoid prohibitive shipping costs. The population within a 100-mile radius was not too big for requirements of safety (if something went wrong) or security (to discourage any who might try to make something go wrong). It had access to power, water, fuel, and utilities but was too far from any seacoast to invite submarine or commando attack. The site provided an awesome view of the Jemez Mountains, which are part of the Rocky Mountain system, and the Sangre de Cristo ("Blood of Christ") range, barely 40 miles away and rising

13,000 feet. Slicing through the mesa land were canyons 100–500 feet deep.

Getting there took some determination. Sante Fe, twenty air miles southeast, was served by a branch of the Atchison, Topeka & Santa Fe Railway. By road, the drive from Santa Fe covered thirty-five miles over State Highway 4, a narrow, bumpy strip subject to flooding, or forty-five miles over State Highway 5, which was smoother and usually drier.

Early arrivals at Los Alamos paid the price of a schedule breakdown. They found no housing or facilities to feed them, and many scientists and their families were assigned temporary quarters on nearby dude ranches. Daily commuting to work meant a lurching ride over a winding, bumpy road. Once there, they found laboratories still unfinished, equipment still undelivered. A milestone was reached on April 14, 1943, when the contractor installed the pole piece of a cyclotron magnet.[1]

Workers on the Manhattan Project were instructed to avoid references to Los Alamos because the name was classified. They resorted to a variety of nicknames—Site Y, Project Y, the Zia Project, Santa Fe, Area L, Shangri La, Happy Valley. Among Santa Fe regulars and early settlers at the project, it was simply the Hill.[2]

Buildings included thirty-one existing structures and eleven new ones, most of them long, low barracks-type affairs of wood-and-gypsum board. Housing plans emphasized apartments and one- or two-room duplexes. There were also a few stone and log buildings from the ranch school. Unlike the newer buildings, these had bathtubs. The Teller apartment was among those without a tub.

While not primitive, life at Los Alamos was barely civilized when compared with the cosmopolitan environment many of the scientists had known when working on projects at Columbia, Chicago, and California. Personal liberty was limited by rigid security standards. Travel outside the compound was limited to two monthly trips to Santa Fe for shopping or the meager entertainment available there. Mail was censored, and long-distance telephone calls were monitored. This brought jarring memories back to many of the Los Alamos physicists who had fled to this country from Nazi and Communist oppression. Teller cited the response of Richard Feynman, the Princeton luminary who was to win the 1965 Nobel Prize for his discoveries in quantum mechanics.

"He wrote a letter, and in the letter he included a laundry list," Teller told us. "The censors tried to figure what does this mean. They could not believe that this was just a laundry list. But that's all it really was, and we had a good laugh over it."

Soon after their arrival with their infant son, Paul, born in Chicago on

February 10, 1943, the Tellers began uncrating two big items, Edward's Chicago-bargain Steinway and a new automatic washing machine. Because no plumber on the base was qualified to install the washer and security officers refused to allow one to come onto the base from Santa Fe, Mici was saved only by a coincidence from losing the benefit of the machine. The general's wife also happened to have a new baby and the same make of washing machine. When this was called to the attention of the security officers, the ban somehow seemed less important and was relaxed. Mici had even more reason to be grateful for the machine when a second child, a daughter named Wendy, arrived in the summer of 1946.

Besides members of the contingent involved in Oppenheimer's pre–Los Alamos meeting at Berkeley, the Manhattan Project drew to the mesa many other luminaries of the scientific community. Among them were John von Neumann from Hungary, the outstanding mathematician of the era; Emilio Segrè, Enrico Fermi's protégé from Italy; Rolf Landshoff from Germany; Victor Weisskopf from Austria; George Kistiakowsky from Russia; and Niels Bohr from Denmark.

In the group from England were Sir James Chadwick, discoverer of the neutron; Cyril S. Smith; W. G. Penney; and Otto Frisch, Lise Meitner's nephew who had fled from Germany to Denmark, then to Britain. Others included Luis Alvarez, Norman Ramsey, Charles Critchfield, Edwin McMillan, John Manley, Nick Metropolis, and Carson Mark.

Great precautions were taken to disguise this great collection of scientific talent. Even the word "physicist" was restricted for security reasons. Scientists were identified instead as engineers. The most famous members of the group were given code names backed up by false credentials—auto registrations, driver's licenses, food and gasoline ration books, income tax returns. Enrico Fermi was "Henry Farmer." Niels Bohr was "Nick Baker." Teller had no cover name.

The challenges confronting the Los Alamos group were scientific, organizational, and, especially in Teller's case, philosophical.

Now that a nuclear chain reaction had been achieved in the Chicago experiment under great precautions to prevent an explosion, the problem was reversed: How to *cause* an explosion. But the challenge was how to produce an explosion from a nuclear chain reaction at a specific instant, not prematurely and not too late for military effectiveness. This would mean packing enough fissionable material into a container to provide a "critical mass" capable of producing enough flying neutrons to create not the slow chain reaction of the controlled experiment in Chicago but an *instant* chain reaction. But the components of the bomb had to be positioned in such a way as to prevent their becoming a critical mass until the right time for detonation. There was reasonable certainty that pure uranium-235 or plutonium could produce such an instant chain reaction and a resultant explosion of tremendous force. What still remained a mystery to the finest minds in physics was the extremely complex puzzle of how to build the bomb so that a subcritical mass would be converted into a critical mass on command.

The organizational challenge seemed almost as complex. How could the vast reservoir of scientific knowledge and the unlimited creativity of so many finely tuned minds of complicated human beings with widely disparate backgrounds be harnessed in a single project under a gruff military commander? General Groves had a ready solution: Sign them up; make them part of the army chain of command, subject to military discipline, with Oppenheimer over them and Groves over everyone.

Oppenheimer himself had readily agreed to this concept. But largely because of counsel from the highly respected I. I. Rabi and Robert Bacher of the MIT delegation, the plan to militarize the scientists died in infancy. They argued that it would retard achievement of the military objective by stifling the free discussion and open dissent essential to scientific progress. A scientist of lower military rank, they suggested, might hesitate to question the judgment of a superior officer on a scientific question.

Bacher and Rabi were also credited with persuading Oppenheimer to adopt an organizational plan providing some direction for the flow of scientific thought. It called for the creation of four divisions, each headed by a director and subdivided into groups. One was the theoretical division, directed by Bethe and with Teller as leader of one of its groups. Another was the experimental division, headed by Bacher. The third was the chemistry and metallurgy division, directed by Joseph W. Kennedy, a twenty-six-year-old graduate of the Berkeley project in which Glenn Seaborg and Edwin McMillan had created plutonium. The fourth division was ordnance and engineering, headed by navy captain William S. Parsons.

On paper and in practice, the organization plan looked tidy and worked effectively. For Teller, however, this arrangement and the focus of the laboratory itself presented problems. He bristled over what he considered the deception played on him by those who had indicated that he would be allowed to work on the thermonuclear bomb. He resented Oppenheimer's part in this.

"When Los Alamos was established as a separate entity from the Metlab in Chicago," he told us, "one of the arguments was that we would work on the fusion bomb as well as on the fission bomb. We actually didn't, and this was certainly something that I was unhappy about."

He was also unhappy about Bethe's leadership of the theoretical division. Bethe himself traced Teller's chill to the mere fact that Oppenheimer made him subordinate to Bethe. Teller attributed his displeasure to Bethe's style.

"Bethe was given the job to organize the effort, and in my opinion, in which I well may have been wrong, he overorganized it," Teller said. "It was much too much of a military organization, a line organization."

Bethe dated the start of Teller's unhappiness to the creation of the division and his appointment to head it.

"The lab was organized, the theoretical division was formed, and I was made the division leader," he said. "I think it was from this moment on that Edward essentially went on strike. Well, he didn't literally. He continued to work, but from then on he seemed rather disinterested in working on the direct business of the laboratory. . . . I believe maybe he resented my being placed on top of him. He resented even more that there would be an end to free and general discussion. . . . He resented particularly that I was no longer available very much for discussions. I remember one occasion when I was terribly busy and he came in to discuss some problem which sounded to me rather far away from our main problem, and so after an hour or so I looked rather conspicuously at my watch, . . . and he didn't like that at all."

Bethe said Teller resented even more that Oppenheimer, previously one of his favorite discussion partners, was also too busy for the kind of freewheeling, opened-ended sessions they had enjoyed at Berkeley. Finally, a deal was worked out. Teller was allotted one hour a week to kick around ideas with Oppenheimer. "I think from ten to eleven on Monday morning, or some such thing," Bethe said. He felt that Teller "was not a team player."

"That's right," Teller agreed. "I wasn't. . . . I deeply objected to the changes Oppenheimer was bringing about in the physics community." Among these was what Teller perceived as a change in the give-and-take of idea testing among colleagues.

Teller also had a Byzantine theory about the deterioration of his relationship with Oppenheimer. He followed this back to an incident just before they arrived at Los Alamos. Teller's recollection was that Oppenheimer, discussing Groves, spoke disparagingly of his "military spirit" and hinted that while it could be condoned in wartime there were limits. "This kind of military spirit will have to be resisted at some time," he quoted Oppenheimer. "We physicists will have to do something about it. The time will come when that will be necessary."

Without waiting to hear specifically what that "something" was, Teller cut off further discussion of the thought by saying, "I doubt that I would ever want to be part of anything of that kind."

"From that day on, my relations with Oppenheimer were distinctly less good—not on my part but on his," Teller said. By the time Teller arrived at Los Alamos, he considered the friendship "already at a dead end."

But with an administrative deftness drawing admiration even from colleagues who had never considered him a capable organization man, Oppenheimer succeeded remarkably well in keeping the Los Alamos ship on an even keel. Whether at Bethe's request or on his own, he became aware enough of the friction between Bethe and Teller to separate them. He did this not by reassigning Teller to another division but by placing him on his own, except for the welcome task of working with Fermi and John von Neumann. Oppenheimer also recognized Edward's special ability to interest and charm newcomers to Los Alamos and made him the laboratory's official greeter and indoctrinator. "Oppenheimer used me—and I didn't need much pushing—to explain to these people what was going on and to help bring them into the job," he said.

Teller acknowledged that Oppenheimer, apparently determined to keep Teller working on the Los Alamos project, tried to keep him happy. "Our connection was almost exclusively through my work, but he tried to make my work as rewarding as possible," Teller said. "He succeeded, I believe, and for that I should be grateful."

A vivid picture of Teller as the loner of Los Alamos was painted by Enrico Fermi's wife, Laura, in her book about their life together. She wrote:

> Edward had become a prominent figure on the mesa by the time I arrived there. He was often seen walking absent-mindedly, with his heavy, uneven gait. His bushy eyebrows went up and down, as always when he was pursuing a new idea. He also helped his thought with uncoordinated motions of his arms. . . . When he could forget his worries, Edward delighted in simple pleasures. His favorite author was Lewis Carroll, and he started to read Carroll's stories to his son, Paul, long before the child could understand them. Edward could be as playful and as naive as his little boy, and each day the two of them spent some time entertaining each other.[3]

A night person throughout most of his career, Teller found his biological clock unsynchronized with those of his colleagues. "Most of them usually started work at nine; I would start at nine-thirty, sometimes later," he told us.

Just as his postmidnight activity at the University of Leipzig many years earlier might have disturbed the sleep of Professor Heisenberg, his late activity at Los Alamos brought complaints from his neighbors there. But instead of keys on an ancient calculating machine like the one at Leipzig, here he was playing the keys of his battered Steinway to unwind from the day's labors—at 3:00 A.M.

Working with von Neumann provided Teller with one of his few bright spots during this dark period. Von Neumann, "Johnny" to all who knew him, was freely considered a genius by most of the scientific community. At six he could mentally divide one eight-digit number into another. He was twenty-three when he left the University of Berlin, because of the Nazis, and arrived in the United States to teach at Princeton.

Teller and von Neumann worked together on a basic problem of the A-bomb project involving one of the two types of triggers being investigated as a possible means of initiating the chain reaction. Earlier work indicated that the gun-type trigger, firing one portion of U-235 into another to produce a critical mass, could be used to detonate uranium-235 but that the more complex implosion type would be needed to produce fission in plutonium. As von Neumann saw it, implosion would compress the plutonium, increasing the explosive force. Considering the still relatively small supply of plutonium, the possibility of getting a greater yield from the same amount of material was given high priority by project officials, especially including Bethe's theoretical division.

"This seemed terribly urgent and an extremely important problem," Bethe said. "So when I asked Edward to undertake this problem with his group and develop the theory of implosion hydrodynamics and all that—which seemed to me the most important task in the theoretical division—he refused."[4]

Teller had joined von Neumann in working on the implosion calculations and was keenly interested in the compressibility factor. But he did not recall the incident cited by Bethe and denied that he refused his request. "He wanted me to work on calculational details, at which I was not particularly good, while I wanted to continue not only on the hydrogen bomb but on other novel subjects," Teller told us. "He might have asked me to do some portion of the job that he had plenty of other people to do, but I don't recall a single instance like that, and if there was one, it was certainly not major."

Whether Bethe's version or Teller's account of this incident is correct, two points seem clear: First, Teller made important contributions to the Los Alamos project; and second, he might have contributed more if he had been "a team man" and had set aside his differences with Bethe and Oppenheimer.

Although much of his work still remains classified decades later, one of the most important contributions he could discuss involved his implosion research with von Neumann. Describing his Los Alamos activity in a letter to us, he said their collaboration marked the start of "the most significant part of the implosion program."

> The calculation is indeed simple as long as you assume that the material to be accelerated is incompressible, which is the usual assumption of solid matter. . . . In materials driven by high explosives, pressures of more than 100,000 atmospheres occur. (A point with which Johnny was familiar but I was not.) If a shell [such as a shell containing the ingredients of a hydrogen bomb—*eds.*] moves in one-third of the way toward the center, you obtain, under the assumption of an incompressible material, a pressure in excess of eight million atmospheres. This is more than the pressure in the center of the earth and it was known to me (but not to Johnny) that, at these pressures, iron is not incompressible. In fact, I had rough figures for the relevant compressibilities. The result of all this was that in the implosion significant compressions will occur, a point which had not been previously discussed.
>
> The importance of this point is obvious. At higher densities the amount of material needed for a nuclear explosion is decreased. This, of course, had decisive consequences on the time scale needed for the accomplishment of our task, since materials were expected to remain in exceedingly short supply.[5]

Teller's summary of the topics on which he worked also included opacities, the rapid transport of heat by radiation expected at the very high temperatures of nuclear explosions. Another topic involved a potential problem at the gas-diffusion plant at Oak Ridge, Tennessee, for separating nuclear isotopes; could the process result in accumulation of U-235 and produce an unscheduled nuclear explosion?

Also occupying Teller at the time were his further calculations involving the hydrogen bomb, including pursuit of the question about possible cataclysm from an all-consuming, propagating nuclear explosion on earth. "A few of us ([Cloyd H.] Marvin, Konopinski, and myself) made detailed and conclusive calculations showing that such a propagation could not occur.

"Even this incomplete list might give you the impression that I was not unemployed in Los Alamos," Teller wrote. He concluded the report on his activities there with a parting shot at his old, now estranged colleague.

"Neither was I really missed in the calculational effort. Really excellent people, including Victor Weisskopf, Klaus Fuchs, and Richard Feynman, to mention only a few, were ready and willing to do the job. It is conceivable that even Bethe might admit that I had not wasted my time."

For years after the war, Teller and Bethe avoided outright bitterness in their disagreement over whether Teller did the best he could at Los Alamos.

In 1982, however, Bethe became less circumspect and spoke out in the fall issue of *Los Alamos Science*:

> With the pressure of work and lack of staff, the Theoretical Division could ill afford to dispense with the services of any of its members, let alone one of such brilliance and high standing as Teller. Only after two failures to accomplish the necessary work, and only on Teller's own request, was he, together with his group, relieved of further responsibility for work on the wartime development of the atomic bomb.

Oppenheimer, agreeing with Bethe's assessment, wrote General Groves on May 1, 1944, emphasizing the importance of the implosion calculations, calling Teller "unsuited for this responsibility," and asking approval to replace him with Rudolph Peierls. Teller threatened to leave, but Oppenheimer again flashed his rare talent for resolving personality clashes and persuaded Teller to stay and work on the hydrogen bomb.[6]
Teller later wrote:

> It is hard to work apart from others in a scientific community, especially when most people are working toward a goal of the highest interest and urgency. Every one of us considered the present war and the completion of the A-bomb as the problems to which we wanted to contribute most. Nevertheless, Oppenheimer . . . and many of the most prominent men in the laboratory continued to say that the work at Los Alamos would not be complete as long as the feasibility of a thermonuclear bomb remained in doubt.[7]

Freed from the responsibility of the detailed calculations he found so onerous and encouraged to follow up on the hydrogen bomb, Teller pitched into his partnership with von Neumann on the implosion trigger and his work with Fermi. He also joined Manson Benedict of MIT at Oak Ridge to run down the possibility of an unscheduled nuclear explosion through accumulation of U-235 in the gas-diffusion plant. Under the Groves-imposed compartmentalization scheme to tighten security, Benedict was unaware of the overall reason for this project, and Teller was unable to tell him. "He scrupulously avoided asking questions and showed complete understanding when I shut up," Teller said. They completed their inquiry, with Teller feeling certain that a big blow-up because of accumulated U-235 was out of the question. But the assignment reinforced Teller's abhorrence of secrecy in science and his conviction that it works against the best interests of a free society. Even in wartime, he felt, excessive secrecy can hamper free scientific exchange that might speed up vital work without exposing important information to the enemy. But in peacetime it can be especially counterproductive.

"In most cases, there is no valid reason for keeping scientific work secret for more than a year," he told us. "By that time, it is almost certain that the Russians know about it, while we are keeping it from our own people, including many scientists. As a result, we suffer more than they from our inability to exchange information among ourselves."

Much of the pressure for production of the atomic bomb at Los Alamos ended with the surrender of Germany on May 8, 1945. In the race to see which could develop the decisive weapon first, the Allies had stayed far ahead of the country that had chased the cream of her scientific community into the opposing camp. Germany, it was later learned, never got as far as duplicating the chain reaction produced on the University of Chicago squash court before Los Alamos even opened for business. The German program, under the leadership of Werner Heisenberg, Teller's old professor and friend, never hit stride. German physicists had completed the theoretical work and had plotted the technical details, but they had not gotten around to doing the experiment itself. Teller believed that Heisenberg was unenthusiastic about the Nazi cause and this was reflected in either deliberate or subconscious failure to expedite work on the bomb. But Heisenberg, interviewed by the authors after the war, acknowledged that because of intense Allied bombing and its toll on the German industrial capacity the Nazis were unable to build the huge plant necessary for production of the required amount of U-235 or plutonium.

Teller's belief that Heisenberg dragged his feet on the German A-bomb project is buttressed by a report from author David Irving. Teller said Heisenberg received evidence from Fritz Houtermans, a top-level physicist, that the project could be expedited through use of the fissionable man-made element no. 94, known by its U.S. producers as plutonium. But Heisenberg ignored the evidence, Teller told us, adding this theory on why: "This to my mind is characteristic of a man who works on a project but does not want to work on it. In other words, I am not saying that he tried to destroy it. I am not saying either that he was sabotaging the Nazi effort. I am only saying that this was the behavior of a man who was working unwillingly."

Irving, in his book *The German Atomic Bomb*, refers to "a great debate behind the scenes of German science" after September 1941. "Many of the physicists," he wrote, "were now beset with grave anxieties about the moral propriety of working on the uranium project—predominant among them being Heisenberg, Von Weizsaecker, and Fritz Houtermans."[8]

By contrast, with the sluggish development in Germany, a full-steam effort generated progress in technical developments at Los Alamos. This was matched at the Oak Ridge gas-diffusion plant for the separation of

U-235 and at the Hanford facility in Washington state producing pluto-nium. The Los Alamos team worked especially hard on the uranium gun and on the implosion project. By early June, the Critical Assemblies Group working on the gun completed tests strongly indicating that the U-235 projectile and target were efficiently designed to avoid the greatest danger, the danger of building the critical mass prematurely, before scheduled detonation.

A few weeks later, in the predawn hours of Monday, July 16, 1945, the military and scientific leaders of the Manhattan District Project, hunched in observation posts on desert land 200 miles south of Los Alamos to witness the world's first nuclear explosion. Postponed twice earlier because of technical problems, this was the Trinity test shot, the implosion-triggered detonation of a plutonium bomb atop a 100-foot steel tower on the Alamogordo Air Base. Halfway around the world, at Potsdam, an anxious president, Harry Truman, awaited word of the test results as he was about to begin a historic conference with British Prime Minister Winston Churchill and Soviet Marshal Joseph Stalin. With Germany now out of the war, the addition of an atomic bomb in the Allied arsenal against Japan would minimize the need for Soviet help in the Pacific war. It would also thereby give Truman a stronger bargaining position in negotiating a post-war relationship with the Soviets.

Nerves were also taut in Los Alamos on the eve of the Trinity test. To ease the tension, many of the scientists had set up a betting pool pegged to the closest estimate of the force from the Alamogordo explosion.

Teller was among observers stationed in a bunker on Compania Hill, twenty miles northwest of Zero, the site of the steel tower topped by the bomb. The bomb itself was raised by winch to a shacklike structure with an oak platform and three sides of corrugated iron. Leading from the base of the tower were lines of T-poles on which were strung wires linking the explosion point with instruments in reinforced-concrete bunkers miles away. These instruments—cameras, seismographs, geophones, ionization chambers, spectrographs, and various gauges—would provide the raw material for analysis of the explosion. In addition to the photographic record, this would include measurements of the blast, optical and nuclear effects, details of the exploding-wire detonators invented by Luis Alvarez, and radiochemical procedures designed by Herbert Anderson to measure the explosive yield.

Also in the Compania Hill bunker were Ernest Lawrence, Hans Bethe, James Chadwick, Edwin McMillan, Richard Feynman, Robert Serber, and others not needed in this phase of the test. Others, whose technical services or oversight was required until moments before the explosion, had taken up positions in three bunkers closer to the tower. Rain, whipped by

30-mile winds, lashed the area, and lightning danced disturbingly close to the 100-foot steel tower. The initial 4:00 A.M. deadline for the shot was pushed back by ninety minutes at the most. After that, daylight would obscure photographic measurements, forcing still another postponement. When the rain stopped at 3:00 A.M., the firing was set for 5:30.

As the moment of explosion neared, Teller checked his protective gear. Observers had been warned to lie down, feet toward the tower, and to shield their eyes with plates of welder's glass that had been distributed. Teller went beyond the basic instructions. In addition to the welder's glass, he used sunglasses for eye protection. He also rubbed suntan lotion into his hands and face and, for good measure, donned gloves.

The radio frequency used to broadcast the countdown also picked up programming from a commercial station in the area. That explained the faint strains of the *Nutcracker Suite* as lilting counterpoint to the crisp announcements beginning with "It is now zero minus twenty minutes." They continued at five-minute intervals, then, with half a minute left, went into a second-by-second countdown.

At Compania Hill, Teller became puzzled by an interruption in the announcement flow:

> The countdown on the radio from the control center went down to minus five seconds, and then it stopped. Nothing happened. It seemed to me so long a time that I felt certain the shot had misfired.
>
> And then I saw a very faint light point which divided into three—that is, a highpoint and two side lobes—which was the beginning of the mushroom. I clearly remember a feeling of disappointment. "This is all?" Then I remembered—all of this was within a fraction of a second—that I had all these glasses between me and the event. So I tipped the welder's glass lightly to peek out the side. The impression I got was the one that you have if in a completely dark room you raise the curtains and the sunlight comes streaming in. That may have been a couple of seconds after the explosion, and, of course, it was twenty miles away. And by that time, of course, I was impressed. It faded, I took off the glasses, and we saw the mushroom and the cloud developing that the wind blew in various directions."[9]

William L. Laurence, the *New York Times* reporter who was the only journalist invited by Groves to cover the test, remembered from the biblical account of creation "Let there be light." Laurence later reported a euphoric scene of scientists leaping up, laughing, dancing about, shaking hands, and backslapping. It was, he said, "like primitive man dancing at one of his fire festivals at the coming of spring."

In the control bunker, just 10,000 yards south of Zero, Kenneth Bainbridge, the test director, shook Oppenheimer's hand and sadly declared, "Oppie, now we're all sons of bitches."

As the mushroom cloud rose 40,000 feet into the morning sky over the desert, Oppenheimer recalled a line from *Bhagavad-Gita*, the Hindu devotional poem: "I am become death, the shatterer of worlds!"[10]

Teller, whose 45,000-ton bet was more than twice the actual test yield of 20,000 and far off I. I. Rabi's winning guess of 18,000, drew some consolation from the fact that he won nine of ten side wagers.

Chapter 9

DECISION

Scientists made the bomb. Militarists greeted its arrival. But politicians decided when, where, and how it was to be used.

Many of those responsible for the birth of the bomb pleaded for its demonstration over an unpopulated area. They said this would convince the enemy that defeat was inevitable and that he should surrender immediately. Edward Teller was among them; J. Robert Oppenheimer was not.

Many military leaders also preferred such a nonlethal demonstration. Dwight D. Eisenhower, Allied commander in Europe, was among them. Gen. George C. Marshall, chief of staff, was not.

But political leaders, especially President Truman and Prime Minister Winston Churchill, saw the bomb as even more than a means of quickly ending the war with Japan. They saw it also as an atomic ace in the hole for negotiations with the Soviet Union on the postwar shape of Eastern Europe and the Far East. This appraisal of the bomb as a potential element in political decision-shaping became known as "the Russian factor."

Of even greater long-range importance was the question of whether atomic energy was both so dangerous and so valuable to mankind that it should be placed under international control instead of being left in the hands of a single nation.

Teller was invited to play a key role in the campaign by some scientists to influence such decisions. His big opportunity came in June 1945, when Leo Szilard, vigorously lobbying for a bigger say by the scientific community, asked him to help circulate a petition urging the government to demonstrate the bomb before using it against humans.

But after consulting Oppenheimer, Teller rejected the invitation. This, combined with the fact that Szilard's effort failed and that Teller felt deceived by Oppenheimer about the latter's own position on the issue, hurt Teller deeply.

Behind-the-scenes skirmishing over the atomic issue had begun as early as September 1942. Szilard suggested that the Metallurgical Laboratory in Chicago, still absorbed in producing the world's first man-made chain reaction, begin addressing political questions that would inevitably flow from its work. Then, in January 1944, he wrote Vannevar Bush, coupling a plea for speedy completion of the bomb project with an argument for international control. Use of the bomb in the current war, he said, was essential to public understanding of how devastating atomic weapons could be; and without understanding, the public would be less likely to accept international control as vital to future peace. By March 1945, Szilard had also prepared a memorandum contending that its geography made the United States so vulnerable to attack that international control was its best bet for its own security. In the meantime, he added, as insurance against the chance that the Soviet Union might reject the idea of international control, the United States should proceed with development of the next stage, meaning the hydrogen bomb. [1]

As Szilard veered off on his own, other scientists at the Chicago Metlab proceeded along more conventional lines to advocate international control in seminars and in a memorandum, "Prospectus on Nucleonics." Feeble plans for peace, the memorandum warned, were being drawn by politicians who did not understand how nuclear fission had changed the world. And scientists who did understand were being ignored in the planning. [2]

(This has been a recurring theme on both sides of the Iron Curtain. In 1974, Andrei D. Sakharov recorded a similar situation involving Soviet First Secretary Khrushchev. Sakharov, recognized as the father of the Russian hydrogen bomb program, recalled that in 1961 the Soviet Union was preparing a unilateral resumption of H-bomb testing in the atmosphere. Sakharov said he wrote Khrushchev a note urging that the resumption be put off. "To resume tests after a three-year moratorium would undermine the talks on banning tests and on disarmament, and would lead to a new round in the armaments race . . . ," he wrote. The note was sent to Khrushchev during a meeting of atomic scientists with the Soviet leader. At dinner with the scientists that evening Khrushchev made an off-the-cuff speech that Sakharov said went like this: "Sakharov is a good scientist. But leave it to us, who are specialists in this tricky business, to make foreign policy. Only force—only the disorientation of the enemy. We can't say aloud that we are carrying out our policy from a position of strength, but that's the way it must be. I would be a slob, and not chairman of the Council of Ministers, if I listened to the likes of Sakharov." [3])

While Szilard and the Chicago scientists tried to make their voices heard in Washington, Teller brooded in Los Alamos. Finally, a month after the surrender of Germany on May 8, 1945, he received a letter from Szilard asking him to circulate the petition. Addressed to the president, the petition made these points: Scientists in the United States had worked to produce the bomb against a background of fear that the weapon might be developed first by the enemy and used against their country. But that fear dissolved with the defeat of Germany. Therefore, the petitioners said, the "United States should not resort to the use of atomic bombs in this war unless the terms which will be imposed upon Japan have been made public and Japan, knowing those terms, has refused to surrender.

"The development of atomic power will provide the nations with new means of destruction . . . ," the Szilard petition continued. "Thus a nation which sets the precedent of using these newly liberated forces of nature for purposes of destruction may have to bear the responsibility of opening the door to an era of devastation on an unimaginable scale."

In *The Legacy of Hiroshima*, his 1962 book with Allen Brown, Teller said he had agreed fully with the convictions expressed in the petition and intended to circulate it. But he decided to touch base with Oppenheimer before proceeding. He said:

> It was my duty to first discuss the question with the director, Dr. Oppen-
> heimer. He was the constituted authority at Los Alamos, but he was more.
> His brilliant mind, his quick intellect, his penetrating interest in everyone
> in the laboratory made him our natural leader as well. He seemed to be the
> obvious man to turn to with a formidable problem, particularly political.[4]

He said Oppenheimer told him, "in a polite and convincing way, that he thought it improper for a scientist to use his prestige as a platform for political pronouncements." The director also assured him, he added, that the nation's fate should be left in the hands of Washington officials, who were "the best, the most conscientious men" and who "had information which we did not possess."

"Oppenheimer's words lifted a great weight from my heart," Teller wrote. "I was happy to accept his word and authority." But his heart grew heavy again, and his happiness turned to anger.

> I later learned that shortly before that interview Oppenheimer not only had
> used his scientific stature to give political advice in favor of immediate
> bombing but also had put his point of view forward so effectively that he
> gained the reluctant concurrence of his colleagues [on the advisory panel].

He felt that Oppenheimer should at least have given Szilard an opportunity to express his opposing view. "Yet he denied Szilard, a scientist of lesser influence, all justification for expressing his opinion."[5]

As a result of his discussion with Oppenheimer, Teller replied in a remarkable July 2, 1945, letter to Szilard that he had decided not to circulate the petition at Los Alamos.

He wrote:

> First of all let me say that I have no hope of clearing my conscience. The things we are working on are so terrible that no amount of protesting or fiddling with politics will save our souls. . . . But I am not really convinced of your objections.
>
> Our only hope is in getting the facts of our results before the people. This might help to convince everybody that the next war would be fatal. For this purpose actual combat use might even be the best thing.
>
> And this brings me to the main point. The accident that we worked out this dreadful thing should not give us a responsibility of having a voice in how it is used. This responsibility must in the end be shifted to the people as a whole and that can be done only by making the facts known. This is the only cause for which I feel entitled in doing something: the necessity of lifting the secrecy at least as far as the broad issues of our work are concerned.

One remarkable aspect of the letter was its complete omission of any hint that Teller had discussed the subject with Oppenheimer. "There was no need to," he told the authors years later. "It was my decision."[6]

Also notable was his repetition, without attribution, of the position stated—but not followed—by Oppenheimer: Scientists should not become enmeshed in political decisions. Teller's rethinking of this position produced a 180-degree turn. Forty-two years later he wrote:

> I eventually felt strongly that action without prior warning or demonstration [of the bomb] was a mistake. I also came to the conclusion that, although the opinions of scientists on political matters should not be given special weight, neither should scientists stay out of public debates just because they are scientists. In fact, when political decisions involve scientific and technical matters, they have an obligation to speak out.
>
> I failed my first test at Los Alamos, but subsequently I have stood by that conviction.[7]

Still another striking feature of his letter on Szilard's petition is Teller's adoption of a new cause: the abolition of secrecy in science. It became one of his favorite subjects, and he often wove three main points into his argument for free exchange of scientific information. One was that secrecy, whether it involves U.S. preparedness or information on Soviet weapons, often denies U.S. citizens knowledge that Russia already has but which they need to help shape and support a sensible defense policy. A second point was that excessive secrecy retards scientific research in the United States by impeding a potentially valuable dialogue between university scientists and their colleagues in the defense structure. "Unless the flow of information is re-established between our defense establishment and the universities," he warned in a 1972 article, "a primary source of ideas will dry up." Third was the point that the dropping of secrecy on broad scientific issues would serve a useful purpose in disarmament talks and other international negotiations. "It is predictable that Russia is not going to follow suit within a short time span," he said, "but in the course of years Russia will feel the pressure and may open up."[8] This was more than fifteen years before Mikhail Gorbachev proclaimed a new Soviet policy of *glasnost*.

Of all those involved in the decision on how, where, and when to use the bomb, the man who came closest to arguing on every side of the issue was Henry L. Stimson. As secretary of war under both Roosevelt and Truman, he bridged the period between the inception of the Manhattan District Project in the spring of 1943 and the use of its product to destroy Hiroshima and Nagasaki in August 1945.

The son of a wealthy New York surgeon and descendant of New England settlers who had fought in every American war, Stimson was a conservative Republican lawyer. After graduating from Yale, he enlisted in the National Guard at thirty during the Spanish-American War. Between stints as secretary of war under President Howard Taft and as secretary of state under President Herbert Hoover, he commanded an artillery regiment in France during World War I.

When Roosevelt called in June 1940 to offer a cabinet post to him, Stimson, then seventy-three and an outspoken critic of Roosevelt's New Deal, was incredulous. But duty prevailed over age, and he accepted.

Eight months after Szilard had written Bush his January 1944 letter urging that scientists begin pressing Washington to consider the long-range implications of nuclear weaponry, Vannevar Bush and James Conant broached the subject with Stimson. In a letter dated September 30, 1944, they said the atomic bomb would probably be ready by August 1, 1945. They also said that a hydrogen bomb, one thousand times more powerful, was likely in the future, making every major city on earth vulnerable to instant destruction. Although the United States and Great Britain were alone in the field, they warned, any nation with a strong science program could pull abreast within three or four years.

Bush and Conant had hoped that Stimson would present their views to Roosevelt, but the matter did not come up when he met with the president and Brigadier General Groves on December 30. Instead, the meeting dealt with security. In response to a question from Roosevelt, Groves said there was strong evidence that the Soviet Union was spying on the Manhattan District Project, especially at Berkeley.

Stimson raised the issue of control at a meeting with Roosevelt over lunch on March 15, 1945, and left believing that the president agreed on two main points: The question of control should be settled before the bomb was used, and a public statement covering this question should be issued immediately after its use.

Less than a month later, on April 12, Roosevelt was dead, and for all practical purposes so were prospects for any early agreement on international control of nuclear weapons. Truman made that clear soon after being sworn in and receiving a full briefing on the bomb project from Stimson and Groves on April 25. The president then set up an eleven-member committee composed of Stimson, four other defense officials, and six scientists to advise him on whether and how the bomb should be used. They reported on June 1 against a background of Germany's surrender twenty-four days earlier, the crumbling of the Japanese military machine, and indications of difficult postwar negotiations with the Soviet ally.

"It was their recommendation that the bomb be used against the enemy as soon as it could be done," Truman wrote. "They recommended further that it should be used without specific warning and against a target that would clearly show its devastating strength."[9]

A possible alternative suggested by many was that the bomb be exploded at night in a demonstration over rural Japan, flashing across the sky the unmistakable message that surrender was the only hope of survival.

"Would such a nighttime demonstration have convinced the emperor and the dissidents in his inner cabinet that they should seek peace immediately and unconditionally?" Teller later asked. "Could we have avoided the tragedy of Hiroshima? Could we have started the atomic age with clean hands?"[10]

When the advisory committee reported to Truman in early June, he was preparing for a crucial meeting with Churchill and Stalin at Potsdam, on the outskirts of battered Berlin. He rejected suggestions that the reeling Japanese be invited before then to surrender. If issued from the conference itself, he reasoned, the call to surrender would create an impression of Allied unity. Also, by then "we might know more about two matters of significance for our future effort: the participation of the Soviet Union [in the final stages of the Japanese war] and the atomic bomb."[11] With the bomb test scheduled for mid-July, Truman would have the results and a firmer basis for decisions to be made at Potsdam. The significance of this was emphasized by Oppenheimer during his security-clearance hearing in

1954, when he testified, "We were under incredible pressure to get it [the test] done before the Potsdam meeting."

As the Trinity test drew near, Truman was convinced that the atomic bombing would be justified by a quick end to the war and the saving of an estimated 500,000 American lives. Gen. George C. Marshall, the chief of staff, dreaded the idea of invading Japan and agreed with the Joint Chiefs of Staff on a plan combining the use of atomic bombs and an invasion of the southern tip of Japan. Under the plan, crafted without full consideration of either the difficulties in mass production of atomic bombs or the horrible aftereffects of an atomic explosion, one corps and three bombs were to be assigned to each of three areas. Of these nine bombs, one or two were to be dropped before each corps landing, and the rest were to be reserved for use against any Japanese reinforcements that might be sent in. "It was decided that the casualties from the actual fighting would be very much greater than might occur from the aftereffects of the bomb action," Marshall later recalled. For him, use of the atomic bomb was clearly a logical choice.

Churchill shrugged off any alternative as unthinkable. "The historic fact remains . . . that the decision whether or not to use the atomic bomb to compel the surrender of Japan was never even an issue," Churchill wrote in his memoirs. ". . . There was unanimous, automatic, unquestioned agreement around our table, nor did I ever hear the slightest suggestion that we should do otherwise."[12]

One reason for this was that the suggestion never reached the table. The petition signed by Szilard and other Chicago scientists—but not by Teller or others at Los Alamos—was shunted aside, undelivered to the president. But its theme was sounded by other, important military voices.

Eisenhower, in a letter to Stimson, declared his opposition on two counts. "First, the Japanese were ready to surrender and it was not necessary to hit them with that awful thing. Second, I hated to see our country to be the first to use such a weapon."[13]

The question in Truman's mind was not whether to give the order for the bombing—assuming the test went well at Alamogordo—but when to tell Stalin about the bomb. Stalin arrived in Potsdam bearing word that the Japanese had asked him to initiate peace negotiations. He believed that his disclosure of this to Truman would be a surprise, just as Truman believed that his disclosure of the bomb would surprise Stalin. Both were wrong.

Stalin first mentioned the Japanese peace overture to Truman and Secretary of State James F. Byrnes shortly after the July 17 opening of the Potsdam meeting. They pretended to be surprised but in fact were fully informed about it, because the United States had broken the Japanese code early in the war and had intercepted enemy radio messages.[14] Stalin said he had not given the Japanese a definite answer, because they had not indicated they were ready to surrender unconditionally.

The president had received word of the successful Trinity bomb test from Stimson on the afternoon of Monday, July 16. Truman waited until the eighth session, held on July 24, then casually mentioned to Stalin and his interpreter that the United States had "a new weapon of unusual destructive force."

The statement drew hardly a flicker. The reason, of course, was that Stalin, thanks largely to Klaus Fuchs, was almost as knowledgeable about American progress in development of the bomb as Truman himself.

Before the conference was over, Truman had negotiated with Stalin and British Prime Minister Clement R. Attlee (who had replaced Churchill in the talks after the latter's defeat in the July elections) on issues ranging from postwar European and Asian boundaries to the recognition of Soviet satellites, such as Bulgaria, Romania, and Hungary. In the bargaining, Truman exuded an assurance based on the conviction that in the bomb he held the decisive hole card.

"The final decision on where and when to use the atomic bomb was up to me," Truman later wrote. "Let there be no mistake about it."[15]

The first atomic bomb was dropped on Hiroshima at 8:15 A.M., August 6, 1945.

Three days later the second bomb was dropped on Nagasaki.

Japan's surrender announcement was broadcast the next day. Allied radio monitors picked it up at 7:33 A.M., August 10, 1945.

The next lap of the arms race had begun, and Edward Teller was anxious to see that the United States would not be the loser.

Chapter 10

THE ROAD TO FUSION

Few of his peers in the United States shared Edward Teller's obsession with nuclear fusion, the process by which man could create an explosion one thousand times more devastating than the bombs that were dropped on Hiroshima and Nagasaki. But halfway around the world, Soviet physicists were equally absorbed by the subject. Among the foremost of these was Andrei Sakharov, whose heroism in the cause of human rights was to bring him international acclaim and whose life in many respects paralleled Teller's.

Both were sons of professionals. Teller's father was a lawyer; Sakharov's was a teacher. Both were reared in an atmosphere of close-knit family life, with strong emphasis on literature and music. Teller's father played the violin; Sakharov's was talented at the piano. Both physicists achieved early success; Teller was appointed to the faculty of George Washington University at twenty-seven and by then was frequently in the company of the day's leading physicists. Sakharov was graduated from the University of Moscow at twenty-one. Eleven years later, in 1953, he was elected to the USSR Academy of Scientists and was awarded the Order of Lenin for his work on thermonuclear energy.

Both Teller and Sakharov emerged as leading developers of the hydrogen bomb in their respective countries and became even more widely known because of their controversial opinions. Both also paid a heavy price for this.

Teller's advocacy of H-bomb development brought him into conflict with such eminent colleagues as J. Robert Oppenheimer, Hans Bethe, I. I. Rabi, and others. Combined with his appearance as a hostile witness later in the Oppenheimer security-clearance hearings, his position on the H-bomb issue also placed him at odds with leaders of the scientific and liberal political establishments. He was ostracized by a large segment of the scientific community and was cast as a villain by much of the popular press.

Sakharov's controversial opinions had nothing to do with his pioneering of the hydrogen bomb in the Soviet Union. Before his problems arose, he had already gained recognition from his peers and his government for his work with his mentor, I. E. Tamm, in formulating the principles of a controlled thermonuclear reaction based on magnetic containment of a high-temperature plasma.

Instead, what first brought official displeasure down on Sakharov was his confrontation with the Soviet military in 1955. The point at issue was his expression of hope that the nuclear weapon then being tested would never be used. This drew a rebuke from Soviet Air Marshal Mitrofan I. Nedelin, who said that the Soviet leaders responsible for such decisions needed no advice from sideliners such as Sakharov.

Sakharov further aroused the Soviet military establishment by publishing an article in the magazine *The Soviet Union* on the danger of nuclear testing, then by speaking out specifically against nuclear tests, and finally by protesting the Soviet imprisonment of political dissidents. Sakharov himself was arrested in 1980, stripped of his awards and prizes, and kept in isolation until international protests brought his release in 1986.

In the late 1940s and early 1950s, once the nucleus of the atom was split and the theory of nuclear fission was demonstrated, both Teller and Sakharov realized that the means were at hand to produce enough heat and pressure to create hydrogen fusion.

This simple scientific understanding led to differing political responses in the United States and in the Soviet Union. In the United States, Teller found that the scientific community of his adopted country had lost its appetite for designing and developing weapons of war. Congress also had lost interest. The war was over.

But in Moscow the Kremlin leaders recognized the important role that continued nuclear weapons development could play in international politics. Invading Czechoslovakia in February 1948 and cutting off ground access to West Berlin two months later, they consolidated their grip on Eastern Europe. Then, on August 29, 1949, the United States received sobering evidence that its monopoly on the nuclear arsenal was over. [1] Air samples collected from the atmosphere near Japan were discovered to contain unexpectedly great amounts of radioactivity. Analysis confirmed that it resulted from an atomic explosion in the Soviet Union.

Detonation of this nuclear bomb, nicknamed Joe-1, was a signal to the West that the Kremlin was prepared to protect its territorial gains of World War II against any challenge by its former allies. To Andrei Sakharov, the search for the secret to hydrogen fusion was a scientific challenge. To the Kremlin, it was a means of furthering political ends.

Discussing this with Teller twenty-five years later, in 1974, as we drove from downtown Washington to Dulles International Airport in nearby Virginia, we raised a question: Suppose the Soviet Union, instead of the United States, had been the first country to hold an H-bomb monopoly for more than five years. What difference would it have made? Teller had just completed a strenuous period of travel and meetings, and his usually resonant voice was rough with fatigue as he replied.

"I am not saying that they would have attacked us. The men in the Kremlin, unlike Hitler, are very cautious. But there are such things as political blackmail. And the weakness of our position, in that case, would have left us vulnerable to their pressures."

There had been a general belief in Washington that it would take much longer for any other nation to develop a nuclear bomb. Even as late as 1948, J. Robert Oppenheimer underrated the Soviet's technical ability and dedication. In a personal letter to the chairman of the General Board of the Navy he wrote:

> At the present time to the best of my knowledge the Soviet Union is not in a position to effectively attack the United States itself. . . . With all recognition for the need for caution in such predictions, I tend to believe that for a long period of time to come the Soviet Union will not have achieved this objective, nor even the more minor, but also dangerous possibility of radiological warfare.[2]

In 1949, the CIA predicted that the soonest the USSR could produce an A-bomb would be sometime in the late 1950s.

At the end of the war, Teller was invited to join the faculty at the University of Chicago, where he could work with his old friend, Enrico Fermi. He was tempted but decided that because of the Soviet threat he should first explore the possibility of continuing work on weapons development.

The new director at Los Alamos, Norris Bradbury, invited Teller to head up the theoretical division of the laboratory. Discussing this with us in a 1975 interview over dinner in the Washington Hotel, around the corner from the White House, Teller recalled the questions running through his mind on that day three decades earlier. Although the offer was tempting, what did it really mean? Would he have the authority and support to move aggressively ahead in the field of weapons research and development?

Teller expressed his concerns to Bradbury. "I said that I would remain only if the laboratory's intensive level of theoretical work could be maintained and channeled toward either of the goals—development of a hydrogen bomb or refinement of atomic explosions."

In essence, Teller's demand was "a great effort to build a hydrogen bomb* in the shortest possible time or to develop new methods of fission explosion and speed progress by at least a dozen tests a year."

Bradbury recognized the current political realities. The war was over, and people wanted to forget. And so, as Teller recalled it to us, Bradbury responded: "I wish I could say that we will do one or the other, but *the political conditions are such* that I cannot promise you either."[3]

That evening at a party at the home of Adm. William S. Parsons, who had headed the engineering division at Los Alamos, Teller approached Oppenheimer for help. Relating the essence of his conversation with Bradbury, he suggested that the former laboratory director use his prestige and influence on his successor.[4] "This has been your laboratory, and its future depends on you," he told Oppenheimer. "I will stay if you tell me that you will use your influence to help me accomplish either of my goals—that is, will you help enlist support for work toward a hydrogen bomb or further development of the atom bomb?"

Teller bristled with anger as he recalled Oppenheimer's terse reply: "I neither can nor will do so."

Teller recognized the futility of further effort to gain the concessions he needed to make the Los Alamos job acceptable. And so, on February 1, 1946, the Tellers packed their belongings, including Edward's precious Steinway, and headed back to Chicago.

While at Chicago, Teller did not abandon his interest in nuclear fusion. A small theoretical group headed by Robert Richtmyer remained at Los Alamos. Teller, who often visited the laboratory, felt that as long as they kept the idea alive there was some prospect of gaining broader support for it.[5]

Appraisals of Teller's work at Chicago during this period vary widely. One of his most promising students, Marvin L. Goldberger, later to become chairman of the Department of Physics at Princeton, told us, "He was doing, at the time I was at Chicago, virtually no research. Although he kept up with physics and interrelated strongly with people and discussed problems with them, he himself was not doing anything of particular significance."

Goldberger's assessment was not wholly supported by Harold Agnew, another of Teller's students and later director at Los Alamos. "Teller was

---

* The term *hydrogen*, as applied to hydrogen fusion or to a hydrogen bomb, refers not to ordinary hydrogen, but to one of the hydrogen isotopes, deuterium or tritium, sometimes referred to as "heavy hydrogen."

a wonderful lecturer for two types of individuals," he told us in an interview at a 1974 physics conference in Denver, "those who knew absolutely nothing—in basic freshman courses he was a superb lecturer—and those who knew everything. But for the in-between individual, it was very rough."

And contrary to Goldberger's recollection, Edward Teller published fourteen research papers during his tenure at the University of Chicago, many in collaboration with colleagues. They included three papers on mesotrons, one with Fermi, another with Fermi and Victor Weisskopf, and still another with Edwin McMillan. Teller also coauthored a paper on deuterium reactions with Konopinski and wrote two papers in collaboration with Maria Goeppert-Mayer, who later became a Nobel laureate. Other collaborators included Frederic de Hoffmann and Robert Richtmyer.

Goldberger said Teller's fear and distrust of the Russians bordered on paranoia. He said, "I became acquainted with his politics very early and found that even during the period of late 1945, when the glow over U.S.-Soviet relations was rather widespread, he already at that time expressed extreme apprehension about the Soviets and great concern over their growing military strength and their imperialistic tendencies."

Teller credited George Gamow, his associate at George Washington University, with initiating the theoretical work in the United States that ultimately led to the biggest man-made explosion. Teller discussed this during one of our Washington Hotel interviews. This one was conducted over a dinner of coq au vin in the rooftop restaurant of the hotel. As darkness fell over the nation's capital, we looked down on the floodlit Treasury Building next to the White House.

During their association at George Washington University, Teller and Gamow concluded that hydrogen, the lightest of the elements, offered the best hope for thermonuclear reaction. The element was found to be abundant in the stars and the sun. And because it contained only one electron, its single electrical charge would be less likely to repel other nuclei. In the spring of 1938, Gamow used the subject to attract the cream of theoretical physicists to his conference at George Washington. A few months later, Gamow, Bethe, and Charles Critchfield, a former Teller student, published a paper on what reactions kept the stars going.

Teller referred to the subject of thermonuclear reactions as "Gamow's game" but said Bethe made the major contribution to it. "Bethe's work was most remarkable. He made a systematic study of every conceivable thermonuclear reaction, cataloged all of the meager experimental data of that time, and made some marvelously enlightened guesses about nuclear reactions that had not yet been proven in experiments. His treatment was so complete that nothing useful could be added to his work during the next decade. Bethe proved himself the champion at Gamow's game."[6]

A casual first-time meeting with a little old woman in 1948 was to exert a profound influence on Teller's involvement in the development of the H-bomb, and, therefore, on the rest of his life. The meeting took place in the Temple Emanu-El in New York, a house of worship so well known among American Jews that it is referred to simply as The Synagogue. His appearance in a synagogue was a rarity for Teller. As noted earlier, for most of his life he was not a practicing Jew. Another notable point was that this appearance was made not as a worshiper but as a speaker on behalf of the United World Federalists. Teller later broke with the organization. He told us he found it to be "unrealistic," and he preferred the approach of the Atlantic Union, which he described as trying "to have a more moderate aim of pulling together advanced democracies instead of trying to mix fire and water or red and blue."

Teller's speech at the synagogue was preceded by an exchange of amenities, with the rabbi serving as their host, an interlude highlighting the fact that Mici Teller, although of Jewish ancestry, had been raised as a Christian in Hungary and was even less aware of Jewish religious tradition than her husband. "Mici displayed remarkable unfamiliarity about everything connected with the synagogue," Teller recalled, "and the rabbi was visibly scandalized."

After he spoke, in order to accept the greetings and congratulations of his audience, Teller moved to the foot of the bimah, the platform from which he had spoken and from which the Torah, or scroll of Jewish law, is read during religious services. Among those coming forward was the little old woman, who not only congratulated Teller but had a question for him. "She asked me what I thought of the Atomic Energy Commission, which was then still quite newly established," said Teller. "I told her the AEC was very important and very hopeful, and I was glad it was established. She said this was very nice to hear because her son was working for the Atomic Energy Commission and she was worried about whether he was doing the right thing."

Asked whether he would like to meet the son, Teller politely assured her that he would. Within moments the concerned but proud mother was back with her son in tow. He was Lewis Strauss, a charter member of the AEC. For both him and Edward Teller it was the beginning of a lifelong friendship and an alliance that was to carry them through many rugged political battles.

They had little in common. Although both were identified as Jews,

Teller's religious observance in early life was confined mostly to the more important holidays. He spoke of feeling "comfortable" in a synagogue, but his attendance was infrequent. By contrast, Strauss was an Orthodox Jew who prayed twice daily. (Years after their meeting, Teller confessed to us a feeling that "Lewis was disappointed that I did not share his deep religious commitment.") From boyhood on, Teller often preferred intellectual isolation to gregarious fellowship. His disposition as a loner prepared him well for the life of a scholar but not for a career in commerce. By contrast, Strauss entered the business world as a traveling shoe salesman and rose to great wealth as an investment banker with the New York firm of Kuhn Loeb, in which he eventually became a partner. What could have been a career setback early in his employment with Kuhn Loeb turned out to be an advantage for Strauss. One Friday shortly before sundown, Strauss was given a messenger's assignment requiring a subway ride to another part of town. This would have violated the Orthodox Jewish prohibition against riding on the sabbath. Strauss began clearing out his desk in preparation for the dismissal he expected because he felt unable to carry out his assignment. At this moment a senior partner of the firm came on the scene and asked for an explanation. After hearing Strauss out, he assured the young employee that his religious dedication would be respected. The delivery was assigned to someone else, and the incident, combined with his talent for finance, marked Strauss for rapid rise in the firm.[7] By the age of thirty, he was a multimillionaire.

Throughout his career Strauss maintained a keen interest in scientific and government affairs. Because of his own intellectual curiosity and his awareness of the potential link between scientific developments and business opportunities, Strauss occasionally helped fund the work of financially strapped scientists. Among these beneficiaries was Leo Szilard, who frequently reported to Strauss on developments unfolding in physics. After Bohr's announcement on January 26, 1939, that the atomic nucleus had been split, Szilard wrote to Strauss: "This is entirely unexpected and exciting news for the average physicist. The Department of Physics at Princeton [where Szilard was visiting at the time] was like a stirred ant heap."[8]

In World War II, Strauss joined the naval reserve as assistant to the chief of the Naval Bureau of Ordnance. By the end of the war, he had risen to the rank of rear admiral. President Truman appointed him to the AEC in 1946. Even then Strauss shared Edward Teller's distrust of the Soviet leadership. At a meeting of the AEC in April 1947, Strauss presented a memorandum questioning whether the Manhattan District Intelligence Division was monitoring the upper stratosphere for evidence of radioactivity. Contrary to the belief expressed by many of his colleagues in and out of the defense establishment, he did not think it would take the Soviets years to build a nuclear weapon. He proposed the monitoring of air samples as a means of detecting their progress in this field.

On September 15, 1947, Gen. Dwight Eisenhower, as chief of staff, ordered the air force to establish and operate such a system, and it was put into operation in the spring of 1948.

This was the year Soviet troops invaded Czechoslovakia. Tension grew when, in April 1948, the Soviets blockaded the corridors to West Berlin and the Americans and their allies countered with a massive airlift. Also in the same year, Alger Hiss, a former State Department official, was accused of passing department secrets to the Soviets. The Cold War was a reality, and many Americans favored more cautious dealings with the Soviets. Strauss and Edward Teller were among them.

Still, the growing international tensions appeared to have little effect in accelerating work on the next stage of nuclear weapons—the hydrogen bomb. Strauss and Kenneth Nichols, General Groves's deputy on the Manhattan Project, were reported to have joined in recommending that only the current level of effort be maintained in the thermonuclear program.[9] At that time, there was sound basis for their recommendation. The atomic bomb, although still being modified to make it more compact and easier to deliver, was already a fact. The hydrogen bomb was still only a gleam in Teller's eye.

But a convergence of several unrelated events changed all this and swept the nation into an accelerated H-bomb program. One of these events was Harry Truman's surprising victory over Thomas E. Dewey in the 1948 presidential election. Another was the return of the Democratic party to control of Congress in the same election, elevating Connecticut Senator Brien McMahon to the chairmanship of the Joint Committee on Atomic Energy. Still another was McMahon's offering a staff position to William Liscum Borden, author of a book suggesting the development of nuclear-armed long-range rockets.[10]

All this produced a political chemistry favorable to Teller's proposal. Truman, after becoming president on the death of Franklin Roosevelt and then being tagged by major election pollsters as an almost certain loser in his bid for a full term, had won and now began his own administration with a reservoir of experience in dealing with the Soviets as both ally and Cold War adversary. McMahon shared Teller's conviction that it would be foolhardy to abandon the U.S. weapons program in the face of a Soviet buildup. Borden, who was to bring heavy influence to bear on the work of the committee, concurred.

But the catalyst for this political chemistry was supplied by the air force B-29s flying air-sampling missions as a result of Strauss's recommendation and Eisenhower's order. On or about August 29, 1949, a patrol over Japan picked up samples that revealed traces of radioactivity. Analysis showed them to be a by-product of an atomic explosion. Since there had been no American nuclear testing, the message seemed clear: After only four years, the U.S. monopoly on nuclear fission was over.[11]

Truman held on to a shred of doubt and hoped that the evidence had been produced by an atomic accident, but he moved quickly. He appointed a committee of scientists, chaired by Vannevar Bush,* to examine the evidence. In short order, it reported that the Soviets had indeed exploded a nuclear bomb.[12] The USSR had joined the club.

On September 23, Truman issued a statement that reflected his personal skepticism. "I believe that the American people, to the fullest extent consistent with national security, are entitled to be informed of all developments in the atomic energy field," he said. "We have evidence that in recent weeks an atomic explosion occurred in the USSR."

As the statement indicated, Truman was not convinced that the Soviets had actually exploded a bomb. "I am not convinced that the Russians have the bomb," he wrote. "I am not convinced that the Russians have achieved the know-how to put the complicated mechanism together to make an A-bomb work."[13]

Teller did not share Truman's doubt. He knew the Soviets had a group of top-notch physicists and mathematicians. He had read many of their papers and was impressed by their excellence.

Teller's apprehension was shared by other scientists. A few days after Truman's announcement, the subject was being discussed by three veterans of the A-bomb project at the Faculty Club on the Berkeley campus, Luis Alvarez, Ernest O. Lawrence, and Wendell Latimer. With the A-bomb at hand, they agreed, the Soviets seemed certain to take the next logical step and develop the H-bomb. They expressed fear that the U.S. nuclear weapons effort was foundering.[14]

The Berkeley group met at Los Alamos shortly thereafter with Teller, who confirmed their impression that the program was stagnant. But Teller said he was optimistic that if given approval and an adequate supply of tritium it could move forward.

The news about Soviet progress also worried Strauss, and he said so in an October 5, 1949, memorandum to his fellow members of the AEC. "It

---

* Bush had just completed a book predicting that the Soviets would not be ready to test an atomic bomb within ten years. The book, *Modern Arms and Free Men*, was already being printed; the presses were stopped to enable the author to revise the manuscript accordingly.

seems to me that the time has come for . . . intensive effort to get ahead with the super," he said. "By an intensive effort I am thinking of a commitment in talent and money comparable, if necessary, to that which produced the first atomic weapon."

Strauss then recommended that the AEC consult its General Advisory Committee (GAC) for its opinion on "how we can proceed with expedition."[15] This carried an assumption that the committee would support his recommendation. He was wrong.

Latimer learned this while trying to drum up support for the recommendation. He contacted AEC Commissioner Gordon Dean and chemists Kenneth Pitzer and Charles C. Lawritsen in Washington. Then he spoke in Chicago to chemists Willard Libby and Harold Urey. At first the general response seemed positive. But within a few weeks the wind began to change. "There had been a lot of back pressure built up, I think primarily from the General Advisory Committee," Latimer said. "We very quickly were aware of the fact that the General Advisory Committee was opposed."[16]

Alvarez reported in his personal journal that the campaign to build the reactor got off to a good start on October 8, 1949. He recorded favorable meetings with Robert LeBaron, then deputy secretary of defense for atomic affairs, AEC administrator Ralph Johnson, Senator McMahon, and Rep. Carl Hinshaw, among others.

But when they also visited AEC Chairman David Lilienthal, they were shocked. Lilienthal was plainly hostile.

"He did not even want to talk about the program," Alvarez said. "He turned his chair around and looked out the window and indicated that he did not want even to discuss the matter."[17]

Lilienthal also kept a journal. For June 24, 1953, he wrote:

> . . . the issue was what to do about the fact that the Russians had exploded an atomic weapon. One view was that we should make an all-out effort to make . . . an H-bomb. . . . Another item on the program for testing at that time was a more efficient and much more powerful fission bomb. The question I raised before the final meeting of the NSC [National Security Council] Special Committee was: . . . Is this the best way to protect the security of the country? I urged that before we committed ourselves further to what had proved to be a "wasting asset" of super-bombs, we re-examine our whole national policy. . . . In an early memorandum to the President, I expressed my views [at the same time that a majority of the AEC's General Advisory Committee expressed their disapproval for an all-out H-bomb program] in which I stressed the adverse political implications of going

forward along this line, as increasing our emphasis on super-bombs as a policy for world peace.[18]

Although Lilienthal's reception was cold, Alvarez and Lawrence were encouraged by the other four commissioners to proceed. They also came away from a meeting with I. I. Rabi convinced that he supported them.

The next day, October 12, 1949, Alvarez was back in Berkeley, recruiting scientists and engineers. Among those signed up were Don Cooksey, associate director of the University of California Radiation Laboratory; William Brobeck, assistant director and chief engineer of the laboratory; Nobel laureates Edwin McMillan and Glenn Seaborg, and a half-dozen other outstanding scientists.[19]

Although President Truman had announced detection of the Soviet tests more than two weeks earlier, a veil of secrecy hung over much of the discussion among scientists and political leaders on the subject of a stepped-up U.S. nuclear-fusion program. But on October 16, 1949, the veil was ripped away by columnist Drew Pearson, who reported that such a move was being considered. This was followed by more intense lobbying by activists on both sides of the issue, including Teller, in preparation for a meeting of President Truman with the members of the GAC two weeks later.

The critical player in the drama turned out to be Oppenheimer, then chairman of the powerful GAC. Another major role was played by James B. Conant, president of Harvard University. Without the support of either, the program was in trouble. Both were vigorously opposed. Oppenheimer set the tone on October 21, 1949, in a letter addressing Conant as "Dear Uncle Jim."

We are exploring the possibilities for our talk with the President on October 30. . . . Many of us will do some preliminary palavering on the 28th. . . .

On the technical side, as far as I can tell, the Super is not very different from what it was when we first spoke of it more than seven years ago, a weapon of unknown design, cost, deliverability and military value. But a great change has taken place in the climate of opinion. On the one hand two experienced promoters have been at work, i.e., Ernest Lawrence and Edward Teller. The project has long been dear to Teller's heart, and Ernest has convinced himself that we must learn from Operation Joe [the Russian explosion] that the Russians will soon do the Super and that we had better beat them to it.

But the real development has not been of a technical nature. Ernest spoke to Knowland [Sen. William F. Knowland of California] and McMahon, and to some at least of the Joint Chiefs. The Joint Congressional Committee, having tried to find something tangible to chew on ever since September 23rd, has at last found its answers. We must have a Super and we must have it fast. . . . The Joint Chiefs appear informally to have decided to give the development of the Super overriding priority. . . . The climate of opinion among the competent physicists also shows signs of shifting. . . .

What concerns me is really not the technical problem. I am not sure the miserable thing will work, nor that it can be gotten to a target except by ox cart. . . . What does worry me is that this appears to have caught the imagination, both of Congressional and of military people, as the answer to the problem posed by the Russian advance. It would be folly to oppose the exploration of this weapon. We have always known it had to be done, and it does have to be done, though it appears to be singularly proof against any form of experimental approach. But that we become committed to it as the way to save the country and the peace appears to me full of danger.

We will be faced with all this at our meeting; and anything that we do or do not say to the president will have to take it into consideration. . . .[20]

Oppenheimer's frustration as revealed in his letter to Conant suggests that on political grounds he realized he was facing a losing battle. It was true, as he noted, that little progress had been made on the H-bomb in the last seven years. But he ignored the point that it was because of inadequate support that almost no work had been done on the project during that period.

Teller seldom missed an opportunity to deplore this lack of commitment. During the Oppenheimer security hearings, he was asked about this by the AEC's counsel, Roger Robb.

"Doctor, it has been suggested here that the ultimate success on the thermonuclear was the result of a brilliant discovery or invention by you, and that might or might not have taken five or ten years. What can you say about that?"

"I think it was neither a great achievement nor a brilliant one," Teller replied. "It just had to be done. I must say it was not completely easy. There were some pitfalls. But I do believe that if the original plan in Los Alamos, namely, that the laboratory with such excellent people like Fermi and Bethe and others would have gone after the problem, probably some of these people would have either the same idea or another one much sooner. In that case, we would have had the bomb in 1947."[21]

Although both sides agreed that development of the bomb was retarded by Hans Bethe's ultimate decision to withhold his services, the reason for his decision, especially whether it was influenced by Oppenheimer, remained in doubt. As Bethe recalled during the Oppenheimer hearings,

Teller visited him at Cornell in October 1949 and urged him to join the H-bomb team at Los Alamos.

"At the time Teller visited me, I had great internal conflict about what I should do," Bethe said.

"Dr. Teller was presenting to me some ideas . . . which seemed to make technically more feasible one phase of the thermonuclear program. I was quite impressed with his ideas. On the other hand, it seemed to me it was a terrible undertaking to develop a still bigger bomb, and I was entirely undecided and had long discussions with my wife."[22]

Bethe offered more detail on this point in a November 1973 interview.

"It seemed to me then and it seems to me now that it was the wrong thing to do, that we should not have escalated," he said. "It seems to me now very clear that we should have developed the atomic bomb during the war when we had a desperate situation with the Nazis. But in 1949 vis-à-vis the Russians we still held all the cards, and we still held the card of greater production, greater delivery capability of the nuclear weapons. So I think the right direction would have been to say no, we are not going to do it. We may do some further research on it, but let's not make it a crash program. . . .

"So Edward and I were on opposite sides of this point and remained so for a long time to come," Bethe continued.

". . . Edward won the battle by enlisting first the Joint Congressional Committee on Atomic Energy, then some of the Atomic Energy commissioners, and, in the end, of course, President Truman gave the order to pursue."

Teller's version differed from Bethe's. He said that Bethe actually agreed "after a somewhat strenuous discussion" to join the team at Los Alamos and that Oppenheimer played a significant role in Bethe's later decision not to go.

As Teller expected, the GAC, at the late October meeting cited by Oppenheimer in his letter to Conant, unanimously voted to recommend against a crash program to produce an H-bomb.

"We all hope that by one means or another the development of these weapons can be avoided," the committee said. "We are reluctant to see the United States take the initiative in precipitating this development. We are all agreed that it would be wrong to commit ourselves to an all-out effort towards its development."[23]

It was the end of an important round, and Teller had lost it.

Chapter 11

POLITICS AND THE H-BOMB

On Harry Truman's scale of decision, the unanimous recommendation of the GAC weighed heavily. Considerable weight also was given to the AEC vote adopting that recommendation, even though it was split, 3–2. As expected, Lewis Strauss was in the minority of the AEC vote. Also as expected, he lobbied vigorously to have the recommendation rejected in favor of an all-out push for the hydrogen bomb.

In this he joined a powerful alliance that included Sen. Brien McMahon, members of McMahon's Joint Committee on Atomic Energy, and top officials in the Departments of Defense and State. Unnoticed by a public still occupied by peacetime transition, a fierce battle was waged behind the scenes for three months by scientists and politicians on both sides of the issue. In the end, an originally perplexed President Truman had gathered enough information and confidence to decide that despite the recommendations of the commission and its advisory committee a top-priority bomb program was the right choice.

When asked more than two decades later to identify those most influential in helping Truman shape his decision, Teller offered three names: "Brien McMahon, Lewis Strauss—and Klaus Fuchs." He also could have added himself to that group without inviting contradiction, for the part Teller played was significant.

The roles of McMahon and Strauss, as well as Teller's, were obvious to those involved in the debate. But Fuchs was not even in the United States while the debate raged or when it was resolved. As one of the British physicists recruited to the Allied war effort, he had spent more than two years at Los Alamos working on the mysteries of nuclear fission as his contribution to the defeat of the Nazis. Only after his return to England and his assumption of lofty academic status there was he unmasked as a veteran Soviet spy who had become intimate with the deepest secrets of the

Anglo-American nuclear weapons program and had been relaying them to Moscow.

That revelation shocked the intelligence and scientific communities of the English-speaking world. It also erased whatever doubt Harry Truman might still have harbored about whether to press forward with the super-bomb program.

Much of the raw material for his decision began taking shape October 29, 1949, when the GAC met in Washington. As Robert Oppenheimer saw it, the purpose of that meeting was to discuss whether the AEC was "doing what it ought to be doing" and, more specifically, whether a crash H-bomb program was "what it ought to be doing."[1]

Glenn Seaborg, professor of chemistry at the University of California, was traveling in Sweden and was the only absentee from the meeting. Besides Oppenheimer, the participating GAC members were Harvard President James B. Conant; Enrico Fermi, the Nobel Prize–winning Italian physicist; I. I. Rabi, then chairman of physics at Columbia; Lee A. DuBridge, president of Caltech; Hartley Rowe, vice-president and chief engineer of the United Fruit Company; Cyril S. Smith, director of the Institute for the Study of Metals at the University of Chicago; and Oliver E. Buckley, president of Bell Telephone Laboratories.

Joining them for a preliminary phase of the meeting were the five members of the AEC and a panel of advisers. Among these was George F. Kennan, veteran State Department official, who assessed how the recently disclosed nuclear test might affect international relations. Also participating were leaders of the armed forces, including Gen. Omar N. Bradley, chairman of the Joint Chiefs of Staff. They discussed military aspects of the Soviet action.

When the briefing ended, all but the GAC members left the room, and the committee then launched its own discussion. It began with Fermi's coverage of technical questions involved in the H-bomb program. As Fermi later recalled, he saw the chances of success as "of somewhat better than an even probability . . . In other words, it was not a foregone conclusion by any means. . . . On the other hand, it was to be expected that perhaps just with development and some amount of technical luck, the thing might be pulled through."

As each of the others expressed his views, it became clear that the main concern of all was not the technical aspects of hydrogen bomb development but the ethical and moral questions.

Fermi wondered whether an international agreement should be sought to ban the hydrogen bomb. "My opinion at that time," he later said, "was that one should try to outlaw the thing before it was born."[2]

Hartley Rowe, the United Fruit official, had thought of the atomic bomb as merely another weapon of war. But the hydrogen bomb was more than a military weapon. It was an instrument of death for entire populations. "You are using it against civilization and not just against the military," he said. "I don't like to see women and children killed wholesale because the male elements of the human race are so stupid that they can't get out of war and keep out of war."[3]

Rabi joined in condemning the H-bomb project on moral grounds and in arguing that the United States should not initiate such a program.

In one respect the GAC meeting was a throwback to the pre–Los Alamos discussions held by theoretical physicists, especially the freewheeling Berkeley conference frequently mentioned by Teller, a lively affair unrestricted by time pressures or compartmentalized responsibilities. The GAC discussion ran on for three days before producing the unanimous recommendation against an H-bomb crash program.

To many, especially Edward Teller, one of the most striking features of the report was this sentence:

"We are reluctant to see the United States take the initiative in precipitating this development."

This theme, recurring throughout the discussion before its embodiment in the GAC report, seemed to assume not only that the Soviets had yet to begin their own thermonuclear-weapon program but that they would not begin unless and until the United States did so.

Fermi and Rabi were so emphatic on this point that even while agreeing with the majority on the basic recommendation they issued a separate report. They said:

> The fact that no limit exists to the destructiveness of this weapon makes its very existence and the knowledge of its construction a danger to humanity as a whole. For these reasons, we believe it is important for the President of the United States to tell the American people and the world that we think it wrong on fundamental ethical principles to *initiate* the development of such a weapon.

Teller questioned the statement about unlimited destructiveness. "It is possible for scientists even as talented as Rabi and Fermi to be wrong," he told us in a 1987 interview. "The fact is that there is a finite limit to the destructive power of a thermonuclear explosion." On the same subject, he gave the following description, which suggests a cork-and-bottle effect:

> A very big explosive blows the atmosphere within a diameter of ten miles into space. With a further increase in the size of the explosive, practically the same mass of air will be blown into space at a higher velocity. The lateral

effects along the ground expand to an exceedingly small extent. Thus, further escalation in the power of the explosive is ineffectual and useless.[4]

The GAC had barely finished its work before Oppenheimer met with Secretary of State Dean Acheson on October 31, 1949, to brief him on the report. Acheson was mystified. Discussing Oppenheimer's message later with his chief advisor on nuclear matters, he said, "You know, I listened as carefully as I know how, but I don't understand what Oppie is trying to say. How can you persuade a hostile adversary to disarm 'by example'?"[5]

Teller met McMahon in Washington a few days after the advisory committee meeting and found him still livid. "I read this report and it just makes me sick," McMahon said. He vowed that he would do his utmost to get approval of the thermonuclear bomb project.[6]

As one of his first steps, McMahon wrote the president a letter directly appealing for approval of the project. He said he could see no moral difference between the use of one large weapon or a batch of smaller ones if the end results were equally lethal and destructive. In the absence of foolproof inspection, no agreement with the Soviet Union to outlaw the H-bomb would be reliable. And if the Soviets developed the superbomb first, the United States would face unlimited danger and harassment.[7]

That November was a busy month for the pro-thermonuclear forces. Hoping to blunt the effect of the GAC recommendation to the AEC, Lewis Strauss proposed that the commission sound out the Defense and State departments before voting on the issue. This, he suggested, would give the commission a broader overview and make its recommendation more effective. The AEC rejected his suggestion.[8] It then not only split 3–2 in adopting the GAC report but issued seven documents—a majority report, a minority report, and an explanatory statement by each of its five members. Chairman David Lilienthal, Sumner Pike, and Henry DeWolfe Smyth composed the majority. Strauss and Gordon Dean were the minority. Smyth urged that the United States propose an agreement with the Soviet Union to outlaw the bomb and that the AEC postpone its recommendation until this was done.

By November 10, the president, still groping for an answer, decided to get additional counsel from Defense and State department leaders. Inevitably, the infighting grew more intense.

Strauss and McMahon agreed on a strategy meeting at Strauss's hotel room in Beverly Hills, California. Joining them was William Liscum Borden, McMahon's right-hand man and executive director of the Joint Committee on Atomic Energy. Then McMahon and Borden stopped off at Los Alamos for a November meeting with a group of scientists led by Teller.

The scientists had now received copies of the GAC report and were urged to read it closely in preparation for the meeting. Teller found it ironic:

> The GAC report seemed to state the conflict rather bluntly. "As long as you people work very hard and diligently to make a better atomic bomb, you are doing a fine job; but if you succeed in making real progress toward another kind of nuclear explosion, you are doing something immoral." To this the scientists reacted psychologically. They got mad. And their attention was [drawn] toward the thermonuclear bomb, not away from it.[9]

Teller said many of the younger Los Alamos scientists especially resented the report.

On the afternoon of the Los Alamos meeting with McMahon and Borden, Teller presented a technical overview of the bomb, emphasizing that it was still theoretical. There was no experimental basis for concluding that nuclear fusion could be produced on earth, and none could be assumed until it was demonstrated. He drew up a schedule calling for the first attempted demonstration in 1951. As Fermi had estimated before the GAC, Teller told the Los Alamos group there was a slightly better than even chance that the bomb could be built.

Until this stage, deliberations on the program were conducted behind a heavy curtain of secrecy. Some reporters had picked up hints of the controversy but were persuaded that breaking the story at that time could jeopardize national security. For example, Alfred Friendly of the *Washington Post* checked out such a lead with AEC chairman David Lilienthal and, warned that disclosure could weaken national security, withheld publication. But three days after the Los Alamos meeting, Sen. Erwin C. Johnson, a Colorado Democrat, broke the secret. Discussing the nation's military preparedness in a nationally televised interview, he mentioned not only an atomic bomb six times more powerful than the one that destroyed much of Nagasaki but a superbomb one thousand times as powerful. The *Post* duly reported it on November 18.

On the same day, with pressure building for issuance of some official policy statement, President Truman called a meeting of a special committee of the NSC. Its members were Secretary of Defense Louis Johnson, Secretary of State Acheson, and AEC chairman Lilienthal. Truman asked them to assess the proposal for an H-bomb crash program on the basis of political, military, and technical factors. In this process, the Joint Chiefs of Staff were also consulted. They replied that the bomb could deter war. But they added that the United States could not tolerate a situation in which only the Soviet Union had the bomb.

A similar note had been sounded by Karl T. Compton, then chairman of the Research and Development Board of the Department of Defense. "Until an adequate international solution is worked out," he said in a November 9 letter to the president, "it seems to me that our own national security and the protection of the type of civilization which we value require us to proceed. . . ."[10]

Throughout the debate, Teller served as scientific adviser to McMahon and Strauss. After Teller's presentation at the Los Alamos meeting, McMahon again wrote the president, saying, "If we let the Russians get the Super first, catastrophe becomes all but certain—whereas, if we get there first, there exists a chance of saving ourselves."[11]

Strauss also stepped up his campaign. In a November 9 letter to the president, he sounded an urgent note.

"I believe that the United States must be as completely armed as any possible enemy," he said. "I recommend that the President direct the Atomic Energy Commission to proceed with the development of the thermonuclear bomb at highest priority. . . ."

In an accompanying memorandum, Strauss argued that the weapon was scientifically feasible, that the Soviet Union had the technical competence to produce an H-bomb, and that "a government of atheists is not likely to be dissuaded from producing the weapon on moral grounds."

By mid-January public awareness of the debate had increased to a point making the need for a policy statement almost impossible to ignore much longer. Drew Pearson, a leading syndicated columnist and commentator, outlined the issue in a radio broadcast on January 15, 1950. Two days later, James Reston gave a detailed account of the debate in a *New York Times* front-page report.

Also by then, the tide had turned against the GAC report and the AEC recommendation.

Whatever doubt remained was dissolved by the discovery that Klaus Fuchs, one of the most distinguished and knowledgeable scientists engaged for years in the U.S.-British nuclear bomb program, had been spying for the Soviet Union all along. The news was especially shocking to a Fuchs friend and Los Alamos colleague who abhorred communism, Edward Teller.

Born in Germany as the son of a Lutheran minister who was also a liberal Quaker, Klaus embraced communism as a young man and fled to England in 1933 after Hitler came to power. Earning his doctorate at Bristol University, he survived British security screening and joined the nuclear research team under Rudolph Peierls, also a German-born physicist. He swore allegiance to the king, signed the Official Secrets Act, was sworn in as a naturalized British citizen, and almost immediately enlisted in the

Soviet spy apparatus. From then until his arrest seven years later, he funneled to Moscow priceless secrets gathered from his work on nuclear weapons programs in England, New York, and Los Alamos.

Fuchs later estimated that his service to the Soviets shaved several years from the time they needed to produce a hydrogen bomb.[12] In 1950, he was arrested, confessed, and was charged not with treason but, because the Soviet Union was a British ally at the time of his espionage activity, with communicating information of possibly ultimate value to an enemy. He was given the maximum sentence of fourteen years, served nine, and immediately left for East Germany. There he was appointed deputy director of the East German Control Institute for Nuclear Research.

New evidence of his role in accelerating the Soviet atomic and hydrogen bomb programs came in October 1987, when Andrei Sakharov publicly acknowledged his contributions.

While at Los Alamos, Fuchs was often a guest at the Teller apartment. Edward and Mici remembered him as very pleasant company. Fuchs himself described the period as the happiest of his life. Teller later recalled:

> He was by no means an introvert, but he was a quiet man. I rather liked him.
> . . . As a full-fledged member of the British team at Los Alamos, he was entitled to know everything we were doing. . . . He talked with me and others frequently in depth about our intensive efforts to produce an atom bomb. It was easy and pleasant to discuss my work with him. He also made impressive contributions and I learned many technical facts from him. . . .
> Fuchs was popular at Los Alamos because he was kind, helpful, and much interested in the work of others.[13]

A strong thread of rationalization ran through Teller's discussion of Fuchs.

"I neither defend nor excuse Fuchs's spying," he said. "But I am convinced that he spied because he thought he was doing the right thing for the country and for the political philosophy that commanded his allegiance."

Fuchs spied not for love of money but for love of country, even though it was someone else's country. He received only token amounts—the highest was $400—for his services. Teller was oddly contemptuous of the Soviets for sullying Fuchs's amateur status with such niggardly rewards. "In the sordid story of Fuchs's spying," he said, "this payment was the most shameful episode."[14]

Disclosure of the Fuchs case capped the presidential decision-making exercise that had begun with the GAC recommendations four months before his confession. On January 31, 1950, four days after U.S. officials received word of the confession, the president's ad hoc committee of the

NSC met in the old State Department Building to draft its recommendation. Lilienthal again pressed for a delay during which the nation's defense policy could be reassessed. Defense Secretary Johnson and Secretary of State Acheson disagreed. Shortly after noon, at a meeting with the president in his office, the committee members repeated their arguments.

Truman did not deny the desirability of time for a policy reassessment. But in light of Senator Johnson's televised statement and increasing public demand for clarification, he said, such time was not available. When the meeting ended, a press conference was called for that afternoon, and a statement from the president was distributed. It cited the president's responsibility as commander in chief of the armed forces to prepare the nation for defense "against any possible aggressor."

"Accordingly," Truman said, "I have directed the Atomic Energy Commission to continue its work on all forms of atomic weapons, including the so-called hydrogen or superbomb."

Chapter 12

Science and the H-Bomb

The president's announcement of a go-ahead on the hydrogen bomb pleased few and displeased many. Despite this fulfillment of his long-standing hope that Truman would decide in favor of the thermonuclear (hydrogen bomb) program, even Edward Teller was among the displeased.

Truman's statement said he had directed the AEC to "continue" its work on all forms of atomic weapons, including the H-bomb. Like many opponents of the project itself, Teller considered this to be dishonest. Whether intentionally or not, it was an exaggeration and was certain to result in widespread misunderstanding about the prospects of success for the project.

"He gave the impression that we could produce a hydrogen bomb simply by tightening a few screws," Teller later wrote.

"Actually, work had not begun. We had eight years of thermonuclear fantasies, theories, and calculations behind us, but we had established no connection between theory and reality. We needed a thermonuclear test."[1]

Opponents complained on two counts, and I. I. Rabi voiced both of them. One was an echo of Teller's complaint that it was dishonest to ignore the distinct possibility that the bomb could never be built. The other was that regardless of this the announcement was certain to spur the Soviet Union to greater effort in its own nuclear program.

As the dean of American physics and a great contributor to the scientific achievements that made Allied victory possible in World War II, Rabi commanded respect in political and academic circles. But his criticism was aimed primarily at Teller and Ernest Lawrence, not at Truman. He suggested that these two powerful scientists had misled the military and the Congressional Joint Committee on Atomic Energy and thereby had forced Truman's hand.

"They had done an awful thing," an outraged Rabi told us in an interview at his office at Columbia University. ". . . Teller was going for it at all costs. It became doubtful that this thing would work or that it would be a weapon."[2]

Rabi insisted that Teller's actions were based on "faith that somehow this could be made to work" and helped shape a presidential decision "founded on a complete fallacy."

He said, "It really constituted for a time, I thought, an extreme danger to the United States."

How would he define that danger? "To lay down a challenge to the Soviet Union," he said.

Truman's decision was neither hasty nor intentionally deceptive. In the announcement itself he referred to a 1945 declaration in which the United States, Great Britain, and Canada had emphasized that "no single nation could in fact have a monopoly of atomic weapons." In his memoirs Truman also made clear that he fully understood the uncertain status of research on the thermonuclear project at the time of his announcement. He wrote:

> By the early fall of 1949 development of the "super"—the thermonuclear or hydrogen—bomb had progressed to the point *where we were almost ready to put our theories into practice*. I believed that anything that would assure us the lead in the field of atomic energy development for defense had to be tried out. *(Italics added.)*

But he also recognized "a most complicated and baffling problem": How much of its personnel and material resources should the AEC invest in an early test to determine whether the H-bomb would work? Uranium, already tagged for use in production of tried and proven atomic bombs, would have to be diverted.

Truman said:

> Everything pertaining to the hydrogen bomb was at this time still in the realm of the uncertain. It was all theory and assumption. Even the scientists and the commission were divided. And, in addition, the questions with which we were concerned related not only to matters of scientific knowledge but also to our defense strategy and our foreign policy. All of these had to be weighed.[3]

The president's statement, then, was not intended to authorize a full-scale effort but a quickening of the pace at which the H-bomb program was then plodding along.[4]

But the intended distinction between a stepped-up pace on a raw research program and a resolve to "continue" a program nearing completion was lost on media and masses alike. It also provoked Teller's critics and touched off a new round of infighting.

This time the issue was how the president's decision would be implemented. The longer this remained in doubt, the more resistance Teller could anticipate in recruiting the talent and skill needed to push the program forward. The ranks of nuclear weapons scientists involved in the nuclear weapons program at Los Alamos and Berkeley were depleted at Los Alamos shortly after the surrender of Japan. Many had left their wartime laboratories when the threat ended. In the Chicago lab, the military had ordered a cutback in personnel even earlier, shortly after the historic experiment at the Stagg Field grandstand.

Illustrating Teller's recruitment problem was that by 1946 only three scientists working on the thermonuclear projects held postgraduate degrees.

One of his more valuable allies in the effort to move the program off dead center was Robert LeBaron, a Princeton graduate in chemistry and physics who was now deputy to the secretary of defense for atomic energy and chairman of the Military Liaison Committee of the AEC. This committee, like the Congressional Joint Committee on Atomic Energy, was part of the oversight apparatus on nuclear matters. It was charged with keeping the AEC informed about atomic energy activities of the Defense Department. In turn, the commission was required to keep the committee informed of its activities related to military matters.

On a key issue, LeBaron also found himself at odds with Sumner Pike, then acting chairman of the AEC. At an AEC meeting on February 2, 1950, in discussing the implementation of the president's decision, Pike declared that the commission should determine whether construction of the bomb was possible. If so, the Defense Department should then be asked to determine the scale of the program.

LeBaron questioned whether the military should be excluded from judging the feasibility of a weapon it might be called upon to use. He proposed that the Pentagon and the AEC collaborate on the development and testing, and insisted that the commission be responsible for making available enough tritium to test the bomb and to launch production of a combat-ready model.[5]

Such a power struggle between two government agencies was not unusual, but it was played against a background of deep-seated distrust. LeBaron was sensitive to the fact that the commission's chief scientific adviser was Oppenheimer. The hearings that were to result in the withdrawal of Oppenheimer's security clearance still lay ahead, but LeBaron was already aware that throughout Oppenheimer's involvement in the Los Alamos program serious questions had been raised about his loyalty.

At one point in the AEC meeting, Pike asked whether the military "had actually established a requirement for a nuclear weapon." Since the military had pushed for a thermonuclear program, it seemed logical that some specific use had been considered.

"Not yet," LeBaron said. But the Pentagon was analyzing the thermonuclear program to determine its cost and its possible effect on the ongoing fission, or atomic-bomb, program.[6]

Such groping by the military to determine its requirements in the midst of revolutionary scientific developments disturbed Teller. But with his customary drive in projects that interested him, he pressed on with his recruitment effort. Almost immediately, he himself was challenged by a dozen top scientists, including Hans Bethe, who signed a public statement raising the morality issue.

"We believe that no nation has the right to use such a bomb, no matter how righteous its cause," they said. "The bomb is no longer a weapon of war but a means of extermination of whole populations. . . . We urge that the United States . . . make a solemn declaration that we shall never use the bomb first."[7]

Within a few days, the voice of Albert Einstein, dean of the world's scientific community, was added to the chorus of disapproval.

"If [the H-bomb] is successful," he wrote, "radioactive poisoning of the atmosphere and hence annihilation of any life on earth has been brought within the range of technical possibilities. . . . In the end there beckons more and more clearly general annihilation."[8]

Compounding Teller's recruitment problem, Congress was reluctant to provide for the project until it saw evidence that construction of an H-bomb was feasible.

Teller mustered counterarguments. To the politicians he emphasized the Soviet threat. This appeal was particularly effective with McMahon, Strauss, and Borden, who shared Teller's apprehension. To scientists he hammered on the theme that they should not turn their backs on the defense needs of their country and at the same time miss an opportunity to learn more about the cosmos through creation of fusion on this planet.

The strategy worked. The funding logjam was broken, and scientists began trickling back to Los Alamos. Among them was John Wheeler, the longtime collaborator with Niels Bohr and one of the brightest stars in physics. Wheeler had gone back to Princeton after the war and was in France when he was persuaded by Teller and Niels Bohr to return.

If more leaders of the U.S. scientific community had been aware that the Soviets were already at work on the thermonuclear bomb as well as the atomic bomb, would Teller's recruiting job have been so arduous? Probably not. Nevertheless, he managed to round up an effective team. Two of his students, Harris Mayer and John Reitz, signed on early. They were followed by more experienced scientists, such as John Manley, Elizabeth Graves, Marshall G. Holloway, Charles Baker, Egon Bretscher, Frederic de Hoffmann, and Marshall Rosenbluth. Emil Konopinski, one of Teller's colleagues from the Manhattan Project, took a leave of absence from the University of Indiana for another tour at Los Alamos. And, as always, John von Neumann could be counted on for consultation.

Marshall Holloway, a top assistant to Los Alamos director Norris Bradbury, was named to head the team. Its mission was to build an experimental thermonuclear device, transport it to the Pacific, test-fire it, and record the results. The project was code-named Greenhouse.

A basic problem of the Greenhouse team was how to generate enough heat. Thermonuclear reactions in the sun and the stars require temperatures of nearly 20 million degrees Centigrade. Even more was believed necessary for the production of such reactions on earth. Why should this be?

Hans Bethe had an answer.

"The solution to the paradox is as follows: In the stars the nuclear reaction has to proceed slowly, taking a time of the order of ten billion years. In a thermonuclear weapon the reaction must take place fast, taking a time of the order of one billionth of a second. The ratio of these times is about ten-to-the-twenty-sixth-power. In order to make the reaction go fast, one needs much higher temperature than for a slow reaction. In the projected thermonuclear power devices the time for the reaction is not quite as short but perhaps may be of the order of one second. But to compensate for this, the density of the plasma in thermonuclear power producers is perhaps ten-to-the-tenth-power times lower than at the center of the sun."

The magnitude of the problem was further illustrated when the Military Liaison Committee met on February 23, 1950, in Bradbury's office at Los Alamos. To succeed, the scientists needed to fuse the heavier isotopes of hydrogen and thus release energy. An almost limitless supply of one isotope, deuterium, is found in seawater. An economical method of separating it was developed during World War II. But according to scientific theory, the fusion of deuterium nuclei required a temperature of 400 million degrees. This was greater than the temperature generated by a nuclear explosion.[9] Without bridging this gap, a thermonuclear reaction seemed impossible.

But there was reason to hope. Nuclear bombs produced after World War II were more powerful than their primitive predecessors used against Hiroshima and Nagasaki. With the increase in power, they produced more heat and sustained it for a longer period.

Another hydrogen isotope, tritium, would fuse at a lower temperature than its cousin deuterium. What if the two were combined? It was calculated that the deuterium-tritium blend could be fused at a mere 80 million degrees. Tritium, in turn, would create the higher temperatures needed for deuterium to fuse.[10]

Fine, but there was still another problem. Tritium was not found in nature. It had to be created, and doing so was extremely expensive. Bradbury, working under fiscal constraints, was worried. Teller was undaunted. He was convinced that the expense would be justified, and he was willing to try his hand at spreading the conviction where it counted.

Nine days after the Los Alamos meeting of the Military Liaison Committee, he was in Washington, testifying before the Congressional Joint Committee on Atomic Energy. Again he deplored the lost years when practically no work was done on fusion. This lost time must be made up. The scientific community must be persuaded to cooperate. He urged that the United States enlist the talents of scientists in friendly countries.

But the bureaucratic infighting between the AEC and the Department of Defense raged on until March 10, when Truman clarified his earlier directive. In a new order, he assigned the competing agencies well-defined responsibilities. Both the AEC and Defense would jointly plan the production of hydrogen isotopes, but only the AEC would be responsible for quantity production of thermonuclear materials.

To Teller's delight, the order also authorized a "feasibility test" to establish whether the theory of fusion could be demonstrated by experiment. It was the long-awaited green light for Greenhouse.

But as the project shifted into gear, opposition intensified. "Ban the Bomb" signs sprang up across the country. Scientists opposing the project on television panels and campus stages drew huge audiences.

One of the most widely noted discussions was a roundtable featuring Hans Bethe, Leo Szilard, and Frederick Seitz of the University of Pittsburgh. It marked one of the earliest expressions of fear about radiation following a thermonuclear explosion.

Harrison Brown, the moderator, raised the question, "Will dispersal [of population] actually help if H-bombs are used not for blast but for radioactivity?"

"In this case," Szilard answered, "[dispersal] will not help at all."

Bethe then took up the response.

"You are certainly right when you emphasize the radioactivity," he said. "In the H-bomb, neutrons are produced in large numbers. These neutrons will go into the air, and in the air they will make radioactive carbon-14, which is well known to science. This isotope of carbon has a half-life of five thousand years. It may well be that the number of H-bombs will be so large that this will make life impossible."

"Yes," Szilard came back, "that is true, Bethe, but that is not what I had in mind, because it would take a very large number of bombs before life would be in danger from ordinary H-bombs. What I had in mind was this: The H-bomb as it would be made would not cause greater radioactivity than that which is due to carbon; but it is very easy to rig an H-bomb on purpose so that it would produce very dangerous radioactivity. . . ."

Bethe and Szilard were two of Teller's oldest and dearest friends. But their comments disturbed him, for he felt they had exaggerated the dangers of radioactivity.

Triggered by the roundtable discussion, the campaign to sink the H-bomb project spread across the nation. Arguments of opponents dominated the March, April, and May issues of the prestigious *Scientific American*. In the first of these, an article by Louis N. Ridenour deplored the manner in which the president had "foisted" the bomb on the American people.

Unlike the fission of the atomic bomb, the fusion involved in the H-bomb "offers no prospect at the present time of any use except in terms of an explosion," he wrote.

Ridenour then claimed that the H-bomb would be of more value to the Soviets than to the United States. Why? "We have several large targets; the USSR has only one or two."[11]

Bethe took up the beat in the April issue of the magazine. "I believe the most important question is the moral one," he said. "Can we who have always insisted on morality and human decency between nations as well as inside our country introduce this weapon of total annihilation into the world?"

Bethe then referred to how the U.S. project might have already affected Soviet policy. "Our decision to make the H-bomb, which showed that we considered the project feasible, may well have prompted them to make the same decision," he wrote. "For this reason I think that our decision, if taken at all, should have been taken in secret."[12] He added that this underscored the need for international control of atomic weapons.

(From this, it is apparent that Bethe, like leaders of the antibomb movement in general, was unaware of the fact that the Soviets had already embarked on their own H-bomb project.)

In the May 1950 issue of *Scientific American*, Robert F. Bacher, a physicist and former AEC member, pursued the question of radioactivity.

"If the neutrons escape into the air, many of them would be absorbed by the nitrogen and produce radioactive carbon," he wrote. "This material is most disagreeable as a radioactive contaminant, since it has a half-life of many thousands of years."[13]

While the triple assault of the *Scientific American* articles extended from March through May, Teller parried with only one major public response, an article in the March issue of the more narrowly circulated but strategically focused *Bulletin of the Atomic Scientists*. The mounting attack on the H-bomb program had stirred his emotions, and this was evident in the piece. He wrote:

> No one connected with the work on atomic bombs can escape a feeling of grave responsibility. No one will be glad to discover more fuel with which a coming conflagration may be fed. But scientists must find a modest way of looking into an uncertain future. The scientist is not responsible for the laws of nature. It is his job to find out how these laws operate. It is the scientist's job to find ways in which these laws can serve the human will. . . .
> It is not the scientist's job to determine whether a hydrogen bomb should be constructed, whether it should be used, or how it should be used. This responsibility rests with the American people and their chosen representatives. [14]

The *Bulletin* article also reflected Teller's belief that scientists should exercise the free-speech right of all citizens and criticize government policy and actions. Scientists should be free to pursue their own paths of inquiry into nature and its laws, but he hoped that enough would always be working on defense to assure the survival of the nation and its guarantee of freedom, including the freedom of scientific inquiry.

In the H-bomb debate Teller saw a threat that the West might again retreat to the kind of isolation that two decades earlier had made possible Hitler's expansion into much of Europe virtually unopposed. He wrote:

> To my mind we are in a situation not less dangerous than the one we were facing in 1939. . . . We must realize that mere plans are not bombs, and we must realize that democracy will not be saved by ideas alone. . . . If we want to live on the technological capital of the last war, we shall come out second best. [15]

Nearly twenty-five years after this exchange, Teller was asked to reassess those of the opposition from a historical perspective.

"What is most striking to me now is how little the effect of the hydrogen bomb was appreciated, even by experts," he replied. He noted that when the articles were written in 1950 intercontinental rockets were not considered feasible.

> I find it most interesting that the articles in 1950, when we had relatively few atomic bombs, were already filled with the idea of "overkill." The point is that today, after the development of many years, I believe that this idea, when applied to our ability to damage Russia, is still not valid and as long as the Russians continue to take defense seriously, never will be. . . . The

point is that a country which is determined to survive can take very much more punishment than any of us, including myself, likes to think about.[16]

Teller then discussed what had motivated him to press for the thermonuclear project:

Actually one of my main reasons for working on the hydrogen bomb was its novelty. Not knowing how it would influence the future, I wanted both as a scientist and also for practical reasons to know how it would work. Some will perhaps consider this irresponsible because they pretend to be able to see into the future. If you realize that you cannot do so and if you are a little more modest about the influence that a scientist can have on the course of events, then I believe it is not irresponsible to try to work out those technical developments which can be worked out.

Teller's recruitment effort was clearly hampered by criticism of the program from leading physicists such as Bethe and his allies. At one point, the AEC tried to muzzle dissidents through a March 13, 1950, order sent to all field operation managers by AEC General Manager Carroll L. Wilson.

"All AEC and contract employees working on AEC contracts," it said, "are instructed to refrain from publicly stating facts or giving comment on any thermonuclear weapons development."[17]

Because this included scientists whose work was supported at least in part by AEC grants or who might be harboring hopes of obtaining future grants as well as those directly involved in the program, the order was followed by a tapering off of public criticism from within the scientific community. But the opposition continued to smolder, ready to erupt again, as it was certain to do.

In lectures to staff members at Los Alamos, Teller drove home the theory that the most likely method of producing a thermonuclear reaction was through use of the high temperatures from a controlled atomic bomb explosion to fuse the deuterium and tritium isotopes of hydrogen.[18] A key aspect of the problem was whether the fusion, once started, could be sustained or, perhaps because of some still-undetected natural forces, would fizzle.

To get the answer, man would first have to translate both the problem and its possible solutions into the figures, letters, and squiggles that make mathematics the language of physics. For this, pencils and blackboard chalk alone would not do. Mechanical brains must be brought into play.

The first electronic computer was built during World War II at the Aberdeen Proving Ground in Maryland. Known as ENIAC (electronic numerical integrator and calculator), it was a primitive monster whose innards included 19,000 vacuum tubes. It filled an entire room and, unlike some of its five-dollar novelty-store descendants a few years later, could neither store nor recall information.

Teller first learned about electronic computers from John von Neumann in 1944 or 1945 and began to appreciate their value in saving time needed to calculate monumental problems in theoretical and applied physics. "I think it is fair to say that he was ahead of everyone else," Teller told us. "Probably the IBM company owes half of its money to Johnny von Neumann."

By early 1950, one of Teller's earlier designs for the H-bomb, known as the classic super, was ready for mathematical analysis. The analysts worked like two teams digging a mountain tunnel from opposite sides. One team prepared for its task by translating the problem into a recipe that could be fed into and digested by ENIAC. The other team, headed by brilliant mathematicians Stanislaw Ulam and Cornelius Everett, would bore into the mountain through the old-fashioned pencil-and-paper route.

Teller, although the prime mover of the H-bomb project from its inception, was only now formally appointed its leader. Laboratory Director Bradbury named Los Alamos division leaders to a committee responsible for the thermonuclear program and appointed Teller chairman of the committee.

Working at a feverish pace and admittedly using unrefined assumptions to save time, they came up with promising preliminary indications by February. Once fusion started, Ulam felt, there was a fifty-fifty chance that it would continue. But by mid-March Ulam had moved deeply enough into his calculations to come up with a firmer prediction, and it was grim. "The result of the calculations seems to be that the model considered is a fizzle."[19] Ulam then met at Princeton with von Neumann and Enrico Fermi on April 21 to discuss the implications of his work. Von Neumann concluded that if there was to be any chance of success, the amount of tritium, still scarce and expensive, must be greatly increased.

When Ulam delivered this analysis to Teller, the project leader was plainly disturbed. "He was pale with fury," Ulam reported.[20]

Teller placed great faith in von Neumann as a friend and scientist, but he did not extend the same trust to Ulam. He suspected the mathematician's motives and questioned whether Ulam really wished the project to be successful. In an attempt to reassure Teller, von Neumann suggested that the classic supermodel, if moderated, might prove to be a major step toward a workable design. But Ulam's negative view persisted, as he made clear in a May 18, 1950, note to von Neumann. "The thing gives me the impression of being miles away from going," he said.[21]

That summer, Hans Bethe, visiting Los Alamos, reviewed Ulam's calculations. When the computer results became available, he predicted, they would confirm Ulam's findings.* Nevertheless, Bethe said, every effort should be made to meet the thermonuclear-project schedule, which called for the Greenhouse test in the Pacific in the spring of 1952.

These were not the best of times for Teller. Fallout from international developments also began to impede his progress.

On June 25, 1950, when the Communist North Korean army crossed the 38th parallel and invaded South Korea, it prompted a reevaluation of U.S. nuclear priorities. If the war were to spread, as many expected, atomic weapons might be necessary to prevent a Communist victory. This could mean the channeling of limited scientific manpower and materials into the production of fission weapons instead of into the still-unproven hydrogen-bomb effort.

To deal with such questions, the GAC of the AEC met in Washington on September 10. The progress reports it received from Teller and John Wheeler were not encouraging. Theoretical scientists were still in short supply. The GAC also noted China's tense interest in the Korean conflict. The possibility of her direct involvement could not be ignored.

Under these circumstances, it was not surprising that the GAC warned Los Alamos Director Norris Bradbury against interfering with the development and production of fission weapons. Its meaning was unmistakable: Do not rob the Peter of fission to pay the Paul of fusion.[22]

In late October, the GAC met again, this time at Los Alamos, generating more bad news for Teller and his project. Early in the year, von Neumann had designed a computer more sophisticated than the cumbersome ENIAC at Aberdeen. It had been hoped that by now this computer, dubbed MANIAC (mathematical analyzer, numerator, integrator, and computer), might be installed at Princeton and ready to churn out answers to some of the more complex problems stumping the thermonuclear team. But, the GAC was told, MANIAC was still not up and running. Even worse was a report that ENIAC, having ingested the less than complete picture, coughed up calculations confirming Ulam's dark prognosis. Still worse, Carson Mark, the head of the theoretical division at Los Alamos, reported the latest conclusion of Fermi and Ulam: When deuterium was ignited, the fire would burn out well before most of the material was consumed.[23]

---

* Teller's model was not shrugged off by all. Marshall Rosenbluth, interviewed at Princeton by the authors some years later, was among those who believed Ulam's pessimism to be premature. "In fact, the actual calculations, of which von Neumann was in general charge, were done by my wife and myself," he said. "And whereas they certainly did differ by some factors from the kind of rough ideas that Teller had, by and large they indicated that the lines he was following were completely correct and that something approximately as he described would behave as he described and would constitute successful design." Rosenbluth's evaluation eventually proved correct.

When Teller took the floor to present his summary, he had little more to offer than the zeal of a true believer. True, he acknowledged, success or failure hinged on the supply of tritium, and prospects for an adequate supply now looked dim. Also, more theoretical work was essential, and more people were needed both for performance of detailed calculations and production of creative solutions to myriad problems. He himself was drained of new ideas. But there was much more to explore, and success would somehow be drawn within reach. Exactly how, he could not say.[24]

Chapter 13

"IT'S A BOY!"

The widespread notion that Hungarians undergo wilder mood swings than others may be nothing more than a myth. But in the last few months of 1950, Edward Teller did little to dispel that notion.

In October he had stood uncomfortably before the GAC of the AEC at Los Alamos and had made a string of awkward admissions: Without enough tritium, the hydrogen-bomb project would probably fail. Getting enough tritium seemed doubtful. Getting enough good theoretical physicists for the project also seemed doubtful. New ideas were desperately needed, and he had none. Teller was depressed.

Among those concerned about his state was Ferdinand Brickwedde, an old friend of the Tellers' from their Washington days in the 1930s. Brickwedde was a cryogenic physicist, and his expertise in this branch of physics dealing with matter at extremely low temperatures was to be critical in attacking a key problem in the H-bomb program at Los Alamos. In an interview with the authors twenty-five years later, Brickwedde said Teller's mood in the summer and fall of 1950 was on a definite downswing.

"He certainly was disturbed . . . and very unhappy about the way things were going," Brickwedde said. "He was concerned about the safety of our country and he believed it was very important to have [the bomb] early. . . . I am pretty sure he felt the Russians were working on it."[1]

By early 1951, however, Teller's outlook had flashed from despair to elation. He was now convinced that there was a practical solution to the thermonuclear riddle, and he was now bursting with confidence that it could be done. But the road ahead was rough.

As he had admitted to the advisory committee at that difficult meeting in October, the tritium supply was critically short. Also, there was the problem of predetonation, or preventing an uneven, premature explosion that would cause the bomb to fizzle instead of pop.

There were political problems underlain by scientific doubts, as expressed by J. Robert Oppenheimer, the man who had shepherded America into the atomic age. John Wheeler, then at Princeton, recalled that another colleague said Oppenheimer had given him a chain of reasons for holding up on the project:

> Well, it can't be done. Even if it can be done, it will cost too much. And even if it doesn't cost too much, it will take too much scientific manpower to make it. Even if it doesn't cost too much in scientific manpower, it will be too heavy to be delivered. Even if it is not too heavy to be delivered, it will be of more use to the Soviets than to us. So we should not go ahead and make it.[2]

Finally, there was the ugly problem of a dispute over credit for the achievement. For more than two decades the authorship of the technical breakthrough remained a matter of controversy. One version held that mathematician Stanislaw Ulam suggested the concept to Teller and that Teller improved on it enough to make the bomb a reality.

Teller's version in his earlier writings is that Ulam contributed "an imaginative suggestion" that represented a "sign of hope" for solving a major problem in one step of the bomb construction. But in more detailed, later presentations—particularly a statement Teller dictated to George Keyworth after the former suffered a heart attack in 1979—the value of Ulam's contribution shrinks considerably.

Ulam said he discussed his idea with Teller and "at once Edward *took up my suggestions*, hesitantly at first but enthusiastically after a few hours":

> He had seen not only the novel elements, but had found a parallel version, *an alternative* to what I had said, perhaps more convenient and general. From then on pessimism gave way to hope.
>
> In the following days I saw Edward several times. We discussed the problem for half an hour or so each time. I wrote a first sketch of the proposal. Teller *made some changes and additions*, and we wrote a joint report very quickly.
>
> It contained the first engineering sketches of the new possibilities of starting thermonuclear explosions. We wrote about *two parallel schemes* based on these principles. *The report became the fundamental base* for the design of the first successful thermonuclear reactions and the test called "Mike". . . . A more detailed *follow-through report* was written by Teller and [Frederic] de Hoffmann. (*Italics added*.)[3]

Ulam did not flatly say which, if any, of his suggestions survived in the final design. Teller's detailed statement to Keyworth not only has Ulam contributing none that survived but explains why Teller took so long to make this clear. Briefly put, it was because Ulam claimed credit for coauthoring the breakthrough idea, then went around saying he did not think the bomb would work, anyway.

In the summer of 1979, over dinner with the authors in Washington, Teller dismissed Ulam's role. Asked whether Ulam had triggered the breakthrough idea, he snapped, "Ulam triggered nothing."

Teller then offered an anecdote emphasizing his position. The government was willing to issue a joint patent to him and Ulam as co-inventors of the hydrogen bomb, and he considered accepting this "for the sake of peace."

"But I found that under the patent laws I had to make a statement under oath that Ulam and I invented this thing together," he explained. "I knew that taking this oath would be perjury. I therefore refused to take out the patent, and no patent was taken out."

In the statement he later dictated to Keyworth, Teller put it this way:

"Sometime in February, Ulam came into my office and said, 'I have a way to make the Super. Let us compress the material.'

"I said, 'Yes.'

"And then he said, 'Well, you know, we could, for instance, have here a nuclear explosion and then put it around some containers to make a starlike structure and put deuterium in here and they will be compressed by the shock and then it will work.'

". . . I said, 'Stan, the simplest thing and it might work, but I think I know something better. You should not compress *mechanically*. You should compress by *radiation*.' "

(The importance of this difference lies in the need to produce a rapid, symmetrical transfer of the energy triggering a thermonuclear reaction. If too slow or uneven, the transfer would result in the unwanted fizzle. The speed of energy transferred by radiation instead of mechanically might be like comparing the speed of light with the action of a mousetrap.)

Teller went on:

"He wouldn't take it, so I said, 'All right.'

"Stan could talk an awful lot and consume a lot of time, and by that time we did not get along very well. I said, 'Look, I will put down both of these ideas into a paper and we'll both sign it.'

"And in that paper I explained how—and for the first time I wrote it down—that compression would help, that you could compress by shock or else you could compress by radiation, and that it was much better to compress by radiation than to compress by shock.

"I did not say whose idea was the one, whose idea was the other. We both signed it.

"Then I had explained all those things to Freddie de Hoffmann, who wrote a much more detailed description of how actually it should be done, and I think that that report, again, Freddie and I signed. . . .

"One of the things that has occurred only once in my life in connection with the hydrogen bomb is a question of priority: Who thought about it first?

"In general, I am not interested; and if in the collaboration of Ulam and myself there would have been nothing more than what I have told so far, then I would have proceeded and happily acknowledged that this invention is due to Ulam and me. But when the George [test] shot had been fired, Ulam went around and talked to everybody in Los Alamos who would listen that the George shot has proved that the hydrogen bomb could never work. He traveled to the East and carried on this message. Why he did that I don't know. That he did it is beyond question.

"Now you know the situation. Ulam did not have the idea, he did not write the paper, and when it came at last to the decision after the George shot, he declared that he did not believe it.

"To me authorship in a paper or in a report does not mean a question of priority; it means a question of responsibility. If you have signed the paper, you should stand up for it. Or if you don't stand up for it, you should tell why you have changed your mind. And to my knowledge Ulam never did."

In essence, then, Teller said Ulam proposed compression by mechanical means and Teller proposed compression by radiation. He then called on de Hoffmann to probe more deeply into the radiation concept. De Hoffmann recalled the episode in an interview with us more than twenty years later.

"Edward came into my office and discussed an idea of his," he said. De Hoffmann agreed that it was an exciting concept and agreed to do at least preliminary calculations.

"I then remember working a good portion of the night on it. And when Edward came in in the morning, we looked at it and—it's vivid in my memory—somehow the thing didn't quite go the way either of us expected it to be. And Edward, with his usual insight, simply looked at it—and I can't tell you now whether there was a factor of two or four or a *pi*—but I mean one factor was off. You know, it was a quick calculation overnight. And as soon as we had rectified that, the thing [seemed] solved, and we thought the thing was there."[4]

De Hoffmann insisted on addressing the point of who should be credited with what on a joint scientific effort.

"I might tell you a very human story about Edward," he said. He referred to the morning they adjusted the calculations on the breakthrough idea. "Edward said, 'Well, this is very nice, Fred. Why don't we write up an internal report?'

"As internal reports were then set up, which I think was a terribly fair way to do it . . . it said on the left 'Work done by' and on the right 'Report written by.' Because these things need not be the same—and, you know, it's become very fashionable to have all kinds of names appearing, and the poor guy who did the work with the brilliant idea appears as one of the fourteen people.

"So Edward said, 'Let's be sure we have a joint paper.'

"I said, 'Well, Edward, that's very nice of you, but I think if my facts serve me correct, it ought to say on the left 'Work done by Edward Teller' and on the right 'Report written by Fred de Hoffmann.'

"And he said, 'Absolutely not. It's going to be a joint report. You had these things ready. You did them overnight.'

"And I said, 'Well, Edward, we'll talk about this,' and he said, 'No. It's got to be a joint paper. That's absolute and final.' "[5]

De Hoffmann ignored Teller's generous offer and took credit only as the writer. Now, as this account is written thirty-seven years later, the Teller-de Hoffmann report is still classified. But there is no secret about the fact that Teller's name appears after "Work done by."

The official history of the AEC dismisses the suggestion that Teller embraced Ulam's idea:

> He listened to Ulam describe a particular approach to apply his idea. Teller's mind raced over the possibilities. He rejected Ulam's approach as posing enormous technical difficulties. He had a scheme of his own based partly on the nuclear mechanics which were to be used at the Greenhouse test of thermonuclear principles. . . .[6]

The statement Teller made to Keyworth at the Los Alamos meeting held in Keyworth's office on September 20, 1979, runs twenty pages. Teller had requested the meeting after suffering a heart attack seven months earlier. He made the request in a telephone call to Keyworth from his hospital bed, Keyworth told us, and began the conversation by saying, "Jay, listen closely. I have two things to tell you. First, I am not immortal. Second, you should never have a heart attack." When Teller finally visited him in September, Keyworth taped Teller's firsthand account of how he designed the H-bomb.

"This is a short statement concerning an important question," Teller dictated, "and that question is how the idea of implosion emerged."

At the outset of the statement, Teller named Seth Neddermeyer, a young physicist at Los Alamos, as the originator of the proposal to use implosion as a means of avoiding the unwanted predetonation. Neddermeyer made the suggestion at a meeting in 1943, a few weeks after the Los Alamos nuclear weapons program began. Even though the main focus was on building an atomic bomb, the possibility of a thermonuclear reaction was also being given at least standby attention.

"Seth did not have any real idea how important the implosion would become from the point of compressing material," Teller told Keyworth. "All he was after—and it was a very sensible point—[was] that by this high-explosive method you can . . . decrease the probability of predetonation."

The implosion idea drew little more attention until about June 1, when John von Neumann visited Los Alamos to deliver a lecture. He then went to the Teller apartment, where he and Teller discussed Neddermeyer's idea.

"We started to make crude calculations based on an exceedingly simple idea," Teller said, "namely, the obvious idea that solid matter is incompressible." In that precomputer era, the calculations involved myriad complexities—pressures and velocities of highly explosive materials arranged in a certain order within containers of various shapes. Von Neumann came up with a formula.

"Now by the time he had that formula, I remembered something," Teller said. "The pressure that one got that way went into the megabars [units of pressure measurement] and, in fact, on the incompressible assumption you would have reached easily a thousand megabars.

"At that point, I said, 'Wait a moment.' I knew something about geophysics, and I knew that at the center of the earth, at the pressure of maybe five megabars—I do not remember now and did not remember then the precise figure, but a few megabars—iron is compressed twenty or thirty percent. . . . At the pressures which would occur if we assumed incompressible materials, the materials in fact could not remain incompressible.

"It was also by that time very clear to me that a compression by a factor of two would greatly influence the critical mass, and the conclusion was then evident that implosion would be an excellent method not only in order to avoid predetonation but also to save critical materials, of which at that time we had very little, and the earliest time at which nuclear explosives could be used would depend on this compression in a decisive manner."

At one point in the statement, Teller recalls being assigned in the early days at Los Alamos to investigate possible "instabilities"—unexpected behavior of the components of the thermonuclear device. He tells of Enrico Fermi's arrival at the laboratory and, in his role of indoctrinating newly arrived major scientists, sharing the assignment with Fermi.

". . . I pointed out to him that one of our chief worries was to be sure that in the implosion no instabilities developed, and one of my challenges to him . . . was to come up with really hard proof that there would be no instability. And Fermi couldn't do it, and neither could anybody else."

Teller indicated that because no proof against instabilities was produced before the first thermonuclear device was tested in May 1951, the design of the device was modified so that "instabilities could in the end, even if they occurred, do only limited damage."

Throughout the last two months before the experiment known as the George test in the Greenhouse series, few within earshot escaped Teller's sales pitch. "During March and April of 1951," he later wrote in *The Legacy of Hiroshima*, "I urged the feasibility of construction of a hydrogen bomb upon anyone who would listen." Among the first to be approached were Norris Bradbury, the Los Alamos director, and Carson Mark, head of the theoretical division at the laboratory. Their reaction was encouraging.

Among those most pleased by the discovery was John Wheeler, who had cut short his year-long sabbatical in Paris to join the H-bomb team.

"All our ideas about how to create a fusion explosion were based on one premise," he said later. "Within a fixed framework we went through unbelievably clever and subtle distortions to try and make it work, and we couldn't. This [Teller's] new idea changed the framework."[7]

But the ultimate value of the new idea hinged on the results of the George shot, for which months of preparations had already been made. If the principle of fusion could be demonstrated there, with a cumbersome device bearing little resemblance to a deliverable bomb, the doubters might be silenced, and work on the bomb itself could proceed.

The basic problem was how to fuse deuterium and thereby release tremendous energy through the kind of thermonuclear reaction taking place in the sun and the stars. Blocking the achievement of this were almost numberless immediate problems.

For example, some way must be found to convert the deuterium from gaseous to liquid form, which would reduce its volume—and the required size of its container—by 800. But this meant keeping these hydrogen isotopes at very low temperature, for the boiling point of hydrogen is 252 degrees below zero Centigrade, compared with 100 degrees above zero for the boiling point of water. To solve this problem, the cryogenic physicists under Ferdinand Brickwedde cooled the liquid deuterium-tritium cocktail with a flow of liquid hydrogen.

Another problem lay at the other extreme. The temperature required to produce fusion was believed to be about 400 million degrees. It was hoped that an atomic explosion could be used to generate enough heat to produce fusion, but the hope bumped against this reality: The atomic bombs at

Hiroshima and Nagasaki generated only about 50 million degrees of heat for about 1.1 millionth of a second. Later models increased this somewhat.

One promising approach was the use of tritium and deuterium in such a combination that fusion might be produced at 80 million degrees. Later would come such refinements as the introduction of lithium into the equation. In his statement to Keyworth, Teller said he latched on to this idea even before the first device was tested in the George shot.

"I realized that another good fuel for the thermonuclear reaction would be lithium-six deuteride, and the reason is obvious and is known to everybody by now," he said. "That was actually the summer of 1950."[8]

Norman Moss, in *Men Who Play God*, offers this excellent layman's explanation of where Teller's idea was leading:

> One way tritium is created is by bombarding lithium-six, an isotope of the metal, lithium, with neutrons. . . . The idea was to [place with] the atom bomb not deuterium and tritium, but deuterium and lithium-six, combined as lithium deuteride. The explosion of an atom bomb sends out a shower of low-energy neutrons, which would create tritium from the lithium. The tritium would fuse with deuterium explosively at the moment it was created.

But before moving on to the lithium-deuteride, or any other refinement leading to production of an actual bomb, Teller and his colleagues had to face the George test, the third in the Greenhouse series. Failure here could mean the end of the thermonuclear program.

Teller, attributing dark motives to its opponents, was careful to limit expectations from the test and resisted efforts to do otherwise. "When preparing for Greenhouse," he later said, "I was urged by friends of Oppenheimer to make a test which in their opinion would prove more than the test that was actually carried out."

Why?

"At that time, it was my conviction that this suggestion was made in the hope that the test would fail, thereby terminating the program altogether."[9]

One development contributing to Teller's feeling that "opposition among scientists" was forcing the program to swim upstream was a report issued December 29, 1950, by an ad hoc panel under the chairmanship of Oppenheimer. It stressed the significance of continuing work on fission weapons. It noted that production of an H-bomb was not expectable soon. "In fact," the committee concluded, "we believe that only a timely recognition of the *long-range* character of the thermonuclear program will tend to make available for the basic studies of the fission program the resources of the Los Alamos laboratory."

Another negative development came on January 15, 1951, less than three weeks later, when Teller told Bradbury he would like to begin planning the test, taking the program another step closer to actual production of an H-bomb.

Teller recalled:

> Bradbury said it is too late, there is no point until after the test. I found that rather outrageous, the more so because by that time I knew how to solve the problem. . . . There was no question in my mind how the super should be made. We needed a primary, we needed a secondary, we needed a sparkplug. The secondary had to have cylindrical symmetry because that was the symmetry natural to the process. The energy transfer had to go by radiation in order to make it as close to simultaneous as possible. All this was clear to me.[10]

Outrageous or not, Bradbury's refusal to let Teller move on to the next testing phase strengthened Teller's conviction that the thermonuclear program was still drawing too low a priority at Los Alamos.

Teller believed that the thermonuclear program, instead of being a part-time project under the guidance of a committee, should be the sharp focus of a newly created division or laboratory.[11] To push this idea, he went to Washington and met on April 4, 1951, with Gordon Dean, the AEC chairman and one of the strongest scientific supporters of the program. After returning to Los Alamos, Teller summarized his proposal in an April 20 memorandum to Dean: a new laboratory, best located in the area of Boulder, Colorado. It would need 50 senior scientists, 82 junior scientists, and 228 assistants. A theoretical group could set up shop there by the fall of 1951, and routine operation could be achieved by the summer of 1952.[12]

With Teller's proposal still fresh in his mind, Dean two weeks later put aside other work on his desk and set out for the Pacific and a firsthand look at the George shot in the Greenhouse test series.[13]

The Eniwetok test site was a link in the desolate chain of atolls making up the Marshall Islands of the central Pacific. Three hundred miles from the U.S. naval base at Kwajalein, it had been selected in 1947 as a prime location for nuclear weapons tests. It offered a sheltered harbor, ships, and favorable winds and ocean currents. One hundred forty islanders had been evacuated before earlier tests.[14]

On the day before the May 8 test Teller, accompanied by de Hoffmann and stiffly lifting his artificial foot with each step, climbed the 300-foot tower for an inspection of the test equipment. Satisfied that all was in order, they returned to their living quarters and relaxed with a swim in the shallow lagoon.

A tropical rainstorm delayed the shot for three hours. Then, forty-five minutes before firing time, a short was discovered in the monitoring arming circuit. Finally, the go-ahead order was given.

In moments, a blinding sheet of light flashed over the tense observers as they hunched in their observation shelters, and mountainous clouds rolled high into the atmosphere. Beneath them, the atoll had been wiped clean of the tower and the iron and concrete equipment structures at its base. They were now vapor.

Dean was awed by the spectacle, then became absorbed in studying those about him. The reactions of nearly all the scientists ranged from obvious satisfaction to whooping joy. But Teller kept a tight rein on his emotions. Eniwetok atoll, he said, would not be big enough for the next test.

In the meantime, the preliminary results of the test would not be known until the next day. Another fitful night lay ahead of Teller. The next morning brought word from Louis Rosen, a Los Alamos colleague, that early evidence indicated Greenhouse George was a devastating success. The thermonuclear reaction of the sun and the stars could be duplicated on earth without necessarily obliterating the planet.

Teller messaged Los Alamos: "It's a boy!"[15]

Chapter 14

Birth of the Superbomb

With the success of the Greenhouse test, Teller now had firm evidence to support his concept of how a hydrogen bomb could be built. He also had great reason to be optimistic about advancing his prime project. But it was not easy to transfer his optimism to others. This became apparent on June 19, 1951, exactly six weeks after the Greenhouse test, when key players in the nuclear drama gathered for a significant meeting at the Institute for Advanced Study on the Princeton campus.

Gordon Dean had called the two-day meeting as chairman of the AEC for the apparent purpose of determining the best way to build an H-bomb. J. Robert Oppenheimer, as chairman of the Weapons Committee and the advisory committee of the AEC, was host.

Among GAC members attending were Enrico Fermi, I. I. Rabi, Cyril S. Smith, Lee DuBridge, and Walter G. Whitman. The commission itself was present in full force as Dean was joined by H. D. Smyth, Keith Glennan, Thomas Murray, and Sumner Pike. From the Princeton and Los Alamos projects came some of the best minds in the field of nuclear physics—Teller, Hans Bethe, Carson Mark, Darol Froman, Lothar Nordheim, John von Neumann, John Wheeler, and the Los Alamos director, Norris Bradbury.[1]

Teller went into the session with warm anticipation. Against long odds and opposition from many of those present, he had fought hard in the cause of the H-bomb. Now, with many of his most powerful opponents in the audience, he expected an opportunity to trot out the results of the Greenhouse test and to explain them as vindication of his theory. But that expectation was jolted as the meeting agenda unfolded. A dozen participants were called on to speak, but he was not among them. Instead, the job of presenting the Greenhouse data had been assigned to Carson Mark.[2]

The reason for this has been a matter of debate. Richard Hewlett, the AEC historian, said Bradbury was responsible. Bradbury said this was not so.

"For one thing, the meeting was called by the GAC and/or the AEC, and its agenda was not my business," he said. The Los Alamos laboratory was expected to present an assessment of the new bomb proposal and to discuss what it planned and would need to solve problems arising from the proposal. "Since Teller and I had rather different ideas as to the most effective way to proceed, it would not have been appropriate to consider him 'laboratory spokesman' in these respects."

Bradbury brushed aside any suggestion that he tried to muzzle Teller.

"I would have regarded this as highly inappropriate and probably almost impossible," Bradbury wrote. "Edward was hardly known for shyness in such circumstances."[3]

Through the years a remarkably wide range of differences developed in recollections of exactly what happened at that June 1951 conference. In his writings, Teller consistently declared there was an apparent attempt to bypass him. But in addition to Bradbury's denial, there is a conflicting account from Hans Bethe.

After Teller mentioned the incident again in a 1982 letter to *Science*, Bethe wrote his old friend and longtime ideological adversary a letter on December of the same year, giving his version.

Bethe said he even remembered being briefed by Teller on the new concept at least a month before the meeting, then being asked to present part of it. He believed that perhaps others had also agreed to participate, and he was convinced that "none of us would have left the meeting without having [Teller's] Method D discussed."

Bethe remembered no debate on whether Teller himself should be allowed to speak, but he recalled that "after the presentation of your ideas, which was very well received, there was some discussion of the implementation."[4]

Whatever the differences in recollections of the meeting, Bradbury was right on one point: Teller desired to be heard, and his desire grew stronger as the two-day meeting went on and on without his being called to discuss what he considered most important.

"I was amazed when Carson Mark, in his presentation, did not mention the hydrogen bomb report that I had handed him three months before," Teller said. "My amazement multiplied when Gordon Dean, still chairman of the AEC, spoke without mentioning the same report which I had explained to him two months earlier. My amazement approached anger as other scientists and officials who knew of the report spoke without referring to it. Finally, I could contain myself no longer. I insisted on being heard. My demand was met with spirited debate, but it was decided that I should be allowed to speak."

In the debate over whether he should be allowed to address the meeting, Teller said, one of his unlikely allies was H. D. Smyth. They had disagreed on much through the years, since Smyth was Teller's upstairs neighbor in the Los Alamos apartment complex and objected to his postmidnight piano playing. Smyth was also among those who had opposed Teller's insistent push for the H-bomb. But it was Smyth, Teller noted, who now argued conclusively that Edward should be allowed to address the conference as it neared its finish.[5]

Approaching the blackboard in his familiar crab walk, Teller proceeded to explain his theory and the calculations supporting it. Among those involved in producing the latest calculations for several months preceding the conference was a Princeton team headed by physicist John Wheeler. Aided by Kenneth Ford and John Toll, who was later to become president of the University of Maryland, Wheeler had set up shop in quarters across campus from the institute conference room. His group called its assignment Project Matterhorn.

Aware that the presentation of Teller's concept would eventually reach a point where it could be helped by a certain chart of Matterhorn calculations, Toll and Ford retrieved the chart from their shop, hopped into Toll's 1939 Studebaker, and drove the two-mile trip to the conference room. There they slipped the chart through an open window to Wheeler, who took it to the front of the room for ready reference in the Teller presentation.[6]

Some idea of Teller's impact on the meeting was conveyed by Gordon Dean two years later when he testified in the Oppenheimer security hearing:

"Out of the meeting came something which Edward Teller brought into the meeting with his own head, which was an entirely new way of approaching a thermonuclear weapon. . . . I remember leaving the meeting impressed with this fact, that everyone around the table without exception—and this included Dr. Oppenheimer—was enthusiastic."

Oppenheimer himself called Teller's approach "technically so sweet that you could not argue about that."

In one forty-eight-hour conference, Teller had erased long-standing questions about technical feasibility. But the moral question persisted and was to pursue Teller throughout the rest of his career.

Teller's worry that Bradbury was dragging his feet on the nuclear weapons program also persisted. Long before the turnabout Princeton meeting, Teller had grown so impatient that he was actively lobbying for drastic changes. First he proposed that a new division be set up at Los Alamos to work only on the new superbomb. Then, on April 4, 1951—two months before Princeton—came his meeting with Gordon Dean to ask the AEC chairman for support of his proposal to build a completely new laboratory to spearhead the H-bomb effort.

Dean felt pressed on two sides. If he rebuffed Teller and Teller left Los Alamos, his powerful Washington supporters, especially Brien McMahon and Lewis Strauss, would be displeased with those they considered responsible. If Dean backed the idea of a new laboratory, morale at Los Alamos would be damaged by this apparent lack of confidence in its ability to handle the nuclear weapons workload. The AEC chairman asked his fellow commissioners for advice and received it in a report on August 23, 1951. Only one, Thomas Murray, endorsed the proposal for a new lab. Two, H. D. Smyth and Keith Glennan, made no recommendation. The others were not in favor.

Teller seethed, generating rumors that he would quit in protest. He did submit a letter of resignation on September 11, but Frederic de Hoffmann and others persuaded him to withdraw it. Teller then told Robert Oppenheimer that he would stay if Oppenheimer, Bethe, or Fermi took over direction of the fusion program. But none of the three was interested.

Teller's frustration grew. He had felt the pressure of a race ever since the 1949 announcement that the Soviet Union had exploded a nuclear device. Now, less than three years later, came word of another Soviet advance. Walter F. Colby, the AEC director of intelligence, reported on September 18, 1951, that the Soviets had conducted at least a second atomic test. This was publicly announced fifteen days later, on October 3.

Teller was not alone in his unhappiness with the pace of the H-bomb project at Los Alamos. Brien McMahon reacted to the new sign of Soviet advances by contacting Dean and asking, "Couldn't you do more . . . ?"

Dean's response was to call an October 11 meeting of members of the AEC and its GAC to discuss progress at Los Alamos. Overhanging the session was the continuing pressure for a second laboratory. Among those questioning whether there would be enough top-notch scientists to staff both Los Alamos and a second laboratory working on the same project was I. I. Rabi. The issue arose, and the committee turned thumbs down on Teller's second-lab proposal.

Teller now felt that his continued presence at Los Alamos was no longer critical to the H-bomb project there and that he might be more effective as a Los Alamos alumnus lobbying for a new laboratory. To press for one while he continued to work at Los Alamos would present problems both of propriety and in personal relationships with his superiors and colleagues.

Then, on November 1, 1951, his decision to leave was triggered by Bradbury's announcement of a reorganization plan. Marshall Holloway was named coordinator of the theoretical work with engineering design and fabrication on the Los Alamos project. Teller would be in charge of the theoretical work and initial design. Holloway would then pick it up and move the test to completion.

Teller and Holloway had differed often and openly. Holloway felt that preparation of the test would require at least thirteen months. Teller had declared it could be done in nine. He took Holloway's appointment as a sign that Bradbury wanted him to leave. He did, accepting appointment to his former position at the University of Chicago but retaining some ties to Los Alamos as a consultant on call.

There now began another stage in Teller's metamorphosis from strictly theoretical scientist to scientist/political activist. The first stage had clicked when Edward heard President Franklin D. Roosevelt's 1940 speech urging scientists to help their government. Another stage unfolded in 1945 when Teller timidly refrained from joining Leo Szilard's petition movement opposing use of the atomic bomb without warning, then learned that Oppenheimer had worked to influence the outcome of this issue after having told Teller that scientists should not get politically involved.

Shortly after resigning from the Los Alamos staff, Teller braced Oppenheimer for an opportunity to address the GAC on the issue of a second laboratory.[7]

Oppenheimer agreed and arranged for him to speak to the combined membership of the committee and the AEC at a meeting on December 13.

Teller went into the session brimming with optimism and emerged in good spirits. He felt that he had persuasively argued that enough mystery remained in the project to justify the efforts of two laboratories. The friendly competition would be productive, and the work would help sharpen the sense of "curiosity and adventure" possessed by all good scientists.

But the result was another turndown by the GAC, ostensibly because of the Los Alamos morale factor. Instead, the AEC favored a weak substitute proposal, a compromise between setting up a new laboratory and relieving Los Alamos of some nonresearch work by farming it out to other facilities already in operation.[8]

Blocked in this approach, Teller decided it was time for an end around and contacted David T. Griggs, an ally who was a geophysicist and chief scientist for the air force. Teller had consistently received a warm reception at the Pentagon, where his views on preparedness to meet the Soviet challenge drew solid support. After hearing Teller's account of his frustrating efforts to persuade the AEC and its advisory committee, Griggs made no promises. Shortly thereafter, however, he shared the account with Gen. James H. Doolittle at a Florida meeting of the air force's scientific advisory board. Doolittle was better known as an early, unorthodox advocate of air power and as the World War II hero whose exploits were dramatized in the book and motion picture *Thirty Seconds Over Tokyo*. As holder of a doctorate in aeronautical engineering from MIT, he was also no stranger to scientific problems. Doolittle met with Teller a few weeks later but said nothing to indicate approval or disapproval. Occasionally he smiled slightly, perhaps as if remembering his own early uphill battles to gain support for his belief in air power.

Before receiving any feedback from his approaches to Griggs and Doolittle, Teller was invited by Ernest Lawrence to visit him at the University of California and discuss a proposition. Teller's youthful liberalism had long since faded, and his drift to the right was by now quite pronounced. But he was still uneasy about Lawrence's even more conservative slant. Two years earlier, Lawrence had threatened to give Fulton Lewis, Jr., the right-wing national radio commentator, the names of colleagues who had refused to sign a loyalty oath required by a new California law.

But Teller also recognized Lawrence's potential value in pushing for the H-bomb project and decided to accept the invitation to Berkeley. Shortly after his arrival in California, he was taken by Lawrence to Livermore, about forty miles southeast of Berkeley, where the navy had operated a training base in World War II. Lawrence, inventor of the cyclotron, had later taken over some space at Livermore to build one of his particle accelerators.

But there was much more available space, and over dinner at Trader Vic's, Lawrence suggested that he and Teller team up to propose that the space be used for a second laboratory and that Teller supervise establishment of the project.

On his return to Chicago, Teller received a call from Griggs, who said Doolittle had thrown his support behind the proposal and that Air Force Secretary Thomas K. Finletter had agreed to discuss it with Teller.

They met at the Pentagon, and Finletter then flew to Los Alamos for a look at the kind of laboratory Teller had in mind. Next, Teller met in Washington with Robert A. Lovett, the secretary of defense.

"Before I left the secretary's office," Teller later recalled, "I knew that I had won." Lovett not only agreed with Teller's explanation of the need for an accelerated H-bomb program but disclosed that the air force had already been planning to set up a laboratory and was even negotiating for a site.

Word of the air force plan had a catalytic effect on the AEC. "The Atomic Energy Commission at last became interested," Teller said, "and began investigating possible locations for a second laboratory of its own."[9] It chose Livermore.

Applying for and receiving a one-year leave from Chicago, Edward headed west. I. I. Rabi, then at Columbia but in touch with many of Teller's Chicago colleagues, said Teller quipped to some of them, "I am leaving the appeasers to join the fascists." Teller denied saying this even in jest.

The Lawrence Livermore National Laboratory was created in March 1952 by action of the NSC and ratification by the AEC. Its financial support was to come from the AEC, and, like Los Alamos, it was to be an academic affiliate of the University of California. In the midst of summer-long planning and construction at Livermore, Mici and their two children, Paul and Wendy, joined Teller on July 14 at their new home in nearby Diablo.

Herbert F. York, one of Lawrence's Berkeley followers, was appointed director of the laboratory. He, Teller, and Lawrence met September 8 with the AEC to discuss plans for new weapons designs and the relationship between Livermore and Los Alamos.

"I can tell you that from the very beginning," Teller said, "and to a great extent due to my insistence, we tried and did avoid those things in which Los Alamos was doing a decent job. We took seriously our role as competitors who had to open new avenues."

Lawrence made good on his promise to recruit staff for Livermore, assembling 123 scientists within a few months to work on weapons projects. Among those scheduled to report later was Ferdinand Brickwedde, the longtime Teller friend and cryogenics expert, who would play a key role in the upcoming Mike test at Eniwetok. The Mike operation, marking the first real test of Teller's new idea of H-bomb design, would be conducted by the Los Alamos crew and would not directly involve the now departed Teller. Brickwedde was essential because a cryogenic (low-temperature) device was needed to keep the deuterium thermonuclear fuel cool enough to remain in liquid form.

The test was scheduled for the fall of 1952, which presented political problems. The target date, October 31, fell only four days before the presidential election. A postponement was suggested by many, including Vannevar Bush, who headed the nation's scientific research program during World War II. Since Truman was not running for another term, Bush believed the decision on whether to proceed with the test should be left to the new president. He also worried about the effects of the test on U.S.-Soviet relations.

"I felt strongly that the test ended the possibility of the only type of agreement that I thought was possible with Russia at that time, namely, an agreement to make no more tests," Bush later explained.[10]

Gordon Dean shared some of Bush's objections, and he conveyed them to President Truman. Truman asked how long a postponement would be necessary. Told that weather conditions might mean a delay of another month or more, he decided that that was too long and ordered that Mike go off as scheduled.

Preparations for the test were already under way on Elugelab, a small island on Eniwetok atoll in the Marshall Islands group of the central Pacific. One look at the massive thermonuclear device was enough to convince the most casual observer that it was only a test piece and not a deliverable bomb. Its cylindrical housing and the refrigeration equipment surrounding it were so bulky and heavy that the device was accurately dubbed the sixty-five-ton monster.[11]

The contents of that cylinder and the goings-on within were kept from the public for more than thirty years after the Mike shot.

Not until 1987 were secrecy restrictions relaxed enough for Teller to give a relatively detailed description of the H-bomb structure. In an article for the *Encyclopedia of Physical Science and Technology*, he outlined problems in the manufacture of the bomb and their solutions.

As an aside, as if to drive home a point about what impelled him to pursue the unholy grail of nuclear fusion, Teller mentioned Soviet work in the field. He said Andrei Sakharov, the creator of the Soviet hydrogen explosive, was drafted for that project in 1948. "That was more than a year before the beginning of the *debate* in the United States on the hydrogen bomb," he said, "where opponents argued that the fission [atomic] bombs were powerful enough and that if the United States did not undertake the development of the fusion [hydrogen] bomb, the Soviets would not do so either."

Teller also made it clear that the key to his successful concept of a thermonuclear reaction was the process of radiation coupling.

In the chain reaction of fissionable material, such as the uranium or plutonium of the atomic bomb, energy is released in several forms. One is the kinetic energy of the fission products. Another is the energy of the neutrons released from the nucleus of the uranium or plutonium atom. Still another is in the form of gamma rays, or radiation energy of very high frequency. But much of this energy is quickly converted into a "softer" radiation of lower frequency, or X rays in the range of a kilovolt, or 1,000 volts.

After much study, it became doubtful that a large enough release of fusion energy could be accomplished either by trying to burn thermonuclear fuel in its original (i.e., uncompressed) state or by using the fission-fusion approach (i.e., merely relying on the atomic explosion to create fusion in the thermonuclear fuel).

This doubt, Teller said, led to consideration of various ways of trying to *compress* and heat the thermonuclear fuel that was placed in the right relationship to a fission explosive. Because they accounted for most of the energy released in the early stages of fusion and because they traveled so fast (almost with the speed of light), the soft X rays seemed ideally suited for the purpose of compressing and heating the thermonuclear fuel.

This approach was referred to as radiation coupling—using X rays to couple the energy-releasing process of fission and fusion.

The design resulting from this concept involved the strategic placement of the fusion material and the fission material within a radiation case. The only known publicly released illustration of the design shows two circles within a rectangle whose corners are rounded. One circle represents the quantity of fission material, and the other represents the fusion material.

In the written explanation, the "fission explosive" is referred to as the primary, and the "fusion fuel region" is called the secondary. These are so labeled in the diagram. They are also designated by letters, but for some unexplained reason in both the text and the diagram the secondary is designated as A and the primary is designated as B.

The heavy metal case enclosing all this, designated C in the diagram, is designed to contain the fast, powerful flow of X rays as the primary fuel undergoes fission. As this radiation flows through the container, its intensity increases. Before the case ruptures and the radiation escapes—a matter of milliseconds—the fusion-fuel region is compressed and heated enough to ignite the thermonuclear process.[12]

Although details of the process are still classified at this writing, it is known that the radiation-coupling concept cleared the way for the development of thermonuclear weapons that are smaller, lighter, and more powerful than the early atomic bombs. For example, the uranium bomb used at Hiroshima was 12 feet long and 5 feet in diameter, weighed 10,000 pounds, and yielded 15 kilotons. The plutonium bomb used at Nagasaki was roughly a sphere about 5 feet in diameter and also weighed about 10,000 pounds and yielded 15 kilotons.

By contrast, the modern thermonuclear weapon is described as cylindrical, about one foot in diameter and "a few feet" in length, and weighing only a few hundred pounds, with a yield of a few hundred thousand tons of high explosive. Unlike the early fission bombs, this has "highly effective" safety features to prevent inadvertent explosion.[13]

But this model was a far cry from the "sixty-five-ton monster" that, despite advice to the contrary from such experts as Vannevar Bush and

Gordon Dean, was being set up for the Mike test in the distant Pacific on that last October day of 1952. For Edward Teller, the test crystallized a decade-long campaign based on a philosophy and fueled by fear.

The philosophy held that what humankind can explore it will explore. If its exploration leads the species to the brink of extinction, the species also holds the intellectual capacity and moral duty to survive the threat and to make positive use of knowledge gained in the exploration. "We would be unfaithful to the tradition of Western civilization if we shied away from exploring what man can accomplish, if we failed to increase man's control over nature," Teller wrote in his 1987 book *Better a Shield Than a Sword*. "The duty of scientists, specifically, is to explore and to explain. That duty led to the invention of the principles that made the hydrogen bomb a practical reality."[14]

Although invited to witness the test at Eniwetok, Teller did not go. "I very much wanted to see the explosion of the device that had consumed my energies and that had dragged me into so many arguments," he said. "But I knew that I really was not needed at Eniwetok." He compromised by observing the evidence of the test in the seismograph room at the University of California in Berkeley. Sitting in the dark, he fixed his eyes on a photographic film and watched for any change in the fine beam of light shining from it.

"I waited patiently and watched the seismograph make a time signal each minute," he said. It would take about fifteen minutes for the compression wave to travel the thousands of miles under the ocean floor from the test site to the California coast.

"At last the time signal came that had to be followed by the explosion's shock, and there it seemed to be: The spot of light danced wildly and irregularly. . . . Our first hydrogen bomb had been a success."[15]

At Eniwetok the only evidence of success was contained in the instruments used by official observers stationed forty miles and more from the sixty-five-ton monster to record the explosion and its effects. The mile-wide island itself, Elugelab, had vanished.

Less than a month after the Mike test of October 31, 1952, Teller received an unexpected, perplexing suggestion from J. Robert Oppenheimer. It came over lunch at Princeton with Oppenheimer and Rabi during the Thanksgiving holiday.

For more than two years, UN forces had been locked in combat with North Korean and Communist Chinese troops in Korea. What had seemed to be an early victory over the North Korean army in 1950 was checked and erased by the entry of mainland China into the war.

Teller said Oppenheimer raised the subject by asking, "Well, Edward, now that you have your H-bomb, why don't you use it to end the war in Korea?"

Oppenheimer might not have been serious and might well have intended this as an acid comment on Teller's having prevailed in the controversy over building the bomb.

But Teller added this follow-up:

"I remember receiving a phone call from Oppenheimer shortly before Christmas. He said, 'Do you remember the conversation we had over lunch at Princeton? Well, I've been talking to some people in Washington, and I just wanted to tell you that they are aware of the possibilities.' "

Oppenheimer might have been referring to the rumor then current in Washington that Dwight Eisenhower, about to be inaugurated as president, was weighing the possibility of using nuclear weapons to end the Korean War. But was Oppenheimer serious about his own suggestion?

Some indication of Oppenheimer's position on the question might be gleaned from an article he wrote for *Foreign Affairs*. Published in July 1953 under the heading "Atomic Weapons and American Policy," it acknowledged a need for the United States to consult its allies. It added, "This does not mean that we should tie our hands."

Then came this:

> It is not clear that the situation even in the Far East would be wholly unaffected. It is troublesome to read that a principal reason we should not use atomic weapons in Korea is that our allies would not like it. We need not argue here either that it is right or that it is wrong to use them there. In either case, our decision should rest on firmer ground than that other governments who know less than we about the matter should hold a different view than ours. [16]

It was obvious to Teller even then that the successful end of his campaign to build the H-bomb did not mean the end of the controversy dogging him throughout that campaign. It was to play a big part in his climactic confrontation with Oppenheimer in the near future. It was also to be reflected in grander scope down the road in his furious fight over SDI.

Chapter 15

THE RUSSIAN H-BOMB

One of Edward Teller's worst fears was confirmed on August 29, 1949. U.S. scientists, analyzing air samples collected by high-flying patrol planes, discovered that the Soviet Union had exploded a nuclear device.

For years Teller had been convinced that the two superpowers were locked in a race to develop a hydrogen bomb. He knew, and he knew the Russians knew, that the first step in developing an H-bomb one thousand times more powerful than the atomic bombs dropped on Hiroshima and Nagasaki was the making of an atomic bomb to produce enough heat and pressure to trigger the fusion process. Now the Soviets had the trigger. They also had nuclear scientists capable of making the logical progression from A-bomb to H-bomb.

Teller was not alone in this fear. Among President Eisenhower's advisers it was so great that consideration of a "preventive" war against the Soviet Union was suggested at least three times in 1953 and 1954. It was publicly documented in *Strategy and Nuclear Deterrence*, a study published in 1984 by Princeton University Press after first appearing in *International Security*, an MIT Press publication, under the sponsorship of the Center for Science and International Affairs at Harvard.

"Although seldom explicitly discussed in writing," the study said, "preventive war was implicit in some of the major policy deliberations of the time."

It cited the following as one example:

"In the spring of 1953, Eisenhower's top foreign policy advisers rejected a proposal by the SOLARIUM Steering Committee, headed by retired Air Force General James Doolittle, that a . . . policy alternative be studied: giving the Soviet Union two years to agree to terms, with the understanding that failure to cooperate might lead to general war." (SOLARIUM was the code name for a committee set up by Eisenhower to help overhaul national-security policy and, in the process, reduce the record peacetime defense budgets inherited from the Truman administration.) The recommendation of the Doolittle group came less than one year after Doolittle, having met with Teller, agreed to support the establishment of a new laboratory needed in Teller's pressing search for the answer to the H-bomb mystery.

Another example used in the study was a formerly top secret memorandum prepared August 21, 1953, by Maj. Gen. Robert M. Lee for Gen. Nathan F. Twining, air force chief of staff. It said the United States was approaching a time when it would be in a "militarily unmanageable" position. Before that time came, it warned, the nation would have to decide whether to gamble on a future shaped by "the whims of a small group of proven barbarians" in the Soviet Union or "be militarily prepared to support such decisions as might involve general war."

The third and most direct recommendation along this line came in May 1954, when the Joint Chiefs of Staff Advanced Study Group proposed in a briefing paper that the United States consider "deliberately precipitating war with the USSR in the near future" before Soviet development of thermonuclear weaponry posed a "real menace."[1]

Justification for Teller's anxiety and for the mounting apprehension of presidential advisers became apparent on August 12, 1953. That is the date when, the evidence strongly indicates, the world's first H-bomb was exploded—not by the United States but by the Soviet Union. Playing catch-up, the Russians overcame the American advantage and, at least for a brief period, forged ahead.

The first deliverable H-bomb successfully tested by the United States was exploded seven months later, on March 1, 1954. Calculated to yield seven megatons, it actually yielded fifteen. This unexpected yield and the failure of forecasters to predict a change in wind direction resulted in the drifting of radioactive fallout onto several of the Marshall Islands nearly 900 miles east of the Bikini atoll test site in the Pacific. Twenty-six American sailors stationed there and 236 natives were exposed. The sailors, briefed beforehand, donned protective gear and escaped serious illness. The natives developed skin rashes, sores, and severe hair loss. A three-year follow-up disclosed that none had died within that period but that many would be disabled for much longer.

American scientists had set off more cumbersome thermonuclear devices in the Greenhouse test of May 1951 and in the Mike test of October 1952. But in both cases these were sixty-five-ton cryogenic experimental devices and, as Teller explained to us, were designed to examine then current fusion theory.

To this day, tight secrecy restrictions have prevented official confirmation, but nuclear scientists on both sides of the Iron Curtain express no doubt that the Soviets set off at least one thermonuclear test device even before Greenhouse, probably in late 1950. This has been challenged by some U.S. officials and physicists. Teller himself sought out one of them as recently as 1980 in an attempt to be certain, but the effort left him still in doubt.

On one point, however, there is little room for doubt: The Soviets built up a long lead time in research. For as Teller noted after reading Sakharov's book *Sakharov Speaks*, the Soviet development of the fusion bomb was moving ahead under full steam at least eighteen months before the issue was being debated by the GAC of the AEC.

Several independent sources have said that the Soviets were already well on their way toward development of the H-bomb before the United States decided to proceed. One of the sources was Harrison Salisbury of the *New York Times*. On August 20, 1953, he reported from Moscow, "The Soviet Government announced today that it carried out an experimental explosion of a hydrogen bomb within the last few days."

Fifteen years later, in an introduction to a 1968 collection of essays by Andrei Sakharov, Salisbury also wrote this:

> The measure of his achievement is underlined by the fact that while the Russians started far behind the United States in nuclear research, [the USSR] was able to catch up and surpass the Americans in developing the hydrogen bomb. The first Soviet *experiment* in hydrogen fusion occurred months before those of the United States.[2]

Others presenting evidence of early Soviet work on the superbomb have included Theodore F. Walkowicz, physicists Eugene Wigner and Marvin Goldberger, and White House adviser Robert LeBaron.

Walkowicz, who later became president of the National Aviation Corporation, was a major assigned near the end of World War II to the Air Force Scientific Advisory Group. In a 1974 interview, he told us of a mysterious occurrence that came to the attention of the advisory group, probably in early 1950.

"There was a Russian shot fired that we did not understand," he said. ". . . It was a Soviet atomic explosion, and we did the usual thing of collecting air samples. . . . These debris samples were analyzed, and from that there were deductions made as to the nature of the Soviet shot. . . . The implication was that it could be understood only in terms of there having been a fusion component in the shot."

Goldberger was interviewed by us on the subject in 1973, when he was chairman of the Department of Physics at Princeton. He had served as a Defense Department science adviser, held a top-security clearance, and was a close friend of J. Robert Oppenheimer, chairman of the GAC of the AEC.

"Did the Russians explode a hydrogen bomb before the Teller H-bomb was fired?" we asked Goldberger.

"Yes," he replied, "that is a true statement." He then referred to the AFOAT One air-sample collection and analysis.

". . . The diagnosis," Goldberger said, "was complete and incontrovertible." He did not refer to a "device" but used the words "bomb" and "weapon."

Wigner's contribution on the question of the Soviet H-bomb came in a 1974 interview. We asked him about a statement by Soviet Premier Georgi Malenkov to the Supreme Soviet on August 8, 1953, four days before the Soviet thermonuclear bomb explosion. "The Government deems it necessary to report to the Supreme Soviet," Malenkov was quoted, "that the United States has no monopoly on the hydrogen bomb."[3]

Would Malenkov have made such a statement unless he were confident that the shot would be successful? Probably not.

Discussing this with us in his office at Princeton in 1974, Wigner recalled that in 1953 he attended a scientific conference that included several Soviet scientists. "A Russian boasted to me," he said, "that they had the hydrogen weapon before we did. And they did explode something that was probably a hydrogen weapon, not as good as Teller's, before we exploded one."

A short time later, Robert LeBaron told us in a Washington interview that in 1951, when he was chairman of the Military Liaison Committee and served as a link between the Pentagon and the AEC, he was present when the president was verbally informed of a Soviet thermonuclear experiment in late 1950 or early 1951.

LeBaron was urged as early as 1950—just sixteen days after President Truman launched the U.S. H-bomb project—to assume that the Soviets were working on their own H-bomb. The warning came from H. B. Loper, LeBaron's assistant, in a memorandum that was dated February 16 of that year and was declassified on April 3, 1975. It was entitled "A Basis for Estimating Maximum Soviet Capabilities for Atomic Warfare," and it presented these assumptions:

- In the field of basic physics, the Russians matched the United States.
- This may also have been true of applied physics and chemistry.
- The USSR had "been determined since 1945, at the latest, to [have gained] superiority over the rest of the world in the atomic weapon field."

Preteen Edward Teller with his sister, Emmi *(left)*, and mother. *Teller Family Archive.*

Nineteen-year-old Edward Teller as a student in Germany. *Teller Family Archive.*

Edward Teller and his wife, Mici, shortly before he joined the Atomic Bomb Project at Los Alamos. *Teller Family Archive.*

Leo Szilard, fellow Hungarian and physicist who pioneered controlled-fission research and whom Edward Teller described as the one man he would have most liked to imitate and the most stimulating person he ever knew. *U.S. Department of Energy.*

Gen. Leslie L. Groves, director of the Manhattan District Atomic Bomb Project, presents an award to Nobel physicist Enrico Fermi, one of Teller's closest friends and coworkers. *U.S. Department of Energy.*

Enrico Fermi and his wife, Laura, who described Teller as a loner at Los Alamos. *U.S. Department of Energy.*

Edward and Mici Teller at chessboard with son, Paul, as daughter, Wendy, looks on. *Teller Family Archive.*

J. Robert Oppenheimer *(left)* and Edward Teller *(back to camera)* shake hands in 1963 in their first friendly meeting since Teller's testimony ten years earlier as a hostile witness at Oppenheimer's security clearance hearing. Glenn Seaborg, another giant of the golden age of physics, looks on. *U.S. Department of Energy.*

Aerial view of Lawrence Livermore National Laboratory, Livermore, California, whose programs include nuclear weapons design, laser fusion, laser isotope separation, magnetic fusion energy, and biomedical and environmental research. Major facilities include the mirror fusion test facility, the nova laser system, and one of the largest research computer centers in the world. *U.S. Department of Energy.*

Edward Teller *(right)* with Harold Brown *(center)*, director of Lawrence Livermore National Laboratory in 1960, and Sidney Fernback, head of Computation Division at Lawrence Radiation Laboratory. *U.S. Department of Energy.*

Edward Teller at Livermore in its early days with fellow physicists. *Left to right:* Herbert York, Harold Brown, Edward Teller, Edwin McMillan, John Foster, and Kenneth Street. *Lawrence Livermore National Laboratory.*

Edward Teller *(left)* and Yuval Ne'eman, Israeli physicist and government leader, confer in 1985 during one of Teller's frequent visits to the Middle East. *Isaac Freidin.*

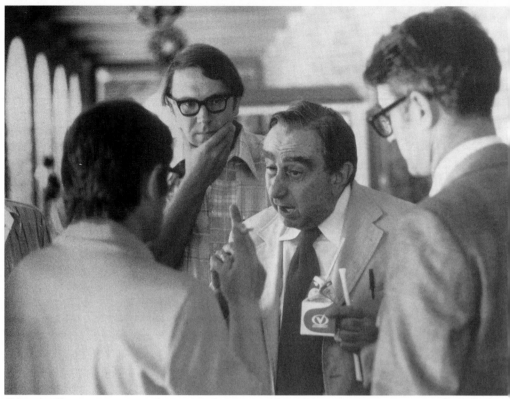

Edward Teller *(center)* engrossed in a 1977 discussion with Soviet scientists Evgeniy N. Yakovlev *(back to camera, left)*, then director of the Institute of High Pressure at Troitsk, USSR, and Vladimir E. Fortov *(rear)*, and with R. Norris Keeler *(right)*, U.S. physicist. *R. Norris Keeler.*

Edward Teller *(left)* and Sen. Rudolph E. Boschwitz of Minnesota, who helped Teller lobby senators on SDI ("Star Wars") funding during a three-day whirlwind tour of Capitol Hill in July 1986. *Senator Boschwitz's Office.*

President Ronald Reagan (*left*) receives congratulations from George A. Keyworth III, his science adviser, on his March 23, 1983, speech proposing the Strategic Defense Initiative. *White House photograph.*

Lowell Wood, chief aide to Edward Teller and top recruiter of young scientists for nuclear weapons programs at Livermore. *Lawrence Livermore National Laboratory.*

John Nuckolls, director of Lawrence Livermore National Laboratory as of May 11, 1988 (appointed 1987). *Lawrence Livermore National Laboratory.*

Edward Teller (*left*) and Caspar Weinberger, former secretary of defense, confer during reception preceding the dinner in Washington, D.C., on November 16, 1988, at which Teller and Andrei Sakharov, Nobel Prize–winning Soviet physicist and human rights champion, met for the first time. © *C. Kane.*

Edward Teller (*left*) is congratulated by Dean Harold Liebowitz after Teller's 1988 commencement address to graduates of George Washington University School of Engineering and Applied Science more than a half-century after Teller taught physics there. *George Washington University.*

- "If there is conclusive evidence of a Russian shortage of uranium . . . it must be assumed that they have attempted to balance that shortage by the development of weapons of higher efficiency per ton of ore available, e.g., a thermonuclear weapon."
- The Soviets were "proceeding with the same sense of urgency and disregard of costs as impelled our war effort."

But as late as the mid-1970s neither Teller nor many other officials involved in the U.S. nuclear weapons program were aware of either the memo to LeBaron or, more important, of Walkowicz's account of the early Soviet thermonuclear shot.

In an attempt to answer the question of who was first with a deliverable H-bomb, Teller wrote in 1980 to Arnold Kramish, who was technical liaison officer for the AEC in 1950 and 1951. He was an intermediary between the commission and government intelligence agencies, including the U.S. Air Force test-sampling agency.

Teller asked Kramish to send him an unclassified account of the thermonuclear events, particularly those of 1951. Teller expressed amazement that he, as the lead physicist on the U.S. H-bomb project, was never informed of any thermonuclear component in the Soviet test conducted at that time.

"The so-called hydrogen component in a Russian test in late 1950 or early 1951," Kramish replied on November 14, 1980, "never existed, and that is why you were never informed. . . . No evidence of another Soviet shot was withheld from you in those days."

Kramish said that after the Joe-1, the Soviet Union test of its first nuclear fission, or atomic, device, "we kept waiting for 'Joe' to drop another shoe." U.S. officials were anxious over whether and when the Soviets would advance from fission to the H-bomb. They were especially vigilant for the next Soviet nuclear test to see whether the resultant air samples contained evidence of thermonuclear components.

"But soon after Joe-1," Kramish continued, "evidence drifted in [later confirmed in the Soviet literature] that the Soviets were engaged in, at least, research on controlled fusion. The air force, particularly, was trying to read something more in this. I was not able to give them something positive as regards weapons until the spring of 1952."

Kramish's explanation for the conclusions of Walkowicz and LeBaron— that the Soviets exploded the first deliverable hydrogen bomb—was that they were mixed up over evidence of *controlled* fusion and evidence of explosion fusion.

"So you see," he wrote Teller, ". . . there was an intertwining of controlled and explosive fusion developments. The passage of time has tended to further fuse these concepts in the minds of many."[4]

Five years after writing Teller, Kramish repeated his conviction in a letter to us. Writing on October 17, 1985, he brushed aside one possible reason for conflicting conclusions as to whether the Soviets were first with the H-bomb. That possibility is that the AEC did not receive all the air-sample collection data from the air force agency, AFOAT One.

"If the latter agency withheld any collection data from the AEC, it would have been nonsensical for them to do that," he said, "for they were dependent on the AEC laboratories to interpret that data. After all, it was the AEC which was building the bombs, not that air force agency."

Kramish added that the United States also had evidence "not from air sampling"—presumably personal intelligence—about whether the Soviets had exploded an H-bomb test device.

The Kramish letters might be considered reason enough to close the book on a thirty-five-year-old debate. But do they?

Walkowicz insisted that the only explanation for material collected by AFOAT One in early 1950 was that the Soviets had set off a thermonuclear explosion. It is difficult to accept Kramish's suggestion that Walkowicz would have confused controlled fusion with a thermonuclear explosion. In the first instance, radiation does not escape into the atmosphere. By contrast, a fusion shot produces radioactive debris that finds its way into the atmosphere, where it can be collected by American planes patrolling for just that purpose.

It is also doubtful that LeBaron, as Kramish suggests, failed "to a greater extent to distinguish [between] the two facets of fusion." In his interview with us, LeBaron was unequivocal about what was reported to the president in his presence.

One possible explanation should not be overlooked: Because of some bureaucratic slip or other reason, Kramish himself might not have received all the results of all the Soviet shots.

In fact, Robert LeBaron indicated to us that this was exactly what happened not only in the case of Kramish but also in the case of Teller. When we interviewed LeBaron in April 1975 over lunch at the Cosmos Club, he spoke of the Soviet fusion shot in late 1950 or early 1951. He said the scientist who analyzed the debris reported his findings to only six air force officers with a need to know and to LeBaron, who received them in his role as presidential adviser and as link between the Pentagon and the AEC. LeBaron said the essence of the report was then passed on verbally to President Truman and Secretary of State

Dean Acheson. Even the secretaries of the services were not told, he said.

Not even the AEC? we asked. Or its GAC or J. Robert Oppenheimer as chairman of the committee or Edward Teller as the lead scientist on the U.S. fusion-bomb program?

LeBaron shook his head. "No," he said, "they were not notified. It was top secret. Any letter of transmittal would have gone over my desk, and I did not sign such a letter."

LeBaron's astounding reply could explain much of the doubt and conflicting discussion on who was ahead at which point in the H-bomb race. It could explain, for example, why there is no paper trail that would convince those who still doubt that the Soviets produced the first deliverable hydrogen bomb.

Another prominent American scientist who expressed no doubt about the Soviet lead over the United States in one phase of nuclear weapons development was Herbert York, the first director of the Lawrence Livermore National Laboratory and author of several books covering his extensive career in nuclear weaponry. In a 1976 report, York referred to the Soviet shot of August 12, 1953.

"It was the first device anywhere to use lithium deuteride as a fuel, and presumably could readily have been converted to a practical weapon if there were any point in doing so," he wrote.[5]

Nine years after York's report, Andrei Sakharov revealed additional details of the Soviet test in a 1985 article for *Foreign Affairs*. "During the ground-level test of the Soviet thermonuclear charge in August 1953," he wrote, "tens of thousands of people were evacuated beforehand from the zone where fallout was possible. People were not allowed to return to the settlement of Kara-Aul until the spring of 1954."[6]

What all this—the frequently conflicting evidence on who was first with the H-bomb—points to is that the Soviets exploded the first deliverable bomb but that it was probably smaller and more crude than the one exploded seven months later by the United States.

During this phase of the nuclear race in the early 1950s, surprisingly to some, Teller was not driven to test a deliverable hydrogen bomb. As he explained in a statement prepared for us in early 1975, he was aware that lithium deuteride was the fuel of choice for such a weapon. But once this was understood, he felt sure, the design of efficient thermonuclear weapons would follow. He felt there was little danger from the Soviet small nuclear arsenal in the short term. So there was time for careful, methodical planning and experimentation.

He wrote:

The 1952 U.S. Mike shot had as its purpose the proving of a principle. No effort had been made at that time to get a deliverable weapon, and the tested configuration was indeed not deliverable. However, it was perfectly clear to all of us that once the principle was proved, a deliverable weapon could be constructed, and all the basic design concepts necessary for its construction were available at that time. The actual test of a deliverable weapon occurred two years later and it worked essentially as we expected. In this whole development the Russian explosion that took place in the summer of 1953 had no effect on our state of technical knowledge or on our planning.[7]

Nearly thirty-five years after the Soviet explosion of a deliverable H-bomb—which the AEC officially brushed off by saying its 1951 Greenhouse and 1952 Mike tests involved "similar reactions"—Soviet scientists attended a May 1988 meeting with American colleagues. Among Americans at the session was physicist Norris Keeler, a former assistant to Edward Teller at the Livermore laboratory. Keeler and several of his Soviet colleagues discussed the nearly parallel approach taken by their countries in development of the H-bomb. The Soviet scientists, he said, freely admitted that they had kept tabs on the progress being made by Teller and his associates. Moreover, like the Americans, they thought it prudent to conduct a thermonuclear burn to test their theory before proceeding to build a deliverable bomb.

This account tends to support the conclusion of Walkowicz and others that there was a Soviet fusion test shot in late 1950, slightly less than three years before the Soviet H-bomb test of 1953. That timetable would have been consistent with the U.S. schedule, under which a fusion shot in 1951 preceded the 1954 explosion of a deliverable H-bomb.

In a statement delivered to us in May of 1988, Keeler made these points:

1. The Soviets carried out a "feasibility experiment" to verify whether fusion could take place under conditions existing in a nuclear-fission device.

2. It is and has been the general understanding among senior Soviet scientists that the Soviet Union fielded a deliverable hydrogen bomb before the United States did so. "Major intellectual lights" in the Soviet program were known to have included Kurchatov, Zeldovich, and Sakharov. "The name of Yuli Khariton [another prominent scientist] has now recently surfaced" and been added to them.

Keeler also relayed reports by Soviet scientists that many of their senior colleagues in the Soviet nuclear weaponry program disagreed with Stalin's politics and were forced to work in the USSR nuclear weapons program.

"It is now a matter of open discussion in the USSR," Keeler said, "that many senior scientists in the Soviet program were operating out of a 'black institute' or were political prisoners. That is, in the fashion of A. N. Tupolev, the eminent aeronautical engineer, they were allowed to work on the program during the day but were required to return to their prison cells at night," Keeler said.

Andrei Sakharov wrote in 1974 that his Soviet research group "became part of a special institute" under the control of Lavrenti P. Beria, head of the KGB and chief enforcer for Stalin, whom Sakharov called "one of the greatest criminals of the sorely tried Twentieth Century." He said, "Until the summer of 1953 the chief of the atomic project was Beria, who ruled over millions of slave-prisoners. Almost all the construction was done with their labor."[8]

Disagreement over early Soviet advances toward construction of an H-bomb, persisting until today, was even sharper during the debate of the 1950s. This explains, in addition to Teller's worry, much of the apprehension and pressure in some quarters of the military establishment for consideration of a first strike or for "deliberately precipitating war with the USSR in the near future," as proposed in the Joint Chiefs of Staff briefing paper of May 1954.

Fortunately, among those who refused to be driven to that form of insanity was the army chief of staff, Gen. Matthew B. Ridgway. He condemned such a proposal as "contrary to every principle upon which our Nation was founded" and "abhorrent to the great mass of American people."

Another was President Eisenhower. Instead, he endorsed a basic national security policy paper which was drawn up a few months later, in the fall of 1954, and rebuffed the Joint Chiefs of Staff Advanced Study Group. "The United States and its allies," it said, "must reject the concept of preventive war or acts intended to provoke war."[9]

Chapter 16

DARK DUTY

Of all the controversies and misfortunes enveloping Edward Teller as a scientist, none was more painful or more potentially devastating than his appearance as a witness in the Oppenheimer security case. It cost him many old friends, much peace of mind, and a good measure of physical health.

On recorded accomplishment alone, J. Robert Oppenheimer might well have lived out his life as a national hero. His brilliance as a theoretical physicist and spellbinding lecturer had earned him international acclaim. The military had overlooked his political eccentricities and his history of unpredictable behavior to appoint him key scientist and administrator of the atomic bomb project. His vast accumulation of honors and praise included President Truman's declaration, "More than any one man, Oppenheimer is to be credited with the achievement of the completed atomic bomb."[1]

But on June 29, 1954, after more than two months of tense hearings and deliberations by its Personnel Security Board, the AEC declared that Oppenheimer was a security risk. The decision, upholding a 2–1 vote of the security board, demolished Oppenheimer's monumental career as a scientist and government adviser. It also split the scientific community into his defenders and detractors, with the defenders in the great majority.

By contrast, the majority condemned Teller's role as a witness whose testimony was interpreted as a telling blow to Oppenheimer. To his critics it mattered little that Teller's testimony was reluctantly given and that Teller's words were far less damaging to Oppenheimer than both the actions and the words of Oppenheimer himself. These critics saw Teller as the villain in the drama, and they virtually ostracized him from their tight inner circle.

This held true despite the fact that Teller was not involved in the years-long investigation of Oppenheimer, was never asked his opinion of Oppenheimer's loyalty until the time of the hearing, and never expressed agreement with the basic accusation against Oppenheimer. In essence, that accusation was that Oppenheimer posed a risk to national security and therefore should not be granted an extension of his one-year contract as a consultant to the AEC.

Oppenheimer's past had been questioned and investigated almost from the moment General Groves selected him in 1943 as scientific director of the Manhattan Project. But not until November 7, 1953, did any of the questioning and investigating propel the issue onto the public stage.

On that date, William Liscum Borden, the former War World II bomber pilot and executive director of Sen. Brien McMahon's Joint Committee on Atomic Energy, addressed a letter to FBI Director J. Edgar Hoover.

"The purpose of this letter," he said, "is to state my own exhaustively considered opinion, based upon years of study of the available classified evidence, that more probably than not J. Robert Oppenheimer is an agent of the Soviet Union."

The factors on which he based his opinion included the following:

- Oppenheimer contributed "substantial monthly sums" to the Communist party.
- His "ties with communism had survived" both the Soviet Union–Nazi nonaggression pact and the Soviet attack on Finland. (This implied that in Oppenheimer's eyes Communist Russia could do no wrong.)
- His wife, his brother, his mistress, all his close friends, and *all* those he recruited for the early wartime atomic project at Berkeley were Communists.
- He "had been instrumental in securing recruits" for the Communist party and "was in frequent contact with Soviet espionage agents."

Borden then cited the emergence of these additional factors after Oppenheimer came under consideration for the Los Alamos post and his name was submitted for security clearance in April 1942:

"In May 1942, he either stopped contributing . . . to the Communist party or . . . made his contributions through a new channel not yet discovered." He also "repeatedly gave false information to General Groves, the Manhattan District, and the FBI concerning his activities during the previous three years."

Borden concluded:

Between 1929 and mid-1942, more probably than not, J. Robert Oppenheimer was such a sufficiently hardened Communist that he either volunteered espionage information to the Soviets or complied with a request for such information. (This includes the possibility that when he singled out the weapons aspect of atomic development as his personal specialty, he was acting under Soviet instructions.)

Hoover and Atty. Gen. Herbert Brownell delivered the letter to the White House together.[2] On December 3, 1953, Eisenhower called an emergency meeting with Brownell, AEC chairman Lewis L. Strauss, Secretary of Defense Charles E. Wilson, Defense Mobilization Director Arthur S. Flemming, and General Robert Cutler, the president's special assistant for national security.

The president directed that hearings be held under Executive Order 10450, "Security Requirements for Government Employment." He also ordered that in the meantime "a blank wall" be placed between Oppenheimer and classified information.

Because they dealt with highly classified material and charges that might unjustly damage the reputation of their subject, the hearings were held behind closed doors, beginning April 12, 1954. On June 16, noting that Oppenheimer himself had given a copy of the charges to the press, the AEC released a transcript of unclassified testimony. The three-member hearing board was headed by Gordon Gray, president of the University of North Carolina.

In the interim, the Gray board had conducted the hearings on Oppenheimer's actions in a political climate far different from the one in which most of those actions were taken.

Borden's document of accusation took Oppenheimer back to 1929 and into the early 1940s. In that period, the popular view of communism was much less severe than during the years following World War II.

During the Spanish Civil War of 1936–39, Oppenheimer was among many Americans supporting opponents of Gen. Francisco Franco, a Fascist who had overthrown an elected government dominated by liberals. Many of Franco's opponents contributed to the support of the Abraham Lincoln Brigade, a unit formed in the United States as a division of the Soviet-sponsored International Brigade.

Oppenheimer frankly reported his contributions to the brigade when he applied for government security clearance six years later to become scientific director of the A-bomb project at Los Alamos. He also reported his contributions to West Coast Communist-front organizations. Also, there was no secret about the Communist party membership of Oppenheimer's wife, brother, and mistress. In the Great Depression of the 1930s, disenchantment with capitalism made communism attractive to many. In the 1940s the Soviet Union was a U.S. wartime ally. Support of Communist-front groups was common among non-Communists and was considered chic among campus intellectuals.

But after World War II, with Soviet encroachment on Eastern Europe and the Baltic States, and with the onset of the Cold War between East and West, the climate changed. Anticommunism became the theme of superpatriots, pseudopatriots, and politicians in search of a publicity touchstone. Foremost among these was Sen. Joseph R. McCarthy, the Wisconsin Republican whose name became synonymous with reckless exploitation of Russophobia. In a speech at Wheeling, West Virginia, on February 9, 1950, McCarthy declared that he knew of 205 Communists employed by the State Department. He amended the charges later by referring to "bad security risks" instead of Communists and reducing the number to fifty-seven. In the end, he failed to supply a single name to support the charge and was publicly censured by formal resolution of the Senate.

But in the meantime, Oppenheimer's affinity for Communists and their causes came under closer scrutiny by security officers as early as the summer of 1943, when he received a warning visit by Lt. Col. John Lansdale, security aide to Brigadier General Groves. Lansdale expressed concern about Oppenheimer's efforts to help a Berkeley scientist receive a draft deferment. Earlier, Oppenheimer had recruited the scientist Giovanni Rossi Lomanitz for the radiation laboratory and now requested he be assigned there instead of going into the army.

Less than one month after Lansdale's visit, Oppenheimer reported to security officials in Berkeley that he had been told a man named George C. Eltenton could channel scientific information to the Russians. Eltenton was a British-born engineer working in Berkeley for the Shell Development Corporation.[3] Oppenheimer said he had been given Eltenton's name by a friend during an informal kitchen conversation at Oppenheimer's home before a dinner party in January or February, more than six months earlier. He did not name the friend.

The disclosure stirred the curiosity of Lt. Col. Boris Pash, counterintelligence chief for the Ninth Army Corps. Why would Oppenheimer wait more than six months to report the conversation? Pash knew that Eltenton was already under surveillance. So why would Oppenheimer name only him and not the person who had brought up the subject in Oppenheimer's home?

At a follow-up session the next day, August 26, 1943, Oppenheimer told Pash that he also had learned of two or three others who had been contacted about channeling information through Eltenton to the Soviet consul.[4] Asked repeatedly to name his informant and the others who had been contacted about supplying information for Eltenton, he refused. Nothing had come of it, so why involve colleagues whose only role had been to hear and reject a suggestion?

Pash expressed regret that Oppenheimer was not more forthcoming. But he marked the enigmatic scientist down for closer investigation. He also took comfort in the knowledge that the conversation with Oppenheimer had been secretly preserved on a wire recorder. Pash sent Groves a message flatly suggesting that Oppenheimer reported the conversation in the first place only because of fear that the Lomanitz situation had brought unwelcome focus on his own activities and he wished to diffuse suspicion about himself. Pash also arranged simultaneously for his security officer at Los Alamos, Capt. Peer de Silva, to send Washington a memorandum saying that Oppenheimer's refusal to supply the requested identities was "playing a key part in the attempts of the Soviet Union to secure, by espionage, highly secret information which is vital to the security of the United States." De Silva concluded that Oppenheimer was either "incredibly naive . . . or extremely clever and disloyal."

Brigadier General Groves, who had pushed Oppenheimer's clearance through in spite of the advice of his security people, was now drawn into the game. In early September, during a sixteen-hour train ride from Cheyenne to Chicago with Oppenheimer and Lansdale, the talk turned to Oppenheimer's refusal to identify his source. He would do so, Oppenheimer said, only if Groves gave him a direct order.

A few days later, on September 13, Lansdale was back at his post in Washington and met with Oppenheimer, who was there on a short visit. The setting was Groves's Pentagon office, and again the conversation was secretly recorded. Also again, Oppenheimer at first refused to identify his source. But he did name several Manhattan Project workers in Berkeley as current or former Communist party members. They included Lomanitz, several former Oppenheimer students, including one Joseph Weinberg, and his own wife and brother. Asked about a friend named Haakon Chevalier, an American-born teacher of French at Berkeley, Oppenheimer replied, "I wouldn't be surprised if he were a member. He's quite a Red." But after a two-hour exchange, Lansdale still had not come up with the key identity.

Then, as the inquiry wore on through several more weeks and tension increased, Lansdale shifted the focus to Groves, who had shrugged off earlier warnings about Oppenheimer. Lansdale urged that Groves, as Oppenheimer had almost invited him to do, order Oppenheimer to identify the contact. Finally, Groves gave Oppenheimer a direct order to do so, and on December 12, 1943, Oppenheimer did.[5]

He named Haakon Chevalier.

But this time around he said Chevalier had approached only him. This differed from the version he had given Colonel Pash four months earlier, when he said that the contact had approached at least two persons on the Los Alamos project and one at Berkeley. The discrepancy, not regarded by Groves as serious enough to offset Oppenheimer's great value to the A-bomb project, would lie dormant for nearly eleven years. Then, combined with others, it would come back to haunt Oppenheimer for the rest of his life.

Oppenheimer's conflicting versions of the Chevalier kitchen conversation did not escape the lawyer chosen to represent the AEC in the case against Oppenheimer before the Personnel Security Board that began proceedings on April 12, 1954. He was Roger Robb, a Washingtonian by birth and known as a tough, thorough adversary in court. Robb's clients had covered a broad political range, from right-wing broadcaster Fulton Lewis, Jr., to the U.S. Communist party chief, Earl Browder.

Robb approached the case without assuming there was enough evidence to sustain the accusation against Oppenheimer. But, he later said, as he dug into the stacks of material during the next two months, that conclusion became inescapable. To gain access to the material, Robb had applied for and received a "Q"—top-secret, need-to-know—security clearance.

Oppenheimer's legal team was headed by Lloyd K. Garrison, a prominent New York lawyer, a member of the Madison Avenue firm of Paul, Weiss, Rifkind, Wharton and Garrison. He was also a member of the board of the Institute for Advanced Studies at Princeton and therefore knew Oppenheimer.

Like Robb, the defense group had applied for a "Q" security clearance. It was granted to Garrison but denied to two of his assistants in the case. On the principle that denial of one was a denial of all, Garrison refused to make use of his clearance and thereby walled himself off from classified material available in advance to the opposing side. When the hearings opened, the defenders were already at a clear disadvantage.

Oppenheimer had barely settled into the witness chair under cross-examination on the third day when Robb began setting snares.

Asked whether he believed that association with the Communist party was "inconsistent with work on a secret war project," Oppenheimer said that he did.

Later Robb brought up the subject of a letter Oppenheimer had written to Colonel Lansdale in 1943 asking whether the recently drafted Rossi Lomanitz could be assigned to the Berkeley Radiation Laboratory. Oppenheimer would not have written that letter if he had known that Lomanitz was a Communist, said Robb, would he?

"No," said Oppenheimer, and the trap was sprung.

All Robb had to do then was to introduce Oppenheimer's own words from the transcript of the interview recorded by Pash and Lansdale:

"I know for a fact, I know, I learned on my last visit to Berkeley, that both Lomanitz and Weinberg were members of the Communist party."

Other Robb questions involved the kitchen conversation with Chevalier.

Did Chevalier mention the use of microfilm to transmit information or its transmission through a Soviet consulate member or that he had discussed the subject with anyone else? Did anyone else tell Oppenheimer that Chevalier had approached someone else on the matter of channeling secret scientific information to the Soviet Union?

Oppenheimer replied in the negative to each of these questions, and the second trap closed behind him.

Robb brought out the transcript of another ten-year-old Pash interview, the one in which Oppenheimer said that two or three others had been approached at Los Alamos and Berkeley.

"Did you tell Pash the truth about this thing?" Robb asked.

"No," said Oppenheimer.

"You lied to him?"

"Yes."

After several more intervening questions, Oppenheimer was asked why he had lied.

"Because," he answered, "I was an idiot."[6]

Robb went on, citing one detail after another from the old interview record, then asked the summary question, closing the last trap.

"Isn't it a fair statement today, Dr. Oppenheimer, that according to your testimony now you told not one lie to Colonel Pash but a whole fabrication and tissue of lies?"

"Right," said Oppenheimer.

Oppenheimer's collapse was not his only dark moment. Another came during the testimony of David Lilienthal, the highly respected former AEC chairman who testified on his behalf. A graduate of Harvard Law School, Lilienthal was an original member of the Tennessee Valley Authority and its chairman from 1941 to 1946, then became first chairman of the AEC. All this was meticulously cited for the record under questioning by Samuel J. Silverman, a member of the Oppenheimer legal team.

Silverman then led Lilienthal up to the circumstances surrounding the security clearance given Oppenheimer in 1947 under the newly adopted Atomic Energy Act. The act provided for retention of clearance by those who had already been cleared to work on the atomic bomb project, but it made the FBI responsible for continuously reviewing and updating their security files. The AEC was to review new information in each file and decide whether to extend a clearance. Oppenheimer's updated file was referred by the FBI to the AEC on March 8, 1947. Lilienthal testified that it contained "derogatory information going back a number of years" but lacked "significant reference" to Oppenheimer's work for the government. (Just four days after the AEC review of his file, Oppenheimer received the Medal of Merit from President Truman "in recognition of his outstanding public service.")

Feeling that the record should include references to Oppenheimer's public service, the commissioners requested opinions from Vannevar Bush, James B. Conant, Secretary of War Robert P. Patterson, and General Groves. All gave Oppenheimer a vote of confidence. Clark Clifford, counsel to the president, was then contacted to make Truman aware of the information in the file.

After testifying to this, Lilienthal was asked under cross-examination by Robb whether he and Bush had suggested to Clifford that a special board be convened to review the Oppenheimer file. "No, we did not," he answered.

Was it ever discussed with Clifford? "No, I believe not."

Was he certain? "I am not sure, but I have no recollection of it."

Robb then fished out an AEC memorandum covering the period and read it aloud: "Dr. Bush and the Chairman [Lilienthal] met with Mr. Clifford and . . . discussed with him the desirability of having a review of this case by a board of distinguished jurists and other citizens." The document said Lilienthal himself suggested that the board include "judges of the Supreme Court."

Now Robb had successfully attacked the credibility of both Oppenheimer and Lilienthal, one of Oppenheimer's staunchest supporters. Combined with the security reports linking Oppenheimer to Communists and Communist causes, this alone would have been enough to sink Oppenheimer.

But when all the record of the hearings was sanitized of classified secrets and was released for public consumption, what created the biggest sensation in the scientific community was not that Oppenheimer and Lilienthal had given damaging testimony. What stood out was the testimony of Edward Teller.

Throughout the weeks leading up to his appearance Teller was in a quandary. Oppenheimer had asked him for support. Teller said the request came when they met at a high-energy conference in Rochester between the time Oppenheimer's clearance was suspended and the start of the security hearings in April.

"When he saw me," Teller said, "he asked me, 'I suppose, I hope, that you don't think that anything I did has sinister implications.' I said I did not think that. After all, the word *sinister* was pretty harsh. Then he asked if I would speak to his lawyer, and I said I would."

Teller also met with Garrison and was not inclined to appear as an unfriendly witness.

"Actually, when I left for Washington," he said, "I was prepared for the question that was going to be asked of me, namely: Do I consider Oppenheimer a security risk? And I was prepared to answer 'no' to that question."[7]

Arriving in Washington on April 27, Teller found a message from Robb asking to speak with him. His inclination was to beg off, because he felt it was "not quite right." But since he had already met with an attorney for Oppenheimer, he did not see how he could refuse the same request from Robb.

Robb first asked the obvious, crucial question. "I told him that I did not consider Oppenheimer a security risk."

Then Robb pulled out a transcript of the proceedings up to that point.

"Robb showed me part of the testimony showing that Oppenheimer had lied to a security person, that he admitted to lying but that he could not now be prosecuted for what was a criminal offense because the statute of limitations had taken effect."[8]

Teller was sworn in the next afternoon. Previous witnesses had included such giants in the field of nuclear energy as Lilienthal, Enrico Fermi, I. I. Rabi, Conant, and Jerrold R. Zacharias, director of the MIT laboratory of nuclear science. Ten years earlier all of them were more prominent than Teller, who did not even rate an assumed name for security purposes while working at Los Alamos. Now he had taken his place in the top rank of theoretical physicists. Regardless of the factual weight of his testimony, his words would be carefully appraised by his colleagues.

One of Robb's first questions was designed to prevent any impression that Teller relished the situation as an opportunity to square an old grudge. Did he want to be there?

"I appear," Teller said, "because I have been asked to and because I consider it my duty upon request to say what I think in the matter. I would have preferred not to appear."

Did he intend that any of his testimony suggest that Dr. Oppenheimer was disloyal to the United States?

"I do not want to suggest anything of the kind. I know Oppenheimer as an intellectually most alert and a very complicated person, and I think it would be presumptuous and wrong on my part if I would try in any way to analyze his motives. But I have always assumed, and I now assume, that he is loyal to the United States. I believe this, and I shall continue to believe it until I see very conclusive proof to the opposite."

Did he believe Oppenheimer was a security risk?

"In a great number of instances I have seen Dr. Oppenheimer act—I understood that Dr. Oppenheimer acted—in a way which for me was exceedingly hard to understand. I thoroughly disagreed with him in numerous issues, and his actions frankly appeared to me confused and complicated. To this extent, I feel that I would like to see the vital interests of this country in hands which I understand better and therefore trust more. In this very limited sense I would like to express a feeling that I would feel personally more secure if public matters would rest in other hands."

This last sentence swept through the scientific community. Lost in most accounts of his appearance was Teller's estimate that because "some people like Oppenheimer" had refused to support the thermonuclear program after World War II, the United States had lost four years in the race to develop the hydrogen bomb. What was remembered, however, was that Teller had appeared as a witness for those accusing Oppenheimer of being unworthy of his nation's trust and that the accusation was sustained.

On June 29, 1954, the AEC adopted the recommendation of its Personnel Security Board that Oppenheimer be denied a renewal of his security clearance.

The AEC action effectively ended Oppenheimer's career as a high-level government servant. In academic circles he retained much of the respect he had held before the hearings. He won reelection as director of the Institute of Advanced Studies at Princeton. Europe welcomed him. He received the Legion of Honor from France and lectured in Belgium, Greece, and Israel.

In 1963, Oppenheimer was selected to receive the coveted Fermi Award, named in memory of the Italian-born physicist who had died a few months after the hearing. Among those recommending Oppenheimer for the award was its 1962 recipient, Edward Teller, who welcomed the opportunity to ease the pervasive pain that still lingered. At a White House ceremony on December 2, President Lyndon B. Johnson presented Oppenheimer the certificate, the medal, and the $50,000 check accompanying the honor. Teller joined those warmly congratulating Oppenheimer in a moment recorded by photographers as both of the old rivals smiled. But nothing more came from this gesture toward reconciliation, and the long-standing chill continued until Oppenheimer's death in 1967.[9]

Ironically, Oppenheimer's friendship with Haakon Chevalier continued until nearly the end. It was broken off only when Chevalier, who had moved to France before the 1954 security hearings, wrote Oppenheimer in 1964 about a book Chevalier planned to write. He intended to record that they had been members of the same Communist party unit, and he asked whether Oppenheimer would object. Writing in reply, Oppenheimer repeated his long-standing denial of such membership and withheld his approval. The friendship ended with a Chevalier letter accusing Oppenheimer of weaving "an elaborate fabric of lies" about him.

Edward Teller was never fully relieved of the burden he carried from AEC hearing room 2022. The first indication of what lay in store came a few weeks after the decision stripping Oppenheimer of his security clearance, when Teller and his wife visited Los Alamos for a scientific conference.

The first event was a social gathering in the dining hall of the central building. As the Tellers prepared to take their seats, Edward spotted Bob Christie, an old friend and colleague from his University of Chicago days in 1942, nearby. Stepping toward Christie and calling out a greeting, Teller extended his hand.

Looking stonily at the hand, the old friend turned away, leaving Teller first stunned, then so hurt that he and his wife quickly left the hall and returned to their room, where Edward Teller wept.

Christie later described his snub as a "spontaneous reaction of the moment," but for Teller it was the beginning of exile from the world of intellectual liberals with whom he had felt closest since his flight from Nazi Germany. Now came the painful process of rebuilding a new world peopled largely by conservatives, militarists, and a few old friends such as Strauss and fellow Hungarians Eugene Wigner and Leo Szilard. To many of them, particularly the conservatives and militarists, he was to assume heroic stature. But the loss of respect and friendship among so many of his former associates caused him and his wife an anguish that he refused to discuss for more than twenty years after its onset. Then, in August 1974, he could contain it no longer. He said:

> If a person leaves his country, leaves his continent, leaves his relatives, leaves his friends, the only people he knows are his professional colleagues. If more than ninety percent of these then come around to consider him an enemy, an outcast, it is bound to have an effect. The truth is it had a profound effect. It affected me, it affected Mici, it even affected her health.[10]

Two years after the hearings, Teller required treatment for colitis, an inflammatory digestive illness frequently associated with stress. The next three decades were to bring many more bouts with it and other illnesses, capped by his 1979 heart attack and later coronary bypass surgery. They were also to bring more crises in an already crisis-ridden career.

Chapter 17

REACTORS

When one of the Soviet Union's most powerful nuclear reactors broke out of control at Chernobyl and sent radioactive poison wafting over much of Europe, Edward Teller was in California monitoring progress on myriad SDI projects. It was April 1986. Like most Americans, Teller received first word about the accident from newspaper and broadcast accounts. But as details began sifting through tight Soviet censorship and scientists outside Russia assembled puzzle pieces in the form of radioactivity measurements and other evidence, it became apparent that Chernobyl was the greatest disaster in the history of the peacetime nuclear energy industry.

In the West, the first four decades of that history were marked by endless controversy over the safety and environmental effects of nuclear energy. Throughout much of this battle, Teller was a central figure. But he was not always on the same side. He consistently supported the development of nuclear energy. But there were times when he opposed specific projects because of the pell-mell rush by their advocates to launch them without due regard for safety.

In fact, forty years before Chernobyl, Teller served as chairman of an advisory committee created by the AEC to plan for a nuclear power industry that could help fill the energy needs of the United States without endangering the environment. The work of that group, known as the Reactor Safeguard Committee, has received much of the credit for the relatively safe record of nuclear reactors built in the Western world. By contrast, industry experts believe that if recommendations of the committee had been followed at Chernobyl, the disaster there would have been averted. Instead, the effects of that event might not be fully measured until well into the next century.

In the non-Soviet world, the first sign of the Chernobyl trouble appears to have been picked up by a technician on April 28, 1986, at the Foresmark nuclear power plant, near Stockholm, Sweden. Chernobyl is sixty miles north of Kiev, a city of 2,489,000 in the Ukraine of the Soviet's southwest. Stockholm is some 750 miles northwest of the Soviet reactor. At 9:00 A.M. the technician at the Foresmark noticed a burst of radiation outside the plant and sounded an alarm. A check of plant personnel turned up no contamination. The plant itself was surveyed for leaks. The results were negative.

But by 10:15 A.M. vegetation surrounding the plant registered radioactivity 500 percent above normal. The Swedish nuclear agency in Stockholm was alerted. A spokesman for the agency later reported, "At about 10:30 A.M. calls were coming in from various radiation monitoring facilities throughout the country. Dangerous radiation levels were confirmed to be in the atmosphere, but the whereabouts of the source was unknown."[1]

Swedish officials considered the possibility of an accident in a neighboring country. They contacted authorities in Finland, Denmark, and Norway. Surveys of reactors there produced no clue.

Weather records for the previous few days were pulled out and examined. Wind patterns were traced back through their northwesterly flow over Scandinavia from the Baltic states, East Germany, Poland, and—the answer: The radiation flowing over much of northern Europe originated in the Soviet Union.

Meanwhile, American scientists working independently of Swedish monitors collected and analyzed samples of air emanating from the Soviet Union. In the fallout they detected a mixture of iodine, cesium, cobalt, xenon, and krypton. The signature was unmistakable. This release could have come only from a nuclear power plant. The assembled clues pointed to the Chernobyl area of the Ukraine.

After refusing for six hours to confirm the mounting evidence, the Soviet Council of Ministers issued a statement on the evening of April 28, admitting, "An accident has occurred at the Chernobyl nuclear power plant. . . ."

Later, it was learned that the accident occurred at 1:23 A.M. on Saturday, April 26, more than two days and eight and one-half hours before the Swedish technician's discovery. Evacuation of the area did not begin until thirty-six hours later.

Problems resulting from this delay were compounded as the Soviet government publicly downplayed the disaster, even while 100,000 persons from farms, villages, and towns within an eighteen-mile radius of Chernobyl were being evacuated. In Poland, the sale of milk and vegetables was banned for fear of radioactive contamination. While children in other Eastern European countries were being given antiradiation drugs, the Soviets delayed similar health measures for thirteen days after the accident.

Only then were warnings issued to citizens of nearby Kiev and farmers of the Chernobyl area to refrain from consumption of vegetables and milk.

Nearly a full year later, on April 6, 1987, an eyewitness description of the accident scene was offered by a fire fighter, Lt. Col. Leonid P. Telyatnikov.[2] Arriving at the Chernobyl reactor No. 4 twenty-five minutes after the explosion, he found fires raging at several levels of the 215-foot-high reactor building. With at least six fire fighters under his command, Telyatnikov fought to control the fire flaring from a hole in the roof. Also on the scene were white-uniformed workers of the reactor station, who warned Telyatnikov and his men of the radiation spewing from the reactor.

"As you were putting out the fire," Telyatnikov said, "you had the impression you could see the radiation. First, a lot of the substances there were glowing, luminescent, a bit like sparklers. There were flashes of light springing from place to place as if they had been thrown. And there was a kind of gas on the roof . . . a kind of fog. It gave off a peculiar smell."

As fatigue overtook the men on the roof, some lost consciousness. With the onset of coughing and vomiting, Telyatnikov realized that he had been zapped by radiation. All six men fighting the fire on the roof with Telyatnikov died within a year. Telyatnikov himself survived until at least early 1989 when he appeared in a televised interview recounting the tragedy. Despite intensive treatment for radiation sickness, he was badly disabled.

Experts differed greatly in assessing the probable effects of Chernobyl. Teller, a world authority on nuclear energy, discounted suggestions that Europeans in the path of the Chernobyl fallout were endangered. On the possible health hazards to Soviet residents themselves, he offered a distinctly more optimistic appraisal than that of Dr. Robert Gale, a U.S. bone-marrow specialist who went to the assistance of Soviet physicians after the accident.

"The accident at Chernobyl unfortunately did involve the loss of life," Teller wrote in *Better a Shield Than a Sword*.

In the first days following the accident, 203 people, all of them exposed at the reactor site, were hospitalized with radiation sickness. At last report, thirty-one people, plant employees in the vicinity of the accident and firefighters who remained throughout the early hours of the accident attempting to limit the damage, have died. In August [1986], when the report was issued, thirty patients were still hospitalized but were expected to recover.

The one really important question is what effect the fallout from the reactor accident will have on life expectancy. Some increase in cancer among the millions exposed, resulting in perhaps as many as 1,000 premature deaths, may occur during the next seventy years. [In the same population, a far greater number of people will die prematurely from smoking cigarettes.] There is no indication that the health of anyone outside the Soviet Union will be adversely affected.[3]

Gale, chairman of the International Bone Marrow Transplant Registry, went to the Soviet Union shortly after the accident to help perform bone-marrow transplants on radiation victims. He had studied the lingering health effects on victims of the World War II atomic bombings of Hiroshima and Nagasaki. Assessing the effects of Chernobyl on Soviet citizens, he told reporters, "I think we can say that there are at least 50,000 to 100,000 people who have had some dose of radiation which might be of long-term concern."[4]

While Teller said there was "no indication" of adverse effects on "anyone outside of the Soviet Union" and Gale did not directly address that point, West German experts raised a question. In April 1987, one year after the accident, they noted that an unusually great number of deformed babies had been born in West Germany since Chernobyl. They called for an inquiry into whether this was the result of fallout from the accident.[5]

Three years after the disaster, the weekly Moscow News reported that some cancer rates among middle-aged residents of a contaminated farm area near Chernobyl had doubled and deformed animals were being born.

In September 1986, the Lawrence Livermore National Laboratory issued a grim report. The reactor breakdown at Chernobyl, it concluded, dispatched as much long-term radiation into the air, topsoil, and water of the earth as all the nuclear bombs and test devices ever exploded.[6]

How could this have happened? Part of the answer lay in the obsolescent design of the Chernobyl reactor, which produced plutonium for nuclear weapons and steam for the generation of electricity. Unlike most of the world's reactors, this one lacked a protective dome of concrete and steel that, in case of accident, could contain radioactive steam and prevent its escape into the atmosphere. International discussions on the need for such safeguards had been held over a period of more than forty years, and the Soviets had been included in these exchanges.

The Advisory Committee on Nuclear Reactor Safeguards first met in June 1947. It soon identified potential dangers facing reactor operators and outlined procedures for coping with them. Its recommendations were also presented in 1955 at the first Atoms for Peace Conference held in Geneva. Teller was pleased that such a conference was called and had argued in discussions with AEC chairman Lewis Strauss that the interests of the United States could be served by a policy of openness. Despite his abhorrence of the Soviets, Teller urged that the United States exchange, even with them, knowledge it had accumulated in this new energy field. The Soviet Union initially declined to attend the Geneva conference but later relented and sent a delegation.

"The United States finally stripped the cloak of secrecy from its nuclear reactor program," Teller later wrote.

> Russian scientists who had been isolated and who were eager for recognition and exchange were anxious to show off their remarkable accomplishments, and they made effective contributions to the conference. They raised the Iron Curtain on extensive areas of Russian science, and delegates from the United States for the first time glimpsed the amazingly rapid progress of the Soviet scientific effort. We realized finally just how much the Russians knew and what they were able to do with what they knew. This realization forced many United States delegates to conclude that science was moving ahead faster in Russia than in America.[7]

But neither this great advance by Soviet scientists nor their receipt of the safety recommendations at Geneva in 1955 prevented the disaster at Chernobyl. For some unknown reason, Teller reported, Soviets operating the Chernobyl reactor ignored several major recommendations prepared by the advisory committee.

As the Soviet Union disdained these recommendations, environmentalists and antiwar demonstrators campaigned against development of nuclear energy in the United States. This opposition spurted in the wake of the March 1979 reactor accident at the Three Mile Island plant near Harrisburg, Pennsylvania.

Combined with rising construction costs and court actions, such opposition led to the abandonment of plants in Indiana, Ohio, Texas, and Washington State. Similar protests were organized in Europe. One plant, built in Austria, was blocked by popular vote from opening at all. Citizen opposition in the 1970s also delayed new projects in West Germany.[8]

But in the Soviet Union plant construction went ahead full tilt without hindrance by antinuclear demonstrations or, as Chernobyl indicated, without adequate concern for safety standards. "We have no Jane Fonda here," a Moscow nuclear engineer told touring Western journalists.

The Muscovite's reference to Jane Fonda carried an ironic note for Edward Teller, who also invoked her name in the aftermath of Three Mile Island. Teller referred to the Hollywood film star in a full-page *Wall Street Journal* advertisement, bitterly taking issue with her and with consumer advocate Ralph Nader for their public opposition to nuclear power plants. Making one of his frequent trips to Washington to counter such opposition and to promote nuclear energy, Teller became ill.

His *Journal* ad carried a 90-point (1¼-inch-high) headline: "I was the only victim of Three Mile Island." Below, in 18-point type framing the photograph of a solemn Teller with folded arms, followed this explanation:

On May 7, a few weeks after the accident at Three Mile Island, I was in Washington. I was there to refute some of the propaganda that Ralph Nader, Jane Fonda and their kind are spewing to the news media in their attempt to frighten people away from nuclear power. I am 71 years old, and I was working 20 hours a day. The strain was too much. The next day, I suffered a heart attack . . .

Now that I am recovering, I feel compelled to use whatever time and strength are left to me to speak out on the energy problem. . . .

I have worked on the hydrogen bomb and on the safety of nuclear reactors. . . . Both are needed for the survival of a free society. If we are to avoid war, we must be strong and we must help to generate the progress that makes it possible for all nations to grow and prosper . . .

Teller's confidence in the safety of nuclear reactors was not easily formed. He was among the many scientists who, in the early stages of the new technology, recognized their potential danger.

In a 1984 interview, Teller acknowledged that he did not readily come by his faith in reactors. "I remained doubtful about the possibility of real safety for many years," he said.[9] Teller's earliest assignment in checking out nuclear reactors came shortly before the successful test of the first nuclear bomb, in 1945. He was sent to Oak Ridge, Tennessee, to investigate whether the accumulation of U-235 in the gaseous diffusion plant might lead to a nuclear explosion. He left convinced that the plant was operating safely.

By the time of Teller's appointment as chairman of the safeguard committee in 1947, six research reactors were being operated in the United States. They were the rebuilt Fermi pile in Chicago; a small heavy-water-moderated reactor at Argonne, in Illinois; two small reactors at Los Alamos; one test reactor at Hanford, in the state of Washington; and the X-10 graphite reactor at Clinton, Tennessee. The Clinton reactor produced large quantities of radioisotopes and radiation for research.[10]

The Hanford reactor resembled the Chernobyl reactor in several features. Both were designed to produce both steam generation of electricity and weapons-grade plutonium. Both were built without a steel-and-concrete containment dome to prevent the escape of radioactive steam in case of accident.

Noting this last point in an interview after the Chernobyl accident, Teller said, "The Hanford reactor would be safer with the installation of a containment dome." The Department of Energy agreed on the need for greater safety. On January 7, 1987, the department announced a shutdown of the Hanford reactor for extensive upgrading—but not for construction of a containment dome. Instead, in a report issued three months later, the department listed several other improvements recommended in a survey report made by six nuclear experts in October 1986. These included many of the same improvements suggested in 1966—twenty years earlier—by R. E. Trumble, a consulting engineer for General Electric, the prime contractor on the project. Among Trumble's recommendations now to be implemented by the Department of Energy were: covering a liquid-waste disposal basin; enabling the reactor's control room to function during an accident; improving the emergency recirculation cooling system; and abandoning the practice of discharging contaminated cooling water directly into the soil. (A separate department document reported that billions of gallons of cooling water laden with thousands of pounds of radioactive material were discharged into the soil in the first twenty-five years of the Hanford plant.)[11]

In ignoring recommendations for a containment dome at Hanford, the U.S. Department of Energy mirrored the position of Soviet officials. They had similarly ignored the suggestion of Andrei Sakharov, their own nation's most eminent physicist, nuclear bomb developer, and atomic energy expert. Sakharov echoed Edward Teller's proposal that nuclear reactors be placed underground. "The idea of underground siting of nuclear reactors is not new," he wrote. "The principal argument against it is the cost factor. But I'm convinced that the cost will be acceptable if modern excavating equipment is used. And, really, no expense should be spared to prevent accidents involving radiation."[12]

Under Teller's chairmanship, the safeguard committee repeatedly threw cold water on proposed nuclear power projects because of what it considered weak protection for the public. His appointment to head the safety unit came at the outset of significant changes in the international political climate and the domestic scientific attitude. During World War II, the development of nuclear power in the United States, especially for weapons, was spurred by fear that the Nazis were racing along their own nuclear path. But risks considered acceptable then became unacceptable later. This was especially true during the peaceful interlude shortly after World War II. Now, as the movement toward a civilian nuclear power industry gained momentum, safety took on new emphasis. Teller's committee recognized this.

Among the committee members were Princeton physicist John Wheeler; Joseph W. Kennedy, chairman of the Department of Chemistry at Washington University (St. Louis, Missouri) and former Los Alamos scientist; Manson Benedict, chemical engineer from Hydrocarbon Research, Inc.; Col. Benjamin G. Holzman, meteorologist and chief of the geophysical sciences branch of the air force; and Abel Wolman, the fiercely independent and outspoken Johns Hopkins University scientist specializing in public health and sanitation engineering.

Wolman, who remained active as a Hopkins professor emeritus almost until his death at ninety-six in 1989, recalled in a 1984 interview with us that he had challenged safety standards at nuclear reactors from the outset. As a member of a committee of the National Research Council, he had raised questions as early as the mid-1940s about whether the AEC was monitoring reactors closely enough. His prodding led David Lilienthal, chairman of the AEC, to appoint an independent committee to review the operation of all reactors under AEC regulation. The committee report, Wolman said, was devastating.

"In simple terms, operations in general were lousy," Wolman told us. "We found that the simplest of specifications for health and safety were completely ignored. Among the worst were the university laboratories— and they were manned by subsequent Nobel Prize winners. They were permitting tremendous violations to exist in their laboratories." He specifically mentioned the government facilities at Oak Ridge, Argonne, and Hanford.[13]

It was shortly after the issuance of this report that the GAC of the AEC, headed by J. Robert Oppenheimer, recommended creation of the Safeguard Advisory Committee, which was to be headed by Teller.

Fifteen years later, but well before the Three Mile Island scare and the Chernobyl disaster, Teller wrote about his concerns on the subject.

> Although there is no chance that a reactor could explode with the force of a nuclear weapon, reactors present an even more serious and insidious threat, the possibility of contaminating the atmosphere with radioactivity. The longer a reactor is run, the greater is the accumulation in the reactor of fission products that have comparatively long radioactive lives—and these longer-lived products are dangerous to humans.[14]

How dangerous? "Released accidentally and gently from a powerful reactor, these radioactive atoms would be more deadly than the same kinds of atoms released explosively from a hydrogen bomb," Teller wrote.

> The intense heat of a hydrogen bomb drives radioactive particles high into the atmosphere, and they are dissipated and diluted before they finally fall back to the earth. . . . But radioactivity escaping from a large nuclear reactor

would not be so diluted. It could expose people in a hundred square miles to full-force, dangerous contamination.

For this reason, Teller added, his committee realized that it had to proceed differently from most oversight committees. "Usually, you proceed and build something with reasonable safety measures without thinking about it a lot. Let accidents happen and then take corrective measures. . . . In our case this was intolerable. The first big accident would have killed the industry."[15]

But the safeguard committee ran into a frustrating problem. Under the curse of compartmentalization, one group of nuclear engineers was prohibited from discussing its problems—and possible solutions—with another group unless they were actually working on the same phase of a project. It was the kind of excessive bureaucratic secrecy that Teller railed against throughout his career.

"I managed to break that down and get permission to have open hearings, open to cleared nuclear engineers," he said. "That is, people with a need to know not only about *their* nuclear reactors but about *any* nuclear reactors."

Another innovation of the committee, Teller said, was its ignoring the routine approach of setting forth do-and-don't rules in favor of a more comprehensive attack. "We said that each proposal should describe the worst possible accident that they could imagine." If the proponents underestimated the possible consequences, as independently envisioned by the committee, or if they failed to recommend countermeasures acceptable to the committee, the proposal was rejected.

During its introduction of these requirements, the committee learned of an accident in Chicago. "It came close to endangering people," Teller said. "It was a water reactor, a very safe reactor. But all the rules had been violated. There were interlocks not allowing people to go in while the reactor was not in a completely shut down condition, not allowing people to manually operate the controls."

A solution to the interlock problem was incorporated into the evolving science of reactor design. There were other examples.

"Oak Ridge had constructed a swimming-pool reactor which they claimed could not explode under any conditions." At Teller's suggestion a similar reactor was built in Idaho and tested. "We yanked out the controls, and the reactor exploded, which was quite unexpected."

At Hanford, when the reactor was being built, property within a five-mile radius was placed off limits. Much of this was valuable, fertile land, and the end of the war brought a petition for its reopening to farming. The committee determined that the reactor was not safe enough for approval of this proposal.

By 1948, the committee had developed a strict formula for creation of an exclusion area around a reactor. It was based on a "worst-possible" scenario of an accident involving uncontained reactors, which included virtually all early government-owned reactors. Under the scenario, with 50 percent of the reactor's fission products released into the environment, a ten-megawatt thermal reactor would require a one-mile exclusion radius, and a 1,000-megawatt electrical reactor would require a seventeen-mile exclusion radius.[16]

On another occasion the AEC planned to build an experimental 30,000 kilowatt reactor at Argonne, near Chicago. The Teller committee expressed concern about the risks involved in building the facility so close to the then 4 million inhabitants of the nation's second largest population center. At a hearing in Washington on April 23, 1948, conflicting views on the proposal were expressed by Abel Wolman, who opposed the project as unsafe, and by Robert Oppenheimer, who insisted that the project was essential to progress in development of the nuclear power industry. In the end, Oppenheimer's view prevailed, but with a compromise calling for a new design with additional safety features.

Teller credited fellow physicist Walter Zinn for developing what became known as the reactor containment dome. This protective structure was first used at the Schenectady reactor. Abel Wolman had refused to sign the committee's report authorizing construction of the reactor without requiring a dome. In retrospect, the committee's insistence on such basic precautions has been cited for preventing relatively minor nuclear-reactor accidents from becoming major catastrophes, notably in the case of Three Mile Island.

But besides appreciating the need for public-safety requirements in the construction of reactors, the safeguard committee also realized the growing commercial need for nuclear power. This would mean a great increase in the number of reactors and, correspondingly, an increase in potential hazards. Although supplies of domestic coal and oil at this time, in the late 1940s and early 1950s, seemed ample, policymakers were being told that the nation must soon choose between dependence on imported oil or development of nuclear energy.

Among those painting this picture were historians George T. Mazuzan and Samuel J. Walker, coauthors of Controlling the Atom: The Beginning of Nuclear Regulation, 1946–47. Even at this early stage, they said, it was apparent that shrinking U.S. resources pointed to an imminent reliance on foreign crude oil. At the same time, the Soviet Union and Great Britain had plunged ahead with development of electrical generating reactors. The leaders in this promising new technology could enjoy an export advantage and thereby contribute to a favorable balance of trade for their countries. The major threat to American dominance in this field was identified not as the Soviet Union but Great Britain.

Against this background, the AEC felt that Teller and his committee were unnecessarily inhibiting U.S. industrial development through excessive restraints in the name of safety. To avoid negative reaction from a public already suspicious of nuclear power, the AEC plotted an end run to neutralize the committee. It created another committee with parallel responsibility. But its chairman, Rogers McCullough, shared many of Teller's worries about safety.

"The second committee did something very peculiar," Teller recalled. "They had no hearings. They asked . . . if they could sit in to listen to our meetings. Later, they had a meeting of their own. They considered the same [safety] questions and came up with the same conclusions. . . ."[17]

Teller and McCullough discussed this overlap and concluded that it was unworthy of either committee's efforts. "We agreed that . . . the two committees should meld into a single committee." Then, in a stroke both sensitive and politically unassailable by the AEC, Teller proposed that McCullough be named chairman of the consolidated committee.

Teller continued serving as a member of the committee and then, as so often in his major endeavors, found himself in the middle of a fight. This one involved his support at that time—he later reversed his position—for the concept of a fast-breeder reactor, one that produces more fissionable material than it consumes.

An application proposing such a reactor was filed with the safeguard committee in June 1956 by the Power Reactor Development Company. The head of the applicant firm was Walker L. Cisler, who was also president of Detroit Edison Co. The company proposed to build in the Lagoona Beach area, near Detroit. It was to be a sodium-cooled fast-breeder reactor costing $40 million. Among advisers on and proponents of the project was Hans Bethe, the eminent physicist who frequently crossed paths—and swords—with Teller.

Also among proponents was Lewis Strauss, who had been appointed chairman of the AEC by President Dwight D. Eisenhower in 1953.

From the outset, the proposal stirred opposition from the safeguard advisory committee on two points. One was the inherent danger of fire or explosion that would result from contact between the liquid-sodium coolant and air or water. The other point was whether such a reactor should be built within thirty miles of both Detroit and Toledo, Ohio, an area inhabited by more than 4 million people. The committee said, ". . . the proposed reactor is not safe for this site."[18]

But after stormy debate the AEC rejected the committee's recommendation and issued the construction permit, touching off a new round of controversy. Walter Reuther, president of the United Automobile Workers, called for public hearings. Adding fuel to the debate, Reuther recalled that Strauss himself, in testimony before a congressional committee, had described the fast-breeder reactor as the most dangerous of all reactors.

During the hearings, Bethe appeared as an expert witness for the Cisler group and said that the plant could be built without greatly endangering the surrounding population. Teller had gradually come to adopt a similar view.

But when the issue was inevitably taken to court by Reuther, and Teller was asked to testify, he ducked. He discussed this years later with a hint of amusement:

> I found out that one can avoid testifying in such a case very simply. When the people from the Atomic Energy Commission came to me, I told them that the reactor would be very dangerous. When the objectors came to me, I told them that the reactor would be very safe. And therefore neither side asked me to testify.[19]

His true feeling on the issue tended to support the applicants. "I felt the reactor was safe. I think it was. It was a little bit clumsy. In the end it had one mishap in which no one was hurt . . . but it never got off the ground."

By 1960, Teller began to believe that the concept of the fast-breeder reactor should be abandoned in favor of one employing the thorium cycle, in which thorium and a small amount of uranium are combined to fuel the reactor. To the safeguard committee he also proposed a study of underground construction. "I personally felt that to put it underground would be an additional safety measure and could be done without too much expense. However, I was voted down."[20]

Although rejected by the safeguard committee, Teller's idea resurfaced more than twenty-five years later. In the fall of 1986, the U.S. Department of Energy, successor to the AEC, was examining the feasibility of two new reactor designs regarded as virtually accident-proof. Without relying on human intervention, both designs provided for fully automatic shutdown of the reactor in case of malfunction. Both designs also dictated underground construction to prevent escape of radiation into the atmosphere.[21]

Edward Teller's confidence that reactors could be built safely jelled in 1970. From that time forward he vigorously promoted the development of nuclear energy as a means of protecting the U.S. economy from the threat of exploitation by foreign oil interests and as a means of strengthening the national defense. "By 1970, we started to accumulate the experience on actual energy producing reactors, in which, by and large, our safety measures had been adopted," he said. "By this time it became quite obvious that the reactors were not in the habit of getting into trouble. And if they are in trouble, it is financial trouble—not human lives."

In the commercial development of nuclear energy, Teller found a valuable ally in Hans Bethe. But in the military aspect, which included especially the development of nuclear power as a vital component of the strategic defense initiative (SDI). Bethe was aligned with the formidable opposition.

The cause of peacetime nuclear energy received a boost in 1973–74, when the Arab oil embargo dramatized how heavily the United States depended on imported fuel. But that same cause was dealt a setback by the Three Mile Island accident in 1979.

Five years later, when the antinuclear movement seemed less volatile and his chief focus had shifted from nuclear reactors to SDI, Teller offered a critique of the nuclear power industry. In assigning blame for problems retarding the industry, he spared very few. Among his main targets were that vaguely identified mass, "the environmentalists," as well as the Nuclear Regulatory Commission (NRC) and, finally, the entire industry itself.[22]

"The environmentalists have introduced unrealistic policies by warning about those things that don't happen," he said. "They have forced upon us the kind of regulation that puts the program in a straitjacket and does not permit rational functioning of everybody. So I think they have been a primarily negative influence."

His criticism of the regulatory commission was simply that it had done "a poor job." He cited an incident that was similar to that of Three Mile Island and had occurred eighteen months earlier: "It was diagnosed and corrected in plenty of time. A report was sent to the NRC, and it was the elementary duty of the NRC to circulate that report. Had that happened, the accident at Three Mile Island would never have occurred. And this was not the only mistake they made. You know, the president called an investigative committee and the NRC called a different one. Both faulted the NRC."

Turning to the utilities industry, Teller said it had failed to adapt its fossil-fuel management patterns to the demands of nuclear power for more imaginative and modern management practices. "They are to be blamed for not having recognized that to run a nuclear reactor is something a little more complicated than to run any other utility plant," he said. "The few operators who have very heavy responsibilities are not sufficiently paid."

Teller also targeted NRC regulations and procedures. "The regulations are so numerous and the utilities are so loaded down with filling out forms and red tape and complying with regulations, which in some cases do not even make sense, that they do not feel responsible for anything else than to comply with NRC regulations. That this is an untenable situation is obvious, and that there should be more competence in the utility industry seems to be obvious."

Teller unloaded his critique in a Washington interview on September 22, 1984. Two and one-half years later, on May 31, 1987, the NRC ordered the closing of the mammoth Peach Bottom nuclear power plant, a 1,065-megawatt facility operated on the Susquehanna River since its 1973 construction by Philadelphia Electric. The NRC said its order, expected to cost the company $5 million a month and to keep the plant unproductive for several years, resulted from safety inspections disclosing repeated violations.

On each inspection, the agency said, employees were found sleeping where they were supposed to be working—in the control room.

Chapter 18

NUCLEAR WINTER

On the afternoon of May 16, 1984, a strange meeting was called to order in Washington, D.C. Under ordinary circumstances, it would have contained all the elements necessary for a typical Capitol Hill extravaganza.

At issue was the question of nuclear winter, the theory that nuclear war would result in a catastrophic reduction of temperatures on the earth's surface. Proponents of the theory warned that it could portend the end of life on this planet. Opponents said evidence to support the theory was basically flawed and should be ignored by government decision makers. Both sides included eminent scientists.

Onstage to lead these opposing arguments were astronomer Carl Sagan, one of the originators of the theory, and physicist Edward Teller, its foremost detractor. Both were known for their spellbinding talents on the lecture platform. Neither was allergic to the limelight.

Sagan and Teller had been invited to this meeting by two congressmen, Republican Newt Gingrich of Georgia and Democrat Timothy E. Wirth of Colorado.

Making up the audience were members of Congress, staff people, and other government officials working on scientific and defense projects.

Throughout the years, except for tricking his way out of testifying in the Detroit nuclear power case, Teller had not been one to duck a fight. But family and friends urged him to avoid this one. Only a few weeks earlier, at seventy-six, he had undergone coronary bypass surgery. There was also the suggestion that locking horns with Sagan on the nuclear-winter issue was a no-win proposition. Physicist Freeman J. Dyson said, "It's an absolutely atrocious piece of science, but I quite despair of setting the public record straight. . . . Who wants to be accused of being in favor of nuclear war?"[1]

One ingredient usually part of a Capitol Hill show was missing this time.

177

Gingrich and Wirth said they were determined to prevent the meeting from fulfilling its circus potential and for this reason barred the press.

Then Gingrich emphasized that the meeting was intended to be a dialogue, not a debate. It turned out to be not quite either, but more of a free-for-all. At one point, Teller dragged personalities into the discussion. He apologized moments later but suffered another tactical setback when an associate sitting in the audience intervened on his behalf, engaging Sagan in a sharp exchange and handing him the sympathetic role of the out-numbered underdog.

Public attention had first been focused on the nuclear-winter concept when an article appeared in the December 1983 edition of *Science* mag-azine. The paper was a joint effort by five scientists—Richard Turco, Brian Toon, Thomas Ackerman, James Pollack, and Sagan. Their hypothesis was simple: A thousand fires from a hundred major cities would produce enough smoke and soot over the Northern Hemisphere to drastically cool the surface of the earth, threatening the survival of plant, animal, and human life on this planet.

The thesis, based on a variety of assumptions, was faithfully accepted by many who favored nuclear disarmament.

Those advancing the nuclear-winter theory had a public-relations ad-vantage in the person of Sagan. A popular astronomer and winner of a Pulitzer Prize in nonfiction, he had become familiar to millions as a host on the *Cosmos* public television series and as a frequent guest on the Johnny Carson television show.

The TTAPS (the abbreviation formed from the initials of their last names) group sought evidence from nature to support their argument. Since there had never been a nuclear exchange and they therefore had no experimental data from such a source, they relied on a Smithsonian Insti-tution study of an 1815 volcanic eruption on the island of Sumbawa in the Indonesian archipelago. It was estimated that the explosion at Mount Tam-boro spewed into the atmosphere some twenty-five cubic miles of earth and rock. The dense smoke and dust blanketed the sun, and total darkness extended over an area of 400 miles. The force of the explosion carried debris far up into the stratosphere, where it was believed to have circled the earth for more than a year. Even though it was estimated that the average cooling of the earth's surface was only six-tenths of one degree Centigrade, the crop damage in New England and northern Europe was exten-sive. It was remembered as "The Year There Was No Summer." In northern New England, frosts were recorded throughout the summer and fall.[2]

Would a nuclear exchange trigger a similar change in climate?

Evidence to support the underlying theory of the nuclear winter started developing in 1981, when the Mariner 9 space probe orbited Mars and began transmitting photographs of the planet. For three months Sagan and other scientists observed and waited for a vast Martian dust storm to subside. Again they noted that at least on Mars dust in the upper atmosphere tended to absorb solar radiation, while the surface of the planet in semidarkness cooled.[3]

In June 1982 came the earliest serious study of possible smoke effects that might result from nuclear warfare. Scientists Paul Crutzen of West Germany and John Birks of the United States reported on this in *Ambio*, the journal of Sweden's Royal Academy of Science. They calculated that a major nuclear war would ignite about 9 million square kilometers of forest in the Northern Hemisphere and that the dust generated would bring about climatic changes by the cooling of the earth's surface.[4]

The 127-page TTAPS paper, which expanded on this by including the estimated effect of smoke from burning cities in addition to the smoke from burning forests, did not come along until eighteen months later. But when it did, it created a sensation. By the time of the Wirth-Gingrich hearing in May 1984, five months after publication of the paper, scientists were engrossed in debate over it, and the military-political power structure was following the debate.

Beginning the dialogue, Sagan said he and his TTAPS colleagues had "stumbled on the idea of nuclear winter absolutely accidentally." Once again he recounted how "when we observed the dust storms on the planet Mars, the atmosphere of the planet got warmer while its surface got colder." Sagan said they found that it was possible to calculate these temperature changes on Mars while at the same time they were able to calculate "how much the global temperature would drop after a major volcanic explosion."

About 1980, Sagan said, he and his colleagues began to consider seriously the climatic changes that would result from a nuclear war. He said, "Here there are two kinds of effects: the fine dust particles that are punched up mainly into the stratosphere by high-yield ground bursts, and the most important effect, the soot from city fires and, to some extent, forest fires, from air bursts of all yields over cities and forests."

The Sagan group, in preparing its model, attempted "to specify how many weapons, of what yields, are exploded on what targets, at what altitudes." They then "calculated" the number of nuclear weapons that would possibly be used from a percentage of 1 percent to one-half of the world's nuclear arsenal. The next part of the computer exercise dealt with the predicted soot and smoke released into the atmosphere. The exercise also examined the light-absorbent properties of the particles and the effect of rain and air turbulence on their dispersion.

Sagan's base line was a 5,000-megaton nuclear exchange, in which "both cities and hardened strategic targets" are attacked.

"In this baseline case, we find that, averaged over the Northern Hemisphere after the various clouds coalesce, the light level drops to less than one percent of the usual light level. That means that at noontime it is already noticeably dark. . . . That light level is sufficiently low that most plants will have some difficulty just in photosynthesis. . . . More severe is the temperature drop. Depending on the uncertainty in the input parameters, we find that the temperature declines on hemispheric average tens of degrees Centigrade from ambient levels, that it takes months to recover average values in the Northern Hemisphere back to the freezing point of water, and it takes something like a year to return fully to the ambient conditions."

Sagan said these calculations were conservative. He contended that the effects would be worldwide, that the "foreign particles" would move very rapidly from the Northern into the Southern Hemisphere. "People and nations far removed from the conflict can be utterly destroyed without a single nuclear weapon dropping on their territory."[5]

In his opening statement, Teller emphasized his points of agreement with Sagan. "There is no issue more serious or more urgent than to prevent another war. I am a little older than Dr. Sagan; I lived through two world wars. I don't want a nuclear war; I don't want any kind of war. . . ."

Teller quoted from Sagan's statement: "Apocalyptic predictions require, to be taken seriously, higher standards of evidence than do assertions on other matters where the stakes are not as great." Teller concluded, "I fully agree. Unfortunately, the evidence, instead of being robust, as Dr. Sagan has said on many occasions, is in my opinion not so. It is flimsy."[6]

Teller questioned the suggestion that as a result of a large-scale nuclear exchange 225 million tons of smoke would go up into the atmosphere.

"Two hundred million tons of smoke go every year into the atmosphere, anyway," he stated, "and that is a quote from Dr. Sagan's paper. He claims—and I fail to see the proof—that these 225 million tons delivered at one time will be at least 100 times as effective as the smoke that is given off into the atmosphere in the course of a year. . . . It is possible that considerably less will be released. It is an unknown quantity."

Teller then raised the question of the effect of rain on the smoke.

"Before nuclear winter can be established . . . several thousand times the mass of the smoke will come down in the form of rain. Will that rain leave the smoke in the air, or will it wash it out? Now, there are good special arguments that the smoke eventually will rise to an altitude where there is no rain, an altitude of ten kilometers approximately, where it is exceedingly cold to begin with, which would be warmed by the smoke, and new meteorological conditions will be established. . . . Before these meteorological conditions can ever be established, the kind of meteorology as we know it is in operation, and during that time several thousand times as much water will come down as smoke is going up. And that this will leave the smoke unchanged is very hard to believe."

Toward the end of his testimony, Teller said, "I am not telling you that Dr. Sagan is wrong in asserting that the possibility of a nuclear winter should be taken seriously. He is wrong in saying that his assertions have been proven."[7]

Teller also questioned the use of dust storms on Mars as a basis for comparison with conditions on earth. "The analogy with Mars, where there are no big water reservoirs, where the amount of air is little and has little heat capacity, is an exceedingly poor analogy," he said.

Digressing, Gingrich asked Teller about SDI. "I'd like to know how your work on the lasers is coming along," he said.[8]

Teller referred to criticism of SDI in a report to Congress by OTA, its Office of Technology Assessment. He questioned a suggestion by the report that SDI would be a failure unless it could provide 100 percent protection against incoming ballistic missiles. He complained that the report was based in part on classified information but that he was prevented from using such information in public rebuttal of the report.

"Every weapon which is shot down, and shot down in such a manner that it will not explode, will fail to light a fire and will further decrease the chance for a nuclear winter," Teller said.[9]

In response, Sagan noted that in addition to the congressional report there was a similarly critical one from the Union of Concerned Scientists. And, he noted, members of the union included such security-cleared scientists and defense officials as Hans Bethe, Richard Garwin, and Adm. Lowell Gayler.

There were five problems with SDI, Sagan said: (1) "It is leaky . . . lets in some fraction of the incoming warheads. . . . About one percent of the strategic arsenal could still trigger nuclear winter"; (2) the Soviets could take "tremendously simple and much cheaper" steps to overwhelm the system; (3) an effective SDI would cost billions, perhaps one trillion dollars, "which seems to me as of some relevance at a time of budgetary deficits"; (4) SDI violates "virtually all of the strategic treaties that the United States has solemnly entered into"; and finally, (5) "it might increase the likelihood of nuclear war by pushing the Soviets into a first-strike strategy" before completion of the U.S. defense system.

"Except for those five things," Sagan quipped, "it's a good idea."[10]

Teller promised his rebuttal would take less than a minute.

"The Soviets are already violating that treaty. They are already developing just the system that Dr. Sagan is talking about. And we—the advocates of strategic defense—are hampered from telling you the truth by the laws of security that do not apply to OTA but apply to our citizens."[11]

Sagan had hit a nerve with his reference to security clearances held by members of the Union of Concerned Scientists.

"To have clearances is nothing," Teller said. "What counts is to use the clearances and to work on it. And these people have used negligible time to work on very difficult problems. For instance, the best among them, Bethe, made strong objections. I invited him to Livermore. Within two days he retracted all his objections. He went home and, under the influence of his friends, he came up with new objections, and did not come back to Livermore to discuss those." Bethe and Sagan were both based at Cornell.[12]

"Now, ladies and gentlemen," Teller continued: "I am not a meteorologist. I have talked more about meteorology than I should. Perhaps Dr. Sagan is a better meteorologist than I am. I am very sure that he knows less about the strategic defense than I do, and he knows less than Garwin does, and Garwin knows less than he could know if he really were diligent."

There followed a quick exchange, with Sagan chastising Teller's personal references. "This is getting very close to ad hominen arguments which I had hoped we would be able to—"

Teller broke in, "They cannot be avoided."

Sagan again referred to the OTA report and to Ashton B. Carter, who prepared it.

"Dr. Teller has been saying for quite a long time that if only we knew what he knew we would be convinced of the effectiveness of the strategic defense initiative. Well, now here is someone who Dr. Teller says does know what Dr. Teller knows, and on the basis of that information he reaches exactly the opposite conclusion."

"He knows it on the basis of a two-hour conversation," Teller answered. "You do not get the same conclusions when you discuss something for years and work on it, or if you have barely understood a question, are prejudiced when you go there, and then write down what you gathered in two hours."[13]

At this point, the battle was joined by a burly, bearded member of the audience who had not been introduced.

"Ash Carter spent a full day at Livermore," he called out.

"A full day," Teller echoed.

"The subject that he spoke of most extensively, X-ray lasers, he spent a couple of hours on it," the stranger added.

Sagan called on the new entry to identify himself.

"I'm Lowell Wood from Lawrence Livermore National Laboratory," he said. "I'm here today as a private citizen and a friend of Edward Teller's."

Wood repeated Teller's statement that Bethe had been invited to revisit Livermore but had not accepted. "I have told him that I will go to any place in the country and meet him for classified discussions on this matter," Wood declared. "The gauntlet is down. The critics of strategic defense are running from it."[14]

Wirth picked up and repeated Wood's declaration "The gauntlet is down," at which point Gingrich moved in to steer the discussion back to its original purpose.

"Let me, in a role I don't often play in the House," he said, "step in as a peacemaker." He recalled Sagan's scenario of 100 burning cities and said his greatest fear, besides the possibility of nuclear weapons in the hands of terrorists, was "the inexorable drift toward launch on warning." As a result, he said, he found the most intriguing aspect of Teller's argument was that a ballistic missile defense offered at least one advantage: "If you could put up a relatively cheap . . . ballistic missile defense whose only purpose was to force them to knock it out, that changes launch on warning to launch on knowledge. . . . You can figure if they use weapons in space and they knock out your ballistic missile defense, that's a pretty good indicator something bad is coming."

Teller followed this up and in the process offered an apology for the remarks criticized by Sagan earlier. "The point is by strategic defense we can make launch on warning unnecessary," he said.

"Secondly, the point that one hundred burning cities will bring about terrible consequences is, in my opinion, exceedingly improbable. We should spend a few million dollars—today we are spending $30 million nationwide—on this kind of research. We should increase that and we should get positive answers on the points on which Dr. Sagan and I differ.

"I believe—I apologize to the extent I was personal—on this point we are in complete agreement that more money should be spent. . . ."

As the debate wound up, Wirth said he sensed that all the principals in the room agreed on "the need to move more openly, directly, expeditiously, on the question of nuclear winter, or the effects of nuclear war, or whatever we might want to call it."

But the note of agreement did not hold for long. Two years later, researchers from the National Center for Atmosphere Research in Boulder, Colorado, challenged the nuclear-winter theory. Writing in the summer

1986 issue of *Foreign Affairs*, Stephen Schneider and Stanley Thompson said that nuclear war could be calculated to produce an average temperature drop of only twelve degrees in the Northern Hemisphere. More like nuclear autumn, they suggested.

"On scientific grounds," Schneider and Thompson concluded, "the global conclusions of the initial nuclear winter hypothesis can now be relegated to a vanishingly low level of probability."

Schneider added: "Carl's idea was brilliant. He proposed an invasion from Mars. It just didn't hold up under scrutiny."[15]

Moreover, that fall, detractors of the nuclear-winter theory drew comfort from a published report that Carl Sagan and his colleagues had hired the Washington public relations firm of Porter-Novell Associates for an $80,000 retainer. The writer, Russell Seitz, a visiting scholar at Harvard University's Center for International Affairs, said that the retainer was paid in 1983 and that in 1984 the Sagan group spent more on video and advertising than on scientific research of their nuclear-winter theory. Seitz's report, one of the more comprehensive and critical evaluations of the theory, was printed in the 1986 fall issue of *National Interest* and then in the November 5, 1986, *Wall Street Journal*.

Seitz also wrote that Sagan and his colleagues revealed the TTAPS study to "a chosen few at a closed meeting in April 1983." He said most participants "did not describe the reception accorded the nuclear winter theory as cordial or consensual." And even though the proceedings were tape-recorded, Seitz said, Sagan refused to release a transcript.[16]

Sagan may have been prudent in denying this request, for according to Dr. Kosta Tsipis of the Massachusetts Institute of Technology, a Soviet scientist at the meeting said, "You guys are fools. You can't use mathematical models like these to model perturbed states of the atmosphere. You're playing with toys."

Also among those Seitz found to have rejected the nuclear-winter theory were Nobel laureate physicist Richard P. Feynman, Harvard professor Michael B. McElroy, and Professor F. George Rathjens of MIT. He quoted them as follows:

FEYNMAN: "I really don't think these guys [the TTAPS group] know what they are talking about."

McELROY: "They stacked the deck."

RATHJENS (who was also chairman of the Council for a Livable World):   "Nuclear winter is the worst example of misrepresentation of science to the public in my memory."[17]

By May 1987 the nuclear-winter theory had not only lost much support among scientific leaders but had given way in some quarters to a theory of *nuclear summer.* Physicist Fred S. Singer suggested that a nuclear war could double airborne water vapor, forming ice crystals in the stratosphere, resulting in the absorption of infrared light and the warming of the earth, thereby creating a greenhouse effect. [18]

In retrospect, Teller's declaration of doubt about the nuclear-winter theory was among the mildest of all.

Chapter 19

A DREAM:
LIFE WITHOUT FEAR

Teller's frustrations over his professional relationships with Oppen-heimer and Bethe at Los Alamos in the early 1940s had been compounded by his concern for the fate of family members he had left behind in Europe. At that time, more than a decade had passed since he fled Hungary in 1933. He and Mici had returned only once, for a visit in 1936. The subsequent forced separation from his parents and his sister, Emmi, was not made easier by word filtering out about conditions in Budapest. Especially discouraging was news about the treatment of Jews, first under the Nazi puppet, Miklós Horthy, then under the Nazis themselves, and, after Hitler's fall, under the heavy-handed rule of Soviet martinets. The experiences of Teller's family under Communist rule were especially bitter, and they helped to harden the mistrust and hostility he directed toward the Soviets well into his later years and to influence his advocacy of nuclear defense and SDI.

Horthy's regime in the 1930s meant quotas and restricted opportunities for Jewish professionals like Max Teller. These were relaxed briefly toward the end of the decade, and Max's law practice picked up again. But the improved atmosphere ended in the fall of 1939 as Hitler's influence spread into Hungary. Although not officially allied with the Third Reich, Hungary assumed a vital importance to Hitler as a staging area for his move against the Balkans and Russia. Even before official creation of the German-Hungarian alliance in 1941, new restrictions were imposed on Hungarian Jews. Among them was a ban on residing in certain areas of Budapest.

With the collapse of the German war machine appearing imminent in

1944 and a weakening of Hungarian support, the Nazis stepped up their anti-Semitic campaign. Horthy himself was ridiculed by Nazi Propaganda Minister Paul Joseph Goebbels as being "strongly infected with Jewish blood." He was kept under close German monitoring tantamount to arrest.

Emmi Teller had been married in 1934 to Andras Kirz, a lawyer. A son, Janos, was born to them three years later. Among the memories Janos was to carry into adulthood was that as a boy of seven he was required to carry a yellow identification card bearing the Jewish Star of David. In interviews with the authors, he also recalled that the Nazis would periodically comb Jewish neighborhoods for young healthy males to be sent to labor camps. In 1944, his father became one of those selected. Andras Kirz is believed to have been killed in 1945 in a Nazi-operated camp in Mauthausen, Austria.

After her husband's arrest, Emmi and her son moved to her parents' apartment. As the Nazis became more desperate and expanded their forced labor roundups to include women, deadly games of cat and mouse developed throughout Budapest. To escape one such sweep, Emmi spent an entire day hiding in a laundry room.

In the final stages of their occupation, the Nazis installed Ferenc Szalasi, an extreme anti-Semite and leader of the Arrow-Cross party, as head of their puppet government in Hungary. As Russian troops streamed into the country and headed toward German-held Budapest, Szalasi intensified his persecution of Jews. Trainloads of Jews were shipped to German extermination camps. In Budapest, execution squads of Szalasi's Arrow guardsmen found a labor-saving method of body disposal. They lined their victims up along the Danube riverbank, shot them, and watched the bodies topple into the river. Rifle-toting boys as young as twelve patrolled the streets, firing at Jews on sight.[1] Estimates of the number who perished in this phase of the Holocaust range from two-thirds to three-fourths of the 800,000 Jews among Hungary's 1941 population.

"The great surprise," Janos Kirz told us, "is not that my father was taken away but that the rest of us survived." Also among those taken away were Mici's brother and Edward's closest boyhood friend, Suki Harkanyi. He was never heard from again.

Janos recalled walking through the city with his mother after the Russians took over in January 1945. "We were trying to get back to my Teller grandparents' home," he said. "I remember, as we walked, the situation in the streets—dead bodies, dead horses, and no windows left in the entire town. Most of the buildings were in absolute ruins."

Not until the war in Europe ended in May 1945 was his family able to get word to Edward Teller in America that his parents and his sister—but not her husband—had survived the Holocaust. Their letters dealt almost wholly with their personal condition and contained only vague references to the political situation. Years passed before Teller was to receive any detailed account of the peril and hardship they had endured under the extremes of both Nazi and Communist dictatorships. But the very absence of such detail was evidence of continuing unsettled conditions in Hungary.

Edward's name frequently came up in family discussions. "He was very much in everyone's thought," Janos Kirz told us. "He was clearly someone who was revered in the family from early on, because his intellectual capabilities were something that not only my mother and grandparents realized, but I certainly remember some family friends who had known him from early days and they were all sort of in awe of his intellectual ability."

Although the end of the war brought improvement in the lot of his family, Max Teller, now seventy-four, was not optimistic about long-range prospects for a good life in Hungary. Even though the Russians occupied the country, military missions were also established in Budapest by Great Britain, France, and the United States. Emmi, who had studied German and English, was hired by the American mission as a translator and interpreter. Max began rebuilding his legal practice.

But Max Teller's dark forecast soon proved correct. The Germans had looted Hungary of much of its gold and other valuables. Now the Russians scoured the country for what the Germans had missed. As an ally of defeated Nazi Germany, Hungary was required to pay war reparations. Accordingly, the Soviets siphoned off the remaining gold and silver reserves. They also dismantled factories built in Hungary by the Germans and shipped trainloads of machinery and equipment to Moscow.[2] Hungary's economy suffered. Negotiable paper such as bank deposits and bonds lost great value. While the worth of gold, silver, and usable items increased, food prices skyrocketed, sometimes rising two and three times a day.

Ironically, the period produced the only taste of electoral democracy that Hungary was to know in her one thousand years of existence. In late 1945 elections were held under the supervision of the Allied Big Four powers. Of 409 seats in the parliament, the moderate Smallholders party won a majority and the Communists won only 70. But for the next three years, bolstered by the presence of Soviet occupation troops throughout the country, they worked ceaselessly to smear non-Communist leaders, to infiltrate and weaken opposing parties, and to take control of the election machinery and the secret police. The general secretary of the Smallholders party and the spiritual head of Hungarian Catholics, Cardinal Joseph Mindszenty, were arrested on charges of conspiring against the government. The head of the Lutheran church was accused of financial fraud and placed under custody. Critics of Communist party leader Mátyás Rákosi were purged. One of the most prominent of these, Foreign Minister Laszlo Rajk, was convicted of treason and hanged.[3]

In the next election, May 15, 1949, the Communists swept 95.6 percent of the votes. On August 20, they proclaimed the nation a "Republic of Workers and Working Peasants," and Hungary's only democratic fling in her entire history was over.

Now, Max Teller told his family, the professorship that had eluded him first because he was too young, then because he was a Jew, would be denied because he was not a Communist. Age and the years-long fight for survival had taken their toll. In early 1950, at seventy-eight, he was hit by pneumonia. With his wife and daughter at his bedside, he died.

The death of Max Teller was the beginning of a new wave of misfortune for Edward Teller's mother and sister. Emmi's job with the American mission in Budapest had lasted only until 1946. Then, after brief stints with CARE, the American relief organization, and with the U.S. embassy, she turned to tutoring students in German and English.

Looking back on that period years later, the Teller family suggested that they had come to the attention of Soviet investigators either because of Emmi's postwar association with the American mission, Edward's emergence as a leader in the U.S. nuclear defense program, or a combination of both. Whatever the reason, it brought a mysterious visit to the Teller apartment at 3:00 A.M. one morning in June 1951. When Emmi responded to the pounding on the door, she was served a warrant ordering the family out of town within twenty-four hours.

The reason, said the authorities, was that the late Max Teller had been an industrialist. Therefore, in this Communist society he and his family were classified as undesirables.

Piecing things together for us, Janos Kirz concluded that the authorities had dredged up a nineteenth-century statute designed to drive prostitutes out of Budapest. They applied this outdated law to Max Teller on the flimsy basis of his having served on the board of a corporate client years earlier. The Communists were using the law to evict known and potential dissidents and, not incidentally, to make apartments available for government and military insiders. In this manner, the Communists displaced about 50,000 persons and helped solve their housing problem.

Emmi and Janos Kirz described to us how many of the displaced Budapest residents were driven by truck to the railroad station and shipped to rural areas. The Tellers wound up in the eastern village of Tallya, where they were assigned, with another displaced family, to a hut occupied by a peasant and his wife.

Janos, who was fourteen at the time, remembered the eighteen-month stay at Tallya as "not particularly rosy." The hut had no indoor plumbing.

Water came from a well, and an outhouse met basic needs. Janos worked in the vineyard and managed to continue his studies with the help of a friend who relayed weekly summaries of school work from Budapest. But the overall experience of being uprooted from their home and thrust into the midst of the hostile farmer's life sharpened the family's decision to emigrate.

"My mother had hopes and desires of coming to America from the time I was born, but when I was a child the idea of leaving one's homeland was a very frightening one," Kirz said. "And so for a number of years the idea of just leaving everyone and everything I knew behind really bothered me. The turning point finally came when we were sent off to this little village. It became very clear that staying in the country was something which certainly was most dangerous.

"I always heard the family talk or dream about life without fear. That did not really sink in, what that meant, until having gone through the experience of living in Tallya and then leaving Hungary."[4]

In December 1952, just as mysteriously as they had been forced out of Budapest, the Tellers were granted permission to return.

Although permitted back into the city, the Tellers could not reoccupy their apartment because it was still under confiscation. They found living quarters with the help of a doctor who had treated Max Teller and who knew of an apartment whose owner had recently died. But they were required to share it with another occupant, a stranger. The fellow tenant later turned out to be an informant who made daily reports about the Tellers to the secret police.

During her employment at the U.S. embassy, Emmi had kept abreast of world events by reading American newspapers and thus had become generally aware of Edward's role in the nuclear weapons program. But sister and brother avoided direct communication with each other. Instead, they relied on their onetime governess, the former Magda Hess, who had moved from Budapest and was now living in Chicago as Mrs. Jacob Schutz. But even in using her as a relay station, they confined their letters to non-political reports on their well-being and general activity.

On the family's return to Budapest, Emmi resumed work as a tutor. She was pleasantly surprised one day by an offer of a position as an official translator and teacher of employees in the Budapest offices of foreign trade organizations. For a year she performed these assignments in the city without incident. She therefore saw no reason for suspicion when she was asked to serve briefly as an interpreter at an industrial center outside Budapest.

Not until she entered the official car ostensibly bound for the center did she realize that she had been tricked. Instead, she was driven to prison. For most of the next three days and nights she was required to sit in a straight-backed chair under harsh lights as secret police peppered her with questions. Some dealt with her former employment at the U.S. embassy. Some dealt with her American friends. But the chief interest of her questioners was her brother—his whereabouts, his travels, his work.

Emmi was able to provide no information of great value on these points. Edward had withheld it precisely because of the possibility that it might increase the vulnerability of his family in Europe. After the third day, Emmi's questioners let her rest and then, with a warning against disclosing the real reason for her absence, released her. But she was to report to them regularly, as if on probation.

Emmi was not harassed again; others became targets of stepped-up police activity as the Communist regime drew widespread criticism. Mátyás Rákosi, the hard-line Stalinist who had given way to Imre Nagy after Stalin's death in 1953, only two years earlier, now regained control. But he had barely settled in before the Soviet world was shaken by uprisings in Poland. Moscow worried that the unrest would spread next door to Budapest. Soviet leaders called on Rákosi to answer accusations that he had mismanaged the government while cavorting with cronies in a lavish life-style, including lakeside villas, curtained limousines, and exclusive access to luxurious department stores. In July 1956, Rákosi was deposed and was succeeded by Erno Gero, another stiff Soviet party-liner.

But Gero was unable to forestall demonstrations by Budapest students demanding political reforms, including free speech, free press, unrestricted travel, and relaxation of Russia's iron grip on the Hungarian economy. On October 23, students demonstrating outside the Budapest Radio Building were fired upon by secret police, and bloody rioting erupted. The rioting escalated to revolution.

Communists and anti-Communists joined in resisting the continued Soviet domination of their country. Hungarian army Col. Pal Malater, popular among his countrymen and respected by the Russians, joined the revolution as commander of its outnumbered, outgunned forces. Also joining were most Hungarian soldiers and police.[5] In the block-by-block fighting that followed, the insurgents, many of them in their early teens, resorted to ingenious tactics in trying to offset superior Soviet armament. In a lethal variation of the old shell game, they placed a line of overturned soup plates—some concealing explosive charges—across a street in the path of approaching tanks. A tank whose driver slowed or stopped rather than risk disablement of his vehicle became an easier target for grenades, Molotov cocktails, and sniper fire.[6]

Imre Nagy, called on to serve as political leader of the movement, had pointed to reform rather than outright secession from the Soviet bloc. But unable to brake the onward rush of the movement, he declared Hungary's repudiation of the Warsaw Treaty and proclaimed his country a neutral in the ideological struggle between East and West. On November 4, fearing similar withdrawals by other Soviet satellites, Moscow sent tanks rolling onto the streets of Budapest. Soviet troops seized control of key transportation and military facilities.

When Nagy called on the United Nations to intercede in support of the self-determination provisions of its charter, Moscow offered to negotiate the withdrawal of its invading units. Hungary agreed, and the negotiations were scheduled at Soviet headquarters in the town of Tokol. Colonel Malater headed the Hungarian delegation. But the negotiation offer unfolded as another example of diplomatic duplicity.

After the apparently successful conclusion of the meeting, the Soviets signaled their security police, who rushed into the banquet hall and arrested the Hungarian officials.[7]

Nagy, forced to flee for his life, found temporary refuge in the Yugoslav embassy. But on leaving the embassy after receiving Russian assurance of his safety, he was abducted by security police. Seven months later, on June 16, 1957, radio stations in Moscow and Budapest simultaneously broadcast that Nagy and Malater had been tried and executed.[8]

Edward Teller's nephew, Janos Kirz, was a sophomore at the University of Budapest during the October 1956 revolution. When it became apparent that the Soviets had put it down, he and his mother decided that he must leave Hungary immediately. On his graduation as an electrical engineer, he would become an essential worker almost certain to be barred from emigrating. Emmi and Ilona Teller also wanted to leave, but at seventy-three Ilona was not strong enough for the rigors of the long, rough trip necessary to elude security forces. So Janos must go alone.

From the underground, Janos learned of an escape route through a farm on the Austrian border. The peasant operating the farm would make periodic trips to Budapest by train, assemble small groups of those wanting to leave the country, and lead them back to his place. To escape detection at the border, they received help from the train crew. The train would make an unscheduled stop short of the border, enabling the one-way passengers to alight near the peasant's farmhouse. There they would be fed dinner. After nightfall, the peasant led them to the border and their Austrian contacts. Janos, carrying a few belongings in a briefcase, took this route. For his escape, Emmi paid 5,000 forints, the Hungarian equivalent of about $200.

It was apparently the last successful mission performed by the peasant farmer. Janos Kirz said that one week after leading him to freedom the farmer was trapped by the Russians while escorting another group to the border. He was executed.[9]

Three weeks later, Janos cabled Magda Hess Schutz in Chicago with word of his safe arrival in Vienna. She telephoned the news to Teller's home in Berkeley. In two more months, Janos arrived at the San Francisco airport on the afternoon of January 15, 1957, just in time to help celebrate his Uncle Edward's forty-ninth birthday.

Kirz later described the reunion as not effusive but warm and rich with news about what had happened to the family on both sides of the Atlantic during the long interim. "Needless to say, it was very interesting, because we had never met and we had to start from scratch."[10]

By February, Janos Kirz had traded a life of danger, hunger, and persecution in Europe for the idyllic existence of a student on the oceanside campus of the University of California, where he laid the foundation for a career as physics professor at the State University of New York at Stony Brook.

Edward Teller now tried a new approach to effect the release of his mother and sister, setting off a strange series of events. After the death of his father, he had made several requests to the State Department for help in setting Ilona and Emmi free. But his new prominence as the lead physicist in the U.S. H-bomb program and his forceful public warnings against the Soviet military buildup had not advanced his popularity behind the Iron Curtain.

"I tried all kinds of things," he said, "but nothing worked."[11]

Something did work later, in 1959, but Teller was never quite certain about exactly what it was. Appropriately, it involved the unpredictable, flamboyant Leo Szilard. It began with a dinner in Washington.

Despite their differences in ideology and style, Teller and Szilard had remained close friends since the early days of their emigration from Hungary. Teller drifted steadily to the anti-Soviet right and pressed for development of the hydrogen bomb; Szilard touted communism as a wholly positive force and spoke out against the U.S. H-bomb program. But Teller greatly respected Szilard's professional brilliance and envied his independent spirit; he chalked off Szilard's admiration of communism to political naïveté.

So it was with genuinely pleasant surprise that Teller bumped into Szilard while visiting Washington. He invited Szilard to dinner, and for much of the evening they enjoyed discussing earlier times in Washington and updating each other on their careers. Then the talk shifted to the future, and Szilard offered a suggestion: Teller should visit Russia.

Recalling the conversation for us later, Teller said he rejected the idea. Szilard called his response unreasonable and demanded an explanation.

"Look," said Teller, "there are many reasons, but one of them is this . . . My mother and sister live in Hungary. Once I'm in Russia, I don't know what the Communists might do to force me into a situation which I don't like, try to extract information from me, whatever. They have kept these two women as hostages, and this alone makes it impossible for me to visit Russia."

Szilard was aghast.

"Teller, you are completely wrong. The Russians would never stoop to such methods. But I understand how you feel. Let me see what I can do."

Teller knew that his eccentric friend had some Soviet connections. He was among scientists from both sides of the Iron Curtain who had met in July 1956 at Pugwash, Nova Scotia, as part of Cleveland industrialist Cyrus Eaton's personal effort to promote understanding and goodwill among the superpowers. But Teller had little reason to expect that much would come of Szilard's cryptic offer of help.

Teller was therefore intrigued to learn later that shortly after their dinner meeting Szilard had attended the second Pugwash Conference and had broached the subject to the head of the Russian delegation.

Three weeks passed. Then Teller's mother and sister received a call from Budapest officials. Passports would be prepared for their departure from Hungary. Why? There was no explanation. As in the case of the family's being given permission years earlier to return to Budapest after banishment to the peasant's vineyard home in the village of Tallya, the reason remained a mystery.[12]

Teller's theory typically ascribed the act more to political expediency than to altruism on the part of the Hungarian Communists. They valued Szilard's friendship because of his influence as an outstanding theoretical physicist and as a defender of communism.

Whatever the reason, Teller and his family were elated by the result. Forty years had passed since Béla Kun's rise to power had opened a long chapter of turmoil and sorrow for them and their compatriots.

Now, for the last of the Tellers in Hungary, life without fear was more than a dream.

Chapter 20

THE DEBATE

PRELUDE

Strategic defense initiative (SDI) is designed to prevent incoming missiles from reaching their targets. In 1983, Edward Teller's first declaration of this objective triggered a global debate involving its technical feasibility, political practicality, and moral desirability that continues unabated even today.

In embracing the concept of SDI as a top priority of his presidency, Ronald Reagan spoke only of its principle, not its detailed application. But in both the U.S. and Soviet Union versions of the concept, unclassified reports point to a similar general scenario:

If a missile is launched, it may be intercepted and destroyed in one of three stages.

The first of these is its *boost* phase immediately after launch, which may last from two to six minutes, depending on the type of rocket used.

Next comes the *mid-course* phase, when the rocket has completed its upward path through the earth's atmosphere. Each rocket may carry three to ten warheads and many times that number of decoys. These may now be released, with the warheads beginning their independently planned runs at altitudes of 100–600 miles toward their targets. This phase may last up to twenty minutes.

Finally, in the *terminal* phase, the warheads and decoys reenter the atmosphere, where the decoys, less durable, may be consumed by friction as the warheads continue toward their target. This last leg of their flight could require five minutes.

The Soviet Union is believed to have about 1,400 ICBM missiles; the United States, about 1,000.

SDI designers speak of a *layered defense* in which several means are used to detect a missile launch, then to compute the point at which it may be intercepted, and finally to intercept and destroy it. The intercepting weapon may be a projectile, or *kinetic-energy* weapon, traveling at great speed, or some *directed-energy* weapon, such as a laser, an X-ray laser, a free-electron laser, or a particle beam traveling even faster, close to the speed of light.

Ideally, SDI contemplates early detection and destruction of a rocket in its boost phase. Some warning may come from prelaunch activity at or near the launch site. Also, seconds after launch, space-based observation satellites may detect the powerful infrared radiation of the rocket exhaust. Or earth-based radar or laser beams may sense atmospheric disturbances caused by the launch.

Missiles escaping detection or interception through the boost phase may be picked up during the longer, mid-course phase. Here sensors can distinguish warheads from decoys and debris, then transmit information about these identified objects to the computing system.

For missiles surviving the first two layers of defense, the SDI concept includes a terminal system of sensing, computerized anticipation of path, and interception before impact on target.

Once the launch is detected and information on the missile path and interception point is fed into the computer and analyzed, the weapon of response is selected. This weapon may be based in space or on the ground. If it is an *antimissile missile*, or high-technology form of artillery, it may be made more effective by arming it with a small nuclear explosive equivalent to ten tons of TNT. Then it can destroy the missile even if it does not make direct contact but comes within several hundred feet.

Another kinetic-energy option is the *rail gun*. This weapon, under development in the United States and Israel, usually drives a bullet with a magnetic force that gives it a greater velocity than the velocity achievable by use of the expanding gas generated by gunpowder.

But even the rail-gun projectile may travel only a fraction of one-thousandth as fast as the beam of a directed-energy weapon flashing through space at nearly the 186,000-miles-per-second speed of light.

Edward Teller suggested that the most promising weapon in this category could be the laser. When tightly focused light passes through a suitable crystal or gas, its atoms may be stimulated, causing amplification and concentration of its waves, which may then be emitted in a narrow, very powerful beam.

Laser-weapon research has included many means of trying to generate the power necessary to make such devices effective against missiles. These have included the use of X rays, chemicals, and free electrons.

X-ray lasers work at wavelengths one thousand times shorter than those of visible light. They may be produced by nuclear explosion, with the resultant energy-laden rays being harnessed and instantly directed at a target.

In the chemical laser, the intense beam of light is generated not by a nuclear explosion but by the violent reactions of gases such as hydrogen and fluorine.

In the free-electron laser, a beam of electrons is subjected to the energy of a magnetic field, accelerating the electrons until they approach the speed of light and pack enough force to destroy solid objects.

Still another form of directed energy is the particle beam, which may be a stream of electrons or of hydrogen atoms. In either case, the beam of particles moves at great speed and can be used to destroy a target at a great distance.

PRO AND CON

The debate begins with a certainty and an assumption. The certainty is that each side has hundreds of missiles aimed at the other. The assumption is that neither superpower trusts the other to confine possible use of its SDI to pure defense without also considering its possible value for *offensive* purposes.

Throughout the debate runs the theme of "What if?"

What if the SDI of one side goads the other side into a first strike?

What if the SDI of the first-struck side works? Or works only partially? Or not at all?

Is all this preferable to the policy of MAD (mutual assured destruction), which has seen both sides, however jittery, refrain from pulling the ultimate trigger?

As the senior and most honored theoretical physicists within the opposing camps, Hans Bethe and Edward Teller naturally accepted the roles of chief nongovernment spokesmen in the debate.

The main thrust of the opposition was summarized by Bethe in this passage from his March 1984 article in *Laser Focus/Electro Optics*:

> A system of laser defenses would be unwieldy, costly, and easily countered. Development of space-based weapons would be destabilizing, because each side would suspect the other of advances it did not know about or of developments it did not fully understand. The likelihood of unlimited war would increase. [1]

Bethe also suggested that much of the system would probably not work and at least one part that probably would—the antisatellite weapon—might do more harm than good.

"The development of strategic missile defenses, including defenses based on 'pop-up' X-ray weapons, poses immense technological problems. They would probably not work," he said. "However, antisatellite weapons are likely to succeed, which is unfortunate, because satellites are a guarantee of stability." This was an apparent reference to the value of observation satellites in keeping each side aware of any hostile action by the other.

Bethe expressed fear that current expenditures of $500 million for laser research and development might balloon into $500 billion in years to come for "a system of very doubtful value." He also hypothesized, "If you have 5,000 lasers in low-earth orbit, they may get in each other's way."

He then added the uncertainty factor:

> You will never really know whether our laser beams will damage the Russian missiles or not. It will be even harder to know what counter-measures the Russians may have taken. This will induce both sides to make worst-case assumptions, and this will lead to an arms race beyond anything we have ever seen.

Teller grimaced with impatience when reviewing Bethe's comments. "I am tired of arguing with Hans," he told us, "but he is putting up a straw man. It is not necessary to predeploy lasers in space."

Addressing this point in *Better a Shield Than a Sword,* he wrote:

> At extremely high intensity, ground-based lasers may be used against approaching missiles. It is also possible to pop up mirrors to redirect the beam of a ground-based laser. . . . In addition, smaller mirrors are sufficient to . . . redirect such beams.[2]

Teller also questioned Bethe's statement that observation satellites should remain inviolate because of their value as stabilizers of the peace. This would amount to a one-sided immunity, he suggested. Then he quoted from the Pentagon's *Soviet Military Power, 1987:* "The Soviets already have ground-based lasers that can damage satellites. . . ."

Teller conceded that ground-based lasers presented problems, but he insisted these could be dealt with. One problem would be the diffusion, or scattering, of the laser beam by vapor droplets in the air. "With appropriate lasers, it is possible to destroy the droplets in a thin cloud, thereby producing a tunnel through the cloud," he said. What about foul weather, which would impede the travel of the laser beam? "To have defense in all weather conditions, multiple laser locations will be needed."

What of Bethe's statement that SDI would destabilize the situation by provoking the Soviets?

"If that is so, the protests should be directed primarily against the Soviet Union," Teller replied. "Soviet leaders have deployed both terminal defenses around Moscow and laser defense at the Sary Shagan weapons site near Lake Balkhash. The argument that defense is destabilizing gained widespread acceptance only after Reagan's [SDI] proposal was criticized by the Soviet Academy of Sciences. It has not been applied to the past or present intensive Soviet defense effort."

As for cost, Teller said Bethe's estimate of a $500 billion outlay for laser research and development down the road was excessive. He noted Reagan's budget proposal of $26 billion—and actual appropriations totaling less than two-thirds—for the first five years of the entire SDI program.

On one point, the required level of laser power, Teller obliquely conceded to Bethe. "You must be able to see and locate the ICBM," Bethe said. "You must distinguish it from the flame behind it, and you must keep your laser beam precisely on one point in that target. It is not good enough to hit the booster somewhere. If your laser beam were only accurate enough to hit the booster somewhere, then you would need a hundred times more power. . . ."

"What Hans points out are real problems that we are working on," Teller commented. "If he wished, he could truly help us solve them. Instead, he throws roadblocks in our path. At this point I can say only that no one really knows what the power requirements are. Any statements to the contrary are nonsense."

A long-range participant in the early part of the debate was Teller's Soviet counterpart in H-bomb development, Andrei Sakharov. After the Reagan-Gorbachev summit of December 1986 at Reykjavik, Iceland, Gorbachev had said that agreement on strategic weapons and medium-range missiles in Europe could not be reached without prior agreement on the limiting of SDI research. Sakharov, who had just returned to Moscow after seven years of restriction to the closed city of Gorky, took issue with the Soviet general secretary. Questions of offensive and defensive weapons and systems should be negotiated separately, said the dissident physicist, and the question of SDI would eventually "die on its own quietly and peacefully."

Teller and his fellow advocates complained that they were hampered in responding to these attacks because security restrictions prevented advocates from using much of the information needed for point-by-point rebuttal. They said it was a classic catch-22 situation.

An example of the problem came in the April 1987 issuance of a 424-page report by a unit of the American Physical Society (APS), its Study Group on Science and Technology of Directed Energy Weapons. The report concluded that technical barriers virtually precluded assembly of an effective SDI and that, even if these were cleared, a few adjustments here and there in the Soviet offensive structure would render the defense obsolescent and ineffective.[3]

Time magazine, quoting from the report eight months later in its issue of December 7, 1987, referred to "the prestigious American Physical Society" and the conclusion that "even in the best of circumstances, a decade or more of intensive research" would be necessary to demonstrate the effectiveness of lasers as weapons.[4]

In other quarters, though, the APS report was criticized as a slanted work whose authors, while distinguished for scientific achievement elsewhere, had never worked in the field of directed-energy-weapons development. Such a criticism was leveled by Angelo M. Codevilla, senior research fellow and Teller's colleague at the Hoover Institution, the conservative think tank housed at Stanford and named for President Herbert Hoover. In the September 1987 issue of *Commentary*, Codevilla said the absence of such weapons experience by its authors could explain "why the report contains so many errors and internal contradictions."

As an example, he noted that in one place the report said the engines of long-range missiles burn for between three and six minutes, "while in another place . . . they burn between two and three minutes. . . ."

Codevilla wrote that the report used a *modus operandi* that "is neither science nor technology" but consists of two key steps:

> Show the near impossibility of our performing technical feats that the report implies are essential to ballistic-missile defense, but that in fact are irrelevant or imaginary. Then use this to argue that more research must be done. . . .
> On the other hand, take it for granted that, on the Soviet side, the most astonishing technical feats . . . can easily be performed to evade a U.S. defense system.

As an example of this, Codevilla cited a passage on the question of missile vulnerability.

> Obviously, the less vulnerable [or "harder"] Soviet missiles are, the more effective must be the directed-energy weapons we design to counter them. . . . Not surprisingly, therefore, the report devotes a good deal of time to creating the impression that the bodies of missiles are very tough and can easily be made even more resistant. The truth, however, is that real missiles happen to be pretty flimsy things.

Most ICBMs, he noted, are made of aluminum and to coat them with laser-resistant materials, as suggested by the report, would increase their weight so much that they would have to be stripped of all but one or two of the ten warheads intended for them.[5]

Another point at issue in the debate was the equipment needed for "battle management," specifically the computers and their software required to analyze the complex intelligence data and to send the appropriate weapons toward the incoming missiles. Software errors could prove disastrous, as described in *Claiming the Heavens,* a special *New York Times* publication on SDI:

> The space agency lost a Mariner probe to Venus because a programmer put a period in the software where there should have been a comma. Similarly, the Gemini V spacecraft splashed down 100 miles off target because a programmer ignored factoring into the program the motion of the earth around the sun.

In 1984, a task force under James C. Fletcher, former administrator of NASA, undertook a study of technical problems confronting SDI. From the outset, the battle-management section of the report was a matter of heated controversy. It projected a software system of global coverage, so vast and complex that its applicability seemed impossible.

But two years later, a simpler, more manageable system was developed on the modular basis of farming out coverage to small clusters of battle stations operating with some degree of independence from each other but linked to a central control point. Lt. Gen. James A. Abrahamson, Jr., SDI director, enthusiastically accepted the revised plan.

Doubts about a computer capability to match the demands of the system nevertheless persisted. A leading doubter was Robert Taylor, head of the Digital Systems Research Center and former chief of computer research programs for the Defense Advanced Research Projects Agency. "The goals of SDI put demands on software that are just absurd in terms of the state of our knowledge," he said.

But there was no shortage of optimists, either. Solomon J. Buchsbaum, executive vice-president of Bell Laboratories and chairman of the White House Science Council, was among them. "Can such a large, robust, and resilient system be designed, and not only designed, but built, tested, deployed, operated and further evolved and improved?" he asked. "I believe the answer is yes."

Even greater confidence was shown by Charles A. Seitz, professor of computer science at the California Institute of Technology. "I don't think there's any question that it can be done," he said. "That is the weight of the most experienced opinion on this issue."

Asked about this mass of conflicting opinion, George Keyworth, the former White House science adviser, told us he had discussed the question with Buchsbaum. He said he had asked the Bell Lab executive about a finding that 20 million lines of computer code would be required to handle computations involved in an all-out attack by the Soviet Union and that this capacity could not be developed.

"I said, 'Sol, answer a question for me. How many lines of code are there in the AT&T operating system to manage the telephone system?' He said 52 million lines.

"So, you see, we are already doing something much more complicated than that just in our everyday switching of our national telephone system."[6]

Even Edward Teller could not accept that comparison. "At present, no computer is fully adequate for the task of battle management," Teller said. "There are computers in existence, however, whose functions are comparable in complexity to those needed for defense. But a defense-management computer would have to be more reliable than that of the telephone system."

Keyworth's use of 20 million as the number of code lines that might be required to process information and directions in the event of attack was more conservative than the figure of David Ritchie, editor of *Star Wars Intelligence Report*. In an article reprinted January 12, 1986, in the Baltimore *Sun*, Ritchie said 100 million lines would be needed to track approximately 300,000 warheads and decoys, then to distinguish the warheads from the decoys, to assign weapons to destroy the warheads, and finally to register which targets were destroyed and which survived.[7]

Emerging from this rain of clashing and confusing opinion of the experts, Edward Teller held up a certainty: "None of our instruments of defense, as envisaged now, are anywhere near perfection. So for the time being, we must aim at establishing *some* defense, if not a perfect defense."

Chapter 21

THE RED SHIELD

Edward Teller was bitter.

In late winter of 1985, he glowered over his dinner at the Cosmos Club and said he was at a complete loss to understand one aspect of opposition to SDI. How could the United States allow the Soviets to continue building *their* SDI shield while being hampered in the effort to build its own shield?

This theme dominates the basic argument of leading SDI proponents, including former military intelligence officers as well as scientists in and outside national defense programs. They use it to attack the opposition argument that deployment of SDI elements might goad the Soviet Union into stepping up its arms development and might even provoke it into a surprise first strike.

Another major point in the debate is whether the key elements of SDI, such as the X-ray laser and supercomputers, will ever work well enough to be effective.

Moreover, could SDI be developed soon enough to be useful? And would its cost be prohibitive when compared with the cost of possible Soviet countermeasures?

Over dinner that evening in 1985, Teller noted that whereas the United States was spending between $3 and $4 billion a year on missile defense, the Soviet was spending about $20 billion.

He suggested that the SDI message should be clarified. "The president's strategic defense initiative should be relabeled strategic defense response," he said, "for that is what we are doing, responding to the Soviet missile-defense initiative."

Teller frequently sounded this theme, occasionally citing the words of Soviet leaders themselves to support his case. In *Better a Shield Than a Sword* he quoted this statement made in London as early as 1967 by Aleksei N. Kosygin, then the Soviet premier:

I think that a defensive system that prevents attack is not a cause of the arms race. . . . Perhaps an anti-missile system is more expensive than an offensive system, but its purpose is not to kill people but to save human lives.[1]

Among those most vigorously agreeing with Teller on this issue was George F. Keegan, who retired in 1977 as a major general and chief of Air Force Intelligence. Two months before President Reagan's SDI speech on March 23, 1983, Keegan offered us his observations in an interview at his home in Fort Washington Station, a Maryland suburb of Washington. Heavyset and ruddy faced, Keegan had surrounded himself with the electronic trappings of his trade—a shortwave radio to pick up Moscow, tape machines, television sets, and video recording equipment.

Keegan declared that the American concept of MAD had been nullified by a nearly impenetrable Soviet "passive" defense system. He said:

"In terms of weapons available to both sides, the United States and the USSR both have enough nuclear power to ruin the societies that now exist. But in terms of operational reality, this is not the case. About 1970, the Soviets began systematically to harden their *underground storage sites, more than 400 of which are at the absolute top of America's list of targets assigned by the White House to our strategic forces.* The missile silos are placed so deep underground and are covered with so much dirt and concrete that they are practically impervious to American bombs." *(Italics added.)*

Keegan estimated that nearly 99 percent of the Soviet's nuclear weapons have been made virtually invulnerable in this manner. He said intelligence had provided details of construction and the number of missile silos.

"With the help of defectors who had actually helped to construct the Soviet missile silos," he said, "and a couple that now reside in New York City who helped design them, we learned, much to our shock, that the new generation of Soviet silos was several times 'harder' than its American counterparts."

Keegan said that under the MAD policy the second most important target for retaliation was the leadership of the Soviet Communist party, but the policy would be useless against defenses built to protect the party hierarchy and military leadership. He traced this construction back to the 1960s, when work was started on new underground shelters in every major city in the USSR. He described one of these as a giant steel-welded sphere buried under several hundred feet of earth and one hundred feet of reinforced concrete.

"Today we could damage no more than probably two or three percent of the Soviet leadership," Keegan said.[2]

The former intelligence chief spoke of a survey he conducted for the

U.S. Air Force in 1976, the year before his retirement. He said it showed that Soviet civil defense had been placed under military control and that Soviet generals command civil defense academies graduating several thousand students a year. He said the Central Intelligence Agency (CIA) and the Defense Intelligence Agency (DIA) accepted his estimate, based on a check of units in several cities, that 100,000 men and women were active in Soviet civil defense.

Keegan was one of the military experts whose arguments, added to those of Teller and other prominent civilians, led to the refusal of the U.S. Senate to ratify the Salt II Treaty. In explaining his opposition, Keegan cited information that he said had never been publicly disclosed concerning brisk Soviet weapons development even while the treaty was being negotiated.

"The Soviets were already secretly developing and testing fifteen major new intercontinental ballistic missile systems," he said. "This fact was never made public for reasons that I consider to this day almost treasonable."[3]

Keegan saw the treaty as inequitable and flawed in many areas. For example, he said, "It would have allowed the Soviet Union to deploy and have in its possession six times the amount of nuclear-delivery firepower possessed by the other side. Also, it would have crippled the development and advancement of the Triad submarine and the B-1 bomber, and would have prevented us from undertaking the development of the MX missile."

Tracing an old bureaucratic rivalry, Keegan said that in the early 1960s the CIA challenged not only the validity of but the need for air force evaluations of Soviet achievements in missile defense. But the challenge softened as evidence mounted.

"We [the air force] had thousands of documents. . . ," he said. "We were able to track the flow of hundreds of top-notch Soviet scientists into these areas of directed-energy weapons research. We had other extremely sensitive intelligence from a number of other sources that I am not able to talk about publicly—involving agents, involving photography, involving sensing techniques, involving some of the most sophisticated intelligence detection and analytical tools ever developed in the West. . . .

"At one point I was able to identify by name nearly two thousand top Soviet scientists involved in an activity much larger than the Manhattan Project."[4]

Keegan acknowledged that despite his thirty-three years of experience in the intelligence field, his evaluation of Soviet antimissile research and deployment was not universally accepted by the American intelligence community. Teller counted himself among those who did not wholly agree with the evaluation, but he later told us, "Keegan has some very valid information."

In early 1985, Teller rushed to the defense of Robert Jastrow, a fellow physicist who had come under fire from many colleagues for suggesting that the peace would be twice as secure with two antimissile defense systems instead of one. The threat of nuclear war, Jastrow said in an article in the March issue of *Commentary*, would be greatly eased if both superpowers developed such defenses.

Jastrow was the founder of the NASA Institute for Space Studies and professor of earth sciences at Dartmouth College. His research included nuclear physics, planetary science, and astrophysics.

In a 1985 book, *How to Make Nuclear Weapons Obsolete*, Jastrow also described the operation of U.S. intelligence satellites and warned of a Soviet threat to their effectiveness. He said the American satellites are geosynchronous, each orbiting at a speed that enables it to hover over the same area of the rotating earth below it, for use in military communications and in an early warning system to detect launches of Soviet missiles. He described other, low-orbit satellites using cameras and television equipment to monitor military and industrial activities. At altitudes below 100 miles, he said, the images "are nearly sharp enough to read the license plates in Red Square."[5]

Jastrow also wrote of American satellites equipped with sensitive electronic equipment designed to detect changes in Soviet radio traffic patterns. An irregular increase in messages between the Kremlin and certain regional outposts, for example, might indicate preparations for new military activity.

In developing a comparable system of satellite surveillance, said Jastrow, the Soviets produced equipment lacking in the American system—a satellite carrying powerful radar equipment that scans the oceans and pinpoints the locations of U.S. naval vessels.[6]

Jastrow also stated that the Soviet Union had tested systems for placing nuclear bombs into orbit.[7] He said:

> This would permit the Soviet Union to initiate an ICBM attack against the United States from any direction, not just over the North Pole. It means that the Soviet nuclear weapons can take the long way around to reach their targets, evading our early-warning satellites as well as the radar picket fence that faces north toward the USSR from Alaska and Canada.[8]

The Soviet Union denied testing this type of weapon, Jastrow said, but U.S. radar detected their intentional detonation of the bomb in orbit and tracked more than 100 pieces of debris as they were scattered into space.[9]

Jastrow's *Commentary* article triggered an exchange of letters by prominent scientists in the same publication. In one passage he had scoffed at *The Fallacy of Star Wars*, a published report prepared for the anti–SDI Union of Concerned Scientists. Those who had submitted the report and now signed the letter criticizing Jastrow were Hans Bethe, Victor Weisskopf, Richard L. Garwin, Kurt Gottfried, Henry W. Kendall, and Carl Sagan.

Defining their position, they questioned the president's goal of defending the U.S. population against nuclear-armed Soviet missiles. "A ballistic missile defense (BMD) of cities is inconceivable," they said, "unless the great majority of Soviet ICBM's could be destroyed while their fragile booster engines are still burning brightly."[10]

Jastrow also came in for criticism by the group on grounds that he lacked clearance for study of classified documents and therefore was "inadequately informed." In defense of Jastrow, Teller said lack of clearance was not necessarily a disadvantage.

"It is important to realize that by abstaining from getting clearance, Mr. Jastrow has retained his freedom of speech," he wrote. "This privilege is one of his main weapons, which is not available to those who have spent years working on the problem of defensive weapons."[11]

In his own response to the Bethe-led group, Jastrow said his argument was supported by history and by the Soviets themselves.

"Andrei Gromyko called for the deployment of a missile defense by the superpowers in a speech to the UN in 1962, in which he criticized the doctrine of mutual assured destruction," Jastrow recalled.

All this helped account for Edward Teller's bitterness at dinner that winter night of 1985.

"If SDI is such a waste of money and effort, why shouldn't the Russians encourage us to waste that money and effort instead of opposing it?" he asked. "That should tell us something. And if they themselves have been doing exactly the same thing to build their own shield—only for a much longer period of time and at many times the cost we are putting into it—that should tell us even more."

Until 1987, Moscow's reticence on the issue and U.S. secrecy require-ments hampered Teller and other defense advocates in their argument that the Soviets believe in SDI strongly enough to have an SDI program of their own. Then the Teller group drew support from several unlikely sources, including the Soviet first secretary himself, Mikhail S. Gorbachev. In an NBC news interview on December 2, 1987, he broke the long Krem-lin silence on American and British press reports that such a program existed.

"Practically, the Soviet Union is doing all that the United States is doing," he said. "And I guess we are engaged in research, basic research, which relates to these aspects which are covered by the SDI of the United States. But we will not build an SDI, we will not deploy SDI, and we call upon the United States to act likewise."[12]

Four days after Gorbachev opened the door a crack on Soviet SDI activity, the *London Sunday Times* scoffed at his limited admission. James Adams, defense correspondent for the paper, wrote in the edition of December 6, 1987, that the Soviets were doing much more than Gorbachev admitted. Gorbachev arrived in London the next day for a meeting with Prime Minister Margaret Thatcher on his way to Washington for a summit meeting with President Reagan.

". . . In fact, the extent of the Russian 'Star Wars' programme—which has been in existence for at least twenty years—has in some key areas gone beyond basic research, into testing and even deployment," Adams wrote.

". . . The work has been going on since the 1960s and already the Russians have a limited capability to shoot down satellites and space stations with rockets, and to blind satellite sensors using lasers."

Adams attributed his report to U.S. intelligence sources and said they had designated the following key sites for Soviet SDI activity:

Moscow. Several centers here concentrate on kinetic energy and particle beam research.

Sary Shagan. Site of the first prototype laser system in the world. "Some of its satellites are able to damage sensors on satellites in low orbit."

Dushanbe. On the Russian border with Afghanistan, site of a 100-million-watt power station. "The U.S. believes a laser is being built that will be able to destroy incoming missiles and attack circling American satellites and battle stations in space. The Russians say Dushanbe will be used only for tracking objects in space."

Troitsk. One thousand miles east of Moscow, the Soviet equivalent of the Los Alamos and Livermore laboratories; built in the 1960s, it includes a huge tunnel for testing high-energy laser weapons.

Tyaratam. "This has two pads capable of launching several missiles a day to attack satellites in orbit."

Azgir. A center for development of technology to generate small nuclear explosions to provide directed energy.

Storozhevaya. A high-energy laser development facility.

Serpukhov. Center for research on computers "to manage battle in space."

Semipalatinsk. Testing site for nuclear weapons and center for underground testing of X-ray lasers.

"The extent of the Russian SDI effort has never been fully understood in Europe or the U.S.," said Adams, "in part because . . . the American government has chosen to underplay the Russian effort."[13]

Even though downplaying it, the White House and the Pentagon have not publicly ignored the Russian effort. Administration officials began publicizing Soviet antimissile defenses shortly after the president's speech of March 23, 1983. By October, 1985, the veil was lifted enough for issuance of a report, "Soviet Strategic Defense Programs," acknowledging that Soviet efforts "in most phases of strategic defense have long been far more extensive than those of the United States."

The report noted that Moscow's unique antiballistic missile defense system was being upgraded and expanded. It also noted construction of the Krasnoyarsk ballistic missile detection and tracking radar system and made the point that this "violates the 1972 ABM treaty." Studding the report are maps and color drawings—but no photographs—of Soviet antimissile systems, radar installations, and ground-based lasers. Another Pentagon document on "Soviet Military Power," issued in 1987, does contain photographs of Soviet defense installations. But the publication emphatically assures its readers, including Kremlin leaders possibly anxious about U.S. spy satellites or overflights of Soviet territory, that the photos were taken by two commercial satellite photography firms, SPOT Image Corporation and EOSTAT, Inc.

Adams's comment that the United States was still underestimating Soviet strategic defense activity was seconded by George Keyworth. At a meeting in early May 1988, he told us that the London Sunday Times account was "amazingly accurate" in its detail.

"What the Soviet Union has done is to carry its air defenses, originally against aircraft, to higher and higher levels of sophistication," Keyworth said. "First against cruise missiles, and most recently—in violation of the ABM Treaty, I must add—they conducted tests to intercept ballistic missile warheads reentering the atmosphere."

Keyworth said two new surface-to-air Soviet missiles, the SA-10 and SA-12, have "significant defensive capability" for terminal defense. "They are putting together a nationally integrated system of radars that allows them to pass off the target from one defensive system to another. So if they detect a warhead coming in they will get a shot at it, and if they miss it they will fire at it from the next place down the line. They will then have a nationally integrated ballistic missile defense system."

Keyworth shook his head. "They already have thousands of air defense systems that are capable of intercepting ballistic missiles—individually. They can only protect a small area, but, integrated together, they provide a defense of the Soviet Union itself."[14]

Gorbachev's admission before the 1987 summit, however limited, eased Teller's burden a bit. With this and subsequent disclosures by the British press and Pentagon reports, he felt less lonely in his campaign to show that SDI was not a made-only-in-America program.

Over trout dinner at the Cosmos in May 1988, Teller quietly discussed the Soviet leader's statement. He recalled those who argued many years ago that U.S. development of the hydrogen bomb might provoke similar action by the Soviets, who had, in fact, already embarked on such a course.

"Do you suppose," Teller asked in mock innocence, "that now the opponents of SDI will still say that if we don't proceed with our program the Russians won't proceed with theirs?"

Chapter 22

LIVERMORE

The Lawrence Livermore National Laboratory sits in a valley an hour's drive east of San Francisco. Seen for the first time on a late afternoon in spring, its tranquil setting belies its reputation as a storm center of debate over whether it is a key to world peace or a threat to human survival. Fleecy clouds drop so low they seem to squat on the surrounding purple hills like tired balloons. Cows and horses graze on gentle slopes. Along the ridges are strung rows of windmills, reminders of a hasty response to the energy crisis of the sixties. Their short blades resembling boomerangs, the windmills spin crazily in the slightest breeze.

From a distance, the barb-topped fence guarding the west flank of the mile-square laboratory grounds is obscured by tall eucalyptus trees rising from just inside. In contrast to the beauty of their natural surroundings, the laboratory buildings are a grab bag of architectural samples—white trailers and olive-drab shacks spotted among sturdier buildings of prestressed concrete, aggregate slab, and glass.

In 1952, Teller sold Washington on the need for a new weapons lab, and Ernest O. Lawrence sold Teller on Livermore as the place for it.

In its early days, Livermore bore the stamp of Lawrence. He had towered over West Coast physics since his invention of the cyclotron and his winning of the Nobel Prize in 1939. One of his former students, Herbert F. York, became the first director of Livermore, and two others, Harold Brown and John Foster, were directors later. Still later, York would write that when Teller became displeased with early plans for the laboratory and indicated he might not join it after all, Lawrence told York, "We would probably be better off without Teller."[1] York left Livermore in 1958 to become assistant secretary of defense for research and development.

After York, Kenneth Street, head of the chemistry division, took over briefly as Livermore director. Teller succeeded him in March 1958. He intended to serve for only a year while preparing to turn the helm over to Mark Mills, a bright young physicist who was being groomed as heir apparent. The need for a smooth transition and for the infusion of new blood was intensified in August 1958 when Lawrence, weakened by a long battle with colitis and the effects of overwork, died. (At the request of Lawrence's family, Teller delivered the first E. O. Lawrence Memorial Address in 1960.) Teller's plan of succession at Livermore was aborted by further tragedy when Mills was killed in a helicopter crash at Eniwetok.[2] Teller remained in the post until 1960, when he resigned and, in accordance with one of Lawrence's last requests to Teller, was succeeded by Harold Brown.

The early performance of Livermore had done little to support Teller's and Lawrence's hopes. Its first product, a new fusion device, failed its first two tests. A third test was canceled because new calculations showed that the device would fail that one, too.[3]

In time, the laboratory took on distinct signs of Teller's influence. He continued to champion its original purpose as a source of new weapons design and was instrumental in attracting talented young physicists to Livermore. Many were signed up under a program supported by the John Hertz Foundation, established in 1956 by the car-rental millionaire who was Teller's friend and fellow native of Hungary. By 1987, the foundation was funding 120 fellowships a year to graduate students in applied sciences. Livermore's staff included twenty-nine Hertz fellows and alumni. Teller and Lowell Wood, his closest associate and chief recruiter, served as foundation directors.

Another longtime Teller associate, John Nuckolls, was elected by the University of California regents in 1988 as director of the Livermore laboratory. He succeeded Roger Batzel, who had defeated Teller for the post by one regent's vote seventeen years earlier and had served in the post ever since.

By 1988 the laboratory employed about 8,000 scientists and other employees on projects costing more than $1 billion a year. Official secrecy shrouds much of their work, inevitably arousing public curiosity concerning the tidbits occasionally dropped about such exotic projects as the X-ray laser, particle beams, kinetic energy, and the like. Lost in the fanfare over these is other, more fundamental work, such as environmental and biomedical research projects seeking answers to vital questions: How do plants respond to chronic low levels of pollutants in the atmosphere? How will chemicals discharged into oceans and streams affect fisheries? How do energy by-products and discharges work their way through the environment and the food chain to affect humans? In looking for the answers, scientists analyze damage to reproductive cells, develop bioassays to detect genetic injury, and do molecular studies on damage and repair of human genes.

In 1987, we spent four days touring Livermore and interviewing many of its key personnel. We had spent much of an earlier day interviewing Lowell Wood, in Washington.

Wood had spoken of Teller's challenging him to find solutions to problems in SDI. He marveled at Teller's acuity in pointing out weak spots in his proposals. "Edward essentially challenges you to go back and find out where in his train of reasoning you find flaws," he said, "and you very seldom do." But this really should not be surprising, Wood suggested.

"Edward received a really fine classical education in physics—physics as it was taught in the heyday of physics," he said. "Edward got through his formal education very quickly, but he had outstanding teachers, some of the great names of the twentieth century, like Bohr and Heisenberg, and he understands physics so well that his physical intuition is highly developed. He not only knows the laws of physics, but he guesses very well how they apply to the world, and that's something that the passage of time doesn't take from you."

Wood recalled an incident involving his report on a fuel project.

"I came in and told him thus and such happened," he said. "We had come up with a marvelous new turn on nuclear fuel that was clean, safe, burned like crazy, no radioactive products, nothing—just ideal. And he looked at it and said, 'It can't be that good.'

"I said, 'Sorry, Edward. You're wrong. These are experimental data.' And he looked at it and said, 'The data are wrong. That's nearly twice as great as it could be theoretically.'

"I said, 'What do you mean, theoretically?'

"He mentioned a particular formula. 'Didn't you check it?' I strolled off, crawled back into the hole, went off and found what the formula was. I dimly remembered it from many years before and went scrambling back to the textbooks, found out what it was, plugged it in—and he was right."

Wood said Teller was a natural for the Red Team in the "What if?" game played interminably at Livermore. He described the Red Team as the one that figuratively "puts on Soviet general staff planning caps and says, 'How in the world are we going to counter this, nullify it, cope with it, defeat it, circumvent it—whatever it is that the U.S. is doing? How are we going to minimize its military and economic impact?' . . . Whereupon the Blue Team comes back, saying, 'No, no. You misunderstood what we were going to do and you didn't know about such and such widget and you didn't know about this technology and this, that, or whatever. Now try to beat it.' And the Red Team works some more on it and tries to beat it. And you go through several cycles of this."

What made Teller such an effective member of the Red Team?

"Because of his huge breadth of knowledge and the length of experience," Wood said, "he knows not only what could be done, but what the Soviets are likely to do, what technological tricks they have, what production complexes they have running in order to do this, that, or whatever, what they've done in the past that's closely related to this. . . . So that's the type of questions he is always asked and that he asks at Livermore and when he goes to Los Alamos or out in the aerospace industry or when he comes back here from the Pentagon or when he sat on the [AEC] advisory committee, the Air Force Scientific Advisory Committee, or the CIA's nuclear intelligence panel. . . . He's a pretty effective Red Team guy."

John Nuckolls, then associate director of physics at Livermore, arrived for our interview at 11:30 A.M. A slight gray-haired man of fifty-five, he was dapper in gray tweed sportcoat, cocoa slacks, and blue and cocoa tie.

In the early 1950s, while still an undergraduate at Columbia, Nuckolls read about Teller's success in developing the hydrogen bomb. The son of an explosives expert with Underwriters Laboratories in Chicago, Nuckolls had been fascinated by explosives since childhood and was impressed by accounts of the thermonuclear bomb project.

"The concept of using nuclear weapons to deter larger conventional wars was one that appealed to me," he told us.

Later, Nuckolls saw a newspaper item about a visit to Columbia by Livermore recruiters. "I just couldn't resist going over to talk to them. So Teller was really the reason for my coming to Livermore."

Nuckolls arrived in 1955 and spent the next five years in the weapons-design program, then transferred to the fusion program. There he and Lowell Wood teamed up on a project aimed at miniaturizing a thermonuclear device. Nuckolls had an idea for producing one not much bigger than a cocktail olive. But some way had to be found to ignite the fuel. In 1969 he and Wood proposed the use of laser beams to compress the fuel into a pellet, causing the fusion of hydrogen isotopes into helium and producing the desired explosion or burst of energy.

The Nuckolls-Wood effort led to a $2 billion federal laser-fusion program centered in a glass-and-aggregate building on the north edge of the laboratory grounds. Its heart is a mammoth chamber rising three stories and jammed with catwalks, huge pipes, and hollow metal spheres, giving it the appearance of a commercial laundry combined with a ship's engine room.

In the vaulted lobby of the building, walls bear colorful pictures and captions illustrating the project. There is also a chart demonstrating progress toward the precious break-even point at which the amount of energy produced by the fusion matches the enormous amounts of energy required by the laser beams used in the process. In 1987, eighteen years after the idea was first proposed, the line on the progress chart was less than two-thirds of the way home.

Nuckolls discussed his work and his association with Teller in a matter-of-fact tone, even when describing the differences he said they had on professional issues. One incident involved another scientist's idea of using a nuclear explosion to put an enormous mass, a 1,000-ton object, into orbit. The idea had taken on special urgency because the Soviets had just proclaimed the success of their Sputnik launch. Nuckolls, then still new at the laboratory, was assigned to evaluate the prospect.

"I hadn't gotten very far when Teller called me down to his office to talk about it," Nuckolls said. ". . . He went to the blackboard, and I began to tell him about my crude, back-of-the-envelope calculations."

Nuckolls was well into his presentation, which involved the firing of a cannonball as an example, when Teller broke in.

"Pretty soon Teller's arms were waving," Nuckolls recalled, "and he was saying, 'Yes, but you haven't given enough weight to the fact that when the gas tries to drive the cannonball down the barrel it will undergo turbulent interaction with the inside of the barrel,' and so on.

"We got into a rather animated discussion, as a result of which I went off and gathered up a lot of books about turbulence, hydrodynamics, drag, and put them all into my calculations. It turned out to be extremely complicated, a much more complicated problem than the fellow who had proposed it imagined." Nuckolls said his evaluation of the idea was "largely negative."

"Another subject we interacted on rather intensely was, could you hide an explosion underground in a cavity," Nuckolls recalled. "For that question, he produced the world's first known computer calculation on the effects of an underground explosion." The subject was of special interest to Teller because the Soviet Union had announced in 1958 that it would suspend nuclear testing if the United States would follow suit. Teller suspected that the Soviets might continue to test underground instead of in the atmosphere, where the tests would be more easily detected.

"Teller and I came to different conclusions on that," Nuckolls said.

Teller's conclusion was that an underground nuclear explosion, while not going unnoticed, could be muffled to disguise its force. "If a twenty-kiloton bomb, with an explosive force equal to twenty thousand tons of TNT, were set off in a hole nearly five hundred feet in diameter located three thousand feet below ground, it would be muffled so as to resemble an explosion of only seventy tons," Nuckolls said. "In addition, the nature of the explosion might remain uncertain because it is difficult to locate deep deposits of radioactivity from aboveground."

These problems contributed to U.S. insistence that any permanent test-ban treaty include provisions for on-site inspection as a safeguard against cheating.

Physicist Ron Hyde, thirty-seven but looking younger, fit the popular image of the Livermore weapons designer. He was slender, and his checked lumberjack shirt, uneven beard, and long, curly hair gave him a campus-fresh look. His deep-set eyes peered through shell-rimmed glasses. Lowell Wood had chosen him to evaluate new ideas, including weapons design, offered by members of the supersecret O Group, Wood's team of young SDI scientists laboring in the olive-drab shacks across the laboratory grounds.

Hyde had come to the laboratory in 1972 as a young mathematics whiz from MIT. His twin passions were space and Soviet study. His distant thoughts were directed not merely to the design of weapons but to entire spaceships. He wanted to help design them and send them aloft as insurance against Soviet control of outer space. He read deeply in Soviet history and tried to interpret the meaning of every latest rumbling from the Kremlin. Hate the Soviets? "I don't hate them," he said. "I just don't trust them."

For George Chapline, another member of O Group, the Livermore mission had taken on a less hostile, more dominantly scientific meaning. At UCLA he was a classmate of Lowell Wood. Later, Wood recruited him for Livermore. He arrived for a look in the summer of 1969.

"I was very impressed by Livermore and the kinds of things people were thinking about—laser fusion and so much else," Chapline told us.

"At that time, Edward interviewed all the people who were employed to work in the physics laboratory," Chapline said. "He made a deep impression. I didn't know much about it before, but the opportunity to find out a lot about nuclear weapons was intriguing to me. Frankly, I hadn't done anything very spectacular or successful until then, so I thought a change of pace might help."

By the early 1970s, he and Teller had coauthored a paper, "The Theory of High-Energy Collision of Nuclei." "It became recognized as a seminal work," Chapline said.

At the same time, much of the effort in laser development revolved around the more conventional power sources, and little progress had been made. But in 1977, Peter Hagelstein, a brilliant MIT graduate in electrical engineering and now an X-ray laser investigator, came up with what Chapline described to us as "a fairly interesting idea."

"It had occurred to a number of people that in general terms one could use a nuclear bomb to pump an X-ray laser, but some idea was needed on how this could be accomplished," Chapline said. "In 1977 I came up with a specific scheme as to how this could be done and showed with simple calculations that it looked fairly plausible."

Official secrecy prevented Chapline from detailed discussion of his "scheme" and Hagelstein's "fairly interesting idea." But the picture emerging from his description was one of two scientists, Chapline the veteran and Hagelstein the newcomer, racing to solve the same problem.

"Laboratory management became fairly excited," Chapline said.

Livermore officials decided that the same test would be used for both Chapline's and Hagelstein's ideas.

"That test," Chapline told us with a whimsical smile, "was successful."

In fact, the test showed that both ideas would work. But Hagelstein's drew wider acclaim. The Department of Energy presented him the 1984 E. O. Lawrence Award for his contribution to national security. The citation referred to his "innovation and creativity in X-ray laser physics." Some even described Hagelstein as the creator of the nuclear X-ray laser, displeasing Lowell Wood and Chapline.

The reason for their displeasure did not become apparent until eight years after the test. In May 1988, it was explained in a letter to the authors by Norris Keeler, former deputy director of Livermore and head of its physics department in 1972–75. At the time, Wood was associate head of the department, assistant to the laboratory director, and head of O Group.

Keeler said Wood began thinking in early 1972 about ways of using the output from nuclear explosions to drive X-ray lasers.

Keeler continued:

> In 1973, Lowell seemed to gain more enthusiasm and repeatedly drew his colleagues into the discussions of the concept. Finally, in late 1974 or early 1975, a comprehensive classified internal document was published by Lowell Wood, with George Chapline and John Nuckolls as co-authors. In this document, all the presently conceptualized nuclear-pumped SDI concepts were presented [except for one developed by Wood in 1979]. I might point out at this time Peter Hagelstein was not even an LLNL [Livermore] employee.[4]

Keeler credited Chapline with "some of the more speculative parts of the 1975 document" and with perhaps helping Wood on the X-ray laser. He said Chapline was liked by Wood "because of his brilliant, innovative, off-the-wall intellectual style . . . but was not the driving force behind the X-ray concept at that time."

"Lowell was always very generous in giving credit to his young colleagues," Keeler said. "He often gave their work high visibility and down-played his own role."

Keeler recalled once having dinner with Wood and listening to him discuss a new concept for computing. Wood mentioned that a particular student could work out the details.

"That, in fact, happened," Keeler said, "and the student got credit for much of the idea. I believe that something similar happened with Hagelstein and the X-ray laser."

However credit is finally allotted for the nuclear X-ray laser, it helped tip Edward Teller's judgment in favor of SDI. He cited this and the development of supercomputers as the two heaviest factors in his decision to urge SDI upon President Reagan.

One of our last stops in the Livermore area was the home of Edward Teller, a heavily landscaped villa on the edge of the Stanford University campus. He led us into a living room with heavy ranch-style furniture, Spanish wall decor, and the battered Steinway in one corner. He had just returned from another exhausting trip and looked it.

His eightieth birthday lay only a few months ahead. Behind him lay nearly half a century of battles over the atomic bomb, the hydrogen bomb, nuclear reactors, and myriad other issues. Now, on the verge of physical exhaustion, against his doctor's advice to ease off, and with time running out, he worked without letup and was drawing lightning in another global debate. His secretary, Genevieve Phillips, had checked his schedule for us and found that he had made forty-four trips in one year. Why, we asked Teller, was he ignoring the doctor's advice? "I plead the Fifth Amendment to that," he said with a smile.

More than half his work time was being spent away from Livermore and the Hoover Institution at Stanford, where he still had offices. And most of his time away, he acknowledged, was devoted to promoting SDI. This included meetings of the White House Science Advisory Council, whose most recent session he had attended the day before our visit to his home.

"That meeting included SDI," he said, "but it was not all SDI." On the evening before that he had flown to New York to address a dinner for Tel Aviv University. "I was asked to talk about SDI. . . . Before that I was in Paris for the same reason, and before that I met with a group of people who were interested in supporting nuclear reactors—and SDI. So wherever I go, the topic cannot be avoided."

Also unavoidable was the question of whether the X-ray laser could be developed soon enough to be an effective component of SDI. Publicly expressed doubts on this point continued to dog Teller.

*   *   *

In February 1988, less than a year after our meeting in his home, Teller seemed not only still optimistic about the X-ray laser but even about the controversy over it. He expressed this rare upbeat view of controversy in an article for the *San Diego Union*, a conservative newspaper that published many of his articles. But he could not have expected that the controversy would reach such intensity that by the end of 1988 it—and he—would attract prime feature coverage by the *New York Times Magazine* and *60 Minutes*, the top-rated CBS television weekly news feature. At the time he made the statement, he felt that controversy would be helpful in the long run because "some of the most important public facts about X-ray lasers have escaped public attention."

"The X-ray laser project represents the most novel scientific endeavor of the entire Strategic Defense Initiative effort," he wrote in the *Union*.[5] Teller noted that he also had doubted the feasibility of lasing, or intensifying the energy of, X rays when Wood and Chapline first proposed it. He said an idea for the lasing of gamma rays, whose wavelength is 1,000 times shorter even than those of X rays, had also been advanced. "As an older and appropriately more conservative physicist, I expressed doubt about both possibilities," he said.

"In the case of the gamma ray laser, my doubts persist. In the case of the X-ray laser, they have been disproved. That is a very great scientific accomplishment."

Also among the doubters was George Keyworth. Teller said Keyworth was not convinced even up to the time he set up Teller's meeting with President Reagan after Teller's 1982 appearance on the William Buckley television program. Teller said Keyworth, after hearing about progress on the X-ray laser at that meeting, merely "agreed that interesting work was being done."

But within a year, Teller was satisfied by additional experiments that the principle of the X-ray laser was firmly established. "It gave me great pleasure," he said, "to write a classified letter to my skeptical friend, Jay Keyworth, which started with the unclassified words 'Merry Christmas.' " The principle was proven, the letter said, and now "we are entering the engineering phase of X-ray lasers. . . ."

Of the $1.044 billion a year in estimated Livermore expenses, including nondefense projects, a breakdown in its *Weekly Bulletin* showed $280 million for weapons research, $73.4 million for magnetic fusion, $62.8 million for inertial confinement fusion, and $80 million for free-electron laser research. There was no separate listing for the X-ray laser.[6]

Teller spoke of using nuclear explosion to supply the vast amount of energy needed to make the X-ray laser feasible for defense, but the White House had consistently refused to accept nuclear explosives for any role in

SDI. That refusal was emphasized by Keyworth when he served as the president's science adviser and in the several interviews he granted us after he left the White House. "The reason," he explained, "is political in the purest sense, meaning the aspect of public acceptability."

Regardless of whether the X-ray laser ever became important in defense, Teller insisted, Washington should be alerted to its technical possibilities and to its importance as a pure discovery in science. Teller said:

> Microscopes using light can view objects of a few thousand atoms. Electron microscopes can almost see atoms, but they can only observe near a surface, not in depth, and not in three dimensions. An X-ray laser can provide three-dimensional pictures of almost atomic-sized objects. . . . A truly high-intensity laser utilizing the energies of a nuclear explosive could open a new chapter in biology.[7]

Teller's "Merry Christmas" letter to Keyworth, dated December 22, 1983, and similar correspondence in 1984 with other high administration officials fed a controversy peaking in late 1988. The issue was whether he oversold the X-ray laser program to President Reagan and defense officials. At the heart of the issue was one of the gravest questions that can be raised about scientists and their work: Did they truthfully represent it to the government and to the public whose support was critical for its continuance?

The question was sharply framed in newspaper headlines, including a *New York Times Magazine* article captioned "Beyond the Bomb: Turmoil in the Labs" and in an interview by Mike Wallace on *60 Minutes*.

Besides the 1983 letter to Keyworth, Teller also wrote two controversial letters that were dated December 28, 1984, and were carried to Washington by Lowell Wood as Teller's personal emissary. One was addressed to Robert McFarlane, then national security adviser to the president. The second went to Paul Nitze, the State Department senior arms-control adviser, who was then preparing for disarmament talks in Geneva. All three letters were labeled "secret," and several paragraphs were deleted from each before they were made available to us in 1988.

The opening paragraph of the 1983 letter to Keyworth says, "Our [Livermore's] Christmas present is a quantitative proof of the . . ." There is then a deletion of about five lines, followed by the lone word *measurements*, at the end of the paragraph. Then comes open space indicating that five lines at the beginning of the next paragraph have been deleted, followed by this concluding sentence of the paragraph: "There is no other theory except that of the laser which could explain these results."[8]

At another point, Teller used a phrase about Livermore researchers "now entering the engineering phase of X-ray lasers"—a statement that would come back to haunt him.

"I do not believe that the X-ray laser is clearly the only means, the best means, or even the most urgent means for defense," Teller wrote Keyworth. "It is clear, however, that it is in this field that the first clear-cut scientific breakthrough has occurred."[9]

The X-ray laser design referred to in the Keyworth letter is known as Excalibur. A few months later, Livermore came up with an advance that was dubbed Super Excalibur. Many times brighter than Excalibur, it would shoot thousands of individual beams to destroy thousands of enemy missiles, Teller said. But, unlike Excalibur, the more sophisticated design had not undergone basic experimental testing underground.

In the letter to McFarlane, Teller referred to the forthcoming negotiations in Geneva. He noted that he had spoken with the president in 1982 about the nuclear bomb–pumped X-ray laser.

"In the meantime, it has become highly probable that this instrument can destroy sharply defined objects at a distance of the order of 1,000 miles and possibly more," Teller wrote. Teller added that given "even moderate support, together with considerable luck, this might be accomplished in principle in as little time as three years."[10]

Teller's letter to Nitze referred to progress in the nuclear bomb–pumped X-ray laser program and to what Teller estimated to be a Soviet lead of up to seven years in the same field.

Undeleted portions of the letters indicate that Teller painted an even more optimistic picture for Nitze than for McFarlane. He wrote:

> The overall military effectiveness of X-ray lasers relative to the hydrogen bombs which energize them may thus be as large as a trillion when directed against sharply defined targets. . . . This approach seems likely to make X-ray lasers a really telling strategic defense technology. For instance, a single X-ray laser module the size of an executive desk which applied this technology could potentially shoot down the entire Soviet land-based missile force, if it were to be launched into the module's field-of-view. . . . A handful of such modules could similarly suppress or shoot down the entire Soviet submarine-based missile force, if it were to be salvo-launched.[11]

The message was clear: Do not give away this potential advance in the disarmament talks.

Teller's optimism about eventual success in developing a militarily effective X-ray laser was not shared by all at Livermore. Among the foremost skeptics was Roy D. Woodruff, director of the nuclear design program. As overseer of the X-ray laser project, he was aware of the many hurdles blocking its advance, especially in the development of sensors to detect and record activity in the microseconds between the instant the laser went off and the time the sensors were destroyed by the great flash of fire.

The *New York Times Magazine* reported on October 9, 1988, that Woodruff's immediate reaction on reading a copy of Teller's letter to Keyworth was to visit Teller's office two floors below his own and to declare that the great physicist's glowing assessment was premature. He urged Teller to send a follow-up letter toning down statements made in the first. Teller refused. Woodruff drafted one himself, but Roger Batzel, the laboratory director, did not approve it. It was never sent.

Woodruff simmered until he became aware of Teller's letters to McFarlane and Nitze one year later. Then he erupted. He drafted a countering letter to Nitze, describing the Super Excalibur as "not impossible, but very unlikely." As in the case of Woodruff's earlier letter, Batzel disapproved it. But Batzel did approve a visit by Woodruff to Nitze in Washington to present his perspective on the X-ray laser program.

In October 1985, Woodruff resigned as associate director for defense systems at Livermore. In a letter to Batzel, he wrote that for nearly two years "potentially misleading" evaluations of the X-ray laser program had been given to the White House. He was then assigned to a less responsible job at the laboratory, which he performed for a year before applying for one with greater responsibility and more pay. Turned down, he filed a grievance with the University of California as the contract operator of the laboratory and won a favorable decision in 1987 from a hearing board composed of Livermore scientists. He was promoted in December of that year to director of the Department of Treaty Verification, a senior position. Batzel retired as director of Livermore a few months later.[12]

In the meantime, Woodruff's cause was taken up by George E. Brown, Jr., Democratic congressman from California. Brown called for an investigation by the General Accounting Office (GAO). Its findings were given to Brown in a classified briefing on February 25, 1988. Four months later, on June 20, the GAO sent Brown a written report stripped of classified material but making these points:

- Woodruff was reported to have told university officials that Batzel had taken "reprisal action" against him, that "technical information about the X-ray laser program had been misrepresented to the administration, and that Teller and Lowell Wood had made 'overly optimistic and technically incorrect' statements regarding this research to the nation's highest policy makers." The GAO found that the Livermore management personnel, including Woodruff, "had made statements about the status and potential of the X-ray laser that were similar to most of the statements identified by Mr. Woodruff as being 'overly optimistic and technically incorrect.' "[13]

- To check the accuracy of the Teller statements challenged by Woodruff, the GAO sought the opinions of "selected [Livermore] scientists, who had specific knowledge about" the X-ray laser program. "From these interviews, we concluded there was no general agreement among these scientists regarding the accuracy of the statements."
- Batzel believed that Keyworth, who had been briefed on the X-ray laser and who knew Teller "to be a technical optimist," was unlikely to misinterpret Teller's letter. Batzel therefore felt that Woodruff's clarifying letter was unnecessary.
- Teller's reference to the engineering phase of the X-ray laser program resulted from his feeling, as a theoretical physicist, that the "basic scientific question, can an X-ray laser be demonstrated, had been answered. Therefore, in his opinion, all that remained to be accomplished was 'engineering.' "[14]

The GAO report delicately avoided direct criticism of Teller for his statements about the X-ray laser program or of Woodruff for calling them "overly optimistic and technically incorrect." As a result, it offered both sides ammunition in support of their opposing views. Brown, who had prompted the GAO investigation, interpreted the report as evidence that "incredible claims were made." Woodruff, disclaiming any personal animosity toward Teller, said, "The laboratory is losing its way. It once stood for technical excellence and technical integrity, but I think it's become politicized during the Reagan administration."

Teller's comment on the affair was uncharacteristically brief: "Let me plead guilty to the great crime of optimism."[15]

One month after publication of the *Times* account, Woodruff's charges were also highlighted on the November 13, 1988, edition of *60 Minutes*. "The failure here is not Dr. Teller's vision," he said. "It's that that vision was the only thing that key advisers, including potentially the President of the United States, heard."[16]

Teller, who was also interviewed for the program, disrupted production momentarily by abruptly breaking off at one point. This occurred when Mike Wallace asked him about possible reasons for his differences with Woodruff and, on Teller's failure to respond, said to him, "You retreat behind silence. When you don't like a question, you retreat behind silence. Why?"

Teller replied, "You will have noticed that I'm not answering your questions when you are asking me about other people's motives. I think you are conducting this interview in an inappropriate manner." Then, beginning to remove his lavaliere microphone, he said, "Shall we stop here?"

"No," Wallace pleaded. But Teller continued stripping the microphone wire from around his neck and, preparing to walk off the set, suggested, "Maybe we sit down and talk a little." They did.

When the interview resumed a few minutes later, Wallace had abandoned the unaccepted subject of Woodruff's motives, leaving 40 million viewers wondering what had transpired during the break in the videotaping of the program. Introducing the next phase of the interview, he said Teller "told us how important it is to the United States to continue work on the X-ray laser program." Teller was then back on camera with his explanation of why: "Because we have good evidence that the Soviets have done so."[17]

The program picked up interviews with Andrei Sakharov, Teller's counterpart as central figure in development of the Soviet hydrogen bomb, and Lt. Gen. James Abrahamson, director of the U.S. SDI program who had recently announced he would retire in early 1989.

Sakharov said he believed that Teller and other SDI advocates "are overestimating work that is being done in the Soviet Union. . . . I think that SDI is a scientific technological monster with no chance for survival because it is pretty easy to be destroyed in orbit."

Abrahamson drew a parallel between SDI and the H-bomb. "If the United States did not go forward with the development of the H-bomb, the Russians would," he said. "They would not restrain themselves just because we restrain ourselves."

So, asked Wallace, Teller was right then?

"Yes."

And he is right now?

"Yes."[18]

Describing the 60 Minutes session to us later, Teller said he was interviewed for nearly five hours and was disappointed that much of his argument on behalf of SDI was edited from the final version of the program. He also said there had been an unpublicized question underlying his disagreement with Woodruff over his letters on the X-ray laser: Since Woodruff was director of the program under which the X ray was being developed, should not he, instead of Teller, initiate any reports on the progress or lack of progress in its development? Teller, noting that he was acting in his capacity as a member of the White House Science Advisory Council reporting directly to White House officials, said he brushed aside Woodruff's protest.

In a general vein, the Woodruff-Times-60 Minutes chapter contributed to a pattern of growing congressional and public skepticism. This was reflected in reduced spending on the program and its relegation to a minor role in the presidential debate of 1988. At that point, funding over the first five years of SDI totaled $16.7 billion. By comparison, estimates of its ultimate cost ranged from $69 billion to $207 billion, depending on how much of the planned three-phase program would ultimately be approved. In the presidential election campaign, the prominence of SDI as an issue was diminished by the U.S.-Soviet Union treaty on reduction of nuclear forces and steps toward further disarmament. Prospects for continued White House backing of the program brightened slightly with the election of George Bush, who, as vice-president in the Reagan administration and as the Republican candidate for president, expressed basic support of SDI. Massachusetts Governor Michael Dukakis, the Democratic candidate, had shifted between outright opposition and narrowly limited support for research only.

Against the background of controversy swirling about Livermore and its weapons programs, we recalled the peaceful last day of our 1987 trip to the laboratory. We had stopped off at nearby Berkeley to visit Emmi Kirz, Teller's sister. She lived alone in a block of frame homes built on a terrace. The living and dining room reflected the quiet elegance of the life she had known in Hungary as a girl before Hitler disrupted the world. Nearly every available surface—the walls, the living-room tables, the dining-room sideboard—bore fading, treasured family photographs, including one of Emmi as a blanket-wrapped infant in her mother's arms. Now spry at eighty-one, Emmi served us tea and Viennese cookies while talking of Edward.

"He has been an excellent brother," she said. "I don't think he has changed much. We talked about that once. He said, 'Maybe I do change, but I'm not aware of it.' He is very warmhearted. Once he is fond of a friend, he is a remarkable friend. And if he has reason to change his mind about somebody, that upsets him very much."

Before leaving Livermore, we drove once more around the laboratory grounds. It was Sunday, and there was little activity, even at the visitors' information center. To give us a few more minutes to inspect an astrophysics exhibit, attendants offered to delay the scheduled showing of a film on the potential value of nondefense projects under way at the laboratory. We hurried through the exhibit, then joined the film audience, which consisted of two other visitors.

Beginning the drive to the airport for our return trip east, we took a last look at the clouds plumped down on the surrounding hilltops and at the grazing cows and horses. Along the ridges, the arms of the windmills spun crazily.

Chapter 23

In Defense of SDI

In his first Capitol Hill argument on behalf of SDI after the president's speech of March 23, 1983, Edward Teller spent an hour as a hearing witness before a unit of the House Armed Services Committee. It should have been his peak performance as a champion of the program, for it traced SDI from a flicker in the mind of then Governor Ronald Reagan seventeen years earlier to its emergence as a sweeping change in the nation's defense policy. But the Teller performance was overshadowed by a hint of scandal and drew little notice.

The hearing was held by the Subcommittee on Research and Development, chaired by Rep. Melvin Price, an Illinois Democrat. Teller appeared before it on April 28, five weeks after the White House SDI dinner. The subject was "third generation" defense systems, those coming after the atomic bomb and the hydrogen bomb.

Even though the day was to end badly, it started out as a pleasant experience for Teller. After forty years of periodic visits to Washington as a staunch advocate of defense, he had established himself among Capitol Hill regulars as an incisive, interesting witness.

On this visit, a warm greeting from Rep. William L. Dickinson of Alabama, the ranking Republican on the committee, was especially welcome. For only a few hours earlier the *New York Times* had come out with a front-page story putting Teller's integrity in question. It suggested that his recommendations on defense policy, especially his persuading President Reagan to adopt SDI, were influenced by his stock holdings in a defense-oriented company.

Dickinson did not mention this. Instead, he said, "I . . . join in the welcome of Dr. Teller and tell you how much I personally appreciate your presence here, and also what you have meant to the security of this country in the past."

The congressman said he felt "very strong" about Teller's efforts in a particular area. "You have been very instrumental in getting data unclassified. . . . Also I think to a very large extent your philosophy and some of the things you have urged on this committee and this administration have been very instrumental in getting us away from the posture of MAD, from mutual assured destruction. . . . You also worked with this committee in getting funds for the advanced computers, S-1 and fifth-generation computers that we are working toward. So the effects of your work will last for many years after you and I are both gone."[1]

Teller spent much of the next hour raking over the history of weapons development since World War I. He also fielded questions ranging from the number of MX missiles that should be retained to how private industry could best be used in the development of a new defense system.

On the whole, Teller's entire stay in the hearing room was a positive experience. Then he left and was questioned further by reporters, including one from the *Times*.

"And what this reporter wanted to know," Teller lamented to us in an interview, "had nothing to do with my testimony, or with SDI, or with anything else that was relevant. What he wanted to know about was my stock in Helionetics." Helionetics, Inc., a small firm based in Irvine, California, specialized in the development of laser and solar-energy products.[2]

The *Times* story described Helionetics as a firm that could benefit from President Reagan's proposal of a futuristic missile system and said its principal owner, Bernard B. Katz, had given stock worth millions to "leading scientific and military experts and others with connections to the Reagan administration."

The report emphasized that Teller had "helped persuade" President Reagan to adopt SDI. It said that in the week before Reagan's SDI speech, trading in Helionetics stock averaged almost 50,000 shares a day, ten times its average trading volume in 1985 and half again the average daily volume up to that point in 1986. The report also noted that the price of the stock rose by 30 percent, from $13.50 to $17.50.

The *Times* account said that contracts with the Departments of Defense and Energy accounted for 70 percent of Helionetics's business over the last three years. It also quoted Jeffrey I. Levatter, president of the company's laser division, as saying that Helionetics's laser technology included a high-powered ultraviolet laser that could be used in space-based weapons and communications and in high-speed integrated circuits. It quoted Norris Keeler, a former director of navy technology and former colleague of Teller's at Livermore, as saying that Helionetics had a "significant role to play" in Livermore's X-ray laser program. It described the program as "one that Dr. Teller has been involved with and that is expected to receive additional financing as a result of the President's initiative."[3]

Interviewed before publication of the story, Teller told the *Times*, "I have not discussed Helionetics in connection with any work at Lawrence Livermore." He also said he had not mentioned Helionetics in any discussions with the president.

The almost inescapable conclusion to be drawn from the *Times* account was that Teller had made a handsome profit on the market as a result of inside information. The *Times* painted a picture of a man who paid nothing for stock in a company, then helped increase the value of that stock to $800,000 by persuading the President of the United States to adopt a program making essential use of the company's products.

Although outraged, Teller issued only a brief, bland response. Keeler, then a Helionetics official, had been quoted as saying there was "collaboration on X-ray lasers" between the Lawrence Livermore National Laboratory and Helionetics. "No collaboration exists," Teller declared. "None is planned, and Keeler told the *New York Times* that no collaboration exists."

Teller said that he was not given the stock but had bought it. And he bought it before Reagan was elected, at a time when the company was facing bankruptcy, during the administration of Jimmy Carter. (It later filed for bankruptcy.) Teller ascribed the increase in the value of the stock to technical advances fostered by the company, particularly in a process for converting direct current to alternating current. "Since the time of my original investment," he said, "I have neither bought nor sold the Helionetics stock."

Addressing what he called the *Times*'s "innuendo," Teller said he did not learn the contents of the president's speech until he arrived at the White House two hours before its delivery and had no opportunity to communicate knowledge of the contents to anyone outside the White House.

As bland as it was, the Teller statement never saw the light of day. The *Times* ignored it. The question overhanging Teller's integrity grew larger.

On the day after Teller's appearance before the subcommittee, the *Stanford Daily* had headlined "White House to Investigate Hoover Fellow."[4] The second-day *Times* story led with a White House statement that Teller "had no involvement whatsoever" in Reagan's SDI speech. Printed on page 12, the account also repeated Katz's statement that he had given stock to Teller and that he understood Teller to have been "part of" the speech preparation. There was no mention of why Teller appeared before the subcommittee or what he said about a defense policy characterized by some national leaders as a key to peace and by others as a threat to human survival.

Three weeks later, the investigation concluded that Teller had done nothing improper in the Helionetics situation.

This was reported in a four-paragraph story on an inside page of the *Times*. By comparison, the original story ran thirty-five inches, half of it on the front page.

This spurred Teller's next response, a full-page advertisement in the May 31, 1983, issue of the *Wall Street Journal*. The cost was $72,531 and was paid by Accuracy in Media, a conservative organization set up in Washington to combat what its supporters regarded as a liberal bias in the press and broadcasting industry.

The inch-high headline of the Teller ad proclaimed, "I was NOT the only victim of the *New York Times*." This was a play on the full-page *Journal* ad Teller had bought in 1979, declaring, "I was the only victim of Three Mile Island," and referring to the heart attack he suffered in his strenuous efforts to defend the cause of nuclear power.

At the outset of the 1983 advertisement, Teller noted that the day after the *Times* story on Helionetics, Radio Moscow broadcast it worldwide "with each misstatement and innuendo embellished."

"The *New York Times*, of course, is not directly responsible for this," the Teller ad acknowledged. "But when the *New York Times*—through misinformation—totally deflects attention from information of utmost national importance, discredits testimony given to Congress, and provides grist for the Soviet propaganda mill, the list of victims includes more than those directly attacked."

Teller then made these points:

- The increase in trading volume during the week preceding the president's announcement was 35 percent over the average weekly volume earlier in the year, not the 50 percent reported by the *Times*. And the reason for the increase was not the upcoming Reagan SDI speech but a promotional trip around the country in the preceding week by Charles Jobbins, the Helionetics president, to tell investment brokers about record sales and earnings for the first quarter.
- Since Teller's retirement in 1975, he had become interested in several high-technology companies and in the case of Helionetics had invested not only time and energy but some of his own capital.
- While the *Times* reported that 70 percent of Helionetics's business over the previous three years was derived from government contracts, in the last

year its "direct sales to the government amounted to 23 percent—13 percent for energy devices, 10 percent for laser development."

- The most outstanding Helionetics product was "a near-perfect device for converting DC power to very precisely controlled AC power." The converter was important in the use of solar cells, in batteries, and in the energy supply to computers and other sensitive apparatus. The *Times* made an "amazing error" in stating that Helionetics laser technology included a high-powered ultraviolet laser that could be used in space-based weapons. "Confusing an annealing—or communications—laser with a weapons laser," Teller said, "is comparable to identifying penknives as armaments."
- He was unaware of the contents of the president's speech until two hours before it was delivered, which was after the New York stock market had closed.

Teller closed with a sweeping conclusion:

. . . that this small but blatant example of the *New York Times*'s mixture of politics with misrepresentation does not stand alone. That the lives of uncounted people in the United States and abroad suffer repercussions from such editorial decisions cannot be questioned.

Indeed, I was not the only victim of the *New York Times*.[5]

But the seeds of suspicion had been sown, and Teller's image had taken a severe hit. As Rep. Francis X. McCloskey, an Indiana Democrat, had told the *Stanford Daily*, "Most Americans don't receive free or discounted blocks of stock," and presidential advisers should "avoid perceptions of conflict of interest."

Teller had a sound basis for his lament that the fireworks over his stock ownership had diverted attention from his testimony before the subcommittee. His eighty-seven-minute presentation, virtually ignored in the press, distilled much of the controversy over SDI. This included such issues as technical feasibility, timely deployment, financial practicality, and possible provocation of the Soviet Union. Also addressed, as a result of questioning by McCloskey, were the origin of Reagan's interest in SDI and the conflict-of-interest issue arising from Teller's stock in Helionetics.

In his statement to the committee, Teller acknowledged the difficultly of making the concept of SDI seem plausible to the lay citizen:

"A great change in the national defense situation is pending," he said. ". . . I have to talk to you about energy concentrations, about temperatures which no untrained person can readily grasp." He referred to the Reagan speech as "a remarkable statement about the fact that mutual assured destruction will not last forever."

"It must be replaced by mutual assured survival, by real defense . . . ,"
he said. "Some people—I am sorry to say, many scientists—whose minds
are stuck in the old concept of 'no defense,' have contradicted him. . . .
The real strategic defense proposals are secret, and they are much too
secret. In fact, we know that the Kremlin knows them, and what the
Kremlin knows, the President rightly says the American people have a right
to know also."

Teller admitted that he was a recent convert to the concept of strategic
defense using third-generation weapons technologies:

"In the 1950s, I taught no defense." he said. "In the 1960s, I was
doubtful. In the 1970s, I was hopeful about defense. And now I know it's
feasible because I have seen at least half a dozen solid defense proposals.
It is a certainty that at least one of them will work. There is the probability
that more than half of them will work."

He then referred to Soviet activity along the same line. "They build up
strategic defense in many places and are improving such defenses around
Moscow. They have operational experience in such matters which we are
totally lacking. By the time their defensive measures will become obvious
to everybody, it will be too late to react."

Teller drew a parallel between Soviet activity in strategic defense and
Soviet development of the hydrogen bomb: The Soviets will proceed,
regardless of whether the U.S. proceeds.

Teller said that in the third generation of weapons what counted even
more than the size of an explosion was "the enormous concentrations of
energy and temperature. . . . Thus, the third-generation weapons can be
used not for mass destruction but to destroy very specific targets such as
offensive weapons in action."

Teller then played the theme that was to consistently underlie public
discussions of SDI feasibility: Although advances in nuclear-explosives
technology and laser technology clearly point to the feasibility of producing
"new kinds of lasers" as components of an effective defense system, these
cannot be explained in open meetings because of official secrecy requirements.

"I *can* mention," he said, "the possibility [of generating], with the use
of nuclear explosives, electromagnetic radiators of new qualities—new
qualities which will give to a nuclear conflict novel dimensions. . . . I am
not talking about orbiting space laser battle stations. I am talking about
third-generation weapons and other instruments that pop up into space
when the time to use them has come. . . . None of these lasers act on
targets like a blowtorch, slowly, but rather act like a hammer, instantly, and
are correspondingly difficult to counter. . . . I am not advocating war on
people. I am advocating war on inanimate, offensive weapons.

"Is all this provocative? What is provocative: a sword or a shield? Gentlemen, I speak for the shield."[6]

Chairman Price asked whether Teller would recommend that "a small number" of MX missiles be deployed in underground silos as a deterrence until third-generation systems could be developed and deployed.

Teller replied, "We cannot give up deterrence by retaliation as long as our defenses are not in place. . . . I know that the transition from retaliation to pure defense must be gradual. . . . It should also be as rapid as ever possible."

Price then asked about criticism of the defense strategy from "a number of scientists and the press." Teller's response was the first in what was to be a long exchange of salvos with his old friend, Hans Bethe.

". . . Their concern arises from their being uninformed," Teller said. "I can quote one example. A very eminent scientist, Dr. Hans Bethe, wrote a few months ago about defense against nuclear weapons and said it was wishful thinking at best." His reaction, he said, was to invite Bethe to the Livermore laboratory for a firsthand look at work on third-generation weapons.

"He listened for a day carefully," Teller recalled. "The morning of the second day he came back with a considerable number of intelligent objections. In the course of the second day, all his objections were answered to his satisfaction. . . . At the end of the second day, Dr. Bethe withdrew his technical objections. He said in front of me, 'You have a splendid idea.'

"But did he change his public position? No.

"Instead of objecting on scientific and technical grounds, which he thoroughly understands, he now objects on the grounds of politics, on grounds of feasibility of military deployment, on other grounds of difficult issues which are quite outside the range of his professional cognizance or mine. . . . For every Bethe there are a hundred others who speak up and who don't even know the basics of what they are talking about."

Dickinson suggested that part of the problem involved the image of the program "as Star Wars games . . . that people conjure up immediately visions of Buck Rogers and the twenty-fifth century."

A similar observation came from Rep. Charles E. Bennett, a Florida Democrat. He said, "There are not very many people at seventy-five . . . who are able to do such a positive, great thing for mankind, which I think you have done with your prestige, your knowledge, your feeling that there is something real that is not Star Wars, that it is something that could at least, in your very modest language, bring about a deterrence because of doubt of success in attack. It doesn't mean you necessarily absolutely preclude some round coming through. But if you made it so expensive and so difficult, it could be a deterrence of that nature. And I think that hope is there. I am glad you articulated that hope."

The question of Soviet activity in laser development was explored after Teller was asked for an assessment.

"The Nobel Prize for the basic discovery in lasers has gone to three people," Teller replied. "One American, Charlie Townes, a good friend of mine, and to two Soviets, Basov and Prochorov. Now I can tell you what these people are doing today. Charlie Townes publishes beautiful papers about what is happening in the center of our galaxy. Basov and Prochorov are working with the Soviet military on lasers. You guess who is currently ahead."

At this point, Teller also said that the Soviets "shut up [silenced] all their people" four years earlier, preventing their scientists from publishing reports on their progress in laser work. But before then, he added, U.S. scientists learned from the Soviets "the most important piece of progress," something so important that he could not discuss it in public session. But he said he believed that the Soviets were ahead in the laser field and in the fabrication of titanium, an element of critical use in modern weaponry.

Among the last to question Teller was McCloskey. He recalled that President Eisenhower, upon leaving office, warned about the "dangers of the military-industrial complex, in effect the military and industry being tied too close together, possibly working against the public good." McCloskey also referred to the *New York Times* story published that morning about the holding of laser-company stock by many military and technical advisers to the president.

"Do you think this could possibly ever provide problems for the public perception of unbiased advice in that area, and is there possibly any need for statutory regulations in that area?"

Teller replied that if he were asked about how much stock he had in the firm or what it was worth he would have to telephone his wife for the answer. "I don't even know what I have," he explained. He then declared that the connection between the kind of laser work done by Helionetics and "destroying missiles, the topic I have addressed here, is simply nonexistent."

But the essence of his remarks was overlooked. It took a White House investigation to clear away some of the cloud raised by the *Times* story. And Teller became more painfully aware of the ancient political maxim that the actions of a public figure must not only *be* right but *look* right.

Chapter 24

In Defense of Israel

In the fall of 1987, Israeli officials grimly decided on a step to protect the nation's children from the dangers of possible chemical-warfare attack. They expanded the school curriculum to include the proper fitting and wearing of gas masks.[1]

That they were willing to subject their youngsters to this discomfort and accompanying psychological stress underscored their conviction that a real danger existed.

As perceived by Jerusalem, the danger flowed from the presence of Soviet short- and medium-range missiles on Syrian soil. Israel's main population centers—Haifa, Tel Aviv, and Jerusalem—lay within easy range of these weapons. The missiles could be fitted to carry either nuclear or chemical explosives, including components of poison gas.[2] Syrian production of chemical warfare weapons was confirmed in December 1987 by Yitzhak Rabin, the Israeli defense minister.[3]

A short time earlier, Aron Moss, an Israeli liaison officer assigned to the U.S. SDI organization, told us that the classroom poison-gas exercises are part of Israel's defense program. Besides such simple precautions as training children in the use of gas masks, the program included a variety of exotic defensive weapons based on new technology. These were so adaptable to the U.S. defense initiative, he said, that it seemed logical for the two nations to cooperate on SDI.

Israel was one of a half-dozen nations involved in such agreements within four years of Reagan's unveiling of SDI. The others were Great Britain, West Germany, France, Italy, and Japan.

Of the six, only Israel was involved in actual hostilities with her neighbors. As the classroom gas-mask exercises indicated, she could overlook no defensive measure, Moss said. Less than one year earlier, Muslims had not hesitated to use poison gas against fellow Muslims. Moss cited Iraq's 1988

IN DEFENSE OF ISRAEL   235

gas attack against Iran. He also referred to the use of gas in an earlier invasion of North Yemen by Egypt's Nasser.

"If they have no moral scruples to prevent them from using this horrible weapon against their co-religionists," he asked, "would they be inhibited from gassing Jews?"[4]

Israel's preoccupation with the multipronged threat from neighboring states and Teller's role in fashioning a defense against that threat predated the SDI concept by twenty years. As early as the mid-1960s, Teller began urging that new scientific technology be applied to the defense of Israel.

Teller had been urged by friends for many years to visit Israel but consistently dismissed the idea. Then, one evening at a party in Berkeley, he met Yuval Ne'eman, a Jewish leader in war, science, and politics. Ne'eman was a sixth-generation Sabra, or native Palestine Jew. At the time of their meeting in 1963, Ne'eman was already known to Teller as a premier physicist.

He had studied engineering at the Technion from 1941 to 1945 and one year later joined the Haganah, the defense organization set up by the Jewish Agency before Israel became a state. At the beginning of the war in 1948, he was a deputy battalion commander. He moved up rapidly before being transferred to the general staff, was assigned to the French Staff College in Paris, and on his return to Israel helped organize the Israeli Staff College.

Ne'eman left the army in 1957 as a colonel and, under the sponsorship of Moshe Dayan, was assigned to the Israeli embassy in London, where he completed work for a doctorate in physics. His thesis offered a new approach to the classification of subnuclear particles and brought him wide recognition from the scientific community, including Edward Teller.

Ne'eman later was chairman of Israel's Atomic Energy Commission, a visiting professor at Caltech, and the 1969 recipient of the Einstein Prize for his work on the classification of subnuclear particles.

Ne'eman's visiting professorship at Caltech lasted two years. It was during this period that he met Teller as a fellow guest in the home of Gerson Goldhaber, director of the Brookhaven National Laboratory.

During a 1987 visit to Washington, Ne'eman discussed with us his first meeting and later close association with Teller. Short and once wiry but now showing a slight paunch, the ruddy-faced Ne'eman smiled behind wire-rimmed glasses and spoke softly.

"He had followed the discoveries that I was involved in," Ne'eman said. "Also . . . Edward had grasped the fact that I had gone beyond the classification to the explanation of why there should be such a classification of particles."[5]

First they talked physics. Then they talked politics. Both believed that the Soviets presented the main danger to the Western world. Ne'eman said that in the eyes of some Israelis this set Teller apart from most Americans, who were regarded as dangerously naive in their assessment of the Soviet Union. "Perhaps," he explained, "because for us the memory of Hitler is overwhelmingly present."[6]

What finally drew Teller to Israel was a proposal for the economical movement of large quantities of earth by means of nuclear explosions. This idea for peaceful use of atomic energy, dubbed Project Plowshare, had been proposed in the mid-1950s.

As Ne'eman recalled, it was during his second meeting with Teller that they discussed Plowshare. Ne'eman, while in London in 1959, had thought of the possibility of generating electric power by channeling water from the Mediterranean to the Dead Sea.

"Edward mentioned that maybe with Plowshare techniques it could be developed," he said.

Teller arrived in 1966. He was not prepared for the feeling that overwhelmed him as he set foot on Israeli soil for the first time. In that instant, a lifelong indifference to religious tradition and ancestry was erased and replaced by a sense of attachment to this unique land with a four-thousand-year history and a new birthright.

"For me," Edward told us, "this was an extremely emotional experience." He was to return again and again, at least once a year, thereafter.

In the office of the Israeli Atomic Energy Commission on that first visit, Teller reviewed the data of the preliminary study initiated by Ne'eman. He estimated that the main portion of the canal could be excavated with 300 nuclear explosions. The proposed route ran from the Mediterranean port city of Ashdod due east to the Dead Sea, a distance of about 250 kilometers.[7] The project looked feasible, Ne'eman said, but it became ensnarled in a political wrangle over funding.

Although the immediate purpose of Edward's trip was therefore unrealized, his visit laid the basis for a long and continuing relationship with the scientific community and government of Israel. Ne'eman introduced him to the board of governors of the University of Tel Aviv, and Teller persuaded them to set up both an applied-science department and a school of engineering. Ne'eman said this suggestion, coming from an outstanding theoretical physicist, helped effect a change necessary to make the work at the institute more effective in meeting the needs of the young country. "He helped correct the bias, so that it made the university leadership feel they should be involved in basic science."

Within two years Teller was elected to the university's board of governors. "He became probably the most important scientific member of the board," said Ne'eman.

Teller also repeated in Israel the success he had enjoyed in the United

States for many years as a lecturer. In 1970, he delivered a series of ten lectures on elemental physics. The first lecture, scheduled for a hall seating five hundred, drew such a crush of people that it was moved to an auditorium with a capacity of one thousand. Even this was not big enough, so loudspeakers were set up on the lawn to accommodate the overflow crowd. Teller continued to draw full houses to the end.[8]

In 1973, Teller also began advising both the university and the government of Israel on the development of science-based firms with emphasis on an industrial-park setting under government sponsorship. The university could offer courses relevant to such industries, he suggested, and they in turn could provide a climate for graduates of these courses to strengthen the economy and develop as scientists.

In October of that year, when Egyptian and Syrian forces attacked by land and sea, Israel demonstrated the value of a balanced strategic defense blending conventional forces and modern technology. In the sea battle, Israeli naval units used newly developed electronic equipment capable of diverting enemy missiles from their targets.[9] Through a combination of this missile-diverting gear, extremely maneuverable missile boats, and highly effective Gabriel missiles, the Israelis avoided the loss of a single vessel while sinking at least nineteen of the enemy, including ten missile boats.[10] By October 19, less than two weeks after the opening round was fired, the tide was reversed, and the invaders were in flight.[11]

Teller, reviewing the battle with us a few months later over dinner in Washington, was alternately grim and upbeat. He sadly noted the loss of life on both sides. Then he blamed the Soviets for making the war possible by supplying weapons to the Syrians and Egyptians.

Finally, he spoke of the courage and resilience of the Israeli defenders.

"I seriously doubt," he said, "that the military forces of many other countries, if any, could have overcome such a major defeat in the early going and then regrouped so quickly to achieve victory."

Still later, in his hotel-room discussion with us, Yuval Ne'eman said Israel's interest in the possible use of specially designed electronic equipment as a means of countering missiles—in effect, an earlier version of SDI—dated back to the Yom Kippur War.

"The Arabs relied very much on antiaircraft missiles, which they used with devastating effect at the canal," he said. "They also used antitank missiles, so Israel was looking for ways to combat these dangers. Israel was always interested in building defensive weapons, and there was work going on in various establishments prior to America's announcement of its strategic defense initiative."

Teller helped stimulate this interest as early as 1975, when, as guest speaker at a Tel Aviv meeting of Israeli scientists engaged in defense research, he stressed the importance of developing pilotless aircraft. Equipped with television cameras, they could be flown behind enemy lines by remote control and transmit live scenes of value to military intelligence. Teller impressed his audience. Ne'eman, sitting in as a defense scientist, gave the project high priority.

The Israelis stepped up the development of these reconnaissance ships and used them to great advantage in the 1982 invasion of Lebanon. After the war, Jerusalem licensed an American firm, AAI Corporation of Cockeysville, Maryland, to build the airframes for additional pilotless aircraft, while the electronic components were being turned out in Israel.

The speed with which Israel developed this item impressed Teller and reinforced his belief that its scientists and engineers could someday contribute to the SDI program. In 1984 he expressed that conviction to Yuval Ne'eman in definite terms.

"Edward called me and said that the United States was going to invite Israel to participate in the SDI program," Ne'eman told us.

"He said there was going to be a formal invitation issued. He felt it was important both for the United States and Israel that the invitation be accepted. Both countries, Edward said, could contribute to each other's and their mutual defense.

"Edward stressed another point. The dedication of the Israeli scientists would be an important factor in contributing to the success of the project. For Israel it is considered an honor for any scientist to be able to contribute to the country's defense. In contrast, in the United States, there appears to be a division in the thinking of the scientific community on this issue.

"Also Teller felt that Israel, always living on the frontier of danger, must have developed techniques that might be important for U.S. application. In particular, Edward was referring to Israel's work in developing countermeasures to stop incoming short-range missiles."

"This Israeli problem," Edward later told us, "was similar to the American potential threat posed by submarine-launched Soviet nuclear missiles off our shores."

After Teller's call, Ne'eman telephoned the director general of the Ministry of Science in Israel to prepare him for the invitation and to urge him to begin lobbying within the Israeli cabinet for acceptance.

But selling the idea was not an automatic exercise. Even though there was general support, a vocal minority opposed the proposition. There were also more quietly expressed doubts in official quarters. For example, Defense Minister Yitzhak Rabin, a former general and chief of staff, shared the traditional military skepticism about new weapons systems, especially those involving untested advanced technologies. Ne'eman helped in the careful building of an Israeli consensus supporting a Washington-Jerusalem partnership in SDI. By the summer of 1985 the time seemed ripe for an open presentation, and Teller was invited to meet with Israeli cabinet officials and to address a seminar on the subject.

En route to the Middle East, he stopped off in West Germany to promote SDI there. In the course of many previous visits to Bonn as a science adviser at meetings of the North Atlantic Treaty Organization (NATO), he had developed extensive contacts in the West German defense establishment and scientific community. On this stop, his purpose was to learn more about possible West German contributions to SDI. He was especially impressed by the potential help of the nation's optical industry.

In Israel, Teller was led by Ne'eman to the office of Yitzhak Rabin in the vast, tightly guarded complex of the Ministry of Defense in north central Tel Aviv. Much of the meeting was consumed by Teller's explanation of how it would be possible for the Jewish state to protect itself from incoming missiles. Rabin was receptive.

"In spite of Rabin's former general opposition to R and D [research and development], this time the minister was positive," Ne'eman said.

Then came a similar meeting with Gideon Patt, the Israeli minister of science. Ne'eman now felt confident that the issue was ready for public airing.

"In Israel there were no serious restraints, with the exception of the extreme left," Ne'eman told us. "They put up a fight in the press, but they were in a small minority. Both Labor and Likud [the conservative party] were for it. This was not an uphill struggle."

Teller addressed the seminar August 15, 1985, in Tel Aviv. Entitled "Introducing the Strategic Defense Initiative in Israel," the program also included Ne'eman and three other Israeli leaders. These were Robert J. Lowenberg, director of the Israeli Institute for Advanced Strategic and Political Studies; Micha Sharir, chairman of the Department of Computer Sciences of Tel Aviv University; and Shaul Yatsiv, representing the Racah Institute of Physics at Hebrew University.

Teller, then seventy-seven, referred at the outset to the development of the atomic bomb. He noted that the bomb had seemed to be only a scientist's dream but in less than seven years had become a reality. The development of this nuclear weapon was "completely unavoidable," he said, and it was fortunate that it was developed first by those living under a democratic government instead of under a Nazi dictatorship.

Teller then acknowledged that in solving the problem of how to defeat the enemies of Western democracy in World War II the birth of atomic weapons had created the new problem of potentially greater devastation in a subsequent war. The West responded to this problem "by not developing a defense" and instead developing, under the policy of MAD, an arsenal that would be even more devastating.

For most of the next hour, Teller led the audience of science and government leaders through a two-level dissertation on SDI. One level dealt with the broad question of whether it would be undertaken. The other was a basic explanation of major SDI technologies and their status at that time.

Teller asked, "Is it better to deter aggression by the existence of defense than to deter aggression by the threat of retaliation?" If one answers this question positively, he said, the "real" question follows: "Is deterrence by defense practical enough?" Then the corollary: "To what extent can it actually be done? This is a technical question, and this is the technical question we want to discuss today."[12]

Teller stated his belief that such a defense is possible but conceded that the means of retaliation should not be abandoned "until there begins to be a real possibility of defense." He recommended a gradual approach, phasing in defense as offensive weapons are reduced.

What of the cost?

"If you produce defense and it costs so much that the aggressor, by increasing his offensive power, can wipe out the advantages of defense, there is no point in doing it. If you develop defense and the aggressor can destroy that defense for less than it has cost to build it, then again there is no point to do it."

But if each of the superpowers can develop an inexpensive, practical, effective defense, the result might be "two armed camps primarily armed with shields and not with swords."

"This obviously would be a more stable situation than the one we have today," Teller suggested.

In this presentation, as in many before and since, Teller gave a reverse spin to the argument of SDI opponents who express fear that SDI is either technologically unfeasible or, if feasible, might provoke the Soviets into a first strike before completion of more advanced SDI components. Repeating his standard theme, he said the Soviets themselves have provided the answer to this argument. He then cited Soviet Premier Aleksei Kosygin's 1967 London declaration that the erection of defenses against intercontinental ballistic missiles (ICBMs) should be regarded as a means of protecting human life, not as a threat. Therefore, Kosygin added, such activity should not be used as an excuse to accelerate the arms race.

Teller then noted with a hint of sarcasm the response of the Soviets to Reagan's SDI speech sixteen years later. "The remarkable thing is that as soon as Reagan said the same thing [as Kosygin], [Soviet General Secretary

Yuri] Andropov promptly . . . disagreed and . . . the Soviet Academy of Science unanimously . . . disagreed as well."

But eleven years earlier, in 1972, the Soviets had built a ring of missile defense units around Moscow, Teller told the seminar. Since then they had continued to upgrade and improve the Moscow strategic defense system while the United States was limiting its activities to research. "Reasonably effective research," he added, citing a demonstration of 1984. "We fired a missile against a missile and intercepted it, after a flight of almost ten thousand kilometers, with great precision."

By contrast with limited U.S. research, Teller added, the Soviets had done more extensive work on sophisticated technology.

Teller warned that the United States and its allies must guard against early overemphasis on experimental technology to the exclusion of defensive measures already at hand. "We already have demonstrated," he said, for example, "that we can shoot down a missile with a missile. A single missile may be fired by mistake. Today, without putting available technology in place, we could do nothing about it." (As might seem inevitable, such an incident was reported in 1985, when an unarmed SN-3 cruise missile was launched in error from a Soviet submarine. After flying over Norway, it landed in Finland. There were no reports of casualties or damage.)

Teller also suggested that such a missile defense might offer protection against the possibility that a lesser power, say a Qaddafi-led Libya, might unleash a missile in a fit of desperation.*

"But that a great attack by the Soviet Union could be so stopped," Teller declared, "—that is, of course, nonsense."

In explaining why he considered this to be "nonsense," Teller lapsed from the subjunctive. "There *will* be many missiles, there *will* be many decoys, things that look like missiles but aren't," he said. Teller said both the United States and the Soviets knew how to make missiles that could take evasive action and still hit the target.

Teller described potential components of SDI and his assessment of them. They included the kinetic energy weapon, which in its simplest form, of course, was known in the Stone Age. "It need not be anything more than a stone that is hurled against whatever target there may be," he said. "But a relatively recent advance in the field of kinetic energy is the rail gun, also more accurately described as the electromagnetic gun. The projectile fired from it achieves much greater velocity than the velocity

---

*In early 1988, the Brazilian government firm ORBITA signed an agreement with Libya to produce a ballistic missile with a range of 600 miles. If based in northwestern Libya, its range would include Algiers and Rome. From eastern Libya, it could reach Athens, Cyprus, western Turkey, the Suez Canal, and Cairo, the capital of Libya's archenemy, Egypt.

obtainable by use of gunpowder." Teller mentioned the velocity of 10 kilometers per second. That would be 32,800 feet per second, compared with the 2,700-foot-per-second muzzle velocity of a commonly used World War II rifle.

"They [kinetic-energy weapons] may turn out to be quite practical weapons in conventional warfare, particularly because these missiles can be emitted, many of them, in one second," Teller said. "It is really a super machine gun. And for conventional weapons, for short-range rockets that do not move too fast, they may be very effective."

Teller then described directed-energy weapons as possibly the best hope for countering weapons of mass destruction. In the directed-energy group are the laser, the X-ray laser, and the free-electron laser. He said lasers "can be made, are *being* made, to move with the velocity of light or nearly the velocity of light." But they also involve two questions: Can they carry enough energy? And can they get through the atmosphere without losing their energy and their strict directional properties? "The answer is yes, it can be done, but it cannot be done easily."

The laser (light amplification by stimulated emission of radiation) involves the concentration of light so that its spread will be less than one-millionth of the distance traveled. It can transmit energy but requires a heavy input of energy for effective use.

The tremendous amount of electricity needed by the basic laser can be suppled by a civilian electrical power grid.

While this might suffice for the common laser, it would not do for the X-ray laser. For this, a small nuclear or thermonuclear explosion would be required. Since the X-ray laser cannot penetrate the denser layers of the earth's atmosphere, it would be of limited use as a space-based weapon against ground targets or missiles in early ascendancy. But at greater altitudes it could penetrate the skin of a missile much more easily than the common laser, Teller said.

Teller said it is possible to distinguish between a missile in space and a decoy. This involves the use of a stream of neutral particles. The stream is aimed at the launched missile or decoy. "The interaction of such a beam with an object in space will give a reaction which will be different if it is a missile, different if it is a light decoy."

In his address to the Tel Aviv seminar, Teller also acknowledged the validity of the argument by SDI critics on a key question: How could a defense system track not one missile but 1,000 missiles and 50,000 decoys? "There is no human way in which it can be done," he admitted.

But in five to ten years, he said, "we can improve the capabilities of computers at least tenfold and introduce programs more complicated than any man can write and perhaps as complicated as only a machine can write." Even that might not work to perfection. "Nothing that we do will work perfectly." But a partial defense is better than no defense, he insisted, and to the degree it discourages aggression, it will be valuable.

After Teller spoke, Micha Sharir, the chairman of the Computer Sciences Department at Tel Aviv University, told the group that the computer problem might be addressed by work already under way. He said the Japanese and the United States even then were developing computers operating in parallel instead of sequentially. "They would rather be constructed by hundreds, thousands, or maybe more, of small, independent computers each doing its own thing. You can get the same results as a single computer, but a thousand times faster."

Before giving way to the other presentations, including Yuval Ne'eman's concluding address, Teller wound up with a story about his appearance before an American audience at Glacier National Park, Montana, in 1969. He said the chairman introduced him with these words:

"Good morning. Dr. Teller, who will address us, had gone for a walk. And maybe a hundred yards here from the hotel he picked up a big stick, a branch. I asked him what the stick was for, and Dr. Teller said, 'That's to use against the grizzly bears.' And I said to him, 'Don't you know that a stick is not good against the grizzly bears?' and Dr. Teller answered, 'I know that, but I hope the grizzly bears don't.' Dr. Teller will talk about the ballistic missile defense."

Six months after this seminar, the government of Israel announced its intention to accept the American invitation to participate in the SDI program. In April 1986 the first Israeli SDI-related contract was made public.

Chapter 25

"A Matter of Survival"

Teller's confidence in the ability of Israel to strengthen the U.S. SDI program was shared by Lt. Gen. James A. Abrahamson, the U.S. Air Force officer in charge of the program. Shortly after Teller's return from the Tel Aviv seminar in August 1985, Abrahamson flew to Israel for a fresh look at the country's defense production.

Before the fifty-year-old Abrahamson assumed the directorship of SDI, he had flown F-100s in Vietnam and more recently directed the space-shuttle program of NASA. He had never met Teller until 1982, when he invited the controversial physicist to Cape Canaveral, Florida, to witness Abrahamson's last involvement in a space shot as a NASA official. They developed a close relationship that continued into their mutual efforts on behalf of SDI in general and Israeli SDI participation in particular.

Abrahamson, a lanky six-footer with short-cropped hair and a boyish face, already had firsthand knowledge of Israeli defense production. He had spent some time in the Middle East earlier in his military career in connection with the F-16 fighter development program.

"Israel was one of our customers in that program," he told us during an interview in his Pentagon office. "They also wanted to be involved in the technology and production of the plane. So I had made, back in those days, a full survey of their industrial capability. This trip was to be an update of what they'd been doing recently and how it could apply to SDI."

Abrahamson's first visit was followed by several more. There were also exchange visits by technical experts from both countries and numerous conferences on both sides of the Atlantic. Then, with Abrahamson's evaluation matching Teller's high rating of this potential partner, came the signing of a memorandum of agreement on Israel's participation.

"Teller recognized, just as I do," said Abrahamson, "that one of the special talents that Israeli industry and Israeli military bring to a program like this is the ability to understand, to creatively put together things that appear impossible, and then to move very quickly on these things. That has been a matter of national survival."[1]

Although the first announcement of an Israeli SDI contract did not come until April 1986, Teller was intensively involved in laying the groundwork for this through much of the preceding year. Israel's SDI representative, Aron Moss, described that involvement when we met him in a conference room of his nation's Washington embassy on May 26, 1987.

Moss, a short and heavyset man of fifty, told of being taken by his parents from their home in Bucharest, Romania, to Palestine in 1944, when he was six. He now remembered their emigration as a dramatic escape by sea just before the Nazis came. They settled in Haifa. After graduating from the Technion in 1959, Moss pursued aeronautical engineering and received his master's degree from Polytechnic Institute of New York in 1963 and his doctorate from the University of Paris in 1972. While in Paris, he negotiated on behalf of Israel the purchase of plans used by that nation to build jet engines for French Mirage planes.

Moss first met Teller in Tel Aviv at a 1975 conference addressed by Teller. He recalled that the audience included about 450 government officials and scientists, the cream of the political-military power structure.[2]

Like Yuval Ne'eman, Moss said Teller had swayed his listeners with his "very convincing way of presenting ideas."

More than a year before the first Israeli SDI contract was signed, Moss had been assigned to survey potential areas in which his country might contribute to the program. He and his colleagues identified nine or ten technologies in which the United States and Israel could work together to mutual advantage.

In May 1985, Teller met in Washington with Moss, Ne'eman, and Ben-Zion Naveh, director of Israeli research and development. The session, lasting over three hours, covered SDI and "what the Israeli participation could be like," Moss said.

After his return to Israel, Moss and his colleagues tackled the subject again. "We identified over fifty proposals that we thought were of sufficient quality and interest to submit to the SDI organization."

A follow-up meeting was held in Teller's room at the Tel Aviv Hilton during his visit to Israel in August for his conference with cabinet members and his address to the SDI seminar. "I gave him an overview of the different proposals that we submitted . . . ," Moss said, "and I did receive some very interesting feedback which helped us later to better identify those fields and technology areas where we could really contribute to the program."

A prime topic at this session was the use of directed-energy beams.

"Teller was always interested mainly in directed energy," Moss said. "And this was a field, he believed, in which Israel could contribute."

Teller discussed such problems as atmospheric turbulence and methods of transmitting energy through space. He mentioned possible approaches to solutions. Moss expressed doubt that Israel could deal with this advanced technology.

"How can we, such a small country," he asked, "be able to contribute to such an advanced program that the United States is managing by using its huge resources?"

Moss recalled this as Teller's response:

"First of all, you probably know that there is a lot of opposition in the scientific community in the United States to the SDI program. . . . Many American scientists do not want to participate for moral or other reasons. You don't have these problems yet in Israel. Your scientists are much more committed to defense programs. . . . So you should have less of a problem organizing the Israeli scientists.

"Secondly, . . . in the past you have not been doing much research work in space-related technology, but I believe that some of your scientists have the potential of doing some retraining and refocusing of their activities and will be able to contribute to this new area of defense.

"Don't worry about the number of scientists, because as a ratio . . . of your own size and population, you can probably put into the program a larger number of scientists than we . . . can. So don't worry about it. You can contribute because you are more dedicated."

Moss said that the Israelis had a special regard for Teller. They respected him for "his scientific genius" and as "an experienced man, a man who had been in and out of all sorts of U.S. projects and activities, a man who has access to the president, a man who has a lot of influence in the United States."

Teller's successful trip to meet the Israeli cabinet members and to address the midsummer SDI seminar paved the way for a two-week familiarization visit to Livermore by a group of Israelis in December 1985. By now the international character of SDI was taking shape. British and German representatives had also visited Livermore.

The Israeli delegation, headed by Aron Moss, was one of two from that country. The other visited Los Alamos. They spent two weeks touring the laboratories and meeting with scientists there.

Moss said the delegation at Livermore was given a stiffly official reception and at first felt uneasy. "Then," he said, "there was a certain moment when Dr. Teller walked into the room and the whole atmosphere of the meeting changed. . . . He told his American coworkers something to the effect that 'these Israelis are our friends and we need to help them get into the program.'. . . The whole thing changed all of a sudden. The atmosphere became very positive, very friendly and informal. It was really his doing, just by his walking into the room and making some statements."

The Israelis met with Teller every three or four months thereafter, usually at the Cosmos Club in Washington or during one of Teller's regular trips to Israel. Moss said they frequently called on him to discuss specific problems.

"Always he would respond and advise how and what should be done," he said. "The man is full of ideas. He has this capability of looking far ahead. Some of his proposals at first seem to be far out, totally imaginary. But then when you think about it, it seems possible."

More recently, Teller had urged the Israelis to consider the development of a ground-based laser as one of the components of their defense system against weapons such as short-range or tactical missiles based in Syria or Iraq. These missiles spend most of their flight in the atmosphere and, compared with intercontinental ballistic missiles, travel relatively slowly.

By the spring of 1988 the Israelis had developed and successfully field-tested an antimissile missile originally designed to intercept sea skimmers. It was adapted to intercept and destroy an antitank missile traveling at a very low level.

"The technology capable of intercepting ballistic missiles is not yet mature," Moss said. "We are not sure, at this point, which of the different candidate technologies is best."

Commenting on this in one of our interviews, Teller noted that Israel's generally fair weather would be a big advantage in the installation of a laser defense system. Clouds resist penetration by laser beams. Teller urged the Israelis "not to be afraid of" laser development, which incidentally could contribute to the U.S. defense effort.

Moss said that one result of Teller's encouragement on this subject was the submission of an Israeli proposal to the United States to demonstrate the use of high-energy laser technology to intercept and destroy incoming missiles.

Asked about the feasibility of the proposal, the Israeli SDI representative again grew cautious.

"Let us say we are confident," he said. "Let us say we are proposing to experiment with this technology in order to be able to demonstrate to ourselves and to the United States whether this technology is feasible."

The Israelis apparently had already examined the possibility that the proposal might be questioned as a violation of the ABM Treaty of 1972 and concluded it was not. They noted that the treaty deals with ICBMs, strategic weapons with a range of 5,000 kilometers.

Such weapons do not constitute as serious a threat to Israel as short-range tactical missiles, which have a range of 500 kilometers and are based in nearby hostile countries. Israel could be expected to avoid any action that might be considered a violation of the ABM Treaty and might thereby jeopardize the U.S. support that accounts for a great portion of the Israeli defense budget.

The tactical-missile threat prompted Israel to enter into a research contract with the United States for "a concept study" dealing with defense against ballistic missiles.

From this and companion studies emerged a joint decision by Washington and Jerusalem to fund development of the Arrow, an antimissile missile designed by Israel Aircraft Industries and regarded as an effective counter to Soviet-built tactical missiles deployed in Syria and Europe. In the United States and abroad, some students of defense considered it of more immediate importance than the overall SDI program. One West German weapons contractor explained, "There's a realization that SDI is so complex that it'll take a long time to put the system in place, . . . and the tactical missile threat is more easily and more immediately solved."[3]

Eighteen months of discussion preceded the decision.[4]

One year later, the ATBM discussion had boiled down to the Arrow. "The Arrow," SDI Director James Abrahamson said in a letter to Rep. Jim Courter, a New Jersey Republican, "is in fact the missile that should be developed to meet the current and projected threat [to Israel]."[5]

The *Washington Times* reported, "[The Arrow is] believed to be a revolutionary system that proponents say could change the military balance in the Middle East and protect Western Europe against very short-range battlefield missiles."

After hard bargaining, an agreement was drawn up calling for the United States to absorb 80 percent of development costs and for Israel to fund the remaining 20 percent.

Asked about a report that he played an important role in the negotiations, Teller said that he was only involved in getting the Israelis and the Americans together in finalizing the agreement. The agreement was signed in Washington in December 1987 by Israeli Defense Minister Yitzhak Rabin and Defense Secretary Frank Carlucci.

The Arrow episode helped demonstrate the leapfrog nature of weapons development. Three months after the signing of the agreement, the United States confirmed in mid-March 1988 that Saudi Arabia was purchasing from China intermediate-range missiles capable of reaching any part of the Middle East. Charles E. Redmon, spokesman for the State Department, identified the weapon as the CSS-2 rocket, also known as the Eastwind.[6] He said it is also capable, from Saudi Arabia, of striking targets as far west as Greece and as far east as India.

The Israelis were fearful that the Eastwind could be used as part of a nuclear weapons system. They said it is capable of carrying a warhead with the explosive power of 2 to 3 million tons of TNT.[7]

Chinese and Saudi Arabian officials denied that the missile was fitted with a nuclear warhead, but the Saudis rejected Washington's request to make an on-site inspection.[8]

The guidance system of the Chinese missile, when fitted with conventional warheads, is not regarded by Western military experts as accurate enough for effective use against military targets. This intensified questions about its planned use, especially the question of whether the use of nuclear warheads might be considered as a means of offsetting its inaccuracy and thereby justifying the great expense.

A similar view was expressed by Yitzhak Modai, a member of the Israeli Knesset and cabinet. "You would easily understand that unless it carries with it an atomic head, it does not pay," he said. "You don't invest that much money in sending a conventional bomb."[9]

Unless, perhaps, the "conventional bomb" is a conventional poison-gas bomb.

It did not take long for the missionary efforts of Teller, Abrahamson, and others on behalf of SDI to produce results. Once the groundwork had been laid, six nations joined up within a one-year period beginning in late 1986.

Israel was the third country and the first outside Europe to become a U.S. partner in SDI. The relationship was formalized May 6, 1986, with the signing of a memorandum of agreement in Washington by Defense Secretary Caspar Weinberger and Israeli Defense Minister Yitzhak Rabin. The agreement covered rules for contract bidding, protection of sensitive data from leaks to unauthorized persons, and a guarantee of U.S. rights to license products resulting from SDI research.[10]

Exactly six months earlier, on December 6, 1985, a similar agreement had made the United Kingdom the first nation to come aboard.[11]

Then, on March 19, 1986, West German Chancellor Helmut Kohl announced that his country and the United States had reached a basic agreement on conditions for cooperation in the research program. It assigned no role to the West German government itself but provided for government backing of private German companies in the program.

In France, members of the Diplomatic Press Association were surprised on May 4 of that year when newly installed Prime Minister Jacques Chirac declared full support of the program as "inevitable, irreversible and justified." Chirac made the statement when asked at a press lunch about differences between his policies and those of French Socialist President François Mitterand. [12]

By the spring of 1988, Europe's own SDI had a name, Eureka, and France was among members negotiating abroad on cooperative arrangements. One of them involved Israel, for which France drew up a list of projects in which Israeli companies might participate as suppliers and subcontractors. The negotiations resulted from early April meetings in Paris between Danny Gillerman, president of the Israeli Federation of Chambers of Commerce, and Alain Madelain, the French minister of industry and trade. [13]

An agreement similar to West Germany's was signed by the U.S. Department of Defense and the Italian foreign and defense ministries on September 19, 1986.

The surge of interest in SDI abroad was attributable in great measure to Teller's efforts. But it also meant a surge of transoceanic activity on his part. In 1987, the first full year after the five nations mentioned above plus Japan had joined in agreements on SDI, the seventy-nine-year-old Teller—after decades of periodic suffering from colitis and less than a decade after a heart attack and coronary bypass surgery—made seven round trips across the Atlantic.

Spurring him on were two convictions: First, European scientists could contribute to the program; also, if Europe could build its own missile-defense system, it would help deter aggression, thereby increasing prospects for peace on the Continent and diminishing the danger of a thermonuclear war.

On these points, General Abrahamson agreed.

"Edward goes all around the world and talks to the political leaders and scientists and tries to show them the logic of what we are doing and to find out if they are interested and if they can contribute to the program," Abrahamson said.

"He addresses public audiences on television, in lecture halls, and interviews. Sometimes he travels at the request of the government. For example, if we need someone to attend a particular conference, we may tap him. At other times, he travels at his own initiative. In either case, we always encourage him." [14]

At bottom, proponents emphasized that SDI relied heavily on a global network of U.S. allies, decreasing the possibility that any first strike could incapacitate all. The greater the spread of the alliance, according to this theory, the more secure each of its members should be.

Or as Teller put it, "The more, the merrier."

Chapter 26

AT WORK ON THE HILL

When young Tom Schroeder arrived for work on July 16, 1986, he was handed a new assignment. Schroeder, the son of a fourth-generation dairy owner from St. Paul, Minnesota, had considered himself lucky. He had been selected as a summer intern in the Washington office of Sen. Rudy Boschwitz, a home-state Republican. Schroeder had spent much of his first few weeks in the capital puzzling over its strange pattern of traffic circles and diagonal arteries. Now that knowledge would come in handy.

Would he mind picking up Edward Teller at the Cosmos Club, over on Massachusetts Avenue, and serving as his aide for the next few days? The senator would lend him his own new Volvo for the assignment.

Schroeder, twenty-one, was awe-struck. He knew of Teller as the prime mover in U.S. development of the hydrogen bomb. He also knew that Teller, now seventy-eight, still cut a wide swath in Washington.

For Teller, this trip had the same general purpose as his many other visits to Washington. But this one was busier than any other. In less than three days he would take part in sixteen meetings on Capitol Hill and at the other end of Pennsylvania Avenue with White House and SDI officials.

Teller's mission this time was to promote SDI in the face of growing doubt and mounting opposition in Congress. Feeding the doubt and fueling the opposition was a spate of unfavorable reports over the preceding weeks.

On May 13, 1986, a physics professor at the University of Illinois-Urbana told a news conference that 6,500 scientists had declared their opposition to SDI and proclaimed their refusal to accept research funds from the program. The educator, John Kogut, said a pledge to this effect had been signed by most of the professors in the nation's top-twenty universities. Among the signers were fifteen Nobel laureates.

Two weeks later Sen. J. James Exon of Nebraska, the ranking Democrat on the Senate Armed Services Committee and a supporter of SDI, bristled over a statement by President Reagan that he would abandon the SALT II arms control agreement later in 1986. Even though it had never been ratified, Exon suggested that the treaty had served to slow the arms race. If the race took off "on a new fast track" as a result of the President's statement, Exon said, "I may have to waver in my general strong support of SDI."

Further problems for SDI developed on June 11 when NASA officials reported that three rockets at their Wallops, Virginia, installation were accidentally launched by lightning. The rockets, designed for weather research, mysteriously lurched off their pads in the middle of a storm and plunked harmlessly into the Atlantic. But their unscheduled flight did little to strengthen public faith in computerized rocketry as a basis for security.

On Capitol Hill the contest over SDI swung back and forth. Supporters scored one good round in early June when thirty defecting or emigrated Soviet scientists told Congress that the Soviet Union had been rapidly developing its own antimissile defense system and that the United States should fully fund the president's SDI proposal.

But prospects for congressional support grew dimmer in late June amid signs of confusion within the administration over the objectives of SDI. At a conference sponsored by *Time* magazine, Assistant Secretary of Defense Richard N. Perle said SDI was intended primarily to defend the nation's ability to retaliate if attacked. This was interpreted as a policy of defending missile silos instead of populated cities, as President Reagan had described the main objective of SDI. Asked about Perle's statement, Paul Nitze, the president's special adviser on arms control, said, "Maybe it's his view, but I can't see any rationale for it."

Clearly, as Edward Teller began his Capitol Hill rounds in search of support for the president's budget request of $4.8 billion for SDI in fiscal 1987, rough going lay ahead. Also ahead was that whirlwind schedule beginning with Tom Schroeder's arrival to pick him up at the Cosmos Club shortly after noon of July 16.

The first stop was a Wednesday lunch session at 1:30 P.M. with the Republican Steering Committee in the Senate dining room. Members of the committee included Senators James A. McClure of Idaho, Paul Laxalt of Nevada, Jesse Helms of North Carolina, Malcolm Wallop of Wyoming, and Robert W. Kasten, Jr., of Wisconsin.

Thirty minutes later Teller was due two blocks away, in the Hart Senate Office Building, for a meeting with New Hampshire's Warren B. Rudman. Then came a 3:00 P.M. conference with the minority staff members of the Senate Armed Services Committee and another at 4:00 P.M. with its majority staff.

Between stops, the elderly scientist chatted amiably with his escort about his mission, about Schroeder's hopes of becoming a historian, and about some of his own experiences.

"The man is a walking history book," the young Minnesotan later wrote in a memo to his colleagues. "His memory is a collage of significant figures—Albert Einstein, Robert Oppenheimer, Niels Bohr, Franklin Roosevelt—and significant events—the Manhattan Project, the development of the H-bomb, and every major defense debate since then."[1]

The next day began at 8:00 A.M with a lox-and-bagel breakfast meeting in Boschwitz's office with Senators Daniel J. Evans, a Washington State Republican; David H. Pryor, an Arkansas Democrat; Frank H. Murkowski, an Alaska Republican; and Chic Hecht, a Nevada Republican. From there, Teller made separate visits to the offices of Senators J. Bennett Johnston, a Louisiana Democrat; Dan Quayle, an Indiana Republican; and Lawton M. Chiles, Jr., a Florida Democrat. In Johnston's office, he also met with Democratic Senator Albert Gore, Jr., of Tennessee.

That afternoon, after a briefing in the offices of the Strategic Defense Organization at Seventeenth Street and Pennsylvania Avenue, he made three more stops. One was at the office of Sen. Sam Nunn, the Georgia Democrat heading the Armed Services Committee. Another was back in Senator Boschwitz's office, from which he telephoned Secretary of State George Shultz and Donald Regan, the White House chief of staff. The last was at the New Executive Office Building for a meeting with security officials. This session was resumed the next day and lasted until lunch, after which Tom Schroeder again picked up Teller and drove him to the office of Sen. John Warner, the Virginia Republican.

Frequently, on the way to the next stop, Teller would ask Schroeder what he knew about a senator's position on SDI. Schroeder was allowed to sit in on some of the meetings. He was sorry that the session in Nunn's office was not one of them.

"Dr. Teller was really disappointed with his meeting with Senator Nunn," Schroeder told us. "Even Rudy was upset."

Upsetting Rudolph E. Boschwitz was not easy. His was one of the Horatio Alger stories of Capitol Hill, and he was known as a can-do, upbeat performer. Born in Berlin in 1930, he was brought to the United States by his parents in 1935 when they fled Nazism. Boschwitz graduated from Johns Hopkins University at nineteen, received his law degree at twenty-two from New York University, and served in the U.S. Army Signal Corps. After practicing law briefly and working in his brother's plywood company in Oshkosh, Wisconsin, he moved to Minneapolis in 1963 and opened a store that grew into Plywood Minnesota, a company with sixty-eight warehouse stores in eight states.

"When they walked out of Nunn's office," Tom Schroeder said, "Rudy kept saying, 'That just isn't like Sam Nunn. I don't understand why he did that.' "

Teller, recalling the incident for us nearly two years later, said it was the most disappointing of all the meetings he had during his three-day campaign.

"I got a fifteen-minute blast, and I didn't know why," he said. "Before I could explain why I support SDI, Nunn said, 'It's complete nonsense to go on researching forever. Tell your friend President Reagan it's time to stop all that and do something real about defense.' "

The last stop on Teller's schedule that trip was a 3:30 P.M. meeting on Friday, July 18, at the White House, where Teller met with Adm. John Poindexter, the president's national security adviser who was soon to become one of the Reagan aides embroiled in the Iran-Contra scandal.

Not all these meetings were absorbing. After one of the longer sessions at the SDI downtown headquarters, Schroeder asked how it had gone. Teller shrugged and muttered, "All right." Then he admitted that at one point, when a dull speaker was raking over old coals, he became distracted and resorted to a little game for diversion.

In one corner of the meeting room a fan labored beneath a fluorescent lamp. Teller noticed that the lamp flickered regularly as the fan blades flashed. By correlating the flickers to the flashes, he tried to determine the number of blades on the fan.

At the end of Thursday, July 17, the longest day, in driving Teller back to the Cosmos Club, Schroeder had overshot the driveway and apologized. Besides being unfamiliar with Washington street patterns, he explained, he had never before driven a car with a stick shift and was momentarily disconcerted.

Teller nodded understandingly. "That," he said, "is a software problem."[2]

A few months later, Teller was recruited by a band of Capitol Hill Republicans to prod President Reagan into stepping up the pace of SDI. They were pressing for a start on the deployment of at least some parts of the system by the early 1990s. They invited Teller to lunch on the Hill. Those gathering for this strategy session with Teller on September 29, 1986, were Senators Wallop, Quayle, and Pete Wilson of California, and Representatives Jack Kemp of New York and Jim Courter of New Jersey.[3]

These five had met with Reagan in August on a similar mission but had succeeded only in drawing his anger by suggesting that he was not pushing hard enough for the program. Neither the Joint Chiefs of Staff nor Defense

Secretary Weinberger believed that a presidential declaration of intent to deploy that early was justified by technical progress. In the absence of their support, the president felt that such a declaration would be premature.

But after being briefed by Lieutenant General Abrahamson on the results of more recent research and testing, Weinberger came around. A key to this change was a September 2 test in which a kinetic-energy weapon hit a missile in flight off the coast of Florida.

The Republican group lunching with Teller on September 29 knew of the test. Teller had been banking on the laser as potentially the prime defensive weapon in the system, but he now recognized the more immediate value of kinetic-energy devices. These devices were already here; as a deployable alternative, strategic laser weaponry was still down the road.

Teller agreed at the Capitol Hill lunch to join the Republicans and other members of Congress and defense officials in sending a letter to the president. It was delivered within the next few days, and this is what it said:

> We are greatly heartened by the research progress being made in the Strategic Defense Initiative (SDI).
>
> At the same time, we are dismayed by indications of large strides being made in Soviet defenses which may soon render U.S. retaliatory capabilities obsolescent. Therefore, in addition to a vigorous continuation of the SDI research program, we urge timely application of SDI technologies to the threats to peace posed by rapidly advancing Soviet offensive and defensive capabilities.
>
> Specifically, employment in the very near term of the most modern defensive means can serve to deter use of Soviet tactical ballistic missiles. In this case, the early fruits of SDI work can be used in the next half-dozen years to deter war in the Middle East, and to defend our European and Asian Allies from attack with shorter-range Soviet ballistic missiles.

The letter added that defensive technology based on interceptor rockets, hypervelocity projectiles, and lasers could be used to defend the entire Western alliance against sea-launched Soviet ballistic missiles "even in the '80's."

"Indeed," the signers warned, "the Soviet Union may employ such defensive technology soon, whether we do or not."

They also urged that 100 defensive launchers be deployed at a single site within the United States, as allowed by the ABM Tready.

The letter also expressed the fear of Teller's hosts at the September 29 luncheon: "We are deeply concerned that an SDI research program which has no definite consequences for defense of America and its Allies within the next ten years will not be politically sustainable."[4]

*   *   *

Teller's base of operations in Washington was more like the noncommissioned officers' room in an army barracks than the accommodations expected for a man who was one of the world's foremost physicists and an influential figure in international politics. It was room 318, a single with shower, in the Cosmos Club, a gray hulk at 2121 Massachusetts Avenue, on Embassy Row.

Until 1988, women were barred from club membership. The front entrance of the club leads abruptly into a large sitting room reminiscent of dingy old-time hotel lobbies. A driveway leading to a side entrance skirts lush growth of dogwood, blue princess holly, and azalea whose petals drift onto a small patio and its white-painted wrought-iron furniture. The walls of an inner hallway in the club are lined with dozens of photographs, one wall with those of members who have been awarded Pulitzer Prizes and another with those of members, including several physicists, who have won the Nobel Prize. Teller passed the pictures every single night on his way to the rickety elevator for the trip upstairs. His room was small and sparsely furnished—a single bed, a shelf-desk with lamp along one wall, a telephone, and a contour swivel chair.

When in Washington, Teller ate most of his evening and weekend meals in the club dining room, which was brightly lit and pleasantly decorated in soft greens and yellows. His diet reflected little concession to age. Sweetening his coffee was a ritual beginning with his cup less than half full. Into this he poured four envelopes of sugar, carefully arranging the empty envelopes on the saucer like overlapping rose petals. By the end of one lunch of broiled flounder, the saucer was overlaid with twelve envelopes. Teller then ordered dessert of peach melba with whipped cream and strawberry syrup.

Teller's stay at the club often lasted a week or more. During one four-week absence from Livermore and his Hoover Institution office at Stanford, he spent several periods of three or four days at the Cosmos between trips to New York, Europe, and Israel. Many of our meetings with him came at the end of a long day in the midst of such a schedule, and he was obviously on the edge of exhaustion.

"You had better hurry with your work," he told us one evening. "I am not going to be functional much longer."

To combat his own weariness and occasional boredom at extended meetings, Teller would sometimes close his eyes and give the appearance of dozing. Richard C. (Mike) Lewin, who served with him on the board of Advance Technology Ventures Limited, told of a meeting at which Teller gave this impression in the Metropolitan Club in New York. But in the middle of the session, the chairman mentioned a particular firm and called on Teller for a report on the work it was doing.

"Teller came alive and started talking," Lewin recalled. "He went on for ten or fifteen minutes in great detail. He seemed to have been alert to what was going on and must have simply closed his eyes in some kind of concentration. Then, when he had finished his presentation, he sat down and closed his eyes again."[5]

Lewin said Teller's reputation as an unusual figure at such button-down-shirt, striped-tie meetings was magnified by his appearance. On this occasion, he wore a long-collared western shirt with metal ornaments. At our meetings he usually wore a pin-striped suit, gray or tan, with gray or maroon striped tie, and black boots. He also wore wash-and-wear white shirts, which he once described to us as "one of man's greatest inventions."

Despite this apparently casual attitude toward dress, he was not without vanity. He steadfastly refused his daughter Wendy's advice that he trim his heavy black eyebrows to soften his forbidding image. He also refused to accept standard makeup before television appearances.

Teller could also be contentious about media coverage. James Houtrides, senior producer for the CBS *Sunday Morning* television program, told us of an interview with Teller in the spring of 1982 for a report on the nuclear freeze movement. Before the cameras began to roll, Teller asked that the interview be shown in its entirety as a safeguard against slanted editing. Houtrides explained that time constraints prevented this. But he assured Teller that the edited version would include his main points.

Teller insisted on all or nothing. Houtrides shrugged and directed the program crew to gather up its gear. At this point Teller relented and reluctantly agreed to proceed. "Then," said Houtrides, "as an afterthought, he added a new condition: 'You will not call me the father of the H-bomb.' We had no intention of doing that, anyway, and I told him so. There was no problem after that."[6]

Within remarkably brief periods, Teller could demonstrate alternate flashes of brusqueness and patience. For one of our meetings, we agreed to pick him up at the old Executive Office Building next to the White House and to drive him to Dulles International Airport. As Teller emerged moments later, a man holding a camera greeted him warmly by name and asked him to pose for a picture. "I'm sorry, I can't, I'm late," he blurted out, then brushed past the man and entered the car.

We drove around the corner to the new Executive Office Building, where we picked up his lone travel bag and the little folding cart on which he wheeled it through airports. As we helped him stow these in the car trunk, we clumsily hooked his pant leg with a lever on the cart. "Wait,

wait," he calmly said. We even more clumsily persisted in trying to load the cart into the trunk, pulling his pant leg up to mid-calf and threatening to topple him. "Wait," he repeated just as calmly as at first. When we finally realized our mistake, lowered the cart to the ground again, and launched into profuse apology, he gently reassured us and patiently explained the physics involved in the force of our efforts to lift the cart and the resistance of the pants fabric to that force. In a time of discomfort, he slipped into his basic role as the consummate teacher.

Through the years, this role was also a source of great personal pleasure and of respect from fellow educators. Hans Froelicher, Jr., headmaster of St. Paul's School in Baltimore, was a prime example. In 1975, while vacationing in Key West, Florida, he learned by chance that Teller was lecturing at Rollins College and decided to drop by. He described the experience in a letter to Gwinn Owens, an author and friend of Teller's.

> What a man, I might say. Charging up and down the platform with no need for any mike or other booster. It had been a long time since we had met a mind that could put a library of a discipline into a paragraph or a formula or a word and still tell you what he means in terms which we could grasp. Of course, in the end he had us farming the oceans to feed the multiplying millions.
>
> It was a 35-minute, packed but slowly paced talk which my watch clocked at an actual 75-minute space of time and no one even squirmed. Questions, after (and some were good), took another 30 minutes. . . . I phrased my question (because he had had enough) as thanks for the best sermon I had ever heard on democracy and its *sine qua non* for compassing this awesome future, and to my surprise and his delight that thanks rang down the curtain.[7]

But as indicated by his rough meeting with Sen. Sam Nunn during that 1986 whirlwind campaign on congressional consideration of the SDI budget, Teller's efforts at teaching and persuasion were not always successful.

On another visit, in February 1988, he testified before the Senate Foreign Relations Committee on the Intermediate Nuclear Force (INF) treaty signed by President Reagan and Mikhail Gorbachev at their summit meeting in December 1987. A few months earlier *Time* magazine, describing Teller's continuing involvement in national affairs over half a century, declared, "The old lion still roars." But on his arrival for the hearing, Teller hardly resembled a lion.

A few days earlier he had suffered a shoulder injury in a swimming accident at his homeside pool. Wearing a cardigan sweater over his cast and with his recently ill wife beside him, he entered the cavernous hearing room almost unnoticed. Like a couple who might have strayed from a senior citizens tourist group, they slowly settled into seats in the rear of the spectators' section. Minutes after the hearing began, they were spotted by a committee aide, who rushed up and escorted them to reserved seats near the witness table.

Although Teller had privately expressed fear that the treaty might prove to be "another Munich," he was listed as a proponent of the INF agreement. For this, he had to swallow his doubts. He had never wavered from his outspoken mistrust of the Soviets, and his unpopularity among the Moscow leadership was just as well established.

A 1983 Tass news dispatch from Moscow had referred to Teller's opposition to a nuclear freeze. It called him "that paid solicitor for nuclear superweapons" and "the recognized 'hawk' of a scientist."[8]

As he prepared to testify on the INF Treaty, Teller might also have recalled a more recent, unpleasant brush with Gorbachev at a White House reception given by President Reagan for the Soviet leader during their summit meeting in December 1987. Teller told us that when he reached the head of the receiving line, the president smiled and said to Gorbachev, "And this is Dr. Teller." Gorbachev did not respond. "This," Reagan explained, "is the *famous* Edward Teller." Gorbachev's voice was cool. "There are many Tellers."

Teller nodded. "I agree," he said, and walked off. "That," he told us, "gave me an excuse not to shake his hand."

Teller was the third person to appear before the Foreign Relations Committee on February 22, 1988. Moving slowly to the witness chair and settling before the microphone, he seemed to undergo a strange transformation from tired old man to ring-wise veteran boxer instinctively responding to the bell.

"Let me start out with a simple unqualified statement," he said, projecting the familiar voice, deep and studded with the rolling "r" of his heavy European accent. "I hope that the INF Treaty will be ratified."

But any U.S. effort designed to prevent war, he emphasized, must be the result of a bipartisan policy. "To enter negotiations with a sophisticated opponent, an opponent who must not be underestimated, in any other way than with a mutual and strong agreement about our aims and about overall strategy, is apt to lead to difficulties in the future," Teller said.

" . . . I would like to see a bipartisan policy that involved agreements on arms control and arms reduction and at the same time included well-conceived, rational defense. To my mind and to the minds of a number of people who have worked on it diligently in the recent past, the strategic defense initiative provides that kind of defense.

"If there is arms reduction, that makes defense easier. If there is strategic defense, that makes circumvention of the treaties less meaningful. The one and the other can and should reinforce each other."[9]

The rest was filler. There were no questions. Having made his point, he thanked the committee and accepted the polite acknowledgments of its members. Then he turned away from the microphone and stiffly rose, once again a tired old man finishing another task.

Taking his wife by the arm, he led her slowly to the door. There was another meeting, and he was late.

Chapter 27

ONE ON ONE

Dear Edward,
    Thanks for your letter . . . I apologize for the remark I made on TV. I had prepared a much better one which was not insulting. But the interviewer would not take it, but provoked me into the one that came over the air. I should know better, but they still get the better of me . . .

So opens a handwritten letter from Hans Bethe to Edward Teller. It is dated January 24, 1987, and the script is jagged and laborious. In content and tone it is consistent with an exchange of revealing correspondence maintained over the years by these two surviving giants of the golden age of physics. Throughout the letters runs a cold public, warm private relationship threaded with harsh differences on policy, frequent reassurances of personal esteem and professional respect, and an occasional expression of hurtful surprise.

In this one, Bethe referred to an open letter published by Teller, one of many in which Teller recounted the history of nuclear weapons and gave his version of clashes with Bethe and Oppenheimer.

"Some of the history in the open letter I agree with," Bethe wrote, "but on much of it I disagree. And of course I don't agree at all on your assessment of SDI, technically as well as politically."

Bethe then noted that he was scheduled to visit the Livermore laboratory within three weeks, on February 11 and 12. Teller and his associates had complained that Bethe's visits to Livermore were too infrequent. They invited him to visit in the hope that bringing him abreast of scientific advances there might soften his public statements doubting the feasibility of some SDI elements.

On February 11, Bethe said, he would be accompanied by two colleagues.

"So," he added, "it would be better if you and I talked on the twelfth (I hope just in private)."

In a similar vein but with less success, Teller had invited his old friend to take a look around the laboratory nearly thirty years earlier, in 1958.

"As far as I remember," he wrote Bethe on June 4 that year, "you have visited Livermore only a single time, which was at the very beginning of our operation [six years earlier]." The place had undergone much change since, and Bethe should be informed about what was going on there, he added.

"We do not agree about a number of very important practical things," Teller said. "It is quite possible that a part of our disagreement is due to the fact that we have seen different parts of the situation. . . .

"Quite apart from that, it would be a real pleasure to see you."

Bethe sent regrets, saying he expected to be tied up much of the summer with other work, including service as a consultant in the U.S.-Soviet negotiations in Geneva on a nuclear test ban agreement. He might be free to visit Livermore sometime next winter, he said.

"I don't believe that a visit to Livermore will make us agree more on political matters," he warned. "I think the difference there is too fundamental to be influenced by technical information. However, as you know, I always like to discuss the work itself, and on this we have always found it easy to agree."

It was inevitable that much of their correspondence touched on the public reports about each other and their work. Just as inevitable was Teller's displeasure with much that was said and written about some of the controversial episodes dotting his career, from his refusal to do calculations assigned to him by Bethe on the atomic bomb to the controversy with Stanislaw Ulam on the idea for the H-bomb. One particularly painful example was the criticism Teller received from his peers after press accounts gave him and the Livermore laboratory virtually all the credit for the success of the 1952 Mike nuclear test explosion at Eniwetok atoll. Los Alamos, where the final preparations for the test were done after Teller left there to help establish Livermore, was shortchanged. The situation worsened with publication of *The Hydrogen Bomb*, a book in which James R. Shepley and Clay Blair, Jr., lauded Teller.

Scientists who had worked at Los Alamos, including Bethe and Teller himself, tried to set the record straight in interviews and in their own writings over the years. Bethe published such a straightforward account in the October 1982 issue of *Los Alamos Science*. Later news reports triggered by Bethe's account painted Teller in a harsh light, and Bethe was upset.

"I want to apologize for the article by Mr. [Philip] Boffey in the New York Times of Saturday, November 13," Bethe wrote two days later.

Teller responded in a chatty letter on November 23, 1982.

"The apology in your letter of November 15 is quite unnecessary," he wrote. "It never occurred to me that you had anything to do with the publicity and distortion of your article that appeared in the national press."

Teller said he "completely" agreed with a portion of Bethe's article criticizing the Shepley-Blair book.

"The following incident, which occurred in 1958, may amuse you," he added. Teller then described having lunch with Sen. Henry (Scoop) Jackson in the Senate Dining Room when Sen. John F. Kennedy approached.

"Scoop stood up and introduced us. Jack Kennedy said to me, 'I read so many wonderful things about you in the book by Shepley and Blair.'

"I became exceedingly angry. I don't quite know why. The main reason may have been that it was quite clear to me that Kennedy was very much less than candid. I think, however, that the real reason was his implicit opinion that I would have welcomed the statements in the book of Shepley and Blair. At any rate, I made a rather improper reply, which I remember exactly. It was a quote from Gilbert and Sullivan's *Yeoman of the Guard*, and my only defense is that I said it in recitativo and did not sing it. This is the precise quote:

> The tales that are narrated of my deeds of derring-do,
> Have been much exaggerated, very much exaggerated.
> Scarce a word of them is true!

"Senator Kennedy smiled a second time, now a little less sweetly, and said, 'Happy to have met you,' turned around, and left. We sat down, and Scoop said to me, 'He may be your next president.' I replied to Scoop, 'I wish you were.' Scoop's index finger came up to his lips, and he made the sound of an emphatic shh."

Later exchanges point to a freeze-thaw cycle in the Teller-Bethe relationship. After they had traded arguments in *Science* magazine over nuclear weapons issues and SDI, Bethe concluded a 750-word letter with this paragraph:

> I am sorry you enlarged the subject of discussion in your letter to *Science*; I am afraid I had to respond to one of the new topics in my comment. I very sincerely believe that the development of defensive weapons to destroy incoming nuclear weapons is doomed to failure. Even if your X-ray laser (which you explained to me) is successful, and I have strong doubts about its feasibility, the real problems will come only afterwards. How will you find the target? This is an extremely difficult task and costs far more than the

weapon actually used to destroy the target. Most important, since the intercept is to be done in space, the offense can put up enormous numbers of light decoys which cannot be distinguished from the actual target because the discrimination by the atmosphere is not available to you. The traffic handling problem would be simply immense.

Teller and Bethe apparently did not speak to each other when they were President Reagan's dinner guests at the White House on the night of the SDI speech, March 23. Teller flatly told us two years later that Bethe did not attend, but he was in error. Bethe's name was on the guest list, and several others who attended told us of conversations they had with him there.

But a chill fell between the two old friends after the president's announcement, and their correspondence tailed off in 1983. Nearly a year after the SDI speech, Bethe wrote Teller to outline his objections to the program.

Teller replied on February 28, 1984:

> It is good to have your objections in writing.
>
> I would have liked to respond in a prompt manner, but this was impossible for three reasons. The first is that your objections deserve a thorough answer.
>
> The second is that my schedule has been even more crowded than usual, and I could not acquire the necessary time. I confess that one unavoidable commitment was to celebrate my fiftieth wedding anniversary with Mici and all our children and grandchildren in Hawaii.
>
> The third and most important reason is that I have gotten into really serious trouble with my heart.
>
> Yesterday I had an exhaustive and exhausting catheterization of my heart. Tomorrow or Thursday, when I have recovered enough from that procedure, I will have a four or five bypass heart surgery . . . If and when I recover I will write to you independently.

By the end of the year, Teller had recovered enough to invite Bethe again to visit Livermore. Bethe accepted on October 3, 1984, writing that he would probably make it sometime in February 1985.

Bethe actually made the visit March 21 and 22, one month later than originally planned. Teller and Lowell Wood later told us in separate interviews that Bethe lavished compliments on the Livermore SDI group and indicated that much of his doubt had been eased. He was quoted by Teller as saying, "You have something splendid here."

But in articles and interviews thereafter Bethe repeated his doubts about the feasibility of SDI. His criticism also extended to Teller himself, prompting a long and painful response dated May 23, 1985.

"This letter is not easily written and not easily read," Teller said, "but I feel that it is better written and better read." He implied a hope that what was to follow would not nullify a recent agreement they had made to collaborate on research on nuclear reactors.

Teller then seized on a recent Bethe reference to the Los Alamos incident forty years earlier in which he had balked at doing calculations assigned to him by Bethe on the atomic bomb project:

> I must tell you I was quite hurt by your article in *Los Alamos Science*, especially your contention that I made no contributions to the war effort. I was reluctant to do calculations which I felt others could do better than I. But I hope you remember that together with Johnny von Neumann (to mention one exa¬nple) I did help move things forward in the implosion problem.

Teller then referred to the article Bethe had recently published with other leaders of the Union of Concerned Scientists in opposition to the SDI.

"That you signed your name to an article by [Richard] Garwin and the Union of Concerned Scientists I find particularly hard to understand," he said. "As you know, this article distorts the situation due to unjustified assumptions." He said Garwin had acknowledged that the article incorrectly represented by a factor of thirty the number of "predeployed objects" needed in the SDI system.

> Whether and in what case predeployment is a reasonable procedure, errors of this kind should not be made credible by your signature. I have stated in our last meeting, and this statement I unfortunately cannot change, that your published stance has made our national effort in a vital field much more difficult. This single fact has a greater influence on me than everything else put together.

Teller then referred to the laudatory comments Bethe had made to the Livermore officials at the end of his March visit:

> I have to assume that at the end of our last meeting your favorable statements were colored by your desire to be kind and pleasant. If this is indeed so, you cannot blame anyone else in case you have been misunderstood.
>
> All of this is most unfortunate and the worst part of it remains that our national effort, which could do a lot towards stability and continued peace, is being impaired. You have looked in detail only into the X-ray laser as far as SDI is concerned, or so it seems to me. It also seems to me that in this one field where you spent at least some time our differences have dimin-

ished. You continue to condemn the many parts of SDI to which, as far as I know, you have paid less attention.

From a personal point of view, all this is very sad and I suspect that our feelings may be similar. At the same time, I must pay more attention to my responsibilities as I see them rather than to my feelings. Indeed, the hope and effort for a useful defense in the strict and narrow sense of the word is the one remaining motivation for which I continue to work.

Bethe's reply was one of the most poignant in the entire record of their correspondence.

"I am happy that you wrote," he wrote Teller on June 20, 1985.

Let me go right to fundamentals. We both want security for the United States and for the world, we both want to prevent a nuclear war. But we differ fundamentally on how to achieve this goal. You think peace will be preserved by inventing ever new weapons and by having a technology race. In my opinion, the arms race has made us less and less secure, especially the big steps of the H-bomb and MIRV.

Bethe said negotiations, however difficult, might at least offer a chance for deep cuts in offensive weapons. He wrote:

President Reagan, in his speech justifying continued adherence to SALT II, mentioned as a major goal predictability. I very much agree with that. It seems to me that a partially effective SDI will destroy predictability.

We are not going to convince each other. . . . You spend full-time on persuading other people, in the United States and abroad. You have the complete support of the present national government. I spend perhaps one-third of my time on SDI, and still try to do physics.

Bethe said he was impressed by the briefing given him on his last Livermore visit. But he said one who is exposed to "so many new and difficult points . . . cannot possibly on the spot form a valid judgment." So he went home, thought it over, and "perceived problems with some fundamental points."

"Certainly, if I was favorably impressed at the meeting, this did not mean a change in my general attitude," he insisted. He added that Teller was right in assuming some of his comments before his departure were colored by his desire to be kind and pleasant. "Do I have to be nasty?"

But what of the short shrift Teller felt he had personally received in Bethe's article? Bethe responded:

I had not come to Livermore to listen to your grievances. As to the past, I recognize that you were a prime mover in getting Los Alamos started and that you made important contributions to the implosion project together with John von Neumann, as well as to the equation of state of compressed solids. I should be glad to make amends to my article in *Los Alamos Science* in this respect.

He had some grievances, too, Bethe said. But he did not think that the middle of a crowd at Livermore was the place to discuss them. As for the publication by the Union of Concerned Scientists and the figure on the number of predeployed objects, Bethe said he and another author, not Garwin, were responsible for the original error, which was corrected to 300 in the final edition of the report. But the figure used by SDI supporters— 100—was also "based on unjustified assumptions," he said.

Bethe said this lower figure assumed that a laser, after destroying one booster, could be retargeted on another booster within one-tenth of a second.

"This is the goal of SDI, but to believe it one has to be the Red Queen," he quipped. He said Garwin estimated three seconds would be more accurate and Edward M. Purcell, "a great designer of apparatus," thought thirty seconds would be closer. Even under Garwin's estimate, Bethe added, more than 1,000 predeployed objects would be required if the Soviets used very rapidly accelerating boosters for their missiles.

"I remember very fondly the years of our friendship, back in the 1930's and 1940's," Bethe said in closing. "I am very sad indeed that politics has separated us so far. But can't we be personally friendly?"

On July 8, Teller replied, "Thank you for your kind letter of June 20." He said that the many points made by Bethe all deserved answers, which he believed would be forthcoming, but that he wanted to discuss immediately the first and most important: "Is peace better assured by negotiation with the Soviets or by working on defense?"

Teller recalled that he had agreed with the Baruch Plan for internal control of atomic resources but that the Soviets had rejected it. Since then, negotiations had repeatedly failed. Whereas Bethe attributed this failure to the arms race, Teller cited the writings of Andrei Sakharov, the architect of the Soviet nuclear program, in rebuttal.

He noted Sakharov's story about being coarsely rebuffed by Khrushchev in 1961 when Sakharov warned that disarmament and test-ban talks would be undermined if the Soviet leader proceeded with plans to resume testing after a three-year moratorium. Teller said this was apparently the turning point for Sakharov, who later emerged as a champion of peace and human rights in the Soviet Union. "I do not hope for a more honest and straightforward approach to arms negotiations from Gorbachev than Sakharov observed in Khrushchev," Teller said in the letter to Bethe.

He then repeated Kosygin's 1967 statement that a defensive system should not be considered cause for an arms race and observed that Reagan's 1983 SDI speech had produced "a sharp change in the Soviet attitude" on this issue.

"Do you think that they protest as they do because they believe that defense is impractical?" he asked. "It seems to me from long experience . . . that the Russians have pursued defense with considerable intensity and for a long time." He cited preparations for defense of Moscow, the deployment of a high-intensity laser at Sary Shagan, and "relevant indications in their open literature prior to 1977 on X-ray lasers."

"I am afraid that right now the Soviets may be far ahead of us in strategic defense and this may lead to a dangerous lack of equilibrium," he wrote. Teller added that the current situation reminded him of the pre–hydrogen-bomb argument that U.S. work to produce the bomb would provoke the Soviets into plunging ahead with their own H-bomb program. But Sakharov himself had written in his book *Sakharov Speaks* that he had been drafted to work on the Soviet H-bomb more than one year before this argument was being voiced by the General Advisory Committee of the U.S. Atomic Energy Commission.

"At this time, I do not urge work on weapons of mass destruction, but rather an effective defense against these weapons," Teller summed up. "That such active defense is technically possible is made much more likely by the loud Soviet protests against our effort. These protests come from people who have substantial experience with these defensive weapons technologies."

Not until his concluding passage did Teller get personal.

"Of all the people who disagree with SDI, you are by far the most effective," he told Bethe. "You are the only one of great scientific accomplishments who has access to classified information, and who has actually made use to some extent of this access."

Teller said he had asked Lowell Wood and others to visit Bethe at Los Alamos before the end of that summer for further discussions of the X-ray lasers with him. "I have likewise asked Greg Canavan [another Livermore expert] to discuss space-based laser technology with you this summer," he said, "so as to correct your misconceptions in this area."

He closed on a somber note:

"Your advocacy with respect to strategic defense may have consequences in world history. Whether you are for or against SDI, there is no question that you carry a great deal of responsibility, perhaps more than any other single individual."

Regardless of whatever additional information Bethe received as a result of this and later efforts by Teller, he was not converted and remained the foremost domestic opponent of SDI.

Bethe made this clear in an August 5, 1985, letter marking the apparent end of this phase in their notable one-on-one private debate.

"Thank you for your good letter of July 8," he wrote. "I am especially glad that you propose to discuss different subjects separately." He then established his own credentials as an opponent of Russian communism, criticizing Soviet treatment of dissidents like Sakharov, their labor camps, their prisons and psychiatric wards, and their coercion of satellite states.

"Your letter gives a logical argument for your hard-line policy. However, the arguments do not convince me."

Bethe then drew a parallel between Khrushchev's rejection of Sakharov's advice and a public statement by U.S. Secretary of State George Shultz "that scientists should not give political advice, including presumably projections of the consequences of certain technical actions." He also suggested that both the United States and the Soviet Union had followed policies of leading from strength.

"The conflict between the Soviets and us strikes me like the religious conflicts and wars lasting from 1517 to at least 1648," Bethe wrote, referring to the start of the Protestant Reformation and the ensuing power struggles throughout Western Europe. ". . . But must we have the analogy of the 30-year war? With nuclear weapons, this would mean the end of civilization in the countries involved, and the ideological differences would become irrelevant."

Acknowledging that the Russians "always wanted to expand," dating back even to the czars preceding communism, he said "they want to do it slowly, continuously, finding opportunities, like Lithuania, etc., and the Eastern European countries. They do not want a cataclysmic war like Hitler, and this is a fundamental difference."

Bethe said that while Soviet expansion should be resisted, especially in Europe and the Middle East, "we should be prepared to resist a potential Russian aggression in Europe with non-nuclear weapons."

Bethe said many Europeans consider the United States "as equally dangerous for starting a war—a nuclear war—as the Soviets." Such thinking leads to neutralism among potential European allies, he suggested. "The best remedy is to change our policy toward 'No First Use' and to change our rhetoric."

Switching to technology, Bethe said the Sary Shagan lasers mentioned by Teller were "much more likely for the purpose of air defense than for SDI."

While estimating that there was a "very slight" chance that the United States could make SDI work, Bethe said Soviet chances in the same field were "enormously smaller still."

"No SDI can work without a super-super-computer for battle management," he said. "Laser weapons cannot be aimed accurately without excellent electron-optical techniques. In both areas, the Soviets are many years behind us. . . . I think we need to have no fear of a Soviet SDI."

In this conclusion, Bethe was obviously excluding such nonweapon components of a strategic defense as the deeply dug shelters.

Bethe's unyielding stance came up during a conversation we had with Teller in his favorite dining room at the Cosmos in May 1988. He shook his head and heaved a sigh. Then he said he hoped to get Bethe out to Livermore for another visit.

Bethe later told us that he did return to Livermore at least once more, in early February 1989, for what he described as "a big [science] meeting" that produced no opportunity for "any personal discussion" with Teller. But he said that his view on SDI had not changed notably and he hoped that an apparent trend toward a reduced emphasis on the program would continue.

One of his last contacts with Teller, said Bethe, came after he and his wife spent part of their 1988 summer vacation at Estes Park in Colorado. He recalled that they and the Tellers had stopped there fifty-one years earlier.

"We sent him a postcard," Bethe said, "and reminisced about our visit there together."

Chapter 28

OUTLOOK

A ridiculously short period may telescope a lifetime. For Edward Teller, that telescopic period could well have been the week of May 1, 1988. It began with his visit to Chicago that Sunday as a father and grandfather. It ended in the nation's capital with his address as an educator to a commencement audience at George Washington University. Sandwiched in between were meetings in Detroit as a scientist consulting for a private company and then a round of Washington meetings as an advocate of SDI. Throughout much of this, Teller's wife of fifty-four years, Mici, now ailing, was at his side. Encompassed within those seven days were fragments from the major chapters of his professional, political, and personal life.

Teller rummaged among these fragments on the evening of Wednesday, May 4. Again, we were at dinner in the Cosmos Club. Again, he looked tired and worn in his rumpled gray suit, white wash-and-wear shirt, and gray striped tie. Again, the volume and projection of his words belied his weariness. The deep, rich tones carried beyond our table. It was as if the voice of a young operatic basso had been planted in an old man's body, and it drew the attention of neighboring diners until Mici urged him to drop down a few decibels.

"These," he was saying, "are questions that are not addressed." His target of the moment was an April 24, 1988, *Washington Post* account of a report recently drafted by the Office of Technology Assessment (OTA). The *Post* story said the report, not yet publicly issued or delivered to Congress, carried the following dark appraisal of SDI:

"In OTA's judgment, there would be a significant probability that the first (and presumably only) time the ballistic missile defense system were used in a real war, it would suffer a catastrophic failure."[1]

Among the questions unaddressed by the report, Teller said, were the usual: How can a program be judged while it is still in the early stages of technical development and largely untested? If it is so impractical, why are the Soviets opposing it while forging ahead with a similar, more comprehensive program of their own? Brushing aside its potential value as a catalyst in disarmament talks, how could one discount its value as insurance against an accidental firing of a Soviet missile or a deliberate firing by some small nation under terrorist control?

Teller had ordered the stuffed rainbow trout. Leaning toward him, Mici softly said, "Be careful of the bones." When we had seen her in their California home two years earlier, she had seemed pale and drawn. Now she alertly joined in the conversation and looked fresh in green cord jacket and slacks topped by a white blouse with lime and blue polka dots.

The year had brought a seesaw of advances and retreats in the fortunes of SDI. Even before the OTA report was leaked and described in the *Post*, the program had been thrown behind schedule by hefty budget cuts. Compared with the five-year $26 billion budget recommended by designers of the program, the amounts actually requested by the Defense and Energy departments totaled only $22.2 billion, with Defense accounting for 90 percent of this. Including an expected allowance of roughly $4 billion for fiscal 1989, actual appropriations totaled only about $16.5 billion. Proponents had hoped that antimissile weapons would be tested in space before Reagan left office in January 1989 and that a decision to begin deploying missile-defense weapons would be made by the end of the next presidential term. Those hopes had faded.

Jack Kemp, the New York congressman who was a strong supporter of SDI and also Teller's personal favorite in the race for the Republican presidential nomination, had been eliminated early in the primary season.

Prospects for help from the White House had shrunk with the president's own dwindling popularity. A *New York Times*/CBS poll showed his approval rating in January 1988 at barely 50 percent, down from 68 percent in May 1986. His administration was reeling from the Iran-Contra scandals, which had led to the prosecution of former national security aides Robert McFarlane, John Poindexter, and Oliver North. They were accused of misleading Congress in its investigation of a hostages-for-weapons exchange. In addition, the president was besieged by calls from within his own party to cut loose Atty. Gen. Edwin Meese, whose personal financial dealings triggered a conflict-of-interest investigation by a special counsel.

The damaging effects of such problems on efforts to muster support for SDI were acknowledged by Lt. Gen. James Abrahamson, the Pentagon director of the program. "At least indirectly, they would have to hurt almost any administration program, especially one based on a defense policy as dramatically different as ours," he told us in an interview at the height of the Iran-Contra investigation.[2]

At a ceremony in March marking the fifth anniversary of SDI, the president had called the congressional budget cuts "irresponsible." With Teller sharing the platform, Reagan told the Institute for Foreign Policy Analysis that Congress had created a self-fulfilling prophecy by reducing funds for SDI on the premise that it would not work. "It won't if we don't develop and test it," Reagan declared.

Reagan then repeated that SDI would not be used merely as a bargaining chip in disarmament negotiations with the Soviets. But he also acknowledged that it was "one of the major factors" in moving the superpowers toward agreement on nuclear arms reduction. He suggested that it could also be a factor in assuring observance of such agreements.

"SDI is . . . a vital insurance against Soviet cheating," he said.

For this reason, among others, he added, "We will continue to research SDI, to develop and test it, and as it becomes ready, we will deploy it." He did not mention the Pentagon's admission that there was little likelihood of deployment during the little time left in his administration.

When Reagan finished, Teller, wearing one of his now familiar cardigan sweaters—this time a vanilla cable-stitch model—stood and applauded awkwardly. Because of the shoulder injury from his swimming accident, he was still unable to wear a suit jacket.

Moments earlier, Teller had given the audience his own appraisal as a theoretical physicist and as an old Washington infighter.[3]

"Let me assure you that I believe that we are going to have a real influence on the future, on stability, and on peace," he told the sympathetic audience. "Through the decades, by now five decades, I have worked for one simple, straightforward purpose, with one simple conviction. This conviction is that in a difficult situation, ignorance will not help. What we need is knowledge—knowledge that atomic explosives could be built (they can), that hydrogen bombs could be built (they can), that defense will now become important (it will)."

On the last point Teller said that times seemed to have changed from the days when attack "was the one reliable winning move." He cited several examples in which defense proved to be the exception to this old rule. He mentioned Vietnam, the grounding of Israeli planes by Soviet-supplied SAMs (surface-to-air missiles) in the early days of the Yom Kippur War of 1973, and the use of the American-made Stinger, a shoulder-fired rocket, to nullify Soviet air superiority in Afghanistan.

True, said Teller, these examples involved defenses against airplanes and helicopters, not missiles. "But SDI . . . in its first five years has embarked on an attempt to prove a point which today is close to being complete: Accuracy, miniaturization, and cost reduction can make defense effective against rockets. . . . And SDI is also effective in bringing the Soviets to the conference table."

Teller then referred to his fiery meeting two years earlier with Sen. Sam Nunn during his whirlwind campaign for support of SDI on Capitol Hill.

"In July 1986, I had the privilege to talk to a famous senator, Sam Nunn," Teller told the institute's audience. "He told me in unmistakable terms that we must do what can be done in a short time. We must do what is militarily effective. And he is right."

Teller recalled his joining Rep. James Courter, the New Jersey Republican, and others in signing the October 1986 letter urging the president to order early deployment of SDI components as a defense against possible Soviet ballistic-missile attack.

"A great number of important people subscribed to [the proposal]," Teller said. "At that time Sam Nunn did not. Today Sam Nunn himself is openly suggesting deployment." He referred to reports that Nunn had modified his outright opposition to SDI by suggesting some deployment as a safeguard against an accidental Soviet missile firing or a terrorist rocket attack.

In this address, Teller admitted that he also had modified his own views, too. Instead of prime emphasis on the X-ray laser, he now agreed that kinetic-energy weapons, "the meeting of the . . . rockets with a defensive object," or "smart rock," could be tactically effective. He still believed that directed-energy weapons, such as the X-ray laser, would work best and that by the year 2000 would provide "really strong and final proof of SDI."

But he said that in the meantime the Israelis would be demonstrating effective deployment of defensive weapons, presumably kinetic-energy types, against Soviet-supplied SS-21 rockets "in the next couple of years."

The key to it all, Teller summed up, was a bipartisan policy supporting the INF Treaty and SDI. "We must develop a bipartisan policy on how to make the world stable. . . ."[4]

Before arriving in Washington on that Wednesday in May 1988, Teller and his wife had spent Sunday in the Chicago area visiting their children, Paul and Wendy, and their families. Paul, a professor at the University of Illinois in Chicago, taught the philosophy of science, specifically quantum mechanics. He had two teenaged sons. Wendy, a Radcliffe graduate in mathematics, worked for Tellabs, Inc., a manufacturer of electronic equipment. She had a daughter by her first marriage, which ended in divorce, and a son by her second.

From Chicago, the Tellers went on to a two-day stay in Detroit, where

Teller met with officials of Energy Conservation Devices, Inc., one of the dozen or so firms for which he worked as consultant. He received expenses but no salary from his government positions. Between his midmorning arrival in Washington and dinner, he had three appointments. One was a meeting of the American Institute of Aviation and Aeronautics. Another was an interview for WNET public television. The third was a meeting in the Old Executive Office Building, where General Abrahamson conducted a status report on SDI before about four hundred Republicans.

At one point in the meeting, Teller was called on by Abrahamson to help answer a pointed question from Daniel O. Graham, the former U.S. Air Force general who had served as Reagan's military adviser in both his presidential campaigns and who later helped found High Frontier, one of the active civilian groups in the promotion of SDI. High Frontier had advocated immediate deployment of available components or use of orbiting space stations armed with kinetic-energy weapons already developed—"off the shelf hardware," Graham called it.

Now Graham noted that President Reagan had told the Institute for Foreign Policy Analysis that SDI would be researched, tested, and deployed "as it becomes ready." But there was talk of deployment in seven to ten years. So, Graham asked, "What do you think the chances are that you will not be ready to deploy within seven years?"

Teller replied that it was more important to continue working toward solutions of technical problems as quickly as possible than to set artificial deadlines as arbitrary evidence of success or failure. "The question should not only be whether you can say you will be ready in seven years," he said. "It should also be, can you say that you will *not* be ready in seven years, or even two years, or one year?"

Relating the incident to us at dinner that evening, Teller said his response was applauded. He could not disguise his pleasure in the telling. Now he returned to the theme of his address the following Sunday, May 8, to the engineering and applied-science graduates of George Washington University. He tried out the general subject on Mici and us. It was to deal with the need for knowledge and the price of ignorance in a dangerous world.

With talk of returning to George Washington University, he brightened again. This was the place where, fifty-three years earlier, he had begun a new life in the United States as a physics professor under the gregarious, unpredictable George Gamow. Before being whisked into the Manhattan Project, he had spent six happy years there, teaching and hosting many gatherings of fellow physicists and students. Through the years he had tried to maintain some ties with the university, but time was always a problem.

In 1987, he cofounded the university's Institute for Technology and Strategic Research. Its mission was to identify potential scientific and technological solutions to national security problems.

Teller had been named an honorary director of the institute. It was the latest in a string of honors that had come his way over a long and busy life. He was especially proud of the 1962 Fermi Award for outstanding contributions to nuclear physics and the 1983 National Medal of Science for his work on molecular physics, stellar energy, fusion reaction, and nuclear safety. Both awards were presented at the White House. In 1986 he also became a unique recipient of the Sylvanus Thayer Award presented by the Association of Graduates from the U.S. Military Academy at West Point. In his acceptance speech, characteristically mixing deeply felt emotion with self-effacing banter, he told why.

"I am conscious of the fact that for the first time the Thayer Award is being given to one whose native tongue is not English," he said. "I have lived in many countries. In only one have I been praised for my beautiful accent. Americans respond in a positive way if somebody mispronounces their language. This is why a refugee can feel completely at home in America. For one who has lost his country, a home is something extremely and acutely valuable. That is why I thank you today with all my heart."

Now the refugee scientist of 1935 sat in an exclusive Washington club more than half a century later as an influential, controversial world leader. Few inhabitants of earth significantly influence the course of history even once. Edward Teller had done this three times, first through his participation in the atomic bomb project, then through his work on the hydrogen bomb, and now through his leadership on behalf of SDI.

In every instance he had been a major figure. He had helped Leo Szilard get Albert Einstein to send the letter persuading Franklin Roosevelt to launch the Manhattan Project, then had worked on that project until it produced the fission bomb. Later, against fierce opposition, he was the prime mover in the development of the hydrogen bomb. Finally, he had helped shape Ronald Reagan's education in the concept of third-generation weapons and had helped persuade him that SDI was a feasible alternative to MAD.

Sitting in the Cosmos Club with his wife and two reporters, Teller had no inkling of how history would judge his efforts. Would he go down as an eccentric genius whose obsession with explosive energy had carried humankind to the brink of extinction? Or as a lonely iconoclast who abhorred war and accurately perceived that the futuristic technology of SDI could be a catalyst to disarmament and a more durable peace?

Whatever the judgment, he had paid a heavy price. His straying from the pack at Los Alamos had stigmatized him as a maverick who could not or would not subordinate his preferences to the common goal, a self-appointed star who rejected the role of supporting player willing to undertake the drudgery of detailed calculations necessary to the success of a project. He had been replaced. In the Oppenheimer affair, his intention to testify in support of the accused was reversed at the last minute by the disclosure that Oppenheimer had lied. He then gave his honest opinion on a matter of national security. For that he was shunned by all but a handful of his colleagues. Finally, he had been derided as the model for the fictional Dr. Strangelove, who chortled insanely as his nuclear weapons demolished the world.

Beyond the cost in terms of lost and damaged friendships was the price Teller had paid through the years in frequent and prolonged absences from his home and family while crisscrossing the country and the oceans in pursuit of peace for the world, power for himself, or both.

Some idea of the isolation felt by Teller was strikingly expressed by Elena Bonner, the wife of Andrei Sakharov, Teller's Soviet counterpart in pioneering development of the hydrogen bomb. Sakharov's wife had been allowed in the spring of 1986 to leave Gorky, where she and her husband had been confined because of Sakharov's dissident views. Elena received permission to travel to the United States for cardiovascular surgery and for treatment of an eye problem.

During her stay, she visited friends in California and, because of her husband's regard for Teller, arranged to visit him before leaving the West Coast for her return trip. The meeting was short, and because of the language barrier an interpreter joined them. But Elena later spoke of the "bond of mutual sympathy" that developed from their meeting. She explained this in a letter written May 14, 1986, just before her departure for the Soviet Union:

> Our meeting was significant for me, not only because of your ideas for releasing my husband from his captivity in Gorky, but also because it confirmed my earlier impression that your fate and my husband's are intertwined and even mirror images of each other.
>
> You worked, however, in different countries, different not just in name and geography. Both of you have gone the limit along the road you believe right and are ready to sacrifice much on that account. Neither of you is influenced by what others think and do, by ideological fashions, or by questions of prestige.
>
> The results: You have been ostracized by your colleagues in the U.S., and my husband in Gorky has not received any support from his colleagues in the USSR Academy of Sciences.

A strong note of disenchantment ran through the letter.

> It does not matter what you say or do with respect to the major issues of our time. The mob decides everything. That was a surprise for me, although for many years I have been skirting the edge of this discovery. Now it has all become clear, partly as a consequence of my many meetings with physicists and other scientists.
>
> I was astonished by the tendency of many of them, including those concerned with disarmament and human rights, to apply different standards to different countries and people. It is simply absurd that some missiles—Western ones—shoot, while the others do not. Some weapons—Western—threaten peace, while others do not. . . .
>
> They simply do not notice that the USSR has never in its history let representatives of the International Red Cross visit Soviet prisons or labor camps. Foreign correspondents have not been admitted to political trials since 1938. It has become a kind of game.
>
> I grow especially irritated by people's attitude toward the Soviet declaration about non-first use of nuclear weapons. How can one believe those words if they are not backed by anything? . . .
>
> I shall return to the USSR in a few days. I confess that I am terrified. I cannot find words to express my full dread of what awaits me.[5]

Two years had passed since Elena Bonner had written the letter. Since then, Mikhail Gorbachev had indicated policy changes ostensibly leading to greater freedom in the Soviet Union. *Glasnost* and *perestroika*, Russian words for openness and change from within, had become familiar references in the Western press. In the United States, the INF Treaty received Senate ratification by a vote of 93–5. Hopes ran high for further steps toward disarmament.

Also, since the Bonner letter, Soviet travel restrictions on her husband had been relaxed, figuratively setting the stage for a historic meeting between Andrei Sakharov and Edward Teller. The stage was literally set on the evening of November 16, 1988, when Sakharov, in the United States for medical treatment, attended a Washington dinner. Sponsored by the Ethics and Public Policy Center, a conservative think tank, the event was held to honor Teller for his work in the development of nuclear energy for peaceful use and for his contributions to national defense. "His motto, 'Better a shield than a sword,' expresses a timeless truth," said the citation presented to him during the dinner. But the presentation was anticlimactic to the first meeting of Teller and Sakharov, the two battle-scarred old lions of nuclear science and nuclear politics.

As hundreds of black-tied government, military, and industrial leaders of the nation's defense establishment and their gowned women stood about, chatting over cocktails in the Washington Hilton reception lounge, Teller patiently sat in an upholstered chair near the lounge entrance. A line of guests wanting to speak and be photographed with him kept Teller busy for half an hour. Then, at 7:10 P.M., he was notified that Sakharov had arrived for their meeting in a room above. Teller excused himself and, clumping behind his wooden staff, made his way to the elevator. For twenty minutes, with Mrs. Teller sitting by, the two men who had led their respective countries in creating the most destructive weapons in history spoke through an interpreter. Then they descended to the main banquet room and joined the guests who had come to see them together.

What Sakharov said in the room upstairs, Teller later told us, differed little from what he said before the microphone at the dinner. Because of his flight schedule, Sakharov was called on before dinner and left for his return trip to Boston before Teller's address. When Sakharov was introduced to speak, the audience stood and applauded warmly for thirty-six seconds. The thrust of his speech was that he and Teller agreed on the important issue of effective but safe development and use of nuclear energy for peaceful purposes. But they disagreed on other issues, he said, and SDI was among these.

"In Dr. Teller I see a man who has always acted, his whole life, in accordance with his convictions," Sakharov began. Tall and portly, he hunched over the microphone. Without text, he spoke in a tired but deep voice. His delivery was occasionally halting, and he used little inflection and few gestures. The audience remained hushed throughout the speech, which, including translation, lasted nine minutes.

"Our lifelines for many years ran a parallel course, and this started a long time ago when Dr. Teller probably had no idea that I even existed," Sakharov said. "At that time I was involved in the work on thermonuclear weapons." Here Sakharov noted that U.S. scientists were doing "the same kind of work" and that each side considered its weapons projects vital to its security.

"But . . . I think that what we were doing at that time was a great tragedy," he said. "It was a tragedy which reflected the tragic state of the world which made it necessary, in order to maintain peace, to do such terrible things. . . ."

Turning to Teller again, Sakharov said they both had "views that coincide." He mentioned the problem of developing safe thermonuclear energy systems. Then he referred to "spheres in which we disagree" on matters of principle.

"One such issue is the issue of space-based antimissile defense," he said. "I consider the creation of such a system to be a grave error. I feel it would destabilize the world situation. . . . If such space-based systems are deployed, even before they are armed with nuclear weapons, there will be a temptation to destroy them, and this in itself might trigger a nuclear war."

Sakharov described SDI as "one of the problems that right now stands in the way of achieving a really profound and deep arms control."

Nearing the end, Sakharov repeated his "profound respect" for Teller and expressed the hope that "such encounters as this" would continue.

"There is a new situation now in the world that has made such meetings possible," he concluded, "and we should explore this possibility to our best ability in order to achieve our profound hope of peace in the world."[6]

As he finished, the audience again rose, more slowly this time, and applauded for almost exactly as long—thirty-five seconds. Teller stood and walked toward Sakharov, Sakharov took a step toward him, and, smiling, they shook hands.

In his response, after Sakharov had departed, Teller paid tribute to the Soviet dissident's courage in speaking out for human rights and peace. He also emphasized their areas of agreement, especially on the need to "get away from the terror too many people, too many publications, have wrongly attached to the mere word *nuclear*" in underestimating the importance of nuclear reactors for energy production.

On his main difference with Sakharov over SDI, Teller said this:

"I will not repeat or explicitly disagree with what he said. I want to state my end of our defense effort, my end of what has been done and must be done—by scientists and by technology—for a stable future.

"My argument has been and continues to be that we must know what can be known."

Teller said this exploration must include nuclear energy, lasers, or devices small and effective enough to stop missiles, which he referred to as "incoming objects." He then emphasized a major difference between his and Sakharov's perspectives on the issue.

"I have enjoyed the possibility to continue to work on all these things. Sakharov has not," Teller said. "Twenty years ago, his clearance was revoked. He has not had the opportunity to work with the remarkable development in the Soviet Union of defensive systems where we have some reason to believe their accomplishments are years ahead of ours. It is not surprising that our points of view should differ, and they cannot be clarified in just a few sentences in a finite number of minutes."[7] Teller said he, too, would like to continue the dialogue.

It was one of our last meetings, again in the Cosmos Club. Clearly, even as the nuclear sword hung overhead, the two superpowers had traveled a heartening distance over the road to a saner world. Teller was among those believing that the strength of U.S. defense—conventional and strategic—

had contributed to the trip. But much more of the road lay ahead, and he was now eighty. When would he stop pressing his weakened body and slow down?

The question took him by surprise. Looking up from his dinner, he smiled. "In eighty more years."

Why did he go on?

"Because I have no choice."

Notes

Chapter 1. The Speech

1. George A. Keyworth, interview, Washington, D.C., December 8, 1986.
2. Ibid.
3. Stanley A. Blumberg and Gwinn Owens, *Energy and Conflict: The Life and Times of Edward Teller* (New York: G.P. Putnam's Sons, 1976), pp. 100–101.
4. Edward Teller, testimony before U.S. Senate Foreign Relations Committee, Washington, D.C., August 20, 1963.
5. Keyworth interview, December 8, 1986.
6. Adm. James Watkins, interview, the Pentagon, Washington, D.C., September 26, 1986.
7. Ibid.

Chapter 2. Culture and Chaos

1. Stanley A. Blumberg and Gwinn Owens, *Energy and Conflict: The Life and Times of Edward Teller* (New York: G.P. Putnam's Sons, 1976), p. 6.
2. Ibid., p. 9.
3. Ibid., p. 21, and Emmi Kirz, interview, Berkeley, Calif., March 25, 1987.
4. Blumberg and Owens, *Energy and Conflict*, p. 16.
5. Emmi Kirz, interview, March 25, 1987; Blumberg and Owens, *Energy and Conflict*, p. 16.
6. Interview, Edward Teller, Washington, D.C., September 20, 1987.
7. Blumberg and Owens, *Energy and Conflict*, p. 14.
8. Emmi Kirz, interview, March 25, 1987.
9. Emil Lengyel, *1,000 Years of Hungary* (New York: John Day, 1958), p. 205.

Chapter 3. The Making of a Scientist

1. David Childs, *Germany Since 1918* (New York: Harper & Row, 1971), p. 35.
2. Herman Mark, tape recording of interview by Stanley A. Blumberg and Gwinn Owens, New York, May, 1973.
3. Hans Mark, interview by Stanley A. Blumberg, Washington, D.C., July 18, 1973.

4. Edward Teller, interview, Washington, D.C., November 23, 1986.
5. Richard Hanser, *Putsch! How Hitler Made Revolution* (New York: Peter H. Wyden, 1970), pp. 353–60, 394.
6. Edward Teller, interview, Washington, D.C., November 23, 1986.
7. Werner Heisenberg, tape recording of interview by Stanley A. Blumberg and Gwinn Owens, Washington, D.C., April 20, 1973.
8. Ibid.
9. Stanley A. Blumberg and Gwinn Owens, *Energy and Conflict: The Life and Times of Edward Teller* (New York: G.P. Putnam's Sons, 1976), pp. 44–45.
10. E. J. Passant, *A Short History of Germany, 1918–1945* (London: Cambridge University Press, 1966), p. 159.
11. Ronald Clark, *Einstein: The Life and Times* (New York: Avon Books, 1971), p. 415.

Chapter 4. CROSSROADS

1. Stanley A. Blumberg and Gwinn Owens, *Energy and Conflict: The Life and Times of Edward Teller* (New York: G.P. Putnam's Sons, 1976), p. 54.
2. Ibid., p. 59.
3. Raymond A. Wohlrabe and Werner E. Krusch, *The Land and People of Denmark* (Philadelphia: J. B. Lippincott Company, 1972), pp. 137–39.
4. Edward Teller, "Niels Bohr and the Idea of Complementarity," in *Great Men of Physics* (Los Angeles: Tinnon-Brown, 1969), pp. 78–97.
5. Blumberg and Owens, *Energy and Conflict*, p. 63.

Chapter 5. STATESIDE

1. Stanley A. Blumberg and Gwinn Owens, *Energy and Conflict: The Life and Times of Edward Teller* (New York: G.P. Putnam's Sons, 1976), p. 68.
2. Jeremy Bernstein, *Hans Bethe: Prophet of Energy* (New York: Basic Books, 1980), p. 55.
3. John Rigden, *Rabi, Scientist & Citizen* (New York: Basic Books, 1987), p. 147.
4. Blumberg and Owens, *Energy and Conflict*, p. 83.
5. Ibid., p. 87–88.

Chapter 6. TO LOS ALAMOS

1. Edward Teller, *Better a Shield Than a Sword* (New York: Free Press, 1987), p. vii.
2. Peter Wyden, *Day One* (New York: Simon & Schuster, 1984), p. 21.
3. Ibid., p. 22.
4. Stanley A. Blumberg and Gwinn Owens, *Energy and Conflict: The Life and Times of Edward Teller* (New York: G.P. Putnam's Sons, 1976), p. 89.
5. Ibid., p. 94.
6. Ibid.
7. Wyden, *Day One*, p. 37.
8. Ibid., p. 41.
9. Richard G. Hewlett and Oscar E. Anderson, Jr., *The New World: A History of the United States Atomic Energy Commission*, vol. 1: *1939–1946* (Springfield, Va.: U.S. Department of Commerce, 1962), p. 35.
10. Ibid., pp. 45–46.

Chapter 7. ASSEMBLY OF A BOMB TEAM

1. Stanley A. Blumberg and Gwinn Owens, *Energy and Conflict: The Life and Times of Edward Teller* (New York: G. P. Putnam's Sons, 1976), p. 108.
2. Ibid., pp. 109–110.
3. Ibid., p. 110.
4. Arnold Esterer and Louise Esterer, *Leo Szilard, Prophet of the Atomic Age* (New York: Julian Messner, 1972), p. 69.
5. Peter Wyden, *Day One* (New York: Simon & Schuster, 1984), p. 56.
6. Edward Teller, *Better a Shield Than a Sword* (New York: Free Press, 1987), p. 69.
7. Ibid.
8. Ibid., p. 70.
9. Nuel Pharr Davis, *Lawrence and Oppenheimer* (New York: Simon & Schuster, 1964), p. 126.
10. Blumberg and Owens, *Energy and Conflict*, p. 117.
11. Richard G. Hewlett and Oscar E. Anderson, Jr., *The New World: A History of the United States Atomic Energy Commission*, vol. 1: *1939–1946* (Springfield, Va.: U.S. Department of Commerce, 1962), p. 104.
12. Blumberg and Owens, *Energy and Conflict*, p. 118.
13. Ibid., p. 112.
14. Ibid., p. 121.
15. Wyden, *Day One*, p. 63.
16. Blumberg and Owens, *Energy and Conflict*, p. 122; Hewlett and Anderson, *The New World*, p. 112.
17. Wyden, *Day One*, pp. 68–69.

Chapter 8. MAVERICK ON THE MESA

1. Richard G. Hewlett and Oscar E. Anderson, Jr., *The New World: A History of the United States Atomic Energy Commission*, vol. 1: *1939–1946* (Springfield, Va.: U.S. Department of Commerce, 1962), p. 233.
2. Edith C. Truslow, *Manhattan District History, Nonscientific Aspects of Los Alamos Project Y, 1942 through 1946* (Springfield, Va.: U.S. Department of Commerce, 1973).
3. Laura Fermi, *Atoms in the Family: My Life with Enrico Fermi* (Chicago: University of Chicago Press, 1954), p. 162.
4. Stanley A. Blumberg and Gwinn Owens, *Energy and Conflict: The Life and Times of Edward Teller* (New York: G. P. Putnam's Sons, 1976), p. 130.
5. Edward Teller, letter to Stanley A. Blumberg, undated.
6. Richard Rhodes, *The Making of the Atomic Bomb* (New York: Simon & Schuster, 1986), pp. 545–46.
7. Edward Teller, *Better a Shield Than a Sword* (New York: Free Press, 1987), p. 71.
8. David Irving, *The German Atomic Bomb* (New York: Simon & Schuster, 1968), p. 102.
9. Blumberg and Owens, *Energy and Conflict*, p. 141.
10. Rhodes, *The Making of the Atomic Bomb*, p. 676; Peter Wyden, *Day One* (New York: Simon & Schuster, 1984), p. 212.

Chapter 9. DECISION

1. Richard G. Hewlett and Oscar E. Anderson, Jr., *The New World: A History of the United States Atomic Energy Commission*, vol. 1: *1939–1946* (Springfield, Va.: U.S. Department of Commerce, 1962), p. 342.
2. Ibid.
3. Andrei Sakharov, *Sakharov Speaks* (New York: Alfred A. Knopf, 1974), p. 31.
4. Edward Teller with Allen Brown, *The Legacy of Hiroshima* (Garden City, N.Y.: Doubleday, 1962), p. 13.
5. Edward Teller, *Better a Shield Than a Sword* (New York: Free Press, 1987), p. 57.
6. Stanley A. Blumberg and Gwinn Owens, *Energy and Conflict: The Life and Times of Edward Teller* (New York: G. P. Putnam's Sons, 1976), p. 158.
7. Teller, *Better a Shield Than a Sword*, p. 60.
8. Edward Teller, "A New Balance Between Secrecy and Openness," 1972 manuscript, and *The Johns Hopkins Magazine* (Baltimore: The Johns Hopkins University), winter 1972.
9. Harry S. Truman, *Year of Decision* (Garden City, N.Y.: Doubleday, 1955), pp. 417–19.
10. Teller, *Better a Shield Than a Sword*, p. 19.
11. Truman, *Year of Decision*, p. 217.
12. Winston Churchill, *The Second World War, Triumph and Tragedy* (Boston: Houghton Mifflin Company, 1953), p. 639.
13. *Newsweek*, November 11, 1963, p. 107.
14. John Toland, *The Rising Sun: The Decline and Fall of the Japanese Empire, 1936–1945*, vol. 2 (New York: Random House, 1970), p. 948.
15. Truman, *Year of Decision*, p. 33.

Chapter 10. THE ROAD TO FUSION

1. Lewis L. Strauss, *Men and Decisions* (Garden City, N.Y.: Doubleday, 1962), p. 216.
2. *In the Matter of J. Robert Oppenheimer: Transcript of Hearings Before Personnel Security Board, April 15–May 6, 1954* (Washington, D.C.: U.S. Government Printing Office, 1954), p. 47.
3. Edward Teller with Allen Brown, *The Legacy of Hiroshima* (Garden City, N.Y.: Doubleday, 1962), p. 22.
4. Stanley A. Blumberg and Gwinn Owens, *Energy and Conflict: The Life and Times of Edward Teller* (New York: G. P. Putnam's Sons, 1976), p. 192.
5. Edward Teller, *Better a Shield Than a Sword* (New York: Free Press, 1987), p. 66.
6. Ibid., p. 68.
7. Maurice Dopkin, interview, June 21, 1974.
8. Strauss, *Men and Decisions*, p. 172.
9. *U.S. News & World Report*, December 24, 1954, p. 101.
10. Philip M. Stern with Harold P. Green, *The Oppenheimer Case: Security on Trial* (New York: Harper & Row, 1969), p. 113.
11. Strauss, *Men and Decisions*, p. 216.
12. Stern, *The Oppenheimer Case*, p. 133.
13. Harry S. Truman, *Years of Trial and Hope* (Garden City, N.Y.: Doubleday, 1956), p. 306.
14. Norman Moss, *Men Who Play God: The Story of the H-Bomb and How the World Came to Live with It* (New York: Harper & Row, 1968), p. 25.

15. Strauss, *Men and Decisions*, p. 217.
16. *In the Matter of J. Robert Oppenheimer*, p. 659.
17. Ibid., pp. 777–78.
18. David E. Lilienthal, *Journals*, vol. 3: *Venturesome Years, 1950–55* (New York: Harper & Row, 1966), p. 406.
19. *In the Matter of J. Robert Oppenheimer*, p. 779.
20. Ibid., p. 242.
21. Ibid., p. 714.
22. Ibid., p. 328.
23. Moss, *Men Who Play God*, p. 21.

Chapter 11. POLITICS AND THE H-BOMB

1. *In the Matter of J. Robert Oppenheimer: Transcript of Hearings Before Personnel Security Board, April 15–May 6, 1954* (Washington, D.C.: U.S. Government Printing Office, 1954), p. 76.
2. Ibid., p. 395.
3. Ibid., p. 513.
4. Edward Teller, *Better a Shield Than a Sword* (New York: Free Press, 1987), p. 5.
5. Edward Teller with Allen Brown, *The Legacy of Hiroshima* (Garden City, N.Y.: Doubleday, 1962), p. 44.
6. Stanley A. Blumberg and Gwinn Owens, *Energy and Conflict: The Life and Times of Edward Teller* (New York: G. P. Putnam's Sons, 1976), p. 220.
7. Ibid., p. 224.
8. Ibid., p. 221.
9. Teller and Brown, *Legacy of Hiroshima*, p. 45.
10. Lewis L. Strauss, *Men and Decisions* (Garden City, N.Y.: Doubleday, 1962), p. 440.
11. Richard G. Hewlett and Francis Duncan, *Atomic Shield: A History of the United States Atomic Energy Commission*, vol. 2: *1947–1952* (Springfield, Va.: U.S. Department of Commerce, 1969), p. 393.
12. Robert J. Lamphere and Tom Shachtman, *The FBI-KGB War* (New York: Random House, 1986), p. 157.
13. Blumberg and Owens, *Energy and Conflict*, p. 228.
14. Teller and Brown, *Legacy of Hiroshima*, p. 29.

Chapter 12. SCIENCE AND THE H-BOMB

1. Edward Teller with Allen Brown, *The Legacy of Hiroshima* (Garden City, N.Y.: Doubleday, 1962), p. 46.
2. Stanley A. Blumberg and Gwinn Owens, *Energy and Conflict: The Life and Times of Edward Teller* (New York: G. P. Putnam's Sons, 1976), p. 233.
3. Harry S. Truman, *Years of Trial and Hope* (Garden City, N.Y.: Doubleday, 1956), p. 308.
4. Philip M. Stern, with Harold P. Green, *The Oppenheimer Case: Security on Trial* (New York: Harper & Row, 1969), p. 154.
5. Richard G. Hewlett and Francis Duncan, *Atomic Shield: A History of the United States Atomic Energy Commission*, vol. 2: *1947–1952* (Springfield, Va.: U.S. Department of Commerce, 1969), p. 411.

6. Ibid., p. 412.
7. James R. Shepley and Clay Blair, Jr., *The Hydrogen Bomb* (New York: David McKay, 1954), p. 105.
8. Ibid., p. 106.
9. Hewlett and Duncan, *Atomic Shield*, p. 414.
10. Norman Moss, *Men Who Play God* (New York: Harper & Row, 1968), p. 45.
11. *Scientific American*, March 1950.
12. *Scientific American*, April 1950.
13. *Scientific American*, May 1950.
14. *Bulletin of the Atomic Scientists*, March 1950.
15. Ibid.
16. Blumberg and Owens, *Energy and Conflict*, pp. 250–251.
17. Shepley and Blair, *The Hydrogen Bomb*, p. 110.
18. Hewlett and Duncan, *Atomic Shield*, p. 438.
19. R. G. Marshak, ed., *Perspectives in Modern Physics: Essays in Honor of Hans Bethe* (New York: Interscience Publishers, 1966), pp. 593–98.
20. Hewlett and Duncan, *Atomic Shield*, p. 440.
21. Ibid.
22. Ibid., p. 528.
23. Ibid., p. 529.
24. Ibid., p. 530.

Chapter 13. "IT'S A BOY!"

1. Stanley A. Blumberg and Gwinn Owens, *Energy and Conflict: The Life and Times of Edward Teller* (New York: G. P. Putnam's Sons, 1976), pp. 256–57.
2. Ibid., p. 256.
3. Herbert York, *The Advisers: Oppenheimer, Teller and the Superbomb* (San Francisco: W. H. Freeman, 1976), p. 79.
4. Blumberg and Owens, *Energy and Conflict*, p. 259.
5. Ibid., p. 260.
6. Richard G. Hewlett and Francis Duncan, *Atomic Shield: A History of the United States Atomic Energy Commission*, vol. 2: *1947–1952* (Springfield, Va.: U.S. Department of Commerce, 1969), p. 537.
7. Norman Moss, *Men Who Play God: The Story of the H-Bomb and How the World Came to Live with It* (New York: Harper & Row, 1968), p. 57.
8. Edward Teller, transcript of September 20, 1979, statement to George A. Keyworth, p. 16.
9. Edward Teller, letter to Stanley A. Blumberg and Gwinn Owens, December 28, 1973.
10. Edward Teller, statement to George A. Keyworth, transcript, p. 14.
11. Hewlett and Duncan, *Atomic Shield*, pp. 540–41.
12. Ibid., p. 541.
13. Ibid., p. 542.
14. Ibid., p. 141.
15. Ibid., p. 542.

Chapter 14. BIRTH OF THE SUPERBOMB

1. Richard G. Hewlett and Oscar E. Anderson, Jr., *The New World: A History of the United States Atomic Energy Commission*, vol. 1: *1939–1946* (Springfield, Va.: U.S. Department of Commerce, 1962), p. 544.
2. Stanley A. Blumberg and Gwinn Owens, *Energy and Conflict: The Life and Times of Edward Teller* (New York: G. P. Putnam's Sons, 1976), p. 275.
3. Ibid., pp. 275–76.
4. Hans Bethe, letter to Edward Teller, December 9, 1982.
5. Edward Teller with Allen Brown, *The Legacy of Hiroshima* (Garden City, N.Y.: Doubleday, 1962), pp. 52–53.
6. Interviews, John Wheeler, October 25, 1987, and John Toll, December 12, 1987.
7. Blumberg and Owens, *Energy and Conflict*, p. 284.
8. Hewlett and Anderson, *The New World*, p. 572.
9. Teller and Brown, *Legacy of Hiroshima*, p. 61.
10. *In the Matter of J. Robert Oppenheimer: Transcript of Hearings Before Personnel Security Board, April 15–May 6, 1954* (Washington, D.C.: U.S. Government Printing Office, 1954), p. 562.
11. Blumberg and Owens, *Energy and Conflict*, p. 293.
12. Edward Teller, article in *Encyclopedia of Physical Science and Technology*, vol. 5 (San Diego, Cal.: Academic Press, 1987), p. 723.
13. Edward Teller, *Better a Shield Than a Sword* (New York: Free Press, 1987), p. 84.
14. Ibid., pp. 83, 84.
15. Blumberg and Owens, *Energy and Conflict*, pp. 296, 297.
16. J. Robert Oppenheimer, *Foreign Affairs Quarterly*, June 1953.

Chapter 15. THE RUSSIAN H-BOMB

1. David A. Rosenberg, *Strategy and Nuclear Deterrence*, edited by Steven E. Miller (Princeton, N.J.: Princeton University Press, 1984), pp. 143–44.
2. Harrison E. Salisbury, introduction to Andrei Sakharov, *Progress, Coexistence and Intellectual Freedom* (New York: W. W. Norton, 1968), p. 11.
3. Norman Moss, *Men Who Play God: The Story of the H-Bomb and How the World Came to Live with It* (New York: Harper & Row, 1968), p. 63.
4. Arnold Kramish, letter to Edward Teller, November 14, 1980.
5. Herbert York, *The Advisers: Oppenheimer, Teller and the Superbomb* (San Francisco: W. H. Freeman, 1976), p. 95.
6. Andrei Sakharov in William P. Bundy, ed., *The Nuclear Controversy: A Foreign Affairs Reader* (New York: New American Library, 1985), p. 104.
7. Stanley A. Blumberg and Gwinn Owens, *Energy and Conflict: The Life and Times of Edward Teller* (New York: G. P. Putnam's Sons, 1976), p. 296.
8. Andrei Sakharov, *Sakharov Speaks* (New York: Alfred A. Knopf, 1974), p. 269.
9. Rosenberg, *Strategy and Nuclear Deterrence*, p. 144.

Chapter 16. DARK DUTY

1. Harry S. Truman, *Year of Decision* (Garden City, N.Y.: Doubleday, 1955), p. 418.
2. Peter Goodchild, *J. Robert Oppenheimer, Shatterer of Worlds* (Boston: Houghton Mifflin, 1981), p. 223.

3. Philip M. Stern, with Harold P. Green, *The Oppenheimer Case: Security on Trial* (New York: Harper & Row, 1969), p. 44.
4. Ibid., pp. 819, 845.
5. *In the Matter of J. Robert Oppenheimer: Transcript of Hearings Before Personnel Security Board, April 15–May 6, 1954* (Washington, D.C.: U.S. Government Printing Office, 1954), p. 889.
6. Ibid., p. 137.
7. Stanley A. Blumberg and Gwinn Owens, *Energy and Conflict: The Life and Times of Edward Teller* (New York: G. P. Putnam's Sons, 1976), p. 361.
8. Ibid.
9. Goodchild, *J. Robert Oppenheimer*, p. 275.
10. Blumberg and Owens, *Energy and Conflict*, p. 365.

Chapter 17. REACTORS

1. Bernard Grossfiels, *The Russian Disaster* (Boulder, Colo.: Paladin Press, 1968), p. 4.
2. *New York Times*, April 6, 1987.
3. Edward Teller, *Better a Shield Than a Sword* (New York: Free Press, 1987), p. 166.
4. The Associated Press, July 11, 1986.
5. Baltimore *Sun*, April 11, 1987.
6. *New York Times* News Service, September 23, 1986.
7. Edward Teller with Allen Brown, *The Legacy of Hiroshima* (Garden City, N.Y.: Doubleday, 1962), p. 109.
8. William Lanouette, "Atomic Energy, 1945–85," *Wilson Quarterly*, winter 1985, p. 192.
9. Edward Teller, interview with author, Washington, D.C., September 22, 1984.
10. Richard G. Hewlett and Francis Duncan, *Atomic Shield: A History of the United States Atomic Energy Commission*, vol. 2: *1947–1952* (Springfield, Va.: U.S. Department of Commerce, 1969), p. 30.
11. *Washington Post*, April 9, 1987.
12. *Time*, March 16, 1987.
13. Abel Wolman, interview with author, September 22, 1984.
14. Teller and Brown, *Legacy of Hiroshima*, p. 103.
15. Edward Teller, interview, September 22, 1984.
16. George T. Mazuzan and Samuel J. Walker, *Controlling the Atom, the Beginning of Nuclear Regulation* (Berkeley: University of California Press, 1985), p. 218.
17. Ibid.
18. Lanouette, "Atomic Energy."
19. Edward Teller, interview, September 22, 1984.
20. Ibid.
21. Baltimore *Sun*, October 19, 1985, "Perspective" section, p. 5.
22. Edward Teller, interview, September 22, 1984.

Chapter 18. NUCLEAR WINTER

1. *Wall Street Journal*, November 5, 1986, p. 36.
2. Hearing before Rep. Newt Gingrich, Washington, D.C., May 16, 1984.
3. *The Atlantic Monthly*, November 1984, p. 56.

4. Ibid., p. 57.
5. Gingrich hearing, May 16, 1984.
6. Ibid.
7. Ibid.
8. Ibid.
9. Ibid.
10. Ibid.
11. Ibid.
12. Ibid.
13. Ibid.
14. Ibid.
15. Baltimore *Sun*, February 6, 1987.
16. *Wall Street Journal*, November 5, 1986.
17. Ibid.
18. Baltimore *Evening Sun*, May 1, 1987.

Chapter 19. A Dream: Life Without Fear

1. Emil Lengyel, *1,000 Years of Hungary* (New York: John Day, 1958), p. 242.
2. Alan Blackwood, *The Hungarian Uprising* (Vero Beach, Fla.: Rourke Enterprises, 1986), p. 20.
3. Ibid., p. 24.
4. Janos Kirz, interview, February 7, 1988.
5. Blackwood, *The Hungarian Uprising*, p. 37.
6. Ibid., p. 43.
7. Ibid., p. 56.
8. Ibid., p. 465.
9. Janos Kirz, interview, February 7, 1988.
10. Ibid..
11. Stanley A. Blumberg and Gwinn Owens, *Energy and Conflict: The Life and Times of Edward Teller* (New York: G. P. Putnam's Sons, 1976), p. 181.
12. Ibid., p. 183.

Chapter 20. The Debate

1. Hans Bethe, "The Case Against Laser ABM Development: Technology and Policy Views," *Laser Focus/Electro Optics*, March 1984, p. 10.
2. Edward Teller, *Better a Shield Than a Sword* (New York: Free Press, 1987), p. 32.
3. Report, American Physical Society, April 1987.
4. *Time*, December 7, 1987.
5. Angelo M. Codevilla, "How Eminent Scientists Have Lent Their Names to a Politicized Report on Strategic Defense," *Commentary*, September 1987, p. 21.
6. Interview, George A. Keyworth, Washington, D.C., May 12, 1988.
7. David Ritchie, Baltimore *Sun*, January 12, 1986.

Chapter 21. The Red Shield

1. Edward Teller, *Better a Shield Than a Sword* (New York: Free Press, 1987), p. 12.
2. George F. Keegan, interview, Fort Washington Station, Md., January 13, 1983.

3. Ibid.
4. Ibid.
5. Robert Jastrow, *How to Make Nuclear Weapons Obsolete* (Boston: Little, Brown, 1985), p. 57.
6. Ibid., pp. 58–60.
7. Ibid., p. 63.
8. Ibid., p. 126.
9. Ibid.
10. Hans A. Bethe, Victor F. Weisskopf, Richard L. Garwin, Kurt Gottfried, Henry W. Kendall, and Carl Sagan, *Commentary,* "Star Wars Letters," March 1985.
11. Edward Teller, *Commentary,* "Star Wars Letters," March 1985.
12. Baltimore *Sun,* December 29, 1987, p. 10.
13. *London Sunday Times,* December 6, 1987, pp. 1, 18.
14. George Keyworth, interview, Washington, D.C., May 12, 1988.

Chapter 22. LIVERMORE

1. Herbert F. York, *Making Weapons, Talking Peace* (New York: Basic Books, 1987), p. 68.
2. Stanley A. Blumberg and Gwinn Owens, *Energy and Conflict: The Life and Times of Edward Teller* (New York: G. P. Putnam's Sons, 1976), p. 405.
3. Edward Teller, *Better a Shield Than a Sword* (New York: Free Press, 1987), p. 122.
4. R. Norris Keeler, undated letter to the author, received May 13, 1988.
5. Edward Teller, article in *San Diego Union,* February 14, 1988.
6. Lawrence Livermore National Laboratory *Weekly Bulletin,* Livermore, Calif., March 17, 1987.
7. *San Diego Union,* February 14, 1988.
8. Letter, Edward Teller to George A. Keyworth, December 22, 1983.
9. Ibid.
10. Letter, Edward Teller to Robert C. McFarlane, December 28, 1984.
11. Letter, Edward Teller to Paul Nitze, December 28, 1984.
12. *New York Times Magazine,* October 9, 1988.
13. U.S. General Accounting Office, *Briefing Report to U.S. Rep. George E. Brown, Jr., House of Representatives, June 20, 1988,* p. 3.
14. Ibid., p. 5.
15. *New York Times Magazine,* October 9, 1988.
16. Transcript, *60 Minutes,* CBS, November 13, 1988, p. 6.
17. Ibid., p. 9.
18. Ibid., p. 10.

Chapter 23. IN DEFENSE OF SDI

1. Transcript, hearing before House Armed Services subcommittee, April 28,1983.
2. Edward Teller, interview, April 15, 1985.
3. *New York Times,* April 28, 1983.
4. *Stanford Daily,* April 29, 1983.
5. *Wall Street Journal,* May 31, 1983.
6. Transcript, hearing before House Armed Services subcommittee, April 28, 1983.

Chapter 24. IN DEFENSE OF ISRAEL

1. Jerusalem *Post*, international edition, December 5, 1987, p. 17.
2. Aron Moss, interview with authors, Israeli Embassy, Washington, D.C., May 26, 1987.
3. Ibid.
4. Ibid.
5. Yuval Ne'eman, interview with author, Washington, D.C., December 19, 1987.
6. Ibid.
7. Ibid.
8. Ibid.
9. Trevor N. Dupuy, *Elusive Victory: The Arab-Israeli Wars, 1947–1974* (New York: Harper & Row, 1978), pp. 401, 402.
10. Ibid., p. 349.
11. Chaim Herzog, *The War of Atonement, October 1973* (Boston: Little, Brown, 1975), p. 263.
12. This Teller quote and all others that follow are taken from a Report of the Israeli Institute for Advanced Strategic & Political Studies, Tel Aviv, Israel, August 15, 1985.

Chapter 25. "A MATTER OF SURVIVAL"

1. James A. Abrahamson, interview, the Pentagon, October 8, 1986.
2. Aron Moss, interview, Washington, D.C., May 26, 1987.
3. *Wall Street Journal*, December 15, 1986.
4. *Wall Street Journal*, May 7, 1986.
5. *Near East Report*, June 15, 1987, p. 97.
6. Jerusalem *Post*, international edition, April 4, 1988.
7. *Near East Report*, March 28, 1988, p. 50.
8. *Wall Street Journal*, March 22, 1988.
9. Ibid.
10. *Near East Report*, March 28, 1988, p. 50.
11. Baltimore *Sun*, May 23, 1986.
12. Kim R. Holmes, Baltimore *Evening Sun*, January 13, 1987.
13. *Wall Street Journal*, March 13, 1988.
14. James A. Abrahamson, interview, October 8, 1986.

Chapter 26. AT WORK ON THE HILL

1. Memorandum, Tom Schroeder, July 19, 1986.
2. Interview, Tom Schroeder, Washington, D.C., August 3, 1986.
3. Fred Barnes, *The New Republic*, January 24, 1987.
4. Edward Teller et al., letter to Ronald Reagan, October 1986.
5. Interview, Richard C. (Mike) Lewin, January 30, 1988.
6. Interview, James Houtrides, February 6, 1988.
7. Hans Bethe, letter to Gwinn Owens, January 24, 1975.
8. *Tass*, March 15, 1983.
9. Transcript, Senate Foreign Relations Committee hearing, February 22, 1988.

Chapter 27. ONE ON ONE

The quoted correspondence is reported from unedited copies made available by Edward Teller.

Chapter 28. OUTLOOK

1. *Washington Post*, April 24, 1988.
2. Interview, James A. Abrahamson, Baltimore, Md., February 18, 1987.
3. *Washington Post*, March 24,1988.
4. Transcript, Institute for Foreign Policy Analysis.
5. Letter, Elena Bonner to Edward Teller, May 14, 1986.
6. Transcript, Ethics and Public Policy Center dinner program, Washington, D.C., November 16, 1988.
7. Ibid.

Bibliography

Alperovitz, Gar. *Atomic Diplomacy, Hiroshima and Potsdam*. New York: Simon & Schuster, 1965.

Bernstein, Jeremy. *Hans Bethe: Prophet of Energy*. New York: Basic Books, 1980.

Blackwood, Alan. *The Hungarian Uprising*. Vero Beach, Fla.: Rourke Enterprises, 1986.

Blumberg, Stanley A., and Owens, Gwinn. *Energy and Conflict: The Life and Times of Edward Teller*. New York: G. P. Putnam's Sons, 1976.

————. *The Survival Factor*. New York: G. P. Putnam's Sons, 1981.

Broad, William J. *Star Warriors*. New York: Simon & Schuster, 1985.

Childs, David. *Germany Since 1918*. New York: Harper & Row, 1971.

Churchill, Winston. *The Second World War, Triumph and Tragedy*. Boston: Houghton Mifflin Company, 1953.

Clark, Ronald. *Einstein: The Life and Times*. New York: Avon Books, 1971.

Compton, Arthur. *Atomic Quest, A Personal Narrative*. New York: Oxford University Press, 1956.

Davis, Nuel Pharr. *Lawrence and Oppenheimer*. New York: Simon & Schuster, 1964.

Donovan, Robert J. *Conflict and Crisis*. New York: W. W. Norton, 1977.

Dupuy, Trevor N. *Elusive Victory: The Arab-Israeli Wars, 1947–1974*. New York: Harper & Row, 1978.

Eisenhower, Dwight D. *The White House Years: Mandate for Change*. Garden City, N.Y.: Doubleday, 1963.

Esterer, Arnold, and Esterer, Louise. *Leo Szilard, Prophet of the Atomic Age*. New York: Julian Messner, 1972.

Fermi, Laura. *Atoms in the Family: My Life with Enrico Fermi*. Chicago: University of Chicago Press, 1954.

Forrestal, James V. *The Forrestal Diaries*, edited by Walter Mills. New York: Viking, 1951.

Franklin, Charles. *The Great Spies*. New York: Hart Publishing Company, 1967.

Gervasi, Tom. *The Myth of Soviet Military Supremacy*. New York: Harper & Row, 1986.

Goodchild, Peter. *J. Robert Oppenheimer, Shatterer of Worlds*. Boston: Houghton Mifflin, 1981.

Grossfiels, Bernard. *The Russian Disaster*. Boulder, Colo.: Paladin Press, 1968.

Hanser, Richard. *Putsch! How Hitler Made Revolution*. New York: Peter H. Wyden, 1970.

Herzog, Chaim. *The War of Atonement, October 1973*. Boston: Little, Brown, 1975.

Hewlett, Richard G., and Anderson, Oscar E., Jr. *The New World: A History of the United*

States Atomic Energy Commission, vol. 1: *1939–1946*. Springfield, Va.: U.S. Department of Commerce, 1962.

Hewlett, Richard G., and Duncan, Francis. *Atomic Shield: A History of the United States Atomic Energy Commission*, vol. 2: *1947–1952*, Springfield, Va.: U.S. Department of Commerce, 1969.

Irving, David. *The German Atomic Bomb*. New York: Simon & Schuster, 1968.

Jastrow, Robert. *How to Make Nuclear Weapons Obsolete*. Boston: Little, Brown, 1985.

Kaplan, Fred. *The Wizards of Armageddon*. New York: Simon & Schuster, 1983.

Kurzman, Dan. *Day of the Bomb, Countdown to Hiroshima*. New York: McGraw-Hill Company, 1986.

Lamphere, Robert J., and Shachtman, Tom. *The FBI-KGB War*. New York: Random House, 1986.

Lengyel, Emil. *1,000 Years of Hungary*. New York: John Day, 1958.

Lilienthal, David E. *Journals*. Vol. 3: *Venturesome Years, 1950–55*. New York: Harper & Row, 1966.

Marshak, R. G., ed. *Perspectives in Modern Physics: Essays in Honor of Hans Bethe*. New York: Interscience Publishers, 1966.

Mazuzan, George T., and Walter, Samuel J. *Controlling the Atom, the Beginning of Nuclear Regulation*. Berkeley: University of California Press, 1985.

Meray, Tibor. *That Day in Budapest*. Translated by Charles Lam Markmann. New York: Funk & Wagnalls, 1969.

Moore, Ruth. *Niels Bohr: The Man, His Science, and the World They Changed*. New York: Alfred A. Knopf, 1966.

Mosley, Leonard. *Marshall, Hero of Our Times*. New York, Hearst Books, 1982.

Moss, Norman. *Men Who Play God: The Story of the H-Bomb and How the World Came to Live with It*. New York: Harper & Row, 1968.

Nagy-Talavera, Nicholas M. *The Green Shirts and Others: A History of Fascism in Hungary and Rumania*. Stanford, Cal.: Hoover Institution Press, 1970.

Nichols, K. D. *The Road to Trinity*. New York: William Morrow, 1987.

Passant, E. J. *A Short History of Germany, 1918–1945*. London: Cambridge University Press, 1966.

Rhodes, Richard. *The Making of the Atomic Bomb*. New York: Simon & Schuster, 1986.

Rigden, John. *Rabi, Scientist and Citizen*. New York: Basic Books, 1987.

Rosenberg, David A. *Strategy and Nuclear Deterrence*, edited by Steven E. Miller. Princeton, N.J.: Princeton University Press, 1984.

Sakharov, Andrei. *Progress, Coexistence and Intellectual Freedom*. New York: W. W. Norton, 1968.

———. *Sakharov Speaks*. New York: Alfred A. Knopf, 1974.

Schlesinger, Arthur M., Jr. *A Thousand Days: John F. Kennedy in the White House*. Boston: Houghton Mifflin Company, 1981.

Shepley, James R., and Blair, Clay, Jr. *The Hydrogen Bomb*. New York: David McKay, 1954.

Stern, Philip M., with Harold P. Green. *The Oppenheimer Case: Security on Trial*. New York: Harper & Row, 1969.

Strauss, Lewis L. *Men and Decisions*. Garden City, N.Y.: Doubleday, 1962.

Teller, Edward. *Better a Shield Than a Sword*. New York: Free Press, 1987.

———. "Niels Bohr and the Idea of Complementarity," in *Great Men of Physics*. Los Angeles: Tinnon-Brown, 1969.

————. Article in *Encyclopedia of Physical Science and Technology*, vol. 5. San Diego, Cal.: Academic Press, 1987.

Teller, Edward, with Brown, Allen. *The Legacy of Hiroshima*. Garden City, N.Y.: Doubleday, 1962.

Teller, Edward, and Latter, Albert L. *Our Nuclear Future—Facts, Dangers, and Opportunities*, New York: Criterion Books, 1958.

Tokes, Rudolph L. *Béla Kun and the Hungarian Soviet Republic*. Stanford, Calif., and Washington, D.C.: Hoover Institution/Frederick A. Praeger, 1967.

Toland, John. *The Rising Sun: The Decline and Fall of the Japanese Empire, 1936–1945*, vol. 2. New York: Random House, 1970.

Truman, Harry S. *Year of Decision*. Garden City, N.Y.: Doubleday, 1955.

————. *Years of Trial and Hope*. Garden City, N.Y.: Doubleday, 1956.

Truslow, Edith C. *Manhattan District History, Nonscientific Aspects of Los Alamos Project Y, 1942 through 1946*. Springfield, Va.: U.S. Department of Commerce, 1973.

Wohlrabe, Raymond A., and Krusch, Werner E. *The Land and People of Denmark*. Philadelphia: J. B. Lippincott Company, 1972.

Wyden, Peter. *Day One*. New York: Simon & Schuster, 1984.

York, Herbert F. *The Advisers: Oppenheimer, Teller and the Superbomb*. San Francisco: W. H. Freeman, 1976.

————. *Making Weapons, Talking Peace*. New York: Basic Books, 1987.

INDEX